Black Notes

Essays of a Musician Writing in a Post-Album Age

William C. Banfield

The Scarecrow Press, Inc.
Lanham, Maryland, Toronto, Oxford
2004

SCARECROW PRESS, INC.

Published in the United States of America
by Scarecrow Press, Inc.
A wholly owned subsidiary of
The Rowman & Littlefield Publishing Group, Inc.
4501 Forbes Boulevard, Suite 200, Lanham, Maryland 20706
www.scarecrowpress.com

PO Box 317
Oxford
OX2 9RU, UK

British Library Cataloguing in Publication Information Available

Library of Congress Cataloging-in-Publication Data

Banfield, William C., 1961–
  Black notes : essays of a musician writing in a post album age / William C. Banfield.
      p. cm.
  Includes bibliographical references (p.) and index.
  ISBN 0-8108-5287-X (pbk. : alk. paper)
  1. African Americans—Music—History and criticism. 2. Music—United States—History and criticism. 3. African Americans in popular culture. I. Title.
  ML3479.B36 2004
  781.64′089′96073—dc22   2004014205

This book is dedicated in loving memory to my uncle James Zeke Tucker, one of the artists whose paintings give this manuscript its illustrative color. While cataloging his near seventy existing paintings near the end of his life, we had hoped he would remain much longer. He taught our family about the importance of recording our lives with a fine eye on expressive details. Zeke, your art keeps us now wrapped in the pocket and in the grooves.

Dear Zeke, our love.

Thank you Harold Cruse for setting me straight on how to be an interpreter of (C)ulture.

Thank you Dr. Ray Browne for helping me to explore the terrain of the academy and plotting courses, meanings, methods, and memories which make up the meat of American cultural studies.

Thank you Dr. Bernice Johnson Reagon for your inspiration and encouragement, tireless work, and examples in instruction in teaching "how music addresses how you go forward."

For my wife Krystal, keeping me clear on where all this fits. I love you.

B

Black music is a Spirit. It rode upon the souls of Black singers, dancers, and musicians trying to find the way home. Then that Spirit opened itself up to all people who could be moved by its creative forces.

Lord, where there is mess, send us a message.

—A praying deacon, Pilgrim Baptist Church, St. Paul

A peaceful face twists with the poisonous nail of thinking. Suppose you loosen your intellectual knot? You waste your life making subject and verb agree. You edit hearsay. You study artifacts and think you know the maker. Mystics arrive at what they know differently; they lay a head upon a person's chest and drift into the answer.

Thinking gives off smoke to prove the existence of fire. A mystic sits inside the burning. But it's a mistake to leave the fire for that filmy sight. Stay here at the flame's core.

—Jelalluvddin Rumi (1207–1273, music teacher, poet, theologian, and mystic), "Thinking and the Heart's Mystic Way"

There is no political solution to our troubled evolution. Our so-called leaders speak with words they try to jail ya. They subjugate the meek, but it's the rhetoric of failure. Where does the answer lie living from day to day? Is there something we can buy? There must be another way.

We are spirits in the material world.

—Sting

What's wrong with the world, people living like they ain't got no mama. . . . People killing, people dying, children hurt and you hear them crying. . . . Can you practice what you preach? Father, father, father help us send some guidance from above, 'cause people got me, got me questioning where is the love? . . . If you never know truth then you never know love. Where is the love? We only got one world, and something's wrong with it.

—Black Eyed Peas

I wanted to be just like them; independent, dignified, proud and fun popular, self-reliant, and cool. Jazz gave black men and women dignity.

—Quincy Jones, *The Autobiography of Quincy Jones*

And without any real conscious work, this was definitely the way I saw music working in the Civil Rights movement. Especially how music addresses how you go forward when you're terrified, or facing real physical danger. It never stopped a bullet . . . but music kept you from being paralyzed, it kept you moving.

—Dr. Bernice Johnson Reagon

Black artists should be addressing the world in terms of black cultural ascendancy, not pulling it down with values of demise and destruction.

—Wynton Marsalis

Contents

Part 3   Two Interviews with the Author

Part 4   Tritone Substitution: Musicians in Tune and in Time

Part 5   Modulations: Talks with and on Contemporary Artists

Acknowledgments

$\mathcal{M}$any thanks to Scott Johnson, Al Mcfarlane, Batala Mcfarlane, Dr. Crystal Keels for their creative support and editorial assistance. My thanks to Scarecrow Press: Ed, Melissa K., Melissa Ray, Niki, Bruce, Mary Jo, and the marketing team, who just keep believing.

I'd also like to thank everyone for your love, inspiration, wise counsel, and support as I finalized my thoughts in this work over the last five years. To dean Tom Connery, Father Denis Dease, my gratitude. There are sooooooo many people who keep up after me. This page is dedicated to these friendships. Your belief in and support of my work has given me this creative springboard and foundation to stretch, speak, and share what I believe. I am coming to see the making of music, artistry, and our shared historical maps have meaning for the contemporary world we live in.

My love and best to all.
Bill B.

1
PRIMARY THEMES

· 1 ·

Opening Song: A Post-Album Age Blues Riff

WAS MUSIC DIFFERENT BACK THEN?

In my university classroom, in a course titled the Theology of American Popular Music, I placed across the blackboard, stretching the length of the room, albums ranging from Earth Wind and Fire, to Chaka Khan, to Bob Marley, to Diana Ross. My students, whose ages range from 18 to 22, were amazed. They had never seen that many album covers before. One student raised her hand and said, "Dr. B, my grandfather has all those albums, did you all enjoy the music back then?" This student was serious! I guess she assumed music in the album age was meant just for socializing the world, not for being listened to as music. Never mind the fact that "back then" was only fifteen or twenty years ago and that she grouped me into a period with her grandfather. But her question about music "back then," in the day, really stuck with me, and my album classroom experiment was cathartic and compelling. Was music different back then?

We are living in an interesting time, post 9/11. As a musician interested in how we live in relationship to music, I call this time a post-album age. The CD, a new technology and a new way of packaging and marketing music, emerged first in 1983. By the 1990s, I began to notice a shift in all sorts of things related to music in popular culture. I define "post-album" in many ways, but in short I think it simply means: in the new millennium, tiny, mass-produced, five-by-four-inch plastic boxes contain recorded music, which squarely fits in the back pocket of the consumer. When music is produced as a convenience, a commercial product, an attachment, a garment to be worn, a flavor, tune, or artist of the week, then it's post-album. The music has evolved; the packaging and marketing, the artistry, the meanings, mind-set, and model of "music-ing," as it were, has shifted. Albums aren't created anymore, but CDs are burned, rapidly. Why, these days you can even select a slice of the recording project and download it for the neat price of 99 cents. So what happens when the centers of your cultural practices, rituals shift artistically?

For me as a musician I am spending most of my thinking time on these issues: the power and pervasiveness of artistry to carry and transform culture.

I am bonded to the flow of creative thought in culture. I believe today many are. So, I am concerned in the post-album time because our popular culture arts seem to be shaped and produced more by market forces seeming more distant than ever from the centers of music making and meaning.

Music and art are among the creator's greatest gifts to wrap around our living. So people who are given creative gifts and opportunities should share in a way worthy of the vocation to

3

which they have been called. This is one of the underlying themes in my Blues-song and essays here. My views on this are shaped I'm sure by my life as a faithful musician from Detroit, my training in theology and philosophy and being an educator.

What happens when the making of music and the mechanisms for its exposure are controlled by people who make decisions based on nothing but constructing and constricting market trends and making more money (A and R, or apples and raspberries people, the executives who, these days, care less about music)? What happens to the music when the majority of young artists projected as recording artists aren't even musicians? That's the confusion I am in with this post-album age. I feel like while there is still great music making moving us on, so much has changed that at least we could talk about it. As a 40-year-old musician who has been making music all my life, a lot of it feels good, but too much of it means something different to me now. This is troubling. So, I wanted to publish some of my essays dealing with these changes while I have been living, creating, and working in a post-album age and ask what does this tell us about the culture we live in and what we value; and what are we, from an artistic side of the question, going to do about these changes, conditions, and the culture of our contexts?

Some of you, my readers, will agree. Many more may not, and it is this group that I am addressing because in this exchange we'll all learn more from one another. I guess for me this is my education moment, because I really care about music making. This post-album age—in CD, popular culture, BET, MTV, TRL, digital editing, MPC, Pro-tools, iPod, Internet file sharing and downloads, the disappearing and reapperaing of Prince and Whitney Houston, the illness of Luther Vandross, the loss of Barry White, Nina Simone, Sam Phillips (He introduced Elvis), Johnny Cash, Ray Brown, Ray Charles, the fall of the "king of pop," the death of Rick James, the literal birth of Justin Timberlake, Britney Spears, Beyonce, and Ashante—constitutes some shifts in popular music culture. I worry too that I will be accused of being an attacker of this generation's art. I am not. As a matter of fact I am blown away by its power. But I am equally an advocate of music with artistic and personal integrity. There was a time not long ago when there was much more engagement in music that shaped, in particular people's lives, holistically.

Bob Marley, in the documentary *Time Will Tell*, says, "My love of music has always been inspired by what we believe in, what we know, and what is happening, what you experience. It's people music, and it's news. It's about your one self, your one history. It's important to understand the words because they have meaning. It carries 'earth Force.'"

My concern is that when we began to lose so many "righteous voices" like Bob Marley's, they (the industry) began replacing our artists with empty commercial rhetoric like "keeping it real" . . . "my new CD drops next" . . . and "thug life." Marley was called, near his death, "The Most dangerous Black man in the world." There are high stakes involved when your music has power and meaning.

In every generation, throughout our history in times when the folks lost their way, it was not the political rhetoric, but the "popular priests" of the times, the musicians, who sang and pointed the way(s).

In every case, those were the "Blackest notes ever," because they were deep with many meanings. So much of what popular music stands for is trivial today and disposable. Why? Given the high visibility and market strength of popular music, why can't our artists use their gifts consciously at this moment and focus that to move us ahead?

In his *Culture Moves*, author Tom Rochon talks about the shifts in history marked by rapid cultural transformation when conflicting values compete for attention. There is a crucial role played by critical thinkers, "actors" who develop new ideas which are disseminated throughout the larger social movement.

This agency, which propels cultural standards and norms, is often about "representing," "ideas, activism, and changing values." In many instances, I argue that artists are the most forward in bringing about a change in attitudes in modern society.

I am noting, though, a real lack of courage in terms of people being willing to stick their neck out and challenge, question, call folks out on these things. Courage to speak as a musician has been placed in a box called "suspect."

What happened to cultural leadership? Collective courage among artists? Artists in the popular marketplace could shut the entire industry down if they refused to participate in this ever-growing madness of "saying nothing with music." Natalie Maines of the Dixie Chicks, Sting, the movements like Rock against War, Russell Simmons's various rallying of Hip Hop artists to "shout out" are noteworthy, if sustained. And since Kurt Cobain and Nirvana's youth angst ministry for smelling out "teen spirit," one cannot miss the torch being taken up in recent days by "therapy rock" bands like Green Day and Blink-182. With a piece like Good Charlotte's "Hold On," the themes of alienation, loneliness, fear, despair, and the resulting rise of suicide among too many youth underline the importance of and need for music with compelling messages and images that inspire.

The new artists of every generation have done this, being courageous artistically and creating music that had something to say. So I look at the work of young artists from Bessie Smith to Dizzy Gillespie; to Bob Dylan, Bob Marley, Hendrix; to John Lennon and uphold the idea that the artists are the creators, cantors, and construction workers, as it were, of many aspects of our culture. As a matter of fact, one could say an entire window of values can be viewed through culture. "I love a man who loves music . . . a man who loves art . . . a man who cares for the spiritual things, and thinks with his heart": Thank you India Irie.

But the majority of the output supported and financed by record companies and the media does not sustain the more positive messages of the artists just mentioned, and therefore the pervasiveness of powerful music is diminished.

What would we say about the time we live in now, looking back twenty years from now? If you look at the song titles alone, the artists and what they sing about, you get your answer. Can you imagine hip hoppers looking back at sixty and singing "Bootylicious," "P.I.M.P.," "Shake Ya Tailfeather," "I Like the Way You Move," or "Gin and Juice"? Or what about the line, "I'm going to have you naked by the end of this song"? While not totally a new idea in popular music culture (Barry White, God rest his soul), the contorted use and projection of the sexual conquest in our daily narrative has gotten so maddeningly demonstrative. Kinda funny huh? But today in this post-album age, what happens to you as a musician when what was the best of values held in the larger society evaporate? When your cultural heroes die? And today where does a musician go to be a musician if the meaning and value of that work has changed direction in culture? How are the record contracts, the traditional "corporate gig," written? And for a Jazz musician who traditionally creates rough, naturally, like the music, what does it feel like now being told that the music is only manufactured, programmed, smooth Jazz? And who do you complain to about any of this when many of the radio stations, clubs, stadiums, distributors, artists, record companies are controlled by the dictates of a few greedy men who could care less about music, you, or me?

MISSING MEANING MINUS MY MUSICAL MEMORY

Certain songs I don't just remember the lyrics but I remember the musical experience, that joy of being taken into that influential lyrical, rhythmic artistry. If the most recent marker of postmodernism is identified by the cultural upshifts of the socially relevant 1960s, then certainly in music markers we are in post-album times. Our times are marked by the proliferation and high-saturation dominance of megamedia cultural prescriptions and formulas in popular culture, business, marketing, finance, information culture, and more and more public and personal entertainment commodities, from flat-screen TV, DVDs, play/culture stations, and, as CNN says, "reporting [on] everything from Baghdad to Beyonce."

The simplest message from my youth could combat these "Shallow Hal" cultural mandates, I think. "You're a shining star, no matter who you are, shining bright to see who you can truly be. Shining star for you to see, what your life can truly be" (Earth Wind and Fire). You didn't need a diamond in the back or a sunroof top, cause you may not have had a car at all, "but remember brothers and sisters, you can still stand tall." Remember that song? No? Well . . . now in the industry, Bentleys and Benjamins rule. That's a post-album value in music, because the music is made meaningful by external market forces, principally.

We take it for granted, but I miss the memory of times when songs on the radio mirrored artistic hope. People in culture are quite literally made, sustained, and propelled by musical image in melody and groove. These are our maps for identity. Musical expression gives glimpses of hope, constructive commentary on despair, makes our values intelligible, spelled out and assigned by our popular culture figures. Every image in fact is an invitation, suggestion, and implication as to how one might hope, the possibility sometimes for one to be or not to be. Image is everything these days, and too much contemporary music carries meaning first not by melodies we all can sing but by images. That's a post-album marker.

THE MEANING OF AN ALBUM

I mean when my crew and I were young growing up in Motown in the 1970s as young musicians, to purchase an album or get an album deal was monumental for us. That huge 12-by-12-inch document with pictures, artwork, meaningful liner notes seemed almost life-size. CDs seem so tiny to me, so dispensable and exchangeable, so tossable and tradable, like a baseball card or something. With an album, it felt big from cover to cover, as if you had something in your hand; you owned something—a sound, a piece of literature, a painting, even, for your wall. It felt like you owned something lasting; the artistry, the music, the history, the images, the musical experience was yours. Now everything is so common and consumer-able, mass quantified and defined, commodified. It doesn't feel quite the same, does it? Anybody now can make a CD. While technology brings us incalculable advantages, the speed with which we raced toward its access did not provide us with the time-honored ethics and critical questions needed to curb our appetites and keep us from falling into the traps of conveniences. Convenience can distort craft, and availability can assume the role of artistry.

It has been reported (*Rolling Stone*, December 25, 2003) that in the industry there are ten billion songs marketed on CDs every year. Sixteen million are now distributed on iPods already. Downloading songs via technology has revolutionized the traditional sources for getting our music. Today's young generation wants speed and instant gratification due to the access technology has provided us. This dramatically affects the meanings in music consumption. Everything, it seems, is becoming a product, and that product is expected to make money, solely. The drive to make money is not new, but music making based on only making money has dramatically taken center stage as a primary value in our culture. This tends to diminish and shrink most message- or positive-image-driven agendas and restricts, in too many cases, creativity and originality.

That's where we are today, and I have concerns about the basic value in the whole exchange of popular music morphing, about the way musicians make music, what they think they are doing, how music is sold and marketed, how ideas of entertainment and media and technology drive music passion in young musicians and consumers instead of imagination and craft. The reason we have music is to touch peoples' lives on the inside; what you drive in, live in, and play in has little to do with what you do and mean as an artist. A show like MTV's *Cribs* is an example of how much young artists are placing value on vast amounts of materiality. Listeners too are searching for the appearance of the most important musical ingredient for artistry, originality. The main difference today is that so much of the music being marketed is not performed by musicians. So, many of the acts are constructed as a marketing package, they don't seem real, they are like microwave acts; pop 'em in and you have music made easy in three minutes and five seconds. Producers don't even use music to make music, they just call up loops and samples from a computer pick box. The singers today who can't really sing in tune, and who don't know it, are fixed with the push of a button in Auto-tune.

And what about talent? Someone said you don't need any talent these days to be a famous musician, you just need a formula, a hook. Is this true? Is this because perhaps we are consumed with consumption and not encouraged to think anymore? This becomes easy if our cultural diet is pressed down on us as a product and option of conveniences. How do you become an American Idol? Clay, Reuben, is that your voice, style, music I heard, or was it imitating American Idols? And what about industry shelf life? Can a new artist last longer than a one hit make? Besides examples like U2, OutKast, or Madonna, will there be a group of artists that will be around ten years from now, still making music?

Too much of what this old boy is hearing is derivative, not only sampling from old school, but just new school artists looping and copying one another. What happened to a culture in the album age that was dripping wet with young creative and talented musicians? My cousin Charles, the main keyboardist for Justin Timberlake, said, "We are the beat generation. We are more interested in manipulating sounds." I am sure there are a lot of young musicians out there, excellent ones like Charles, but this media machine mimics mediocrity and creative people are usually constricted, cursed, and crushed. And so, the possibility of music culture moving us continually forward is slowed due to the boulders of resistance pushed against the hands of artists who strive for and dream about artistic excellence and integrity and originality and innovation against the complacency of market forces.

Louis Armstrong, Bessie Smith, Sister Rosetta Tharpe, Charley Christian, Charlie Parker, Billie Holiday, Miles Davis, Thelonious Monk, Elvis, Jimi Hendrix, George Clinton, Busta Rhymes, Macy Gray, and Erykah Badu; these are sounds that no one has ever created before. This is original voice.

Readers, yes, this is a reflection of a young musician becoming 40 and waking up and wondering why music culture resonates so differently in so many ways. Now what about the consumers of this post-album product? What do they want? I must confess I live almost as an "invisible man making music" in a post-album, CD-formatted popular culture reality.

This post-album reality really does offer some challenges to old ways of thinking about the noble role of music culture among consumers. These days, the musicians who are center stage aren't really musicians anymore, and the fans seem to want and expect something different. Don't get me wrong, as a teacher I can't afford to stay far from the actors on the stage of this new post-album drama. I mentor many younger musicians and I ask them this stuff all the time. For example, as I mentioned earlier, my cousin, who I watched and encouraged as a young musician is the main keyboardist for Justin Timberlake. During the fall of 2003, I went to see the Justin/Christina tour. People were screaming for Justin and Christina Aguilera, but as a musician it was hard for me to know if they were moved by the personality, the music, the likeness of the video to what they were seeing on stage, the actual videos that were playing on the screen, the acrobatics, the smoke and firebombs, the motorcycles on stage, cages, lights, dancers, the volume, the macroevent. I could not explain what I witnessed on stage and was sure I could never keep an audience's attention like that without all that stuff going on. These audiences are accustomed to total sensory saturation, and musicians cannot compete with that. That is a reality in a post-album age.

SO WHERE DO WE GO FROM HERE?

So, I have to ask myself, "Bill, how will you deal with your old musician's dilemma? How do I live in a world that is post-album, bearing a critique but engaging in discovery and growth, and respecting new music, artists, and presentations fully without sounding like an old man?"

Everywhere I perform I make sure I speak at college campuses. Being a visiting artist/scholar in places such as Harvard, Princeton, University of Texas, Howard, Fisk, Morehouse, and Bishop State College in Alabama, I speak to hundreds of college-age students. As the director of the American Cultural Studies program and professor of music at my own university, I teach and advise 200-plus students a year.

Students immediately recognize the difference between 50 Cent and Black Eyed Peas, or see the relevance in the mentality of Nina Simone or Tracy Chapman. They can hear the meaning in the music, its presentation.

Yet they don't have the power to turn off the cultural programming that would lead us to believe that because of the "pump," Lil Kim is a better cultural selection, keeping it real, than Yolanda Adams or Jill Scott. So it is clear to me that this generation—the millenniums, or the Hip Hop generation, all born in the 1980s—do value quality, desire empowerment and identity, and strive for their excellence. It's just that in a post-album age they are powerless to ignore the deafening barrage of some very messed-up ideas, images, and impressions of the media saturation.

In popular culture there is a four-part player rule: artistry, audience, industry (record companies, media, MTV), technology and the times. Music rarely rises outside of the influential context of these forces. But who is to blame for the post-album age madness? I definitely have "21 questions." For our future directions, I put my money on an informed and engaged artist block coming up and out of communities across the country that will be informed, innovative, and poised to make a change. I am definitely advocating for a change of direction in popular culture mentality, first from young artists. The answer to much of these problems is, as I argue, a better linking to the older generation of music makers, who can have more "hands on" and effectively pass onto this generation some of the values of music discipline and business.

There has been over the past few years such an incredible distance, so that the interests of music makers, consumers older than 23, and those not doing Hip Hop or Rock have been muted. The 2004 36th Grammy Awards show was a refreshing glimpse into what may be a positive direction (Prince with Beyonce, Pharell Williams with Sting, Justin Timberlake with Auturo Sandival).

So, in these essays I float through a range of cultural celebrations and critiques, hoping for engagement and discovery from multiple angles. I decided a few years ago, no matter how difficult it would be, to shape the lives of younger people by showing the range, power, and the importance of our music history and linking that with the best engaging of contemporary music. One powerful example of musical artistry with social consciousness in modern history is Black music. But Black here incorporates "all colors (styles)," so Woody Guthrie, Bob Dylan, Carole King, Bonnie Raitt, and Dave Matthews—all of whom take their dippin' from rural Spirituals and Blues—really matter in this discussion.

So, in the following 48 essays I deal with music as a cultural study involving broader interests in art and movement of ideas in our culture through and over times. I ask some compelling questions which circle in and around what it means to be an artist interested in making music. I talk to artists (Bernice Johnson Reagon, Bobby McFerrin), artist-educators (Dr. Billy Taylor), industry heads (Russell Simmons, Patrice Rushen) and try to pinpoint where we are going, look to critical models in our literature and movements in music history to gauge with and some "working ideas" to ground and critique with. In 2004, it is a challenging time, when peoples' mess and dirt outshine the good in the majority of us. But together, we musicians and consumers in specific communities with local radio, stores, concert venues (many of us have abandoned our chase of record companies and distributors and are creating market niches, fan bases in local regions, concert halls), through education, can rewrite the changes of the music culture in a post-album age. We can create grooves that move people, inspire the times, write music that moves folks' hearts to joy, keep the party pumping, illuminate evil and stupidity, and ensure our future as a society. This is my post-album Blues-song, heard in the key of all modes.

· 2 ·

Reflection: Prelude

Writing the book confirmed ideas that had been rolling around in my head for years and that now, given the opportunity, flashed out upon the page with a stunning self exhilaration and certainty. That is, how to measure this world in which we find ourselves, where we are not at all happy, but clearly able to understand and hopefully, one day transform. How to measure my own learning and experience and to set out a system of evaluation, weights and meaning. . . . The Music. The Music, this is our history.

—Amiri Baraka, introduction to the 1999 edition of *Blues People*

*A*miri Baraka's book *Blues People* has wrapped itself around my soul and mind so many times I have felt that I owed him a certain pay for my becoming an aware musician. As an artist, I have long contemplated my own straightforward talk, shout out, and response to the call that *Blues People* evokes in so many of us, over and over again. *Black Notes* is talk about Black music culture. This work is written as a short collection of essays and reflections and should be read as one Black artist's perspective on creating, defining, and considering direction(s) in contemporary musical culture.

Everybody wants to talk about Black music but they don't talk enough to Black musicians. The assumption is always that there is one kind of Black musician, with one experience and representing one community of Black American artistry. Not havin' it! There simply needs to be more dialogue from Black artists about their music(s) because the music is so rich and has such a pervasive cultural force. Insights come from and at so many angles. Black artistry is multifaceted and multidirectional. As I am doing music I get a chance to see and work within the practice from wider views. I share this because too many times people are unaware of the width and participation of music practitioners. I wanted to highlight this point because rarely do musicians get a chance to speak about the levels of diversity, venues, styles, and opportunities afforded to them as artists. Many times the general public is simply cut off from seeing and hearing about music outside of radio, commercial TV, and video programming. There is lack of support and lack of access to the inner circles of other parts of the industry outside of performing gospel, doing Rap, Hip Hop, and R&B. What about being a composer or writing a radio program? What does a musician consider his or her role in all this to be, besides making money and being famous? In my view, educational institutions and the industry gatekeepers participate in a dangerously pervasive and insidious practice of "locking images" and placing people and culture in boxes for a predetermined shelf life. These days the gatekeepers are usually young MBAs who know only bottom-line sales formulas and business-driven market surveys which attempt to interpret consumer impulses.

This narrative represents a take, a spin on musical creation and culture and how this has been navigated through the evolution of Black music's many forms (Spirituals, Blues, Jazz, Black symphonic and chamber music, gospel, R&B, Soul, Funk, Hip Hop). But, I want to also take a leap and talk about the hope in a future direction of this cultural sounding.

Speaking creatively, artistically, is a way to regain ownership of who you are—your inside story. This is Music Philosophy 101. This reclaiming is particularly significant if who you are has been caught up and tangled in a sticky web of history, race, economics, class crashes, and identity crisis. Sound like a common problem? It is. In his *Hip Hop America*, writer Nelson George hints at this need to tell a new narrative through art forms in Black culture. He writes, "'I' is a powerful word in the vocabulary of the African American male. . . . Black male pride is profoundly manifested in the renaming of oneself. This renaming is an extension of a long tradition by which African-Americans have new 'I's' that speak to how they see themselves or wish to be seen."[1] For example, in the following, notice how the artist focuses on the issue of identity: "My Name is Prince" by Prince; "I'm Bad," by Michael Jackson; "R.E.S.P.E.C.T.," by Aretha Franklin; "Say It Loud, I'm Black and I'm Proud," by James Brown; the album *Who Is Jill Scott?* by Jill Scott. As early as 1925, Bessie Smith asserted, "Here's my plan. I ain't gonna play no second fiddle." In a contemporary shout out from the grave, perhaps, Bessie's sentiment continues on Macy Gray's 2001 album, *How Life Is*. Gray's banner of independence states, "There is a conversation I need to have with me . . . it's a moment to myself." This (I)dentity, or reclaiming control of destiny and "performing the manifesto," is powerful business and a major theme in Black music culture.

Because of a distinctively painful but rich historical tradition, when we experience a Black creative form of culture it manifests itself and represents in subtle and direct ways a continuous and deep stream of experiences and expressions. This collective consciousness is consistent with the needs of this particular human conditioning. We cannot forget that in every generation, Black music has been the representational form of what some important voices have to say. As Baraka told us in 1963, "This recent music is significant of more radical changes and re-evaluations of . . . emotional attitudes toward the general environment. . . . Negro music is always radical in the context of formal American culture."[2] Perhaps this has just been our most available forum in the West to rattle the cages, shake and question foundations, to show it and speak it as it was and as it is.

Black social condition, evolution, and history in the Diaspora are very, very different. Each generation of musicians reflects on this difference. Struggle is universal, yet struggles are also culturally coded. The cultural coding of Black experience can be found in the arts, especially in music. This music and its creative processes therefore are unique and still transforming. To stay on target as a viewer and admirer of Black culture is exhilarating and daunting. This is why I think we respond to what is being communicated and expressed in Black music culture with the thirst of one who has come to the end of a long desert journey.

There is no other group of people who love and live for their music like Black people. You can sense the entire being of Black people in their arts, from song to sculpture, poetry to dance. They live in the vitality and power of their expressive forms. No other "despised group"—(Black slaves) to this extent has with their voices humanized and transformed others and thus reconstructed their perceptions—and obtained then a new worth and self-dignity culturally, aesthetically, intellectually—with music. Now that's the deep thing about the history of Black music in the West. Rarely, if ever, have a group of people used their music to say to the rest of the world, "Yes, we are here, yes we are human, yes, we have a rich culture and just listen and be in our music."

As musicians muse about what their music says about who they are, what they're about, where their "home" is, what being "real" or authentic means, and as they create images, reclaim identity, and "represent" through musical form, their art becomes powerful windows of culture. This is evident from William Grant Still's *Afro-American Symphony* of 1930 to Tupac's *All Eyez on Me* of 1996. We are actually looking through a cultural chamber, watching folks create then navigate, negotiate, and formulate cultural value.

My own inquiry these days is leading me to ask the questions of an aspiring Black music aesthetician. That is, I am someone who is committed to exploring the artistic and philosophical meaning of music making and to developing an understanding or sensibility which helps to not only interpret but gauge, if possible, where the music is headed and what the culture is saying about who it is. "Aesthetics" in my way of speaking here is simply talk about music and its culture. This talking one should assume comes from a sincere concern about music qualities and how music culture moves, feels, walks, talks, and sings among people. At various times I hope to approach this through at least six frames of inquiry: who, what, where, when, why, and how. This effort is a historical inquiry and projection primarily seeing culture in its making(s). I want to suggest strongly, in this inquiry and sharing of essays, that there is a continuum from slave hollers to contemporary Hip Hop artists. Despite the ugly commercial monster that controls our culture(s), many of us ain't giving up on the music and its potential to mean something again. There still exists a thread of creative performance aesthetic firmly grounded in the traditions of Black artistic practice related to purpose, function, creative expression, social navigation, critique of cultural domination (hegemony), and theological relevance. Black art is a continuous expression of evolving modernity and a primal reflection of our human histories.

In a classic treatment of Black American culture, James Cone's *The Spirituals and the Blues* (1972) points to Black arts as "the truth of Black American experience." He goes on to state that Black music combines a powerful mix of music and verse/poetry and is the response to the chaos and beauty of the Black social condition. Black music culture represents conscious constructions of beauty, which symbolize solidarity and identity formation, codified by musicians, or "griots," who hone their craft, practice their trade, and see themselves as artists. While this is true of many cultures, Black American arts continue to converge at many points of meaningful expression, cultural sounding, and personal and communal definition. These expressions are of marked significance. Not only do they mark the continuation of life within the culture, but they signal death(s) as well.

Too often, of late, the expressions of our popular culture celebrate blindly. Young recording artists substitute nonmusical ideas like "keepin' it real," "getting paid phat," "bling bling" (the drowning of oneself in monetary flash and jewels) for musicality. These are problematic pathologies that are worn as a barrier against a cruel materialistic society that fuels the craze. This cultural apparatus "industry," a term used by Harold Cruse, author of *The Crisis of the Negro Intellectual*, exploits celebrations, picks, publishes, produces, promotes, and projects pains and anxieties as commodities to be believed in as the only point of expression and culture. This can be seen in music, film, plays, and books. We have to continue to celebrate and critique, to be on watch and be critical. Black music culture is a clock, a map, and a bloodline. Music and art making in their various forms are illustrative of a culture's health, reflecting both ills and genius. Black musical arts and culture are revelatory and transformative, having a tremendous impact today, as in decades past, on world culture. Black musical arts have revolutionized musical expression in the West and continue to emerge as a vibrant cultural tradition, a moving force and sensibility.

I remain, along with many friends, anxious about the culture's potential to respond to its vitality and its "sores." Will Black music continue to reverberate with new expressive powers as we make and wait for new directions of culture in the emerging of this new century? Those of us involved in creating, asking, and teaching stand in a unique period that comes only once every one hundred years or so. We all get to assess what happened, why, who, when, and then look forward and ask, Where is it going? We are members of a generation of musicians who sit right in the middle of a cultural transformation, both technologically and in terms of musical function, practice, and style. Being post–Civil Rights artists we are trained in traditional music and Black music practice, but have to "give it up" to a new movement in music: Hip Hop culture. Many of the artists who make up contemporary Black music impulses in popular music are not musicians at all. Today the times' most important music is performed and fronted by a different kind of griot. But, they have all the rights and privileges, the "proppers," all that we have worked hard and dreamed to obtain—rappers with record contracts!

In discussing some aspects of Black popular culture, to critique and gauge directions, I've needed a set of eyeglasses. I find the perspectives of cultural studies as a system of exploring folks in culture to be most helpful. There is a subtext here that underlines my own interests: defining the business of cultural studies. Cultural studies is the examination of "people stories"—in this case, people stories told in musical form. These sharings also attempt to connect to larger historical questions on creating music in contemporary culture.

This book operates on the premise that artists create and reflect in ways that generate social, cultural meaning as well as creative expression. These are meanings which are persuasive, instructive, and important, and which reflect on our contemporary social construct and evolution forward. The idea as well is where we could be going. While reflection on these connections is not new to the discourse in social/aesthetic criticism, what is unique about this book is that it is written from the perspective of a practicing, performing artist/scholar whose multidimensional musical voice focuses on perspectives from popular, jazz, and concert traditions, and contemporary arts philosophy in education.

This book should be of interest to people looking at American music, culture, and history through the lens of cultural studies—that is, art practice and ritual, related to creative expression, social navigation, critique of cultural domination (hegemony), and theological relevance. In this way there are at least five communities of readers whom *Black Notes* is written for.

1. The academy. As a scholar I address, in the form of a narrative/discussion, the history, aesthetic theory, function, meaning(s), and contexts of Black music culture.
2. The professional artistic community. This is talk from another practicing artist, a composer and performing jazz musician.
3. The church. It is crucial to pay very close attention to connections and expressions in contemporary popular culture. Our culture is informed by many impulses. Prophecy has always come from outside the church. For many artists making music is not merely a "pastime but a priesthood." In other words, the musician can be seen as a sort of popular priest. Musical expressions dealing with the human condition (spirituality, love, society) become relevant for theological examination and spiritual reflection. Black American music creation is always closely aligned with African theology, Black music functionality, and the duality of secular and sacred musical activity. Gospel singer Kirk Franklin took it all the way to the edge, asserted the reasons why "we sing": the eye stays on the sparrow as well as the fallen, hurting neighbor with broken wings.
4. The general reading public interested in Black popular music culture. One of the most powerful and influential agencies of social contact and discourse is popular music. In

American culture, music is in our daily interactive mix. Music coats our culture. As Gamble and Huff wrote some twenty-five years ago, "In this day of confusion, we must find the root of the problem in order to solve it. The problem is the lack of truth and communication among man and woman. The word of music is one of the strongest means of communication on the planet. The message is Peace, Love, Wisdom, Understanding and Unity."[3] Author Albert Murray has also written, "The artist (writer) never ceases being concerned with human fulfillment . . . provide the most adequate frame of reference for coming to terms with contemporary experience."[4] Popular culture and expression is so important and compelling because it's where people are expressing in vibrant, innovative ways their uncompromising willingness to be alive. It is within these forms that people celebrate the victories of being human.

5. Young musicians. I want a younger generation of musicians to be able to read this and see themselves in continuous streams of Black music culture. I would like for young musicians to read and listen to the tradition and be empowered to speak relevantly and powerfully because we are armed, prepared, and have an urgency to participate in the making of great music and a great society. Youth songs and movements turn the world around. But again, I want to ask, What's the next note and what's the right next note?

Throughout this writing, in addition to advocating the importance of music practice, I refer to this map for cultural evolution. Watching the culture of Black music and people provides at times very powerful formulas for doing and sustaining identity in the modern world. Everything that I have come to believe in, that which I teach and share, has come to me by dipping into the deep wells of Black music culture and artistry to shape my perspective. And this book is a discussion of Black music from a musician's perspective.

In my first book, *Landscapes in Color*, I interviewed and had dialogue with forty Black composers. With everyone, from Bobby McFerrin to Bernice Johnson Reagon to Herbie Hancock, there was a sense that the music still is the primary cultural force. My experience as an educator looking at these issues began when I taught Harold Cruse's course American Culture and Gender as a doctoral candidate at the University of Michigan in Ann Arbor (1988–1992); I continued on to become a professor of Afro-American studies and music at Indiana University (1992–1998). This trajectory of inquiry continues as I currently serve as director of American cultural studies and professor of music at the University of Saint Thomas in Saint Paul.

With Cruse's recent charge to me, as well as a great meeting in 2000 with Amiri Baraka, I have been moved to ask the questions these great thinkers showed us it is necessary to continue to ask, but in new ways. I travel widely as a composer, teacher, and performer, and I see evidence of a need for continuous reenergizing and focusing on social/cultural directions in Black music. The clock is ticking.

The writing of this book began in an old-fashioned way by contemplating and pulling things together in a secluded cabin while at Marian Wright Elderman's retreat in Clinton, Tennessee, in 1999. I reflected on some of my experiences as an artist/educator, reactions to the performances of my music all over the country, my writings over ten-plus years, and the things I have gained from speaking with and working with so many people in our business. I had made trips to speak with old and young musicians in the South. I lectured at Duke, Morehouse, University of Texas, and Harvard and encountered the contemporary surge of new Black music in Philadelphia. Black music makes a difference in our world. In the attacks on the World Trade Center on September 11, 2001, America's most visible symbols of material and might were destroyed. It seems to me that we should look toward the resurrection of our centers of human value. Consequently there is within this writing the discussion and the question of defining the role of the artist in contemporary society, as well as creative processes by artists who are informed and driven by cultural themes and consider how those themes are, again, shifting. This is our most important discussion: the future of contemporary popular music creation, where things are headed. I can only imagine that this inquiry will continue and this is chapter 1.

In 1963, some forty years ago, Baraka asked at the conclusion of *Blues People*: What are artists (Black people) being asked to protect and to believe in? What do "we" value? By the 1970s, the answer, I believe, came back in the music: our communities ("Ain't no stopping us now, we're on the move," in the words of McFadden and Whitehead). I wonder today: What are we being asked to believe in? What are the artists singing about? The answer to the question in 2004 is money, power, possessions, your sexual conquests, fame, and the glory of "I." And this is where too many young artists in popular culture, circa 2004, have erred. Massa's steak is poison! It can't be all about getting paid, fame, and going for the glory of I. The common thread for Black music in particular—Spirituals, Blues, Gospel, segments of Swing and Bebop, Soul, and early Hip Hop—was interest in the wholeness and well-being of people, and that didn't mean making bad music. Keeping it real meant being musical with a passion for excellence, a passion and love for music making, and a real understanding and connection with the people being moved. I don't mean to preach, but I just can't help myself!

I am very much aware of the numerous pieces that have explored and continue to explore the terrain of Black American music. The more ways to probe, the better. As well, there is the awareness here of the limitedness of containing the discussion to just Black American music in the States. Watching the *Buena Vista Social Club*, man, that film on the mixture of peoples of color, their traditions, and the richness and density of cultural matrices, makes this point clear. Everywhere Black people take music, we take it to the next level. The blurring of cultural borders via the Internet and the sharing of music, aesthetics, styles, and languages in our now very smart and connected global pop market underlines this, as seen from New York to Brazil to South Africa to Germany to Haiti. This is the most salient arena of interest for cultural reporting and observation: the power of Black artistic/spiritual presence in the modern world. So, again, this spiritual gifting and artistry for the purpose of moving people becomes a most important inquiry. I'm not interested so much in what music is, but in marking what our music making does through creative artistry for people purpose; that is, music focused on folks. As an educator and artist working within American institutions and culture—serving the communities of the young people I reach directly and the colleagues I engage with most fiercely—I focus on Black American music in the United States in this sharing. Miles to go befo' we rest. I hope you enjoy.

· 3 ·

Introduction

A VOICE

$\mathscr{I}$ begin this extended essay by speaking as an artist, more specifically a composer and an educator concerned with creating, defining, and in some ways critiquing contemporary popular American musical expression(s) and culture at this moment in the early years of the twenty-first century. Artists are a group of the most important carriers and definers of nondiscursive, encoded knowledge(s) and meanings in contemporary times. That is, artists create and reflect meaning, which is infused with nontangible, expressive, imaginative, and intellectually charged "messages." So important are these "meanings" that any accurate indication or description of where or what American society is, or what it will become, must include the musings, ramblings, and voicings of artists. While none of this is new, every generation that raises the issue raises it more powerfully, and this is what helps to move the entire culture so that it can see itself more clearly as human. We have buried too much of our capacity to be humane deep beneath our skins, and it may be that part of the "soul-ution" is allowing the space for arts to unearth this as they have always done throughout time. But is this unearthing of the human spirit still a part of the agenda of contemporary music culture, as it has been in the past?

ROLE OF ART/CULTURAL REFLECTION

I am primarily interested in the exploration of the fact that art is an expression representing one's understanding of how people move in the world; that is, how they relate to it. Popular music is clearly an expressive outlet for how one sees the world, finds love, screams out at society, feels Spirit, and celebrates or worships one's God(s). In short, I focus here on the melody makers sometimes referred to as the "popular priests," who are inextricably bound by circumstance and choice to major human movements. Musical expression is a reflection of not only artistic choices and thrusts but social, intellectual, political, economic, and eschatological choices as well. My ideas on these things are reflective of the insights and experiences held in common among many of the artists I have interviewed, performed with, and held friendships with, including Bobby McFerrin, Nnenna Freelon, Leonard Bernstein, Dr. Billy Taylor, Ysaye Barnwell, and many others. Some of these artists' ideas will be presented here. Creators in our society, specifically musical artists, carry significant weight in shaping meaningful and lasting impressions of what our "deeper reality" or humanity is.

With the proliferation of media driven culture, a real decline in the influence of the traditional church, and an obviously corrupted political and legal system, contemporary society is once again significantly represented by the artists who sing and muse about who they are and "long to be." When no one else understands or can deal or cope, it is a song or video image that embraces our soul more significantly, yells at the world which is constantly closing in on us, choking our identity, and bashing our sensibilities. The music in many cases delivers us, without question.

CULTURAL CRITIQUE

There are other sides to the question of the function and effect of music as well, as many claimed these artistic "projections" were in part the cause of a culture in decay at the close of 1999 and wondered what this signaled as we moved into a new century. Author Cornel West hinted at this in his early writing *Prophetic Fragments*:

> The impact of mass culture, especially through radio and television has diminished the influence of the family and church. Among large numbers of Black youth, it is Black music that serves as the central influence regarding values and sensibilities. Since little of this music is spiritually inspiring, people have fewer and fewer resources to serve them in periods of crisis.[1]

Part of the commentary in these reflections serves as a contemporary cultural critique as well. My feeling is that unlike the Rock and Roll era, which produced for many young people a modern youth identity expressing the values of the new generation emerging in the late 1950s and 1960s, much of today's music serves as a replacement of values for all kinds of reasons. The difference between the two eras is that the earlier generation accepted a challenge and believed in a world they could grow in, affect, and change. In today's generation there is a feeling that there is little at risk here because so much is possible and accessible, and maybe the world's not worth changing. The best way to deal with it is to just adapt to it by a quick and easy fix. This societal ambivalence is acceptable. Without sounding too much to the right, the notion of values—that is, working for excellence, self-determination, pride, and a care for a community—has been lost. Whatever we thought was gained socially as a culture after the Civil Rights movement, the 1970s, and 1980s, perhaps we had lost by the close of the twentieth century. Where do we find our "truth platform" today? We must face the reality that these new values and cultural constructs in music and contemporary sensibilities engage a growing many of us more faithfully than our once tried-and-true foundations. For this reason I have a particular, though not exclusive, interest in discussing the musical artistry of Black American artists because I know this "work" and I am familiar with the foundations. I am convinced that some of the most profound and important music in American popular culture has been created by Black artists, and this work has significant cultural meaning.

In Black popular music we find a "prophetic place," and in examining this work one does encounter a significant pulse of contemporary culture and its evolution throughout the twentieth century and into the twenty-first. As Leroi Jones pointed out long ago in *Blues People*, Black music not only reveals the "sociological soul" of Black Americans, but also tells us much about the soul or "soul-less-ness" of American society in general.

While Black music is my staring place, these essays move outward to a larger discussion of music and artists in our contemporary culture.

Reflecting on a broader cultural front, Tupac Shakur, Biggie Smalls, Kurt Cobain, Princess Diana, Gianni Versace, John Denver, Chris Farley, Michael Kennedy, Sonny Bono, Jaki Byard, Phil Hartman, John F. Kennedy Jr., Aaliyah, and Lisa "Left Eye" Lopez all died by murder or accidental deaths within seven years (1996–2003). In my way of thinking, this is yet another indication that the cultural foundations are quaking around us and the times are signaling that something significant is going on. For many these people were the best examples of what our contemporary society is producing, at least in terms of commercial, political, and social success. What does it mean when your cultural heroes and "she-roes" die? Some cultural critique, examination in its most "raw and real" expression, is necessary to hopefully produce a read on who we are becoming and as well turn questions back on the art and address its "ugly" reflection and projection.

In a recent conversation I had with the author of the groundbreaking *Crisis of the Negro Intellectual*, Harold Cruse told me:

> Well, you have to look at it like this; all music using words and voices is a reflection of the culture that it comes out of. That's what opera is. If you read closely into the history, you will see various instances in which people were moved not so much by the music, but by the cultural situation the music portrayed. It's not the whole of black culture that is represented in rap. The rappers imply that their message reflects the sentiment of black youth, but it isn't so. So, you have to deal with it in very strict and specific terms. The average black person in America is no more favorable of rap than the average white person is to Richard Wagner. Rap is a phenomenon, but you've got to deal with it and explain it! As a critic of our art, you cannot condemn it! You have to attempt to explain its implication, the implication of the message and why the message has become what it is. Rap will either die out or develop according to our own internal force. That's how you become a critic of the art form. We need you.

While the proliferation of new musical sensibilities, new forms, new ways of doing music raises in me, a confirmed musician, a bit of angst, my publisher thought it wise that I invite some of my close friends to help me if not comprehend what's going down, at least weather the storm. The storm is a new generation of music makers, a new popular music industry, and new audiences: 200,000 White fans cheer and recite the words to a DMX tune, "My Niggas" (Woodstock, 1999). And a confirmed nonmusician named Puff Daddy (P. Diddy) can make 200 million dollars as a top-selling producer by giving the musical instruction to his engineer, "Make it sound real dark and shit."[2] Things are different now. I'm down with poetic nuance, but I struggle with where music making, especially among a younger generation of popular artists, is headed. So I've put out a prophetic call to friends to have an open dialogue from various perspectives about music of various kinds, in order to simply talk about music making as it has been, as it is, and possibly what it is becoming. What will music in the popular marketplace mean in 2010 and what will artists have to say?

CULTURE AND AESTHETICS REVISITED

It is important to lay new groundwork by talking about the way in which artists are constructing the philosophical and methodological premises they work within. An aesthetic perspective takes into account what contemporary artists are saying their art is doing. Some survey and discussion with various artists is recorded here from numerous conversations about these issues.

Culture and aesthetics must be addressed from many sides, especially in education. There needs to be a concerted effort spent on reflecting and addressing our contemporary challenges, searching for solutions within the realm of our sharing. One major challenge for us today is figuring out a way to comprehend the diversity of confusing contemporary definitions and images of "self." These projections, which include the use of media (cable, the Internet, MTV) and informational technologies, seem to force a race to get "to it" fast to make it yours, via an economic system that's been constructed to support and motivate these new definitions of the contemporary self. The challenge is twofold: sometimes combat and critique, and other times dance with the popular rhetoric that legitimates who we are by our involvement in these contemporary frameworks. A comprehensive view of artistic process through discussion and exploration of artistic product can be helpful in keeping in place the importance of human creativity as a prerequisite to human achievement. It illustrates the congruency in creative work and social progress, that this two-step dance with artists' (musicians') work is relevant, important, and a reflection of who we are as citizens.

Further, these same challenges from the current popular music(s) are connected to megacultural drives. These drives call us in our own ways to:

1. Challenge and question the media saturation of negative and shallow rhetoric, images and ideology of contemporary culture which does not examine the full range and possibilities of the human story it reports on. Challenge the artists to be accountable for the images and messages inherent in their popular expression.
2. Arm ourselves with tools of interpretation in order to deal with the diversity and social/spiritual complexities of our time.
3. Keep a watch on the intoxicating lure of our present race toward fast access, automation, and push-button ideologies with pretty lights. But simultaneously harness the creative, intellectual, and innovative work for the pursuit of "usable knowledge."

We need to teach people in our society that being creative and taking time to explore one's inner voice and thought has great rewards, but that it is as well a great challenge because society has reduced the importance of creative arts to mere entertainment or specialty interests. In contemporary culture the majority of the emphasis on training for success is for gaining access to money and power in business, information technology, sales, service, and finance. Consequently our society is bereft of places where our humanity gets explored, pampered, and developed. If we are not careful we will become more and more a nation filled with angry, frustrated people driven by impulses that push us to dangerous realities.

WHY NOW A PROPHETIC CALL?

There is a growing urgency in our society to hear, heal, and revisit the idea of meaningful exchanges between people. Our society has become a common playground for violence, selfishness, social ambivalence, complacency, mean-spiritedness, and political and spiritual emptiness. There is definitely a cry, a need for prophetic voices, impulses, and movements. These needs have driven us to rely on waves of bad substitute teachers who take the role and the money and write "mess" on the chalkboard. It is important to identify places in our culture that have meaning, and also to unearth compelling figures, expressions, and movements which slow the downward spin and provide more moments of "truth platforms." Is making it "more dark and shit" just the kind of coded sensibility that is needed to unmask the unreal and unearth the resting answers we desperately seek in many ways? I don't know. That's why I'm asking. Artists continue to be among the most fluid examples of human achievement in this arena of societal exchanges. So I have made here a prophetic call. What should we be looking and wanting to hear from artists?

What's the right note? What are the signposts? How do we decode the handwriting that's on the wall? In the last hundred years we have seen extraordinary musical and historical movements and revolutions. Consider the Jazz Age, the Harlem Renaissance, Bebop, the social protest and action in the sixties, early seventies, Hip Hop, MTV, and the Internet. How do we continue in this prophetic vein? Have we lost our way and our sensibility too?

We are all witnesses to the potential and power of popular culture and its role in shaping who we have become to a large degree, post-1970. Popular culture in its various shapes is the most influential human agency in contemporary society. Political ideology in this country, as far as the public mainstream is concerned, is nothing but selfish and empty rhetoric that few really have come to expect anything significant from. We watch political madmen and star-hungry candidates rise up to claim they represent a new voice in American politics and slowly witness the decimation of civic accountability. While we wait, the church in its various denominational divides hardly moves toward its prophetic self. Yet Paul Tillich in his *Theology of Culture* many years back concerned himself with "hearing" voices from outside the walls of the institution that he believed were relevant and worthy of our attention.

Artists in the past have "called up" the spiritual, intellectual, and aesthetic power to represent authentic and vivid examples of human need and meaning. They have reflected and projected prophetic musings which have moved us in times to consider who we were, and today are fast becoming. For example, Carlos Santana on his 1999 *Supernatural* CD refers to a writing by Gabrielle Roth which states: "Many of my favorite shamans are rock stars. They probably don't even know they're shamans but they know how to get to ecstasy and back, and they know how to take others with them. They may not have a license but they know how to drive." In his liner notes he thanks all his musicians with similar gratitude for their "songs which capture our mission to spread hope, peace, love, light and the joy to the heart of the listener." Likewise, on Paula Cole's 1999 release, *Amen*, in a song entitled "God Is Watching," she states, "God is watching us play our ghetto wars. God is watching us play our games. God is waiting for us to overcome. God is waiting for us to just love one another." Another example of a popular priestess is Lauryn Hill, who on her song "Superstar" from the 1998 release *The Mis-Education of Lauryn Hill* states, "Come on baby light my fire. Everything you drop is so tired. Music is supposed to inspire, how come we ain't getting no higher? Now tell me your philosophy on exactly what the artist should be? Should they become someone with prosperity and no concept of reality?"

Artists through their musing provide a space for people to be moved, touched, and inspired through song. As John Lovell has written in his *Black Song: The Forge and the Flame*, "Song always expands the man who creates it and through him the men he inspires. Without song through the ages men would be dwarfs, working at their best only to fulfill tasks at hand. Song enables man to explore his undiscovered world within and brings that world under active command."[3] Perhaps it is this song which will inspire politicians to legislate for peoples' causes and churches to empower their folks to engage meaningfully in the society in which they live and move. We have to ask ourselves constantly what it means to live in a time when money and convenience are the dominant cultural theme or rule, or to live in a time when image is everything and content is secondary, or when an investment company advertises that we should take faith in the Internet as the dominant force of our future? What does it mean to live in a time in which we see the arts industries run by number-crunching young MBAs who know only that their bottom line depends on asking advertisers what music they believe will attract new buyers, before they consult the musician about what she or he can create?

There's a lot of musical masturbation going on right now—a whole lot of titillation for the pleasure of momentary attention. There isn't enough substantive, sustaining, and sincere musician doing. And I see this going on not only in popular music (Rap, Rock and Pop, Garage, R&B, Smooth Jazz), but in new concert music as well, by supposedly educated composers who can talk "enlightened," but who generate computer-programmed stuff. But it ain't music because it doesn't speak.

This book is not an analysis of popular culture or a history, not even a critique or assessment of music, popular culture, and artists, but a prophetic call. It does embrace culture, retrace some steps in our musical history, and celebrate cultural expressions, but it also "pinches" culture, hoping it yells and evokes glimpses of authentic reality which are deeply rooted in human meaning. Music and art don't really belong to artists; they are the captains or conductors on a vehicle that is meant to transport, transform, and translate. I am not suggesting that every artist is consumed with messages and purpose or has acknowledged or professes his or her role as popular priest. Many times artists exorcise demons of social despair and transport folks by simply being there and being aware of joy, pain, triumph, imagination, and spirit—because they operate the vehicle, the music, the art. If there is any voice in these times that cuts across our social, racial, sexual, political, and ethnic divides, it is the crosscurrents of contemporary musical artists. So here is my prophetic place. This is where I start. Now I have asked friends to share their perspectives in an attempt to understand the meanings and the "places" from which the artists speak.

We have in a small way begun a dialogue or prophetic call to make, draw from, and share in appreciating expressions that should move us toward being more humane, responsive, intact, and in touch. It is here that we begin again to become better citizens and better participants in shaping our combined destinies. This being in touch is what resulted with music during the war protests and Civil Rights movements, the 1967–1969 music festivals, Motown, Soul, and the beloved community music of the seventies (for example, "Celebration" by Kool and the Gang).

But what do we make of the current cultural revolution of the combined power industries of popular music, media, and information technology? For whatever we may think about it, again, popular cultural expressions and the media have become the most dominant mainstream ideological forces of our times. Dr. Ray Browne (one of the pioneers in popular cultural study) some thirty years ago called for a class-action suit against the academy. He put out a call for thinkers and people with "new questions and frames of mind" who could draw attention to the importance of the study of contemporary culture and life. I too firmly believe that contemporary "cultu-real expression" will continue to reflect and project our societal images, which properly understood are mirrors of ourselves.

As this relates to discussing Black musical expression, the main reason for critics like Alan Bloom and others to dismiss the contribution of these ethnic formulations of self is that they have not taken the time to view these expressions as culture, thinking communities with a history, conventions, an aesthetic. There is little consideration of popular arts and their relevance as expressions of social/political values, and certainly not from a theological standpoint.

The value in this writing is in the dialogue around informed and sensitive insights which simply inspire us to consider from an artistic perspective: What's the right note?

What can we expect to hear from artists in the coming years? In short, we have to continually embrace the work of artists and we have to continually look closely at what the art and the artists are saying about who we are in our times. But, we also have to be critical in a caring sense, if for nothing else maintaining a balance between evolving reflections of our humanity and discovering and disarming problematic projections of our inhumanity.

No one person can claim to have an authority, but we must maintain an informed sensibility to what art is, who it is for, and what is communicated in contemporary life and culture. What's the right note in a post-album age?

IN THE POCKET AND
ON THE DOWNBEAT

"African Music" by James Zeke Tucker

Black Music: A Historical Survey (The Dippin' Pool)

*B*lack music is a Black Spirit. It rode upon the souls of Black singers, dancers, and musicians trying to find a way home. To speak about the music is to speak about it not simply as a history or a record of artists or style distinctions, but to speak of the embodiment of a cultural Spirit, a significant cultural movement, still evolving and providing modern modes of being in the world. Then that Spirit (Black expression) opened itself up to all people who could be moved by its creative forces. Now, as Quincy Jones has stated, "Black music is the music the whole world has adopted as the voice of their Soul."

When I listen to the musics of Black America, that is, Spirituals, Jazz, Blues, Gospel and the songs of R&B from the mid-1960s through the 1980s, I am amazed at the scope and size of the repository of melodies, songs, and musical materials recorded. This music is a collective, in this short time period, equal or near equal the variety of output we see in printed Western art music. Much of this is due to the increased amount of technological production and mass marketing of American popular music, thus allowing more musicians the opportunity to be supported and disseminated. But, as an inquiry into places where the music can be viewed or surveyed reveals, the vault of Black music materials is seemingly endless. While western European art music scholars have researched centuries of their own musical traditions, a comprehensive view of Black musical culture reveals art and a narrative of development deep with cultural, philosophical, and artistic meaning. There are numerous writings which help to clarify, or even identify, a Black musical arts ideology, a philosophy, an aesthetic stance, but the continuous defining of a working Black aesthetic is an extremely challenging task because of the overall breadth of music being created around the world. The other reason is that Black music and cultural creation has been so rapid and responsive to social conditions and times that it continues to "mutate." One can't keep up with it! The influence of technology and media transmission of popular as well as academic or the music of the "trained" composer blurs the lines of cultural, regional, and time period distinctions. Terms like "cross-fertilization," "eclecticism," and of late "sampling" underscore this difficulty.

So where does a Black aesthetic begin and where is the principle activity taking place which continues to define what it is? Do we look to Hip Hop music of the late part of the twentieth century? To the trained Black academics writing about Black "art" music? Is it best defined by dance and video media or TV and movie culture, which in many ways are joined at the hip with new creative ventures being produced daily in the culture? It is important to visit lasting statements made by some leading thinkers who have contributed significant ideological definitions and descriptive narratives which have brought us a bit closer to understanding, if possible, a philosophy of Black musical art making. Some suggestions were made for reviewing some of these earlier. Black cultural activity is so wide, in addition to the examples of music(s), poetry, dance, and sermons, an aesthetic would have to include historical, literary, theological, and sociological discussions interpreting the meaning and function of Black musical culture seen over the last 200-plus years in American musical production. Perhaps this is a suggestion for a historical, cultural, aesthetic map of Black musical making in modern society.

What I would like to do here is take a survey, a sampling of some of the major periods and genres, and as a recap trace certain artistic movements within Black American musical development. We can't really speak about American music from a Black historical perspective without some idea about the contexts from which so much American music has sprung. Music rises and has meaning only in the context of social/cultural movements. But these essays are not an attempt to write a history, but more a way to ask about and suggest ways to interpret what the culture, Black artistry, might be "meaning" and where it may head next. I want here to introduce some themes and some connections that have given rise to Black thought in music, hoping to, as stated earlier, be one journeyer and investigator into this very important and multipronged history.

THE JOURNEY: REFLECTING BLACK
AND THE DIPPIN' POOL

Over the past several years I have taken many trips to New Orleans. I come away knowing that this is one of the only places in the world that celebrates, at least in concept, the beauty and majesty of Black creative musicianship. Visually, the images and the spirit of Black creativity and innovation in expressive arts are everywhere. This is expressed through historical and culturally specific ways, regionally, in food, tastes, religious practices (syncretic), and of course in music and performance practices. For the first time I began reflecting again on the beauty and power of black creative expression purely from a humanistic expressive position apart from any political or sociological meaning. I have come to understand that in terms of a national identity, Black American artistic expression is this nation's classic creative treasure. Jazz as the embodiment of the most "sophisticated," studied, and researched of the musical forms out of the Black arts traditions, is a unique manifestation of cultural expression and modern society particularly grown out of the emergence of the industrialized West in the twentieth century. It's hard to imagine the modern musical West without its (Black) structural, rhythmic, sonorous, and expressive dimensions. It is not only Jazz music, but an entire gamut of Black expressive forms in literature, poetry, preaching politics, dance, visual arts, intellectual/social writings, social movements, institutions, and thinkers that all share a common thread, a "dippin' pool" as I call it. The movements within Black American music culture are tracked in artistic, social, religious, and intellectual activities among the folks in America from the late 1690s to the late 1990s, some 300 years of Black American creating.

Much of the music, which many times accompanied social movements, grew out of resistance to problematic social/human contexts. Unfortunately, American White society has viewed Black humanity as dispensable and disposable, and so much of our accomplishments as invisible. The irony of course is that on the other hand, Black accomplishment is worshipped and documented, especially in "entertainment" arenas and sports and seen as indispensable to definitions of Americanism. Despite the continuous attacks on Black humanity, to the suffocation, sometimes, of the potential of young people to see sustained positive and productive images of themselves (add to this a couple hundred years of a lack of opportunity and access to consistent, nurturing, supportive cultural mechanisms in education and finance), these folks have created indigenous cultural structures for spiritual self-imaging and expression. And despite the intended attempt to diminish and silence the protests, Black American aesthetic and social movements have remained the most persuasive macrocultural moments of the American twentieth-century cultural evolution.

From the the Jazz Age, through the Harlem Renaissance, to Rock and Roll, the Civil Rights movement, to the close of the twentieth century with Hip Hop and Rap, America's most vibrant and socially relevant cultural movements have been created, accompanied, and shaped by Black artistic thought and innovation. How can this be explained sociologically? What is it that inspires, compels, then propels Black artistic product within American then international psyches and marketplaces? How do we account for the fact that in 2004 more than 80 percent of Hip Hop music created by Black urban youth is being purchased by White suburban youth? While one explanation has to do with the fact that there is a far greater number of young White record buyers, a closer examination would reveal a historical precedent for America's attraction to Black artistic product, from Minstrelsy to Rock and Roll.

I am reminded of nineteenth-century author J. Kinnard's comments in 1845:

> Who are our true rulers? The Negro poets to be sure. Do they not set the fashion and give laws to the public taste? Let one of them in the swamps of Carolina compose a new song, and it no sooner reaches the ear of a white amateur, than it is written down, amended (almost spoilt), printed then put upon a course of rapid dissemination to cease only with utmost bounds of Anglo-Saxondom, perhaps with the world. Meanwhile the poor author digs away with his hoe, utterly ignorant of his greatness.[1]

In contemporary creation, while much of the exploitation and the distortions of the Black American image and identity still exist, the "poor Negro" is acutely aware of the financial potential of his "song." Again, as Puff Daddy "P. Diddy" Combs has asserted, "It's all about the Benjamins, baby." Yet even in this scenario the artists still sing. Or as author Vincent Harding asks in his *There Is a River*, "How in the permanent, and grueling exile could a people dance and create songs of art, fashion institutions of hope and bear so many children of beauty?"[2] As we continue to examine creative expression in our culture and consider the social contexts we move through, one begins to have a greater understanding for the relevance of this cultural movement, called Black American music.

While the Duboisian notion of the division of the twentieth century was that of the color line, the challenge of the twenty-first century will be the dismantling of social, class, race, economic, religious, and gender categories and divisions bequeathed to us from the twentieth-century cultural sprawl. The creation, at least here in America (as that continues to expand and change in shape and color), of cultural constructs of nationhood and self should be based on the belief and faith of our shared identities and spiritual quests. Arts exploration through cultural construct, expression, and identity is one way to cement meanings, and build a "lived-in culture" in the twenty-first century. For our discussion, the specific focus on Black artistic development and analysis provides not only a window and a framework for projecting identity, but a model, universally understood and respected as poignantly human, and poignantly profound and moving with meaning(s) relevant for absorption.

Using again Henry Louis Gates's insightful example of approaches to literary texts, he writes, "Each tradition at least implicitly, contains within it an argument for how it can be read. . . . Ours is an extraordinarily self-reflective tradition, a tradition exceptionally conscious of its history and simultaneity of its canonical texts which tend to be taken as verbal (expressive, mine) models of African American social condition revised."[3] These expressions had to be all encompassing without the luxury to be "art for arts sake." Black art is existence art and this is its most salient point. "I ain't got no money. I ain't got no honey. I got the blues. Why am I singing? 'Cause I got the blues. How am I going to get on with it? By singing the blues." Not only did the Blues get sung, the corporate faith and mobilization socially, politically, and spiritually empowered groups of men and women called three-fifths of a human being in the American Constitution to overturn an evil and selfish system, while making converts along the way. Those Blues and Spiritual singers transformed a nation and the whole world. They took joy in singing, then in moving along. With these aesthetic, social creations, Black Americans were the "freest," as Charles Murray has stated, "to make a synthesis of all the elements that their condition challenged them with. They moved beyond enslavement and social invisibility to became the 'Omni-American,' the quintessential example of American personhood and character."[4] This is what is meant by cultural study: investigating artistic expression in historical, social, and political contexts; such an investigation provides us with a framework for exploring the meaning and complexities of "lived stories."

THE AFRICAN ROOT

A full appreciation and understanding of Black music is possible only when first looking at the African cultural, aesthetic root. All Black arts created within the Diaspora (Europe, West Indies, North and South America) are all cultural derivatives of traditional West African practice, philosophy, and worldview; these arts include dance, music, sculpture, poetry, quilting, storytelling, instrument building, and religious practices. The African spiritual worldview and practice are the roots of Black music and African American cultural practices. Africans in most traditional belief systems have held a particular philosophy about life that grows from their understanding of human community in relation to the divine, directed communal spirit. For our purposes, arts, life, and religion are not separate operations; they are equal mirrors, expressions of reality.

Music and artistic expression are used as extensions of the thinking about who "we" are in relation to a divine Spirit and each other. As John Miller Chernoff, in *African Rhythm and African Sensibilities: Aesthetic and Social Action in Musical Idioms* puts it, "The depth of music's integration into almost all of the various aspects of African social life is an indication that music helps to provide an appropriate framework through which people may relate to each other when they pursue activities they judge to be important and common place."[5] Music as a cultural expression is a by-product primarily of this world/community view, and is used to help keep these sensibilities in place.

The African saying "the Spirit will descend with a good song" is an outgrowth of an understanding that when the song is a reflection of the thinking of the whole community in relation to divine interaction, God's Spirit descends among the people. When experiencing particularly traditional African music, it carries a wide variety of expressions. Also, one can't help but notice the colors, shapes, textures of African arts in sculpture, instrument making, costume, and daily dress adornments, all of which signify the spectacular resonance of life which is a reflection of African worldview. All this can be seen, heard, and felt in the vibrancy of African music heard principally as rhythmic dynamism. When considering the horrific African slave trade and system (approximately 1440–1860, 420 years plus 100 years of legalized segregation and racial separation ending in the 1960s), there is a heavy concentration of enslaved Africans coming out of West Africa (Senegal, Guinea, Ivory Coast, Ghana, Nigeria, Cameroon, Gabon, Congo, Zaire, Angola). There is a direct line or route from West Africa that leads to South America, the West Indies, Haiti, Cuba, the Southern states, and, for our purposes, very notably, New Orleans.

Once the West (Europe, the Americas) was in contact with Africans, which represented a huge number of peoples, languages, and cultural practices in this context of contact, Western culture would be influenced, changed, and reshaped drastically. The very ignorant assertion by historians that Blacks have not contributed positively to any civilization is now understood as mindless racist theory.

One of the most enduring and dominant influences in the West is African and African American musical culture and practice. Because the music is such an important part of the African worldview, it is not surprising that much of this practice was brought with Africans to their new homes and environments. During the middle passage the estimate is that ten million Africans survived from high estimates of close to 50 million brought out of the African continent. Through this mix of customs and inhumane breeding practices imposed on Africans by Europeans, and then Southern slave plantation owners, music would become the one linguistic/spiritual link that could unite African peoples in the new environments.

Because in traditional African life music accompanies every social, political, and communal activity, it continued to serve as a life-support system, sustaining Blacks through the activities American slaves had to adapt to. The principle carrier or tradition bearer of musical cultural/practice in West Africa was the griot, also called the *jali*. It is from such people that our notions of the role of artists have been handed down. Coupled with the Western European model of the artist as "cultural hero," promoted by philosophers such as Arthur Schopenhauer and Friedrich Nietzsche, and the composer Richard Wagner, the representation of myth, symbols, histories, moralities, and people stories by the artist reveals the importance and power of the musician in contemporary times.

In traditional belief systems, African realities are seen as structured by musical expression(s) which are synonymous with speech as communication. This gives a variety, a flexibility to tones, pitches, rhythms, pitches that are so important to African language and speech as expression. When you hear Blacks in the Diaspora expressing themselves in musical ways, it carries with it this emphasis on expressive meaning(s) synonymous with speech. This is one of the most salient points of African and African American artistic expression. African musicians are required to have a good ear, a sense of timing, an excellent memory, and a superb command of their art or craft. In writing from the Western-educated slave Olaudah Equiano, he states in 1789, "We are almost a nation of musicians, dancers and poets. Thus every great event . . . is celebrated in public dances, which are accompanied with song and music."[6] Musical practices in West Africa alone included song, scale, and rhythmic conventions and traditions with a staggering array of instrumental families and subgroups, including: xylophones and marimbas (pitched wooden pianos), stringed instruments, zithers, bows, the 21-stringed kora, brass, wind flutes, bells, rattles, whistles, and one of the world's largest assortment of drums used for every communicable purpose imaginable. It is interesting to see the speed of amalgamation of so many diverse African musical practices with Western musical instruments and practices, the outcome of which has revolutionized music making in modern times. The most enduring and influential forms were manifested in the American slave creations: the Spirituals and Blues which expanded to become Ragtime, Jazz, Gospel, R&B, Rock and Roll, Soul, Pop, and Hip Hop. These styles of African American practice gave rise to some of the most important creative artists of the Western world.

There are many performance and expressive concepts that help us to speak about definable characteristics that shape African American music. These African retentions have become staples of African American music, thought, and performance practices.

Consider the following elements found in African American music which are based on African roots: the music is communally based; it reflects collective and individual improvisation; it is spirit led; it exhibits rhythmic dynamism; it features the "sound" of the Black voice or uses the horn as an extension of the Black voice; it includes social commentary and employs inexhaustible variations of repetition and metric layering which includes guttural expression (moans, groans, screams, shrills) as beautiful; it encourages active listener participation and reaction; and the expressions incorporate physical movement as part of the performance practice.

The communal aspect of group participation is key and evident in every example of Black musical performance. (It would not be proper to stand up and say "Play it" during an orchestra concert.) As this relates to our discussion, the communal activity which accompanies music and dance has as much meaning and importance as a medium to exchange information as the music and dance itself. As a result of this basic premise, music helps to provide the "appropriate framework through which people may relate to each other" (Chernoff), and this characterizes most Black music making in the creative Diaspora.

After examining traditional West African culture, spiritual worldview, and musical arts, some fundamental aesthetic and musical staples emerge that shape Black musical thought and practice in the Diaspora.

Music and dance expression are a shared or "corporate faith experience," what we could call active artistic activity.

This corporate faith, expression, experience is for our understanding artistic, social/political, religious, individual, and collective expression. The performance can be innovative at each new happening, yet upholds traditionally respected, accepted conventions and standards of practice with a high value placed on performance execution and expression. All this is understood as mystical/spiritual, mythical, and historic truth telling in one. Music and artistic expression is noncategorically defined; that is, music equals life's expression to serve as entertainment, worship, or information sharing and is one function. Music is music and it is crucial to life.

Rhythmic dynamism or diversity is an important idea, practice in Black musical expression and execution. As a matter of fact rhythm is primary and is a way of order associated with ideas, a philosophy, the meaning of life or how life resonates. It is like the Native American notion of the drum as "heartbeat." ("It don't mean a thing, if it ain't got that swing"—Duke Ellington.)

Music, dance, sculpture, singing, and instrument making are interdependent and aesthetically congruent.

There is an inextricable union of spoken, sung musical, and instrumental expression as bound with the human vocal line. For Blacks in the Diaspora, expressing in musical ways carries with it this emphasis on expressive meaning(s) synonymous with speech. Music is the examination and the probe of personal and corporate experiences. "That's why I sing d' blues."

In short, these things taken together form a constitutive body of elements shaping and defining Black expressions throughout the Diaspora from voodoo, to Jazz, to literature, to

Romere Beardon, to break dancing, Gospel music, and Rap, to Ellington and the symphonic works of William Grant Still.

THE CULTURAL KITCHEN: MUSIC AND CULTURAL EXPRESSION IN SLAVERY (SPIRITUALS AND THEIR MEANING)

The Spirituals: Definitions

The Spirituals are a body of slave religious songs created by plantation Blacks who fused western European harmonies and forms with preexisting West African songs, modalities, and practices, making an African American slave church tradition. The result was Black American slave songs used in religious meetings among slaves. These represent the first collectible body of newly formed African American music.

The definition of religion (Latin, *religare*) is to tie together again. As we examine the musical, theological, and cultural meaning of one great body of Black music created in the United States, we have to remember that we are simultaneously fusing two major religious-cultural-social-philosophical musical worldviews and practices together; one from Africa and one from western Europe. Religion is further defined by sociologists as a set of ideas, values, and beliefs that shape how a group of people understands the world and therefore affect their behavior. Religion is always the concretized belief system, the institution that mechanizes and gives structural function to the collective beliefs. The sociologist divides religion into a substantive definition that focuses on the essence, the essentials, the belief in spiritual beings, God, and the functional definition that explains how it (religion) operates. In short, religion is a unified system of beliefs and practices relative to sacred things. These beliefs and practices unite into a single moral community or church including all that adheres to them. The community or church helps people cope with the perplexities of life by offering an explanation and by providing a strategy to overcome despair, hopelessness, and futility. This is one way to begin to explain the binding of practices and beliefs behind the unique formation of Black Christianity and its supporting musical and ritual conventions.

In traditional West African belief, the values, religious, and communal ethos are believed to be integrated in the musical and social exchange. The musical participation embodies one's commitment and beliefs, and is a part of the communal exchange, including values, wisdom, and cultural practice. Music is a part of this sensibility. The Black Spiritual(s) encompassed the "newly accepted" Christian beliefs and symbols in song text, but wrapped them up within the African notions of spirituality, functionality, performance practice, and sounds.

The formation of the Negro American Spiritual provides a place in history where cultural amalgamation gets played out on a more universal stage: the meeting of the West with Black reflection in spiritual and social experiences in the more than 400-year period of slavery. Black music practice has an appeal that transcends its culture, and the prevailing issue is the human struggle to survive and hope to overcome. This is the universal message of the Spiritual song traditions.

Within the rise of global exports and interests in a world market, there erupted Black people and their aesthetic creations, which became part of the commodification of goods and services in the great transatlantic slave trade, the first global economic experiment. Within this experiment, Black people with tremendous cultural systems were left to reorient themselves around and within a new cosmology. Music as a belief and language system becomes the primary and first anchor on which a foundation for reaffirming human worth, dignity, and power could be established. And much of the power of communication could be found in musical expression, early on.

The relevance of the Spiritual songs and their theological significance and power can be seen among Black believers. That is, the idea of an abstract understanding of a European version of Jesus Christ was transformed into a direct and personal identification with the pain, power, and the resurrected Spirit of the Christ figure. Scholars have called this Black identification with the Jesus event "Black Theology." Slaves identified their struggle with the Israelites and their bondage. One of the major concerns of the slave system was the "Christianization" of the slaves. By the earliest baptizing (1641), there was an indoctrination of enslaved Africans by colonists with biblical stories and Western Christian concepts. And while this escaped the slaveholders, it is easy to see how the savior figure in Jesus became a saving figure for slavery. Christ's triumph over death became Black triumph over the evils of the slave system. The biblical cultural hero Moses delivering his people out of bondage became another obvious powerful example of this forced cultural transfer. So we have the creation of a body of works by Blacks in the Spirituals, which are at once a cry for liberation, spiritual/religious/cultural expression, and artistic individualism. Therefore the art piece becomes a place of extreme meanings intertwined.

Songs such as "Freedom Train," "Oh Freedom over Me," and "Swing Low" are examples of a mix of religious sentiment and social/political expression. For instance, the words to "Go Down Moses" read: "Go down Moses, way down in Egypt land. Tell ol' Pharaoh to let my people go." These songs reinvented, placed a premium on using the song to convey, contextually, the realism of the singer's trials. It is also easy to trace the principal performers from traditional African songsters, griots, and *jalis* to the slave preacher, Blues singer, Gospel singer, and Soul singer to the rapper and to mark how the traditions and African retentions remained:

1. African griot (retold and kept history, culture, religion)
2. Slave singer (work songs release)
3. Plantation preacher (social gospel)
4. Plantation fiddler, singer (diversion and social entertainment)
5. American minstrel traditions (slave life mimicked on stage)
6. Bluesmen and -women (psychological, social)
7. Jazz singer (Black American popular song)
8. Political poets (1960s and 1970s revolutionary poetry, Gil Scott Heron)
9. Contemporary R&B singers and rappers (post-1970s urban social experience of Blacks)

In the Spirituals we have a people screaming out, pushing boundaries, and transcending their condition, wrestling with the meaning of their existence, challenging the times. These are the essential meanings of the Spirituals. Or, as Ray Pratt has observed in his *Rhythm and Resistance*, "The Spirituals suggest music may function in a profoundly utopian way, seeking to transcend the existing order . . . music is that space, that realm of freedom." The Spirituals were "impressive creations of an oppressed minority who used the music as a mode of psychological revitalization."[7]

Process

But how did they get "cooked up"? The Spirituals as musical expressions are the amalgamation of African scales, rhythmic and style sensibility, and the European hymn traditions of Isaac

Watts and others. As slaves were required to participate in the White religious services, they adapted and transformed creatively the song traditions they heard. Slaves were exposed to these traditions through examples seen in the Bay Psalm Book of the colonies (1651) and later Watt's hymns (1707) and John Wesley's psalms, hymns, and spiritual songs (1742). The later evangelical songs were livelier, as they were used in religious revival contexts. These later Christian songs had more rhythm, were more "loose," and were adaptable. This was a perfect opportunity for African embellishment and appropriation to combine with an African formulation of song expression and performance. There are numerous accounts of observers who began to point out that the slaves were doing something quite different with the religious music.

Beyond the religious, individual yearning for meaning and artistic considerations, there also is the all-important context of the slave plantation system. As scholar Roger Abrahams has written, in *Singing the Master: The Emergence of African American Culture in the Slave South*:

> I see the events as being characteristic of a dynamic process taking place on the plantation in which the slaves neither divested themselves of their African cultural heritage nor acculturated to the behaviors and patterns of their White masters. The practices emerged as forms of resistance, not in the sense that they attacked the system but rather in ways in which they maintained alternatives toward time, work, and status. In the process new cultural forms emerged. . . . An African American culture was developed by slaves in counterpoint to "planter" ideology. . . . A good deal of culture building then was taking place in the yard between the Big House and the slave quarters, in contested areas betwixt and between two worlds.[8]

Examples beyond music include food traditions (chitterlings, yams, greens), new complexities of sexual relations (slave women and slave men with White lovers, round-up breeding), corn shucking and dance contests, and certainly the social protest/Black Theology that developed in the "invisible institution."

The "invisible institution," or underground Black church was developed by slaves in resistance to and independently of the "traditional" church. After hours, the slaves would gather together and create their own services. The music they created in spiritual resistance was the Black church music that has been the foundation of most Black American music forms. In the colonies, the East and North, the independent Black churches emerged more fully in the 1790s; an example of this is Richard Allen and AME (African Methodist Episcopal). But the large body of Spirituals were essentially slave songs and were developed orally first on the plantation.

Types

There are generally three kinds of Spirituals which are performed: the Folk Spiritual, still sung in many traditional rural churches; the Hymn Spiritual, sung as a regular part of congregational hymn books; and the Concert Spiritual, represented by choral arrangements and performances by the likes of Paul Robeson, Robert McFerrin, William Warfield, or contemporary opera greats Jesse Norman, Kathleen Battle, or Denise Graves.

One of the Spiritual song traditions which survives today is the more "artistic" notated rendition sung by trained concert singers and choirs. These "notated" Spirituals began to be collected and preserved and given international exposure, first through the Fisk Jubilee Singers (1870s) and other Black college groups which emerged after the Civil War.

In regard to music making, slaves for sale were listed in newspapers as "very fine fiddlers and banjo players," and this musical element increased their marketability. All kinds of music making was happening, and many shapes of this synthesis of traditions by Black Americans were evident as early as the late seventeenth century. There are examples early on of Black composers of African descent working in Europe, such as Chevalier de St. George (1745–1794), who directed the Parisian orchestra in the late 1700s, or English-born Samuel Coleridge Taylor (1875–1912), who was called during his lifetime "the greatest living composer since Beethoven." In both of these cases, we have Black artists combining the tradition of Western art music with the identity, expression, and cultural traditions of Black people. These efforts were first crystallized in our American form with the numerous arrangements and spiritual compositions penned by early American practitioners like William Wesley Work. This music was "raised" to the concert repertoire again in the early part of the century with the efforts of traditional Black (-trained) concert singers who performed this repertoire of the "Negro Spirituals" in recitals or liturgical services. Following the successful concretizing and worldwide appearances by the Fisk Jubilee Singers in the 1870s, Black American singers helped to make this work a part of what has become mainstream repertoire.

European composer Anton Dvorak wrote praises of the American slave music, and on hearing it commented, "[These are] the most striking and appealing melodies that have yet been found on this side of the water unrecognized by most Americans."[9]

The pure utilitarianism of holding up a people, assuring dignity and hope in the face of physical and emotional abandonment and psychological terror is an extraordinary and fascinating art piece. The genius in the form is that it is the concretization of the themes of suffering, hope, plans of insurrection, and spiritual empowerment and faith, all at once.

When we listen to Spirituals as a special stylized music, this new twist in expression is before the Blues, before Broadway and Jazz, and American popular singing. The spirituals are the great foundation for forms that were to emerge out of this road map. These works represent a three-stream tradition: western European, Black American vernacular, both sacred and secular music practices.

These are the ingredients for original and new cultural traditions, truly "American" and truly, in a sense, African American. These elements, the building blocks of culture, include: the social/political context (slavery), a religious worldview where Christianity fused with African notions of "in tuned" gods who work in natural connection with human destiny (ancestors), musical traditions, and importantly, family and community bonds (slave breeding). So here emerges the Spiritual, a religious song tradition shaped simultaneously by European structures and sonorities and African scales and melodic traditions within Black rhythmic performance traditions. These songs were sung and performed by Blacks to give spiritual meaning and expression. Simultaneously the slaves used the Spiritual as encoded message pieces which eventually served as resistance songs carrying the message of human freedom and liberation. There are several things to keep in mind in summation of the exploration of the Spirituals as Black cultural product.

From about the 1690s to the 1890s there developed, largely from slave singing, a repertoire of some six thousand religious songs known today as Negro Spirituals. These songs are the earliest style that emerged from what were called "field hollers" and "work songs" but were the fusing together of African tradition, practice, and worldview and principally European religious hymnal traditions that slaves were expected to learn as they attended their master's religious services.

The Spirituals contain numerous themes that are conscious and are evidence of literary wit and personal, communal resolve in terms of the songs being protest construction. The themes of liberation and freedom, divine justice, living in exile, having faith in adversity, death and suffering, Jesus as friend and salvation, and clear articulation of antislavery sentiment are contained in the Spirituals. There is the widespread use of metaphors and double meanings in the texts such as: train (a way of escape), chariot (group of escapees heading North), cloud (the other side of the cloud is heaven), Jordan (the North), and pharaoh (slave master). All of this is a clear articulation of Black Theology in song and religious practice. This is a unique form of Black Christianity among Black believers. Jesus Christ was transformed into the embodiment of pain, power, and resurrection synonymous with the slave experience. This provided Black identification with the Jesus event, where slaves saw their struggle and triumph as identical with those of the Israelites and their bondage and freedom as depicted in the Bible. In this way the slaves' freedom was to be realized in due time, just as in the biblical promise that was made to Israel.

Amiri Baraka has asserted, "Black musical arts reveal something simultaneously about the nature of Black weighted psyches, as well as the nature of this country." It should follow that Black music by Black creators in America carries with it an irrefutable beauty and depth which demands a more critical view. The music itself is a set of eyeglasses into dimensions of the "souls of Black folks," an understanding of their history and of a peculiar sociological context. Because of the profundity and diversity of Black experience in America, the cultural expressions are at once filled with glory, triumph, pain and despair, beauty and ugliness; they are lyrical and dissonant, liberated and enslaved. The expressions are democratic, pluralistic, ethnically molded, religious, and spiritually reverberant, rich and dirt poor. Coupled with the facts we explored about the representative nature of art (that art and life's experiences are intertwined), Black music by aesthetic and sociological design is profoundly unparalleled by its "own" definition.

The Blues

The Blues, in short, is a music form and style of playing that evolved out of the Spiritual and slave hollers and can be thought of as plantation and Black rural songs taken on the road to the streets. The Blues are song/poetry concerned with common experience and instrumentally driven by a sole nonspecialist folk singer on the banjo/guitar, which extends later to piano, horns, and eventually ensembles. This is common, country, Black folk music. But the most salient point of the Blues is how it sounds and how it functions to give a "deep down real feeling" about experiences in the world, usually troubling, but always meant to be uplifting, to "play the trouble away." There is great power in art's ability to identify "misery," name it, and then deal with it by "operating on it." The Blues is expressed in slurred, moaning, gutsy singing and playing, using what are sometimes referred to as "blued" or minor tones within a scale. This "singing between the pitches" was a uniquely African embellishment to the European musical scale theoretically characterized by lowering (flatting) the third, fifth, and seventh pitches of a major scale even against the major chord sonority or sound. But the courage of the Blues singer and the profundity of the form and singing is that the Blues addresses expressively in song how Black people were feeling and "dealin' wid'" it. It has been said that Blues music, bluesy expression, is "Black music speaking language," inner beliefs and feelings the musician is playing, telling the story. Blues is the "mother tongue" of all Black popular music, thus American popular music.

We can see the transfer in terms of the role of the musician who handles the forms going from the griot or *jali*, to slave plantation musician and lead singer, shouter, or slave preacher, to now the wandering, individual Bluesman. There were numerous slave musicians who apparently were very skilled and generated folk traditions on fiddle and guitar, mixing these with rural, poor, White English and Irish ballads and jig traditions. These musical traditions were eventually taken to the cities. The Blues became the foundation or root in many ways of all other forms to grow out of the Black vernacular, from Gospel to urban contemporary. Due to the decentralization of Blacks via the emancipation after the Civil War (1860s through the 1920s), the worldview, the daily experience, now extended beyond the plantation and plantation church experience. Now we had "roaming Negroes," men in search of jobs and for the first time solely responsible for providing for a family. This was a new experience. The downside of it, the angst and powerlessness of this new identity, provided a new social context. Mixed in was the reality of broken love, sex, tragedy in interpersonal relationships, death, and travel.

And while there was much movement to the big cities of New York, Chicago, Pittsburgh, and Philadelphia, there was also a lot of movement to larger Southern cities like Jackson, Mississippi; Atlanta, Georgia; Charlotte, North Carolina; and elsewhere. The American social reality was now a South and North thrown into a completely new understanding of a multiethnic society. This is another example of Black American creative musing which articulates through song, Black presence. These songs began to contribute to the dynamics of social, political, economic identity and forced America to truly live up to its "believed in" creeds of freedom and justice for all. The issues surfaced through song. Soon separate but equal facilities of segregation emerged. What was a Black person's human place in such a society? It was worked out first in song. During this time even in the South, the Black community was divided into several social/work classes including tenant farmers, migrant laborers, clergy, tradesmen (cobblers, locksmiths, iron men, storekeepers), and professional men—teachers, dentists, lawyers, and doctors who were descendants of several generations of freed educated Blacks.

Before the migration of so many Blacks after the Civil War to the cities in the late 1890s, the largest concentration of Black migrant workers who were largely isolated was the farmers of the Mississippi Delta region. Here we find an isolated and dense population that sustained older remaining African traditions cultivated during slave life, and again the Blues was the dominant musical style and tradition. Many of these traditions are still practiced up until today. Here you can still find the drum and fife bands, instrument making, and some of the retained African song traditions. W. C. Handy (1873–1958), a Northern-trained Black musician, first heard these styles, the Blues, in Cleveland, Mississippi, during a stay in the Delta (1903–1908). Soon after Handy published his "Memphis Blues" in 1912 and "St. Louis Blues" in 1914. They put into notation a 12-bar form, based on a I–IV–V chord sequence that became the standard practice among musicians. The evolution, migrations, and decisions (mostly imposed due to American social construction) about what would be the best path to integration caused a split in the psyche, disposition, and temperament of American Blacks; this split is still evident today. How much was to be abandoned on the "altar of assimilation and progress"?

Musically, the structural and stylistic limitations of the work song and traditional spiritual forms could no longer contain the experiences the wandering singer-poets began to respond to. The Blues as an expressive form became more elastic and improvisational; it became an elusive, somewhat structured, somewhat free poetic/musical form that contained Black experience from about the 1870s into the first years of the twentieth century. The form began to evolve and grow up. It is this form and expressive styling that became the most persuasive American music form created here on this soil. Every derivative popular form from Country Western to Broadway and the film megaproductions of the 1930s and 1940s have developed from and deeply dipped into the Blues. Much of what is contained in the Blues (form and structure, style, musical syntax) has become the foundation for music written by composers, from William Grant Still to the Beatles. The Blues is the equivalent of a standard blueprint which an architect might use to construct a new building.

The insistence and focus of the Blues verse on the life of the individual and his individual trials and successes on the earth is a manifestation of the whole concept of man's life and its development. The Blues gives the emotional meaning to the individual, to one's complete personal life and death. It is musical existentialism! Americans didn't have a music that was so personal, so introspective, the "real deal." This is a part of its appeal.

Cultural critic/historian Gerald Early commented that if Black people in the West had only just given the world the musical artistry of the Blues, that would have been enough to cement their place in the evolution of the modern world. On another front from about the 1830s is the growth of the exploitative form called Minstrelsy. Minstrelsy is a mix of European stage and parlor music with Black music styles; it included grotesque and degrading mimicking of slave music traditions. This hybrid form swept the country during the nineteenth century and found its way transformed into urban vaudeville shows, the father of Broadway musical traditions. White minstrel performers used burnt cork to darken their faces and performed Black folk songs, dances, jokes, and stage acts they witnessed in simple rural exchange. They distorted this and made mimicry of it for profit. This material produced the first all-American entertainment variety show. Again this material was based on Black "cultural stuff." This is really the beginning of American popular music traditions. It is a complex tale of appropriation and commercialization, a battlefield for cultural politics, and America's best form of diversion. Even here, Minstrelsy never stopped being a place where Black expression asserted "meaning(s)."

TRAVELS

The Mississippi

While there were significant Black music traditions being established and practiced from the eighteenth century in places like colonial Boston, Philadelphia, and New York, and certainly in the rural South, another extremely significant development happened in the seaport city of New Orleans. These traditions traveled upward on the Mississippi River. In New Orleans, many Black traditions; European, Native American, and Creole music culture; along with the Blues thrived in the streets and communities. This cultural stirring was a big part of the nineteenth-century mix. The migratory period of Blacks moving in various ways northbound after the Civil War created the public awareness and dissemination of what began as rural slave music and became the internationally respected, sought after, and imitated American popular music(s).

Out of New Orleans, the Mississippi represents figuratively as well as literally a great transport of culture. For Black people, as portrayed in the Langston Hughes poem "The Negro Speak of Rivers," the river, the Nile, the Mississippi, ole man river has represented a deep wellspring of spiritual meaning, the flow of life and vitality. This theme comes up consistently in vernacular form (lyrics) and was a constant companion psychologically for these peoples on their various pilgrimages northbound. As mentioned earlier, the Blues is also an example and sonic result of people who take song and music and travel. The rich land of the Delta was fertile and Black farmers and laborers picked cotton for 40 cents a day, 35 cents for two hundred pounds. One farmer recollected that his father was picking in 1900 for 20 cents a day.

That's the Blues! Cotton for the South was big business. At the close of the eighteenth century, it was reported that cotton exports produced 57 percent of the nation's economy. Southern towns along the Mississippi became playgrounds for millionaires and investors. Once again, as in the life of the plantation, it was Southern rural Black music that provided the cultural icing, the diversion.

The urban cosmopolitan result is the urban Blues heard in Chicago, which eventually transformed to Jazz, R&B, and Gospel. These more urban versions of the Black vernacular rural Blues of the Mississippi Delta farmer are the result symbolically of a turbulent ride up the Mississippi, the result of social hardships, loss of love, and an endless search for new roots, better economics, and identity. To understand the Mississippi in this light is to keep in mind what it represented as a vehicle to escape one version only to find newer, sometimes even more harsh versions of White hatred in the Northern cities. The urban Blues is the musical result of the Black awakening to this new social reality.

The music (Blues) of these Mississippi Delta farmers now looking for work in the cities is the "reporting on" the travels of these displaced workers/singers, urban soothsayers. It was not all gloom and doom, though. There was freedom and there was the excitement of exploring the Mississippi and the lure of work and opportunity in very vibrant Northern towns such as Memphis, St. Louis, and of course Chicago. The plantation music of Blacks hit the road during a time of prosperity at the close of the nineteenth century, with the macrocultural growth of the U.S. economy and life; it is easy to see the musical transformation and the carrying of Blacks up the Mississippi northbound to settle in the cities. The reality of travel and exploration and industry, cultural transformation, cross-pollination, sharing, technology, and evolution of style resulted in newer forms of musical expression.

New Orleans

The year 1897 is said to be the year that the New Orleans red-light district, later called Storyville, was allowed to exist and be open for business. Travelers, sailors, and those locals who wanted to dabble in the "delights" were entertained by musicians who had been developing a syncretistic dance and instrumental style which came to be known as New Orleans band style. The music was performed by trained musicians or at least musicians who were exchanging ideas with European professionals in a rich environment that was more tolerant than others of exchanges of all kinds between Whites and Blacks. Keep in mind many of the styles, sounds, forms, and practices (Spirituals and Blues) among Black musicians from the rural South were similar and had been preserved and shared among Black people. Various "Black ways" of doing music had been established for nearly two centuries already. More exchanges in New Orleans produced a music that apparently allowed a European instrumental–Black fusion to emerge, flourish, and develop performing conventions. There are so many great musicians and mythical folk heroes who forged the styles, such as Buddy Bolden and Jass-bo Brown (who, some report, gave us the name "Jazz"), and most certainly the great traveling New Orleans musicians like Jelly Roll Morton (1890–1941) and King Oliver (1885–1938), who spread the sound, style, and influence of New Orleans Rag-Blues-early Jazz as far as Chicago and California in the early twentieth century.

New Orleans is a mix of many different cultures, and one model for how Black, European, and indigenous music(s) coexisted. One great artistic example of this syncretism is the internationally recognized composer and pianist, Louis Moreau Gottschalk. Born in New Orleans in 1829, still reported by some historians to be in fact a Creole (of mixed race), by the age of 13 he was sent to Paris to study. By the 1840s at the height of the steamboat culture he began to compose a mixture of plantation melodies, Caribbean rhythms, and traditions he had learned. He is a great example of the New Orleans syncretic workings which provided the basis for how future American music would be formed and fashioned. His music was a hit in European circles and exemplary of Black forms being disseminated internationally, just as the Fisk Jubilee singers were able to do with the Spiritual in Europe about this same time.

Another musical example of New Orleans traditions being carried further northward up the Mississippi by performers is the great Louis Armstrong, born 73 years later in 1901. Armstrong played first on steamboats, moved to Chicago, settled in New York, moved back to Chicago, then moved back again to New York. By considering musical personalities who "speak" the art it is easy to see how these forms spread up the Mississippi, went across land then back down the Mississippi again, ultimately influencing the way these forms gelled and established several performance practices recognized today as Black music styles. The more pure vernacular folk traditions (traditional Blues) of the rural Delta moved up the Mississippi to St. Louis and Chicago as well. Industry and people moved back and forth and up and down the Mississippi again. Consequently you have groups of musicians settling in those cities yet still traveling back to the South. And there are the technologies of the new century and the culture of radio and entertainment that are beginning to emerge at the same time. Traveling musicians were hearing the big city musicians whose urban cultural kitchens heated up in places like Washington, D.C., and of course Harlem, New York. There began by the 1920s to be an industry, a market for recorded Black vernacular music. The Mississippi Delta Blues once again proved to be rich in music and cultural resources.

All kinds of industry by the early part of the century can be compared to a "river float," and American popular musical culture got its boosts along the river in towns where the people were entertained, as in the red-light districts of New Orleans, Natchez, Memphis, St. Louis, and again, later, Chicago. As people stopped along the Mississippi, a part of the experience was town entertainment. And it is in these places where much music gets manufactured, refined, then sent again up the river as those musicians traveled within the steamboat commodities industry. Consequently farmers made "midstream" career changes as they found their rural lamenting could have marketability. This is how much of the rural Blues from the Delta created by Black southerners became urban products to be subsumed under American popular cultural product. Some of the best examples of traditional Blues singers from Southern regions are Charley Patton (1880s–1934), Son House (1902–1988), John Lee Hooker (1917/20–2001), Muddy Waters (1915–1983), the great Robert Johnson (1911–1938), and B. B. King (b. 1925). These musicians have made a most impressionable mark on our culture with American Blues traditions.

THE URBAN SPRAWL: MORE MIGRATIONS

"I got stones in my passway, and my road seems dark as night. I have pains in my heart, they have taken my appetite."

—Blues singer Robert Johnson, "Stones in My Passway"

Historian Paul Oliver writes,

The Mississippi Delta is often regarded as the birthplace of the Blues. Many Blues singers came from this area, where the Black population equaled and in many cases far outnumbered Whites.

The proximity to Memphis and the relative ease with which record executives could reach the area by rail from Chicago also meant that it was well placed for location recording. Similarly, many Mississippi Blues singers were able to migrate to Chicago.[10]

As stated earlier, during the first half of the Reconstruction period (1867–1877), there emerged the wandering Bluesman who performed and adapted Black song traditions for comment on and expression of his secular condition. While the earlier rural Blues and work songs were created to accompany the needs of the worker (created to give expressive vent to these migrant farmer/workers looking for work and homes, lost in the city), they could no longer contain the new experiences of Black people as they began to participate more fully in American society. Migrant, out-of-work laborers toward the end of the century approaching World War I numbered in the hundreds of thousands and set into motion a new socioeconomic urban life pursuit. All this is reflected in the music.

The South during this time enacted Black Codes and vagrancy laws prohibiting the movement of Black men, instituting jail sentences and prison work camps for men found without having proof of work. This condition is mirrored in the text of the Blues as well. In 1857's infamous Dred Scott decision, Supreme Court Justice Roger B. Taney declared, "Blacks have for more than a century been regarded as beings of an inferior order and altogether unfit to associate with the White race either in social or political relations, and so far inferior that they had no rights which the white man was bound to respect." In 1896 the courts further upheld a doctrine of "separate but equal," mandating segregation in public transportation and facilities. Between 1889 and 1899, with the terrorism of the Ku Klux Klan, the public spectacle of lynchings numbered around 189 per year. This precipitated a series of great migrations of Blacks from the South, in which hundreds of thousands of men and women moved to the North. They brought their music with them.

As we will continue to see, the notes still resonate with meanings connected to and reflective of people migrating with stories of hope.

The Classic Blues, another development of Black Blues, were born in this urban entertainment mix; they were notated and recorded by White rural music collectors and then disseminated through a new industry called race records. As mentioned earlier, W. C. Handy, who had lived in Memphis, heard Blues singing as early as 1903 and published his "Memphis Blues" and "St. Louis Blues." By this time the practices and tradition had moved up the river to the major urban areas. These so-called Classic or Urban Blues were sung many times by more lovely and glamorous versions of lamenting women, often on the stage and in front of cameras.

The first race records (Okeh, Columbia, Victor, Paramount, Decca), a regular series of commercial recordings of Black popular music, were initiated by Perry Bradford, a songwriter and manager of a traveling singer named Mamie Smith (1883–1946). Okeh Records released her single, "Crazy Blues," which became a hit. Soon other White recording companies began to record and issue series which were catalogs of Black performers. Mamie Smith then is credited as the first commercially successful popular music recording artist, as many would soon after follow this pattern. Black Swan records and the Pace Music Company should be mentioned here, because it was the only completely Black owned and operated recording company which produced diverse recordings from Blues to concert singers. Its great staff arranger was the celebrated dean of African American classical concert composers, William Grant Still (Afro-American Symphony).

It is during this period that Black singing and "style" became a performance characteristic that established a unique Black popular projection, image, sass, and flavor. Other singers, such as Ma Rainey (1886–1939), Bessie Smith (1895–1937), Alberta Hunter (1895–1984), and Ethel Waters (1896–1979), had helped to cement Blues traditions and style. The contribution of these ladies greatly enhanced the popular presence of Black artistry and made it a significant artistic achievement in the West.

Ragtime

Ragtime is another urban musical form/style which is largely instrumental (piano) and personified by the most known Black Ragtime composer, Scott Joplin. While most of my discussion here has been on the migration of people who carried and settled in places carrying the Blues, the other extremely relevant Black music form that developed in Black communities was Ragtime. Ragging a piece of music is "Blacking it up." This refers to Black style(s) principally giving music a dance jig, or jump. Later this would mean jazzing something up, giving it the personal, "Black feel." Trained Black musicians who settled in the East and North who perhaps were able to take some form of music lessons applied their own ethnic/vernacular feel to European parlor piano music, or band music. The result was a notated, written form pulling from the two worlds, and the music phenomenon became Ragtime. At first it was principally a piano music, but later it became instituted in band, chamber, and even orchestral music. Actually, one of the ways newly freed Eastern- or Northern-settled Black families showed their independence was to purchase a piano. This was an American, largely Northern show of middle-class values. But the style emerged also out of necessity. Many Black musicians were hired to provide music for saloons, eateries, and such, and, as W. C. Handy noted, these Black players were piano thumpers.

They were a one-man band, consequently developing a style of piano playing that was dance orientated, while simultaneously steeped in traditional European melodic and harmonic stability and grounding. The "two worlds" on piano became rag-piano or "Ragtime." This is clearly a holdover from slave dancing and fiddling. The most notable creator of the high form of piano rag was composer Scott Joplin (1868–1917). The point is that he was a trained Black pianist who settled in Missouri, conducted a piano studio, attended George Smith College for Blacks, toured, and in 1899 found a publisher to publish his "Maple Leaf Rag," which sold a reported one million copies! Joplin went on to work and live in New York and composed the first Black American opera, *Treemonisha*, in 1911. Joplin was the first widely known Black American trained composer of critical acclaim. His work made a major imprint on American music and introduced a pre-Jazz Black form respected throughout the world. This was a major marker of Black artistry in modern society. One point that should be made, particularly in these early American music stages, is that new music is developing and overlapping all the time. So style discussion must be seen as a pendulum across these decades, threaded between and within these traditions, regions. It is not as if the Spirituals, Blues, Ragtime ever dried up and went away; they are a continuum in the evolution of the music, as we will see in Jazz.

Jazz and the New Negro

The Blues was initially vocal-based music and, as mentioned earlier, a form as well as a style. Jazz music was first born out of the Blues styling as instrumentalists were emulating the vocal tradition, making the horns "talk" and speak like a Blues singer's sentiment and riff. While Blues singing may well represent a traditional, vernacular, folk-based style during the early years of the twentieth century, there is the emergence of the assimilated, educated Black communities and their interests. The sentiment of the New Negro was largely reflected in a manifesto by university professor and writer Alain Locke. The New Negro, this modern, urban, self-liberated Negro, created the need for new forms which were more refined, urban, and sophisticated to accommodate the expression of this new identity socially. Jazz music, particularly in places like New York or D.C., where middle-class, urban Blacks lived and produced in greater numbers, is the form more closely associated with this move. Jazz is the highly stylized instrumental musical form that evolved and grew from the vernacular slave song traditions of the Spirituals, slave hollers, Blues, and Ragtime.

While many of these forms "grew up" nurtured in the diversity of the New Orleans atmosphere and then traveled north, Ragtime in particular developed as a Northern musical expression. The musician-bandleader who is credited with not only bridging the transformation of early, New Orleans Jazz to the modern big band, but with creating the modern Jazz orchestra, is Fletcher Henderson (1897–1952). As he organized his band for playing entertainment venues in New York, during the early 1920s, he formed the model of Jazz band organization: separate sections of five saxophones, horns, and rhythm instruments. He is called the father of big band.

Jazz music as a form was now purely an urban music, slick and refined and highly commercial. It was the natural result of yet another cultural amalgamation of European aesthetic standards and forms and the artistic individuality of Black musicians by the end of the nineteenth century. What is most timely for Black artistry is that Jazz music emerged as the popular voice of the newly industrialized, "cultured," and rich America. From about the time of the 1920s through the 1950s, this new American style, seen through the artistry of Jazz, helped to socialize the country in ways that made acceptable for the first time Black artistry and imagery. Again, the artistry of figures like Louis Armstrong as an early ambassador projected this American art/human-expressive style internationally. In modern life "image" is everything. Before the new Negro Jazz image, Blacks were portrayed in cartoons as monkeys, dumb hairy creatures and happy, overweight, cooking mammies. Jazz music allowed the carrying of Black accomplishment and artistry exported internationally. Jazz art became America's popular music, to which everybody danced, loved, and dreamed. Of all the indigenous Black musical forms, Jazz is the most highly developed from a craftsman's perspective. Yet, Jazz also maintained most of the aesthetic, artistic standards, and staples of the other forms, including improvisation, rhythmic dynamism, group interaction, and African-derived expressions of scoops, growls, and blued scale formations. In every way, Jazz is an attempt to emulate Black vocal styling. Secondly, Jazz is move and groove music and it must swing because it accompanies Black people moving.

An important phase of Jazz as a recognized American form was its acceptance by elitist White musical circles. In his essay which appeared in the 1925 book *The New Negro*, J. A. Rodgers quotes the internationally renown conductor Leopold Stokowski:

> Jazz has come to stay because it is an expression of the times, of the breathless, energetic, super active times in which we are living, it is useless to fight against it. The Negro musicians of America are playing a great part in this change. They have an open mind, and unbiased outlook. They are not hampered by conventions or traditions, and with their new ideas, their constant experiment, they are causing new blood to flow in the veins of music. . . . They are pathfinders into new realms.[11]

As early as 1893, European composer Anton Dvorak had written, "The future music of this nation [America] must be founded upon what are called the Negro melodies. These can be the foundation of a serious and original school of composition."[12] This should be proof enough that Black expressive forms had begun to make a significant imprint on American cultural identity: "the right notes." But Jazz had many detractors as well. The White American press and cultural critics, unfortunately, saw Jazz as music for monkeys and a degradation of culture.

Duke Ellington

One of the most respected, popular, and productive musicians to develop during the 1920s, 1930s, and 1940s was the composer, pianist, and bandleader Duke Ellington. Born in Washington, D.C., Duke (1899–1974) emerged in Harlem at the time of Harlem's Cotton Club (1927), a hot music and entertainment spot in New York which had a national radio broadcast. This helped to gain for Duke national status as a music radio star at a time when New York was being recognized as a cultural center of the world. Secondly, Duke emerged during the height of the New Negro movement among artists in Harlem in the 1920s. In this way Jazz as seen through the work of Ellington and many other artists heightened the image of Blacks as thinkers, accomplished, respectable, and "cultured." Jazz as a Black art form carried with it the hopes and aspirations of the newborn, early-twentieth-century, urban, cosmopolitan, Black America. Jazz was the right music to be associated with a social movement called the New Negro movement or the Harlem Renaissance. Several writers by the early 1920s, including James Weldon Johnson and Alain Locke, proclaimed Harlem as a cultural community with an intense life, Black diversity, and holding the greatest promise for the revival of the arts, a "crossroads of culture." Locke in his *New Negro* wrote, "In Harlem Negro life is seizing upon its first chances for group expression and self determination. It is the race capital. . . . The Negro celebrates the attainment of a significant and satisfactory new phase of group development."[13]

Writers, artists, poets, playwrights, choreographers, and composers worked toward the end of proving the greatness of the Black race through arts and literature. As a musical and cultural figure, Duke Ellington emerged as a central icon exemplifying these images and themes.

Actually, many accomplished people of color who were active during the nineteenth century focused their work, writings, music, and social protests on the behalf of their people. Called race men, they mechanized the rhetoric of Black pride and accomplishment in education, the arts, and society one hundred years or more before the Civil Rights period. Works such as David Walker's *Appeal* (1829), Henry Highland Garret's *Address to the Slaves of the United States* (1843), Martin Delany's *The Condition, Elevation and Destiny of the Colored People of the United States Politically Considered* (1858) were passionate and scathing attacks on the racist and hate-filled American system that deprived nearly 20 percent of its population of human dignity and public accommodations as basic as education or dining facilities. Black intellectuals (race men) such as George Washington Williams, W. E. B. DuBois (1868–1963), and Carter G. Woodson (1875–1950) began traditions of scholarship devoted to the research of the historic and heroic past of Blacks. There was also emerging an aggressive Black press, including Frederick Douglass's *North Star*, T. Thomas Fortune's *New York Globe* of 1874, William Monroe Trotter's *Boston Garden*, and the *Chicago Defender*, a Chicago-based paper which played a huge role in encouraging hundreds of thousands of Blacks to move north from the South. Also of importance was Marcus Garvey and his movement, which by 1920 had over one million followers. His message was one of race pride, economic self-sufficiency, and an Africa for Africans.

Bebop

Post-1940 there were Jazz artists who had become detached from the bubbling or "entertainment diversions" on the top. The Jazz styles beginning in the middle 1940s and especially Bebop represent a movement of musician or artist ideas. The beboppers consciously attempted to create an approach to Jazz playing that was more than mere entertainment. It was faster and more harmonically, melodically, and rhythmically challenging, with new tone colors and twists on old Jazz standards. A new emphasis was placed on altered chords, for example a flatted, or lowered, 5th, 7th, 9th, 11th, or 13th interval. This altering introduced chords that became more dense, and these altered notes began to appear more and more as normative properties of the music. And in this way, the beboppers were the first great revolution within the larger movement of Black music culture. It is during this period some of the most important architects of newer American popular musical styles emerged. Dizzy Gillespie (1917–1993) commented, "What we were doing at Minton's was . . . creating a new dialogue, blending our ideas into a new style of music. Our phrases were different, we were changing the way we spoke to reflect what we felt. The new phrasing came with the new accent, our music had a new accent."[14] That accent is called "Bop."

As Jazz music developed post–Harlem Renaissance, it began to be "its own" self, a music apart from a commercial entertainment art and the implications of it as social progress music. This was something the beboppers would bring out as the ingredient that fueled their devotions. Dizzy Gillespie in his *To Be or Not to Bop* speaks of this, as does one of his protégés, Quincy Jones (b. 1934). Bebop represents a Black, sophisticated, liberated, smart, and stylish art with attitude, a social philosophy, and dress. It becomes an even more difficult task to trace what is happening at every moment with Black music adequately because American culture and society have stepped into hyperdrive, driven by economics, global relations, technology, and a tremendous number of exchanges, innovations, and experiments by many artists—Black, White, and international. As fast as artists create, there are markets demanding the next thing. American music in a way accompanies society, but it pacifies it as well. There becomes with this capitalistic surge the need for "cultural diversions." This is where popular culture got its start and became cemented as an American entertainment phenomenon. Music making simply became a part of the social matrix.

The Jazz art has become the "most sophisticated" or refined of the forms within the Black arts continuum. There are several reasons for this. Because it is instrumental music, it requires a great amount of technical, craftsperson facility, as well as it being a form associated with accompanying and emulating Black vocal style. Further it has developed as a form which places a premium on an artist, focusing in on the expression and craft of interpreting and performing at rapid speeds simultaneously. It left its vernacular folk form and developed into a hybrid of other cultural perspectives erupting during a time of great social awareness, as America searched for her cultural identity. Coupled with the economic and technological booms in the early twentieth century, these early urban expressions helped to define what writer F. Scott Fitzgerald termed the "Jazz Age." To probe through this art in even more philosophical ways, Jazz forms as they developed later could further be described as:

Focused musical language in connection with human, emotive, expressive ideas
Melodic inventiveness
Rhythmic dynamism
Mastery of the instrument and art form

Harmonic inventiveness, a freshness as if you can hear the artist discovering as you hear it
A mix of wit, pathos, childhood playfulness, and maturity
Elegant expression
Engaging group dialogue
Focused individual interpreting and inventing while commenting on an upheld tradition
Lushness

The Jazz musician is a great example of an artist at the highest level. In hearing the advanced soloist you get the sense of what it "costs" to speak, that in some profound way improvisation emphasizes why it is dehumanizing to have the liberty of speech somehow taken away. There were some sacrifices in being allowed to speak. So there is this great sense of the importance of "saying something." This is likened to the Black church experience where a parishioner may shout out to a preacher, "Ahh, you saying something now." The opportunity to speak is not taken for granted and actually the solo is the great benchmark of the Jazz artist's ability. Black music, especially in Jazz, is so very profound in this way because it relies on one's lived experience for its meaning and the quality of its expressiveness. As Charlie Parker (1920–1955) often said, "Music is your own experience. If you don't live it, it won't come out of your horn."[15] Popular music got this heightened sense of an individual's artistic expression from the Jazz musician, especially the beboppers, with Bebop being the grandfather form of Hip Hop.

Beboppers evolved into a "class" of skilled musicians who thought of themselves as artistically and socially revolutionary. They constructed a conscious protest against the old commercialism of Big Band and moved the idea of Jazz as entertainment to Jazz as art. They brought up the standard of Jazz and as well the idea of Jazz as social consciousness. This seeped into all kinds of aspects, like being "modern," being "hip," and dressing with a flair, which became the trademarks of their style. They believed they were reinventing Jazz tradition, and so the place for experimentation became late-night "jam" sessions. In these sessions, the musicians would hang out in a place like Minton's or Monroe's Uptown House in Harlem. These happenings have been called "the Jazz man's true academy."

Certainly there was the styling of the post Classic Blues ladies such as Billie Holiday (1954–1959), Ella Fitzgerald (1918–1996), and Sarah Vaughn (1921–1990), who blossomed as stylists along with Duke Ellington, bandleader/pianist Count Basie (1904–1984), and others. As with the earlier evaluations of vernacular Black music, Jazz was the continued attempt to emulate the sound of the Black voice. These ladies represent the "sound" Jazz was attempting to get to. But the Bebop approach was a cultural movement within Jazz, complete with a new aesthetic, language, even a dress code. And as Miles Davis put it, in his autobiography, "The movement was like reading a textbook to the future of jazz music."

Miles Davis

Miles Davis (1926–1991) represents the next wave of artistry beyond Duke Ellington and was the protégé in many ways of the beboppers Charlie Parker and Dizzy Gillespie.

If we could use Miles Davis for a moment only to try to grasp some other movement in Jazz, this would be illuminating, as the forms evolve and move even closer to the American cultural center. Miles Davis was an instrumentalist (trumpeter), conceptualist, and one of the principal players to emerge in New York in the 1940s and to be recognized as a major leader and shaper of Jazz culture from an aesthetic, cultural, and historical, as well as from the media's, perspective. But Miles is surrounded and influenced by the likes of Charlie Parker, Dizzy Gillespie, Thelonious Monk and schools of players following throughout the 1950s well into the 1980s, such as Cannonball Adderly (1928–1975), John Coltrane (1926–1967), Wayne Shorter (b. 1933), Herbie Hancock (b. 1940) and Tony Williams (1940–1997). Together these voices along with the media propelled an artistic emergence of the Black art forms of Bebop and several derivative Jazz styles.

While there are many ways to see the next phases, Miles Davis represents as an artist the quintessential or most characteristic example of the art form as culture and as style. While not always the originator of these aesthetic movements and manifestos (BeBop, Cool School, Modal, Fusion), Davis's contribution and participation in these places him as a seminal figure in the history. For example, the Bebop movement (1943–1948) represented a break with the audience-pleasing commerciality of the swing band musicians represented by Ellington and Count Basie. Davis, along with mentors Charlie Parker and Dizzy Gillespie, was there in the forefront of the movement. The Cool School movement (1949–1955) represented a break with the fast, complicated musician orientated approach of Bebop. The approach to playing Jazz was less excited, less busy, a more smooth, detached, and reflective sound. The grouping of instruments included a French horn, Tuba, and no piano, giving it a more European, chamberlike sound. Davis not only organized a unique ensemble to record and project this new approach, he made for himself a projected "cool" media image which characterized his public persona until his death. His record *The Birth of the Cool* was recorded in 1955.

The large orchestrations in Davis recordings (*Miles Ahead*, 1957; *Porgy and Bess*, 1958; and *Sketches of Spain*, 1959) of arranger Gil Evans were a foreshadowing of Third Stream. The Third Stream was the mixing of formal European large-range ideas and Jazz music with the avant-garde tendencies in concert music seen in the later experiments by Gunther Schuller and the Modern Jazz Quartet. Modal Jazz, as exemplified on Davis's *Kind of Blue* record (1960), is another attempt to move away from the density which is represented in his orchestral experiments and mainstream jazz. In Miles's words, from his autobiography, "The music had gotten thick. . . . I think a movement in jazz beginning away from conventional string of chords, and a return to emphasis on melodic rather than harmonic variation . . . fewer chords but infinite possibilities as to what to do with them."

There was yet another period, his classic quintet, where Miles surrounded himself with younger players Herbie Hancock, Wayne Shorter, Ron Carter, and Tony Williams, and formed a refined, sophisticated performing unit. These recordings, which took place between 1963 and 1968, provided a model for group excellence which became the staple for modern Jazz performance. There was a return to making music that was "in tune" with the social movements of the times. Prior to this period, Miles had also been returning to Paris frequently and made visits to the home of social activist/author James Baldwin. Davis often spoke of his rising concern for the social plight of Black people in the States.

Miles's album *Bitches Brew* was a turn away from wearing the "establishment suit" to dashikis, Afros, and the creation of Fusion music. Fusion, or Rock-Jazz, brought a hardened electric edge to the music, forging at once artistic expression of the social rage of the 1960s and the technological experiments of the period. In this way Miles's experiments looked to incorporate what was going on in popular rock exemplified in someone like Jimi Hendrix or a band like the Who, and social unrest heard in the music of the period. It was a turn toward the impulses of the younger generation, who had become devoted to Rock and Roll and the protest music of the period.

A final stage from about the late 1970s until Davis's death was his belief in adopting the stylistic and aesthetic resources of popular culture, now called Pop, Urban-Contemporary, and finally Hip Hop. His new young model for artistic excellence was Prince. From his emergence in New York's Bop rage in 1944 until his death in 1991, Miles Davis's creative career spanned nearly fifty years. This is why I see him, as do many others, as representing the emergence of Jazz as a cultural style. There was the culture of Jazz, its approach, the sound of his horn (the wispy/airy sound of the stemless Harmon mute), the use of "cool" phrasing, relaxed nonspeedy playing, the use of media to project the image of the hipster, dress and attitude, and these were equally a part of the Davis persona and image, as style. Miles Davis became a millionaire. Miles's life as style and music made him the most commercially successful Jazz artist of his generation.

Black musicians making a million dollars is proof that the art form had reached an important place in the societal configuration of success, marketability, and cultural stability.

POST-MONK: HARD, FREE, AND BEYOND

Creative movements always unearth innovators who are memorable personalities we associate with the spirit, values, and ideas of a time. Thelonious Monk (1917–1982), because of the sheer uniqueness of his performance and compositional approach to playing, is clearly one of the most innovative voices to come out of the Bebop and beyond era, remaining a potent force in more progressive Jazz until the 1970s. His Five Spot performances, Town Hall concerts, and subsequent albums and European tours provided a rich recording legacy of his contribution. In Monk's music the tonal structure from chord to chord is sometimes unpredictable, so one's base as a listener is constantly shifting. Monk, according to historian Gunther Schuller, propelled the language beyond the traditional chord systems and pushed it, like the European avant-garde movements, toward nontonality; that is, music without any fixed tonal center. Bebop, perhaps the first great American music revolution, helped to institute a social sensibility that helped Black musicians shrug off their total dependence on the older strictly vernacular forms. Many boppers were heard to say, "We don't care if you don't listen."

This musician-orientated experimentation continued to manifest itself in creative voices throughout the 1960s and 1970s, and with the advent of Black social consciousness of the Civil Rights era.

Hard Bop and Free Jazz, the next Black musical movements, were attempts by musicians to reestablish the dominance of the rhythmic vitality of Black music, clearly homogenized in the Cool School and now largely dominated by White Jazz players. Hard Bop players in particular insisted on the heavy reliance on the vernacular sounds of the Blues, and even Gospel, as in saxophonist Cannonball Adderley's piece "Mercy, Mercy, Mercy" (composed by Joe Zawinul). In Free Jazz, another movement in modern Jazz, there is also a focus on African identity, ethnic aesthetics and instruments, free improvisation, and collective group improvisation. All of these help to define what this music is about and what it sounds like. Other characteristics include the absence of tonality and predetermined chords, loose structural design, suspense of regular beats of time signature, and fragmented melodic textures rather than dependence on melody. While there are many artists who take in various strains of these movements, several stand out: John Coltrane (1926–1967), Ornette Coleman (b. 1930), Anthony Braxton (b. 1945), the Association for the Advancement of Creative Musicians (AACM), Richard Muhal Abrams, the Art Ensemble of Chicago, Cecil Taylor, Albert Ayler (1936–1970), Sun Ra (1914–1993), and later Charles Mingus (1922–1979).

The Free Jazz movement again grew closely to nonmainstream sentiment which emphasized distance from commercial Jazz movements at the time, particularly Cool Jazz. Some called it "Avant-Garde Jazz" or "Action Jazz" because of its emphasis on rhythmic energy and vitality. A principal player in this movement, Ornette Coleman began in the late 1950s to fuse Blues and vernacular music with European notions of atonality and the avant-garde "emancipation of dissonance" and aleatoric principals (chance occurrence) music. He recorded in 1960 *Free Jazz*, from which the name emerges.

The Art Ensemble of Chicago was formed in 1965 and emerged full-blown in 1969, created from and out of the support of the AACM. This collective of musicians began to experiment actively, formed a record company, and found a base for concert support and scholarship. The Art Ensemble of Chicago's motto was "Great Black Music—Ancient to Modern." This signals a real understanding among musicians that a continuum of styles, approaches, and cultural and aesthetic conventions had been upheld in African American experience and substantiated a cultural forum and identity in creative musical form.

With the emergence of Spirituals, Blues, Ragtime, and Jazz, Black music has created for itself a vibrant style, international cultural icons, and a cultural standard which has ignited its countrymen and -women. Poetry, literature, dance, painting, drama, film, and sculpture have been created and inspired by these musical forms. These arts were engagement in the cultivation of social-political-artistic platforms to support and illuminate the lives of Americans and their social realities. Further, these expressions spawned a multimillion-dollar entertainment industry.

The notes are right for a multitude of reasons encompassing a wide variety of experiences, attitudes, journeys, and hardships, as well as the intellectual, cultural, and artistic triumphs of Black people.

A VIEW OF GOSPEL MUSIC

Gospel music is known and accepted today as a contemporary musical category and style, the continuation of commercial/popular manifestations of Black church singing traditions. I place it here because, although it emerged fully several decades earlier, Gospel music, like Urban Blues, R&B, Rock and Roll, and many aspects of Jazz culture became in the 1960s a part of the great wave of Black mainstreaming that marks this period as a revolution in terms of the cultural projection of Black identity in the modern world. Thomas Dorsey (1899–1993) is recognized as the father of Gospel music mainly because of his devotion to making the style known to the masses. But the emergence of Gospel music follows much the same transitional evolution as all Black music; it began with folks creating home traditions and evolves with the musical and commercial developments of American society. That is, masses move into urban areas and new cultural forms evolve to accommodate that move. The product is then created, bought, and sold. One view is that Gospel music is the Spirituals "gassed up" to incorporate stylistic, musical, and performance conventions already established in the Blues, Jazz, and popular music. Once these popular styles were brought into the spiritual singing context and commercialized, Gospel music as a style emerged. In truth the performers were just "evangelizing," taking the message to mobile communities but using the technology of their time and evolving like any other absorbent creative form. There are of course other distinctions. One of Gospel's most salient and rich distinctions is the textual emphasis placed on "personal testimony." And as the urban experience became sometimes unbearable, Jesus, again as in the slave experience, was able to deliver. Another distinction is the continued "celebratory ritual," as heard in the recordings.

It's as if the ritual is a part of the music-making experience, so that the "live" church experience, even the conversions, are a part of the aesthetic, the meaning. Gospel music is only as meaningful as the shared ritual it brings the folks to. But contrary to this natural evolutionary theory, many Gospel music historians argue that Gospel music has its own codified musical language, the "Gospel style," based on years of good church signing and playing; it is not simply a "jazzed up" Spiritual song. These distinctions are musical and are seen in performance practices used by Gospel artists. One such distinction is their embrace, use, and development of vocal and textual improvisation taken to musical and technical virtuosity. This is very, very skilled vocal expression highlighting moans, groans, and extemporaneous textual illumination and "musical screaming" heard in few other traditions in the world. This at first was seen as "devil music."

But the masses of Black urban audiences were drawn to Gospel because it more closely aligned with their contemporary, faster urban environments. As early as 1938 concert promoter John Hammond was organizing Black Gospel concerts at Carnegie Hall in New York, where figures such as Sister Rosetta Tharpe (1915–1973) were mixing up Blues and church singing styles with little separation. This helped to further cement and codify multiple regional and stylistic approaches, mainly among Black musicians, and helped to fortify Black art as a cultural foundation which again provided a strengthened identity and ideology.

The Black mainstream church's institutionalization of Gospel music happened in 1930 at the National Baptist Convention in Chicago with the work "If You See My Savior" by Thomas A. Dorsey. It was a huge success, and soon after the convention adopted Gospel tradition as its main musical "devotion device," providing support for conference activities of "praise and worship" as well as Christian affirmation. It is worth noting that Thomas Dorsey was a recognized Blues composer and performer who was the pianist and musical director for the well-established Blues singer Ma Rainey. Again with Gospel music this is exemplary of the inseparable practices of spiritual and secular Black traditions and conventions among Black practitioners. Dorsey and others fused the more commercial, secular, worldly styles and rhythms and used those to uniquely shape the church singing traditions which were increasingly more urban anyway. In 1932, Dorsey began the publishing company Dorsey House of Music for the sole purpose of selling the music of Gospel composers. There are three main factors that have led to the influence and growth of the style:

1. The migration of rural Blacks from the rural areas who brought singing traditions to the North urban areas during World War I
2. The National Baptist Convention's public endorsement of Gospel music
3. The organizing efforts of Thomas Dorsey and contemporaries, who formed a publishing company and established paid music concerts, organized choirs, and music festivals for the performance of gospel music

Additional support for this emerging mainstream style could be seen in 1940s radio programs like *Gospel Train* on WLIB in New York and others across the country.

In 1957, the Clara Ward Singers, a Gospel chorale, appeared with major Jazz figures at the Newport Jazz Festival. This event brought another form of Black music to the mainstream masses. The radio shows included national sponsors, and there were even organized "Gospel clubs," after-church nightspots where you could go and hear Gospel music.

Another voice and a major artistic figure in the popularization of the music was that of Gospel great Mahalia Jackson (1911–1972). Mahalia Jackson, who is known as the queen of Gospel music, actually began as a protégée of Thomas Dorsey. Jackson catapulted Gospel singing to higher visibility by appearing on the nationally syndicated *Ed Sullivan Show*. Jackson was later seen in her own *Mahalia Jackson Show* in 1954 on CBS. In 1961, Mahalia Jackson was invited to perform at President Kennedy's inauguration party, and in 1963, a TV show entitled *Gospel Time* emerged. In 1969, James Cleveland, actually a second-generation Dorsey, created in California the Gospel Music Workshop of America, which brought together thousands of singers and songwriters to be trained in the Gospel tradition.

As the Black student Civil Rights organizations mobilized in the late 1960s and 1970s, the choice musical ensemble to establish was the Gospel choir. By the mid-1960s, Gospel style could be heard in the folk, protest, church singing traditions which carried the King Montgomery bus protests to international audiences. Gospel music got yet another boost and advanced to a more marketable, mainstream, popular category, Contemporary Gospel. The work that gave it the boost was the Edwin Hawkins Singers' "Oh Happy Day," which rose in the popular charts as a top-ten single, a first for a "religious-based" song.

This song helped establish Gospel music as a commercially stable mainstream sound. Soon after, as happens with every other Black popular music form, Rock groups and mainstream popular artists such as Elton John used Gospel harmonies and styling as well as Black Gospel choirs to sing on background verses. TV commercials use Gospel tracks in the background when absolutely nothing is being represented as religious or spiritual.

"For those of you who thought gospel music has gone too far . . ." This is the opening line from late-1990s Gospel Hip Hop star, singer, and impresario Kirk Franklin. In his work he samples 1970s bass lines from George Clinton, layers in the hype and noise of Hip Hop production to emulate the energy in urban contemporary Black popular culture, and claims that it is just a Holy Ghost party, and a way to reach a younger, disenchanted, searching generation. This is yet another demonstration of why the challenge in tracking Black music is so daunting—because of its unlimited life vibrancy and its unstoppable morphing. The older traditions as well continue to remake themselves within Black life as needed. The notes continue to ring with human purpose.

RHYTHM AND BLUES, ROCK AND ROLL, AND A BIT OF SOUL AND HIP HOP: THE EMERGENCE OF BLACK POPULAR MUSICAL CULTURE

They always keep exquisite time and tune and no words seem hard for them to adapt to their tunes . . . so that they can sing a long meter tune without any difficulty . . . with the most perfect time and rarely without any discord.

—Fanny Kemble, *Journal of a Life on a Georgia Plantation*, 1835

I use this diary excerpt frequently because it illustrates the ignorant, "they the other," shallow depiction of Black artistry by White observers of the often perceived Negro's "natural abilities." But, it is also a record of an observation of unique performance qualities that set Black expressive works apart. This quote underlines the points about the use of music by folks to accompany and adapt to "lived in" environments. It has always been the case that the outside observer of Black art making has been fascinated or intrigued or curious about Black music practice. But much of what Blacks were doing was not seen by the majority of mainstream Americans, aside from the Black church experience, or the elite Whites who witnessed Black performers in Harlem's Cotton Club in the 1920s or danced to the Swing music of the 1930s.

Black music was for mainstream, White America a curious and foreign experience up until the explosion of Rock and Roll in the 1950s. Even then, the real demons against Black music and culture came out, as this was seen by many as a concerted effort by Blacks and liberals to destroy the "purity" of White youth. Most of the urban Black music—the Blues, Boogie Woogie, and secular Gospel traditions—was captured on race records from the 1920s, distributed mainly in Black communities. Nevertheless, Original Race Records and the larger companies prepared White American consumers and began a feeding frenzy that would change American culture forever. The radio Gospel shows of the 1940s and 1950s featured Black jubilee quartet groups heavily steeped in the Spiritual-Blues traditions. As mentioned earlier, this is a noted occurrence of cross-fertilization of styles and techniques between Black sacred church traditions and Blues-secular Jazz traditions. Black musicians were still traveling from the South to Northern cities, and whole Black communities were searching for better economic/social conditions and were traveling as well. Faith communities were working communities, and the energy and social environments were married and mirrored each other, allowing so much of Black cultural practice to flow.

Rhythm and Blues

By 1949, a secular popular Blues tradition and category could be noted by *Billboard* magazine as Rhythm and Blues. This style and sound has grown to become the popular format that mainstream Black performers identify as Black pop/dance, outside of Jazz and Gospel. Jazz can largely be seen as the carrier of mostly instrumental expression, whereas Rhythm and Blues focuses on the popular singing/dance traditions emphasizing love and contemporary life. As for mainstream White America in the late 1940s, there were still the large White dance Jazz orchestras (Harry James, Glenn Miller), and, as my father described to me recently, "They had a dreamy mainstream, white cottage house with a picket fence kind of music."

Most Black youth got this R&B, post–War World II, from jukeboxes, where so much of the dance and slow-dance romance music was heard which reflected the domestic hopes of returning Black soldiers. The postwar bands were transformed from a larger Cab Calloway (1907–1994) Orchestra to the slicker, big beat, commercial love rhyme of someone like a Louis Jordan (1908–1975), the 1940s pioneering performer. His group the Timpani Five had a reduced big band, down to rhythm section and three horns, Louis on sax and singing. Louis Jordan had 80 singles on the R&B charts, many of which crossed over. He set the pattern for modern R&B as a trendsetter crossover artist with catchy comic lyrics, dance steps, and style; he was a great entertainer. Other groups include the likes of the Orioles, Ruth Brown, Solomon Burke, Big Joe Turner, the Ink Spots, and many others. Rhythm and Blues then is the urban popular dance, song, and celebration of Black communities rejoined with loved ones after the war. This music was captured on "race records" sold primarily in Black communities.

Rock and Roll

Rock and Roll, a term coined by a White DJ, Alan Freed, represents the awakening and attraction of "young America," mainly White America, in the 1950s to Black popular dance music. While many Black artists had been ignored by the mainstream industry up until this point,

Black music performed by Whites, on the other hand, allowed many Black artists to gain for the first time a larger public acceptance. Thus Little Richard (b. 1935), Chuck Berry (b. 1926), and Fats Domino (b. 1929) became huge crossover acts. But this Rock and Roll was really the second wave of popular Black forms and styles after the "Jazz period." Artists mentioned earlier, such as Cab Calloway and Louis Jordan, were performing a faster, more dance-orientated version of Swing called "Jump" in the 1940s. It was Alan Freed's "discovery" of these race records in 1951 and then his move to New York in 1955, playing this music during prime radio time at night, that caught the attention of young White listeners. Of course, yet again, the next step was the industry jumping onto the opportunity, and a "new" style of American entertainment was born. In order to make this acceptable to a very plain mainstream American culture, the industry supplied White American youth with a string of acts that were more palatable to White tastes. The media projected images of Bill Haley in 1955 and Pat Boone, essentially covering older Black artists' pieces, and America had a "new" music. But it was Elvis Presley who became the most recognizable and influential "rock star" teen idol. He is the musical amalgamation of White Southern folk and country traditions, all "shaken up" with rural-Black Blues and Rhythm and Blues forms. He became the "new" American cultural music phenomenon in 1956 with "Heartbreak Hotel." Something must be said of the importance of rural, country music and its impact on all kinds of singers, including Elvis. Black people loved country music as well. You can't miss the country music influence on someone like Chuck Berry. So there was a lot of cross-influence and exchange among White and Black Southern rural folk, and this cross-cultural fertilization is largely unspoken of, especially as it relates to Black artistry owing much to White country music tradition, vocally and instrumentally.

Elvis Presley, Jerry Lee Lewis, Johnny Cash, Carl Perkins (all a part of Sam Phillips's big Sun Records million-dollar quartet), Bill Haley, and others became the catalysts for Rock and Roll as a public mainstream musical-cultural expression. But the real fathers of this music of Rock and Roll were Black creators who had been evolving out of race records traditions. These race or color categories, while they have remained a permanent institution in America, have as well been responsible for breaking down cultural barriers. The story through the lens of our mainstream cultural screen, the TV, reads similarly. After the rejection of a decade or so of Hollywood's narrow versions of White-bleached suburban mediocrity, or "Pleasantville," after the war, Rock and Roll music and culture became a central catalyst for young White America's search for their own real identity apart from that of their parents. TV and films in the 1960s catapulted "American pop" (the twist) into mainstream hearts and living rooms.

Music again is the great cultural catchall and catalyst. This further illustrates the transformative role of popular music and culture. The image and voice of young America exploded largely because youth came alive with the rhythms and expressive liberties provided by the forms of popular music. From the late 1950s through the 1960s, 1970s, and 1980s came the emergence of the more commercially acceptable sounds of Motown, Soul music, and Rap, all of which are carried by the same foundation: the performance conventions of common folks expressing human experience. James Brown's (b. 1928) "Soul Power" anthem of 1968, "Say It Loud, I'm Black and I'm Proud," sums it up best.

Soul Music

For our discussion, Soul music as a movement, musical style, and an approach to life that incorporates ideology, spirit, and political consciousness is the best example and illustration of most of the themes in this narrative: the potent force and meaning of Black popular cultural forms of music. This important music period of Soul, between 1965 and 1975, represented for Black people and artists many things: cultural and political empowerment, a musical/style category, spiritual/expressive depth and meaning, race pride, and social and civic responsibility and accountability. This was articulated in the concepts of Soul music: soul brother, having soul, soul food, soul hair, singing with soul, and getting down to the soul of the matter. Authenticity, image, and identity were the dominant expressive and creative themes. In this turbulent period in American history music sought to uphold a social consciousness about race, class, gender issues, police brutality, civil rights, integration, war protests, and serving your common brother or sister. In 1969 *Billboard* magazine revamped its categories and instituted Soul as the overall category for Black popular music. As musicologist Portia Maultsby points out,

> The Soul era was a productive period for Black Americans. Group cohesion, political activism and community self help programs were responses to the messages of soul singers and leaders of the Black Power movement. The music created by Blacks and for Blacks during this era communicated a general philosophy of refusal to accept the undesirable and a determination to create a better future.[16]

Maultsby further outlines some characteristics of the period:

1. Music and artists were the agents for social change.
2. This work, more than early music, paved the way for Black people to enter mainstream American culture.
3. Black American music was no longer a fringe music but "charting" in pop, and Black artists were on the rosters at Warner, Columbia, ABC, Epic, and other labels.

Quincy Jones was hired as the first director of Artists and Repertoire by Mercury Records, in 1961. There was a sense that Black music, and therefore Black people, had now arrived and counted in American culture. Soon there was *Soul Train*, a nationally syndicated TV show which highlighted and projected the very powerful and influential images of Black artists in the mainstream in positive ways. *Soul Train* competed for the attention of White viewers who traditionally looked at *American Bandstand*, the Dick Clark music show innovation of the 1950s, both preceding, of course, MTV.

For me, the song titles of this period tell the story of what Soul music songwriters and performers of the time were about:

"Say It Loud, I'm Black and I'm Proud" (James Brown)
"A Change Is Gonna Come" (Sam Cooke/Otis Redding)
"Wake Up Everybody" (Harold Melvin and the Bluenotes)
"War" (Edwin Star)
"Higher Ground" (Stevie Wonder)
"What's Going On" (Marvin Gaye)
"Ball of Confusion; That's What the World Is Today" (Temptations)
"Message in Our Music" (O'Jays)
"Yes We Can" (Pointer Sisters)
"Ain't No Stopping Us Now" (McFadden and Whitehead)
"I Will Survive" (Gloria Gaynor)

"Everyday People" (Sly and the Family Stone)
"Fight the Power" (Isley Brothers)

Of all the periods we've examined, this period is the one for me where the notes are the "Blackest" and the berries are the juiciest. This is because so much comes together that defines the elements of Black music aesthetic, functionality, and meaning. Spirituals, Blues, Gospel, R&B; instrumental facility, training, and technique; innovative artistry; international recognition and appreciation; and the power of a relevant social dynamic.

The Soul music period included, in addition to the examples above, artists such as Aretha Franklin; Earth, Wind and Fire; Al Green; the Supremes; the Jackson Five; and early Parliament-Funkadelic. Their work set up all the basic foundations for the new innovations in the late 1970s and 1980s, the urban contemporary music and later stylistic developments in Hip Hop of the 1990s and beyond.

This period of music production most succinctly mirrored what Black people, and thus America, were thinking and feeling about living in this culture. It was all told in the music, inextricably bound to the way people were living. The issues, concerns, worldviews, political perspectives, styles, and social customs were all embedded in and carried by the music. The simultaneous explosion of Black identity and America's acceptance of this presence could be seen, felt, and heard in volume. Even the best "American" model of hard work, dreams, and cultural productivity was imaged in Black American music culture, for instance, Motown records.

How Berry Gordy Jr. (b. 1929) created his million-dollar talent reserves reads like an American family fortunes legacy. Berry Gordy began writing songs in the late 1950s and, encouraged by some success, took out an $800 family loan (from his parents) and founded Motown Records. That $800 investment, from a Black "bank," allowed him to introduce to the world one of the most amazing stables of music talent, ever. This Motown explosion was, I believe, the most image- and culture-stabilizing expression Black people had had. In 1988, Berry sold that multimillion-dollar company, and in its final sell, in 1993, it went for 301 million dollars. Millions and millions of dollars later, we still have our Soul impacted by that music. The first Berry Gordy (b. 1854) was a slave who purchased land and built a farm in Georgia. The business he started on his land included a blacksmith shop, general store, and houses. He sold cattle, peanuts, and vegetables. His son, the second Berry Gordy (b. 1888), took over the business, sold a load of timber for a large amount of money, and then "took the money and ran" from oppression and terror in the South, and with family settled in Detroit—a classic pattern, moving in the great migrations northward. (My dad's grandfather [b. 1850s], a slave, sent my grandmother and her eight brothers and sisters with savings he had from his farm as a former sharecropper. In 1990, when I began this writing, I was still hanging out with the youngest of those siblings. He was 104.) The wife of the second Berry Gordy, Bertha Fuller, was a schoolteacher who became a successful businessperson, and they began to build businesses and sell real estate. The third Berry Gordy (Berry Gordy Jr.) purchased a small record store, began writing songs while working on the Ford assembly plant. These three elements in the family background—entrepreneurship, assembly-line detail, and a love of music—became the elements which built one of the most successful Black business enterprises in modern history, the music corporation Motown. This business was built on the principle of American ingenuity, talent, and hard work, in addition to some very important ideological concepts in Berry's music/culture experiment: Black owned, directed and operated; first Black portrayal of "regular American teenage angst"; entrepreneurship; family values; teenage corpo-

Nowel Family (my wife's family), circa 1910

rate "tailor-made acts" who were immaculate, well groomed, and well dressed; hard teamwork; a Black music writing/production/playing team (Holland-Dossier-Holland, the Funk Brothers); making music with a "great beat with great stories that anybody can listen to"; and "the Sound of Young America."

The signature artists who represented the successful, internationally known sound of Motown helped to make a major impression on the world with Black musical artistry of the 1960s. Diana Ross (b. 1944) and the Supremes, Smokey Robinson (b. 1940) and the Miracles, Marvin Gaye (1939–1984), Gladys Knight (b. 1940) and the Pips, Stevie Wonder (b. 1950), and of course Michael Jackson (b. 1958) and the Jackson Five—these were the living, singing embodiments of what dreams were made of in the old-fashioned American way. It was a story of simple hard work, from rags to riches and glory.

Beyond the 1960s and 1970s, Black musical artistry continued to crystallize and be shaped by advances in recoding technology and electronic innovations like the synthesizer. All this broadened the scope of the music, the narratives, and the sound. New forms grew, such as Funk and Techno Funk (Parliament-Funkadelic). The newer 1970s Funk was driven by an even harder beat, with a bigger dominance of the rhythm section, featuring electric bass, punctuating guitar, drum, synthesizer, and funky horn sections. The music, with strong vocal leads, revolved around a repetitive, driving, syncopated feel which was created largely for social party-dance, which became big in the post–Civil Rights era, as Black people spent more time cele-

O'Neal Family (my dad's family), circa 1920

brating the "anticipated" freedoms of the late 1970s and 1980s. This begins the Disco period. Disco was intended for people to come together to have fun, release tension from the social unrest of the past decades. Funk-dance music allowed for social interactions; the musical themes, the poetry within the music, still advocated social consciousness, but you just danced to it instead of standing around listening or holding hands marching in the streets. "Dance to the music. Forget your troubles and dance. . . . Forget your sickness, weakness. . . . Dance to the music" (Bob Marley [1945–1981], "Them Belly Full").

The narratives were larger too. The human experience in this music included humor (Bertha Butt and the Butt Sisters), fun, fantasy, folly, and foolishness (Funkadelic and the Mothership Connection). We are not completely romanticizing the era; there were destructive demons and demise in the lives of Robert Johnson to Parker, Holiday to Janis Joplin, Hendrix (1942–1970) to Marvin Gaye. The artistic seduction to drugs, sex, suicide still plagues the artists' lives, so that Jim Morrison to Kurt Cobain remind us of the tremendous battles these artists wage. Despite the start and growing rise of a "glorified rock and roll lifestyle," in my way of looking at this, the music was still broad and symbolized for people a wider pallet of cultural experience to define their realities.

Black popular music, while distinctly remaining identifiably "Black" (sound, performers, performance practice, methods, delivery), throughout the 1980s became even more mainstream and was titled Funk/R&B and Urban Contemporary. Most of its meanings, despite the period's offstage antics, were focused on uplifting people in some way.

Rap and Hip Hop Culture

Hip Hop or Rap music, as it first was titled, began commercially with the release of "Rappers Delight" in 1979 by the Sugar Hill Gang. But the music/culture was a movement that emerged in the consciousness of communities much earlier. Again, through sharing experiences, and by diasporic connections from Jamaica to the Bronx, there emerged a new Black impulse in art. This particular expressive form grew out of neighborhood parties in the early 1970s where the DJs spinning records used to talk with the audience during a break between records. DJs would challenge each other by capping on their opponents, thereby creating a contemporary urban debate session couched in slang word battles, rhyme schemes, and humorous ways of telling a story. This really was a Jamaican DJ tradition brought here to the States. (See *You Call That Music!*) Young street poets expressing themselves artistically through Black style supported by the best of Black popular music created a public arena and performance stage for claiming authenticity, reflecting (I)dentity and projecting image. You had to have "skills" to keep the party going, and what made you better was your ability "to mix it up" while keeping the party going on during breaks.

Rap became a big practice among youth, and translated into big money once again for the profit-opportunist industry. We learned this lesson from Rock and Roll. A *New York Times* writer reported,

> Rap like most everything from the Blues to alternative rock before it has been officially embraced by those who originally ostracized it, or avariciously consumed by those from whom it sought independence . . . White young people (who make up 70% of hip hop sales) are listening to and using elements of rap not for theft but because they relate to it, because the music is a legitimate part of their cultural heritage. Black and white fans are flipping back and forth between the local rock and rap radio stations, simply in search of the best song.[17]

There are many reasons to investigate Hip Hop and to see this as one of the most vibrant and meaningful musical expressions in contemporary American musical culture. Besides the fact that it is clearly the most provocative musical art form of the last decade of the twentieth century, the real meaning of this new cultural activity is found among the "folks," where the operative meanings I've suggested (language and behavior) are used, created, and worked out daily. There are a lot of social, political, new, postmodern aesthetics at work in "da hood" where urban youth breathe. Sociologically there is no difference from the hippie generation of the 1960s (Rock and Roll), or the British youth in the 1970s (Punk, Slam). Part of the Hip Hop aesthetic is a performer's flow in rhyme. Rhythm is the qualifying ingredient. Rhythmic movement in this late-twentieth-century art form is the self-conscious mode of intellectual creative expression. Despite its ugly commercial exploits, and its sometimes harsh language, Hip Hop truly stands in the same camp as all other "welcomed" branches of the family of Black arts traditions.

The emergence of new language forms (Hip Hop jargon) and modes of expression (both in music and movement, dance, and poetry) can be seen. Language, movement, and new aesthetic sensibilities create musical form, structure, syntax, and style. These elements are based on the "rhythmic way" in which another generation of young Black people speak. For Hip

Hop or Rap music I want to suggest eight elements that seem to be consistent in the music and constitute conventions within the style:

- Back beat (the undeniable groove which is the makeup of the dynamic tension of multiple rhythms and the unifying power of those relationships)
- The rapper/trickster poet (from the Yoruban demigod, Esu-Elegbara)
- Gestural timing or the flow of the rhyme
- The message; the coded play on language (signifyin')
- Urban Black self-renewal, life affirmation (postmodern secular spiritual empowerment)
- New York and New Jersey tonality; language accents
- Covering, sampling, quoting, troping, speaking with other texts and musical grooves
- Communal affirmation; the Hip Hop song, or Black reign, descends on you: "Heyyyy!"

The role of the rapper here and actually the roles of all Black creative agents in the Diaspora are connected to an ancient African creative ancestor, Esu-Elegbara. As Henry Louis Gates points out in his *The Signifying Monkey: A Theory of African American Literary Criticism*,

> There can be little doubt that certain fundamental terms for order that the black enslaved brought with them from Africa, and maintained through the mnemonic devices peculiar to oral literature, continued to function both as meaningful units of New World belief systems. Esu is the sole messenger of the Gods who interprets the will of God to man . . . is the guardian of the crossroads, master of style and of stylus . . . the divine linguist, he who speaks all languages. . . . Esu's discourse, metaphorically, is double-voiced . . . connects the grammar of divination with its rhetorical structures. . . . He keeps one leg anchored in the realm of the Gods while the other rests in this, our human world.[18]

Many of the lyrics in Hip Hop seem to suggest "Listen to me now" or, in other words, "WAKE UP!" To many this may seem simpleminded and vacuous but to those within the cultural ritual these meanings are premium in experience because they give life. The rhythm dictates worldview and taste, sensibilities and values. The "sign" brings affirmation, self worth, liberation, dignity in Blackness, and new subcultural identity.

This segment of the Rap/Hip Hop community of artists mirrors thirty years earlier a similar movement of a need for cultural expression among that generation of Black youth. Both generations do this through the creation of new musical forms in which they navigate and formulate identity and image. This is expressed through the music, the beat, the vibe, the message, the dance move, and the rhyme.

The presence of the beat represents one's acknowledgment of the need to be inextricably bound with movement in the universe. Even if the rappers don't know or acknowledge this themselves they are trapped in the unavoidable web of cultural osmosis and transfer. Put in a larger Black worldview, movement then is like God-Spirit and represents vitality and life force. In being "traditional musicians" and even in our notions of speaking and being, we have to reckon with the challenges posed by a generation of poetic, frustrated, and sometimes angry youth searching for identity in a world that has defined them as "the enemy." The rhythm, the compelling imagery that is inextricably bound with the music and its expressive medium, the smart rhyme schemes and phrasing which again challenge and infuse all English colloquiums and slang, the lyrics, symbol structuring (something every Black arts form has done to the West), the sonic density and layering of sounds, the technique of the technology used to produce this incredible sound art are all new boundaries of expression. Here you can see new music with old-school identity as it emerged in Rap's earlier days, so that the work of Public Enemy, KRS-1, or Sister Soiljah, Queen Latifah through Arrested Development and Mos Def, underscores the points regarding the tradition's continuum.

As well, the huge popularity all over the world, the problematic definitions of self and sexual worldviews, the worshipping of purely monetary success, the money the form generates, its seeming lack of concern for the opportunity to advance a more "positive image" of the young Black self, particularly male, and its competition with and smothering of the more established forms of Black music within the record industry are huge challenges to overcome. We're still sorting through the duplicity of the music.

But, authenticity, image, and (I)dentity are the humanistic ideological themes that are the mechanism that guides so much of the artistic expression of contemporary Rap and Hip Hop music. It's another generation's way of navigating "Black being" in American society, but it maintains all, if not producing more, of the fire, spirit, and meaning of Black music that preceded it. All popular American musical expressions are really the result of groups of people expressing joy or angst, or celebrating their humanity or protesting their restriction of humanity. This is the case with the post–War World II cultural revolution of Rock and Roll and the social protest movements of Soul music and revolutionary folk traditions as seen in the work of Bob Dylan, Joan Baez, Bob Marley, and others. These efforts brought common people together, prompting yet more explosive ritualistic exchanges in the Folk and Rock festivals at Monterey and Woodstock in 1969. Thirty years later, in 1999, we have a *New York Times* writer who attended the premillennium festival writing

> Black rappers are finding it possible to serve both Black and White audiences without betraying either. They are finding that any adolescent who has ever felt victimized can relate to most rap lyrics because pop music always has communicated through metaphor, innuendo and fantasy. . . . It is a birthright, a standard by which they calibrate their lifetime notion of pop music.

1990s AND BEYOND

There have been five major developments that have come into play that extend the power of the presentation of ideas, images, and messages in popular music, during the Rap/Hip Hop emergence and continuing to the present:

1. In 1981 the introduction of MTV (Music Television)
2. Digital technology to sharpen images and audio clarity updated music video production to big budget movie quality
3. Globalization of American Music culture, so that there are shared aesthetic values, increasing the volume and synergy of popular artistry as never before; an unprecedented degree of interest in global sales
4. Complete industry saturation with youth culture—so much so that "youth narratives" (e.g., Alanis Morrisette, Tupac) become markers for national interest in (I)dentity, me in process
5. The process of corporate consolidation, so that even record labels consider themselves as "subdepartments of huge transnational corporations."

Artists have multitiered agreements. This alone shapes how they write, perform, produce, and market their product. For example; in pre-1995 an artist was recorded with a video and a tour sponsor, for instance, New Kids on the Block.

Post-1995, Will Smith, as an example, had a record deal, a major-studio movie deal, and videos; he was in TV ads and had his image on Burger King cups. Puffy Combs, Missy Elliot, Eve, and Russell Simmons have been in clothes ads or started their own clothing lines. Some artists run nonprofit corporations and others run magazines; there is total industry crossover in twenty-first-century music art. Today, a little more than 80 years after Mamie Smith sang "Crazy Blues" in 1920, and James Reece Europe complained of Black musicians not being paid, it can probably be shown that Black artists make more money from the sale of their music than any other living artists in the world.

Lastly, since the advent of videos produced to support records, many mainstream artists compose for the video story simultaneously or just for the visual narrative. Isn't this a switch? The technologically crafted visual narrative in film has literally in some cases replaced the imagined, dreamed narrative of the heart that before just needed the lone strum of a chord and a lyric to evoke meaning. What does the song need music for if what we are expected to hear can now be seen first in a big-budget video production?

Contemporary commercial music has since the early days exploded into a multibillion-dollar industry mixing and mangling love stories, interpersonal exploration, art, social protest themes, and entertainment fantasy, which have all become synonymous with the idea of American popular culture. If there is one to be found, Black music is the true melting pot of American culture. Black Blues, Jazz, Gospel, White-Anglo ballad forms, and European Classical music sensibilities carried by the expressive rhythmic fervor of Black music within a popular projection is the total sum of American popular music. Or a Folk formula might look something like this: Black Folk traditions from the Mississippi move to Chicago and other places where musicians settle; as well, White-Anglo ballads are mixed with Southern Spirituals and Blues (Country and Western), and the result is American popular music. This connection, this living in the expression of American popular music sentiment, reminds us that this is a prophetic place. It's where people live and should be considered when assessing the value of the right note. So music making in the twenty-first century is connected to an enormous amount of image, message, music, and value capital. This changes the meaning and the "value" process of artistry tremendously, and for me raises critical questions about the consequences of these more impactful meaning(s) in popular music/culture consumption.

CONCLUSION

There have been many contributors to the evolution of this music, many cultures and many social and artistic impulses. One of the delicate issues that has arisen is this: Who proudly claims rightful ownership, or authentic authorship, from a cultural standpoint, of Jazz? The idea of Jazz as "America's Classical music," brought home very powerfully in the documentary film by Ken Burns, has created a public discourse among musicians, historians, and popular music aficionados. Is it rightfully called Black music or does the homogenization and categorization of this music within American or Jazz studies rightfully save the form from "ghettoization" and false claims of ethnic art purity? Certainly I have tried to show that all this music is the result of an intense baking and stirring. While all that is clear, it's still Black music. This music sounds and manifests itself much in the same way that Black people speak, interact, move, and feel in the world. The rest of the contributors took their cues from this first. The greatest innovators, those who decided their worth in the world was dependent on these expressions of their culture, were Black. The color of the Blues is Black for sure. Art must be reshaped, reblended at all times, and certainly Western language conception and other non-Black players extended the formation and dialogue of Black music culture. But at its center, Black music contains the lives of Black people who provide the heartbeat, from Spirituals to Hip Hop.

Alongside Spirituals, Blues, Ragtime, Jazz, Gospel, R&B, Soul, and Hip Hop there is Reggae, Funk, Go-Go, Dance (Disco, House), and the regional impulses of Motown, Philly, Minneapolis, or Texas. There's a lot of music I did not explore in this essay, and I know much was missed in this summation. This is not to mention all the visiting impulses both internally and from outside, such as the British invasion in the 1960s, the World Beat impulse (such as Afro-Cuban), Youth Punk, 1990s Grunge, or African Pop. I still maintain that all these movements are evidence of the diversity, variety, and volume of Black American artists and artistry in popular culture, from Bessie Smith to Lauryn Hill and from the Ink Spots to Boyz II Men. You could take all of our people's economic, intellectual, and social movements and together they would not match the contribution, influence, and lasting imprint Black musical artistry has made on Black peoples and on the world. This is our existence mapping, the music.

Popular Culture in Non-Theory: Seeing Ourselves, Revealing Ourselves, Knowing Ourselves

The creation of new ideas occurs within a relatively small community of critical thinkers who have developed a sensitivity to some problem, an analysis of the sources of the problem, and a prescription for what should be done about the problem. These critical thinkers do not necessarily belong to a formally constituted organization, but they are a part of a self-aware, mutually interacting group of critical communities.

—Thomas Rochon, *Culture Moves*[1]

NON-THEORY

To speak about an interpretation of culture in the present time is a difficult issue. Culture is always changing and our interests, or "what's in," and what we value constantly evolves. In attempting to discover and explore culture, I don't trust or invest too much in one theory or way of assessing what is, or who's narrative or song is important. Instead I try to keep in mind some "working ideas" about what makes a cultural happening matter to people. I depend upon sites and places where people are or where they have lived, and instead use this lens of reference. I ask a series of questions which help to understand who, why, how, when, where, and what happened. So by the end of a particular exploration, perhaps a conclusion can be drawn which helps to understand something about such rises in cultural activity.

It's important here as well to consider the social, economic, political (cultural) forces that impacted, collided with, forced, compelled, or inspired human creativity. This gives us a sense of recognizing human patterns of expression, beliefs, values, and rituals, which help to say what may be going on with these people at this time or another. But even that attempt at an interpretation is subject to fault because we weren't there. So, personal narrative, the (I) story becomes crucial to cultural interpretation. In short, what does that song say? What does it mean? What do the artists, people stand for, believe, and hope in?

The "buzz" today is in contemporary popular culture. Most writers, academics in any field these days have become seduced and rightfully so by the excitement and relevance of what's happening in the world today. Certainly arts, celebrity, politics, advertising images (TV), movies, and media in culture factor very high on the list.

Popular culture allows us to see so many meaningful elements, fixtures, and symbols of our culture. This is the means by which our identities are concretized in many ways. As one writer puts it, popular culture represents the unseen and unspoken convictions and worldviews which form collective mind-sets. Jack Nachbar, in *Popular Culture, An Introductory Text*, writes:

Cultural study demands that we examine elements not as ends in themselves but as a means of unlocking meanings in culture as a whole . . . is a quest for meaning. . . . It reflects our image back to us but alters our image in the process . . . for we may thereby be able to exercise a greater element of control over what we believe. Culture provides the reflections necessary to expose and highlight our beliefs and values.[2]

Because of the amounts of money we invest in cultural production, we are able to use this as an important place of inquiry into who we are and possibly where we are headed. But as well as the industry, the cultural apparatus must be critiqued because its motivations must be factored in as well. Many times these interests are in conflict with the artists' or communities' goals and best interests, so consumer mentality and industry impulses have to be considered to define culture completely.

Because of the fluidity of cultural activity and our immediate responses to what's around us, "what's in" many times is what informs us about who we are today and is of great value. One makes decisions every day based on sets of cultural values which swarm around our heads via popular, common culture; they constantly define us. Nothing we do is absent from cultural shaping in these various forms and expressions.

WORKING IDEAS

The discipline of cultural studies formally began as a form of analysis and critique in the 1950s by British scholars who recognized that common people who work in a capitalistic society are governed by powerful forces. These instituted powers determine and therefore usually suppress individual freedoms. These thinkers began to then look more closely at how the larger "cultural force"(mainstream society, industry, government) shapes and controls people in relation to their individual lives, and how there always exists some form of struggle against power. So a lot of the study became focused on how to give agency back to those in society governed by oppressive social forces. The subjective, inner voice of individuals becomes valued. The idea of giving and assuring agency to common individuals and in those human spaces organic systems of expression and living emerge. This is the positive side of cultural creation by the folk, the common people. The dominant idea and focus of cultural studies has become seeing then through the "matrix," unpacking and deconstructing and ensuring that we live in a democracy focused on the betterment of society for all people. So culture study in this way is a study of critiques of systems as well as a study of life practices and celebrations made despite the presence of "controlling systems." The crucial component of cultural studies is the critique and resistance to the blinding deafness of hegemony, "the man's" subscription to the "how you must live like magazine" at every level.

It is easy then to see how poetry, work songs, and protest movements become a "lens" and "sites" for communal agency.

Today, the study of various aspects of popular culture expressions provides a rich history, a view of contemporary life, a philosophy that grounds in these same kinds of agency values but as well allows a critical read on the cultures we participate in and with. This is because popular culture has served to ensure that common people critique and celebrate culture. Cultural studies is a type of exploring which advocates the opportunity to see the world differently, to peel back the layers, a continual breaking open of the "wrapper." Doing this allows a kind of a healthy resistance that systems often impose on our ideas and visions of the world. What we breathe and take in reaches far into the zones of familiarity, but then we have to process it and see ourselves as better equipping the world, creating change, and establishing, as each new generation must do, maps for finding new places in this world. You cannot live in a world you don't understand. And you can't commit to living in one without appreciating all that is going into what makes our world go around.

So because of the inevitable change that occurs in culture and the flexible and rapid responses people have to cultural shifts, I prefer not to hold onto one theory of investigation or explanation, but simply keep track of impulses or working ideas that inform.

American culture has been and is being shaped by a series of myths and beliefs, some sour, some sad, and some not all bad (individual freedom, achievement, land of dreams, America the beautiful and the endlessly abundant . . .). These beliefs, myths, and values are for each of us a piece of the map for the world we enter and exit each day. We then want to look at the carriers of these myths, the symbols, practices, icons, and personalities that help construct and maintain our ideas of culture. These are all reflections of important ideas. What is being said if a generation sings, "Born in the USA" or "Say It Loud, I'm Black and I'm Proud"? Or what do we value when actors who have appeared before us as action heroes suddenly become elected governing officials who then determine and define crucial aspects of our living conditions through legislation, taxes, and political agendas?

WHAT IS CULTURE?

Culture is traditionally defined as the social and religious institutions created as well as the intellectual and artistic manifestations that characterize a society woven into a "web of meanings, values, and significance." Cultural studies then examines the products and processes of culture, human work, and thought produced by a given society and in a given time. Culture is ethnicity, nationhood, creative enterprises and practices (Jazz music), creative sites such as a museum, human rituals (Mass, football games), artifacts (songs, a doll, a magazine). Culture is, as well, behavioral tendencies, laws, rules, and ideologies that govern us, story and legends which give expression to beliefs, aspirations, and perceptions, all of which serve to explain national phenomenon or the origins of people.

What then are the central debates in modern American culture? Are we still a melting pot of cultures? Whose interests are served with the historical presentation of the past? What are the central themes that are contained in a song, poem, play, or movie—for example, identity, power, values, definitions of America, definitions of race, class, gender, and ethnicity? How are these themes presented then worked out in our daily life practices, heard in our historical narratives, media, popular culture and TV, politics and policy? What is the role of art (i.e., music, sculpture, literature, and dance) in shaping and carrying ideas about American culture and values? Who are some of the central figures who have shaped this identity, and how do these constructed icons send messages about what our citizenry and identity is?

Even looking at art practices and the function of media allows us to see how culture manipulates our ideas, causes fear, or makes us "marginally dissatisfied with our personal lives, suggesting that if we purchase a product that it has the possibility of improving our 'sad' lot in life."[3] Think about generations of little girls who grew up seeing themselves as Barbie. A simple example of a toy illustrates the very powerful ways in which a culture assigns its attitudes about sexuality, spending and living, work-worth or not, values, gender roles, and behavior, through an identity based on a constructed plastic American icon.

This way of looking at our culture provides a serious view with "ways to think about the world" (Michael Eric Dyson).[4] It also provides us with ways to view our politics, religion, news, athletics, and education. These ideas are expressed through the "conversation of our culture, our most convenient expression and thus become the content of our culture" (Neil Postman).[5]

MUSICAL EXPRESSION AS A CONVERSATION ABOUT BEING AMERICAN

Artistic expression in society as I've mentioned is more than entertainment and diversion but is an engagement and conversation about living in culture at a particular time. Black American music as one example of this has come from a two-parented household of Black life and music culture wed to ideas, conventions, and traditions inherited from the West and wrapped lushly in American historical experience and society. Billy Taylor's often debated saying, "Jazz is America's classical music," rings true. The perception and minimization of this cultural product as a mere "popular commodity" is limiting. Music is inextricably bound to so many human, social, poetic, intellectual, and spiritual thrusts in our culture. So many of the watershed historic points of the music, cultural, and social experiences really helped define what American culture has become. The concepts of liberty, democracy, social rights, artistic expression, economic and legal maturation, migrations and manifest destiny, the power of youth movements, and the potency of people moved by spiritual empowerment ("working ideas") can be seen through the development of American music. From rural narratives to big city life, the realization of American dreams to the social-cultural battlefronts, all these define American character. Woody Guthrie (whose guitar had written across it, "This machine kills fascists") sings, "This land is my land, this land is your land. This land is made for you and me" (1940). In "American Life" (2003), pop artist Madonna's lyric, states, "American life, I live the American dream. You are the best I've seen. I'm just living out the American dream, and I just realized nothing is as it seems."

American music is an amalgamation of many cultural attributes. Local, common peoples from Europe and the enslaved Africans, along with Native Americans and, as well, Asian and Latin American journeyers, all struggled within the challenged and difficult social/political environment they made, and these interactions created American culture and spirit. America is a place where culture has meaning because of its "ethnic presences," its strivings and yelling. It's a very complex weaving and matrix of yearnings, migrations, and mixes. This is what makes the concept of culture difficult when assessing the "what" of what it is. As this cultural quest to define culture concerns the contribution of American artists within the American social context, there are so many things to point to.

Music is the great culture carrier catalyst. A peeling back of the lid of music reveals it as an activity of:

Human expression
Religious and faith experience
Political protest
Intellectual structuring
Reflections on the nature of beauty
Organization of expressive symbols

Personal and communal identity
Social mobility

Any sustained exploration, analysis, or critical viewing of artistic expression reveals a great many examples of layers upon layers of cultural activity where people maintained identity, spiritual, and intellectual reflections of themselves and communities they grew within. Artistic expressions reflect cultural activity and project cultural identity and action. Black music in particular is the catchall and catalyst of culture. The great achievement of Black music is its profundity in the simultaneous expression of pathos and pain with the liberating spirit of human achievement and joy in adversity. These expressive banners made for powerful music and a powerful people and culture that have been a transforming and inspiring voice in human history. These music traditions are dense and moving music-psyche narratives of Black American culture through which Black people poured detailed accounts of their spiritual, social, political, personal, and communal evolutions. The best examples are the Spirituals and Blues, and modern-day Hip Hop follows the same paths. "Hip hop is for real, 'cause it's dealing with the truth/All over the world it's aggravated youth" (Queen Latifah).

This story style and expressive music became a significant human art recognized as a deep multivoiced tradition becoming as well the foundation in many ways for music, literature, myth, poetry, drama, dance, sculpture, painting, and rhetorical speaking traditions used in pulpits, political platforms, and academic debate and discourse.

Singularly, the Spiritual/Blues/Jazz traditions have impacted nearly every kind of expressive styling in Western development since the opening up of the global exchange which began during the African slave trade in the 1440s. It is very clear, looking back over the last 150 years of American culture, that many of the most influential humanistic movements (music, cultural, social) have been mechanized around, about, by, and for Black people, and with music. These activities and social constructs transcend their ethnic social identity and have been embraced by all Americans.

American culture knows its soul because of the impulses of American popular culture. And music is popular culture's most celebrated expression and form.

These music(s)—Spirituals, Blues, Ragtime, Jazz, Bebop, Rhythm and Blues, Rock and Roll, Soul, and Hip Hop—have inspired so many people. These cultural soundings have allowed us in the past the opportunity to examine the simultaneous rise of great music(s), incredible artists, and powerful movements of ideas and cultural practices which embody noble and meaningful motion in human creativity, social action, and individual and collective spiritual transformation. So I want to continue to ask if this is changing.

AMERICAN CULTURAL STUDIES:
HIS-STORY IS OUT, OUR-STORY IS IN

Within the scope of the larger questions of society, this dialogue involves a broader examination of American culture and specific contexts people move within.

A study of American cultural history and expression is a search for places where identity and nationhood are being formulated, authenticated, ritualized, and represented.

The exploration of these various expressions is what culture and cultural study is about. Today one of the most revealing approaches to this complex narrative is to think of oneself as a cultural reporter or journalist. One has to hang out on the playground where things are being worked out. Some of the most engaging and significant ideas in contemporary popular culture are expressed through the media, advertising, music, and the culture arising through the Internet and information technology. Of significance as well is the demographic swing we see in the growth and convergence of multiple ethnic groups (Hispanic, Asian, Arab, biracial mixing between Blacks, Whites, and Asian Americans), particularly this generation moving in and around urban areas. Their formulations of identity and the macro-American cultural response is the significant pulse of cultural study and activity. As Farai Chideya has written recently,

> We can't understand America without first understanding it as a cross section of cultures. . . . Our idea of "American-ness" has always been linked with "whiteness," from tales of the Pilgrims forward. . . . The future will be created by the Millennium Generation, today's fifteen- to twenty-five-year-olds. They are the most racially mixed generation this country has ever seen—the face of the new America. (*The Color of Our Future*)[6]

I frequent a Thai restaurant in St. Paul, Minnesota. Most of the young people working there are area college students working to support themselves while keeping "in touch." One second they take an order and converse with the cooks in their native tongue. The next moment they are speaking to each other in urban vernacular: "Yo what up Boy!!!!!" In the background the restaurant has piped in comfortably Hip Hop, R&B, and pop Thai and Vietnamese artists. One verse is in Vietnamese, but the hook of the song, "Baby I need your love," is in English. Their style of dress is FUBU (the Black urban designers For Us By Us) and the Gap. This is a primary example of how American cultural identity is being defined in the twenty-first century: it is in the grind. This is part of the complex narrative of new millennium rituals of culture and identity. As author Ronald Takaki has written, "This changing demographic diversity has raised fundamental questions about America's identity and culture. . . . Americans have been constantly redefining their national identity from the moment of first contact on the Virginia shore."[7]

In the past too much of the cultural interpretation has been from he who has analyzed, defined, and looked down from the ivory tower from afar and here at home to curiously report on those who walk on the pavement. Or American cultural identity has simply been viewed as a European outpost, a further defined, more productive White society containing colorful minorities who bubble up and offer a moment of entertainment or diversion.

Today a more real picture of who "we are" and where "we are going" must come from the common stories of folks constantly creating and defining culture. The idea of culture being reported through "his-story" seems quite out of step with the more real telling(s) of "our-story" as it is happening.

Moving back from our contemporary current pulses, there are several other historic watershed moments or windows through which we see American culture grappling with itself to reflect, then project, its identity. One kind of historical snapshot or overview looks like this:

1. After the settling of Jamestown in 1607, nineteen enslaved Africans and indentured European servants arrived in 1619.
2. Following the establishment of Boston (1620) and the eastern coast, America rises as a nation.
3. 1770s: The Declaration of Independence as a separate country, thus a huge cultural empire.
4. 1860s: Civil War and the amendments to the Constitution.

5. 1870–1900: Opening of the Midwest and West, clashes with Native Americans.
6. 1900–teens: Migrations of some 13 million Europeans (Germans, Russian Jews, Irish, Italians, Poles) searching for political, economic, and religious freedom and hope, World War I, New York as a cultural/advertising/capital mecca.
7. 1920s: The Jazz Age, Harlem Renaissance, and the New Negro.
8. 1929, 1930s: Stock market crash, 1930–1933 depression, New Deal, emergence of Hitler and start of War World II.
9. 1940s: Prominence of Swing music, Glenn Miller, radio programming and Hollywood's visions, Pearl Harbor in 1941, the bombing of Hiroshima and Nagasaki in 1945, Bebop, Cab Calloway, Louis Jordan, and the early roots of Jump, Rock and Roll.
10. 1950s: Postwar returns, suburbia, baby boomers boom, Alan Freed and Rock and Roll in 1955, television.
11. 1960s: Civil Rights; the assassinations of King, Kennedy, Malcolm X; Andy Warhol's thesis of the art of the common object and "pop art"; Bob Dylan; Monterey Peace and Woodstock festivals.
12. 1970s: Soul, war protests, Disco.
13. 1980s: Reaganomics, Rap, Punk, Grunge, in resistance ("Rappers Delight," 1979).
14. 1990s–200_?: Urban and global cultural explosion in media, information technology, Internet, music television, and popular culture; the final consolidation of buyouts, mergers, and megacompanies that control everything.

When we examine how these periods sprang up and how generations are negotiating their spaces, a serious look at any number of questions about our identity as citizens provides us with a fuller understanding of what the culture is truly made of. Of course there are many other factors that shape culture, but as an artist I focus on the humanistic and expressive attributes of American society. Again, by investigating and exploring creative cultural product, we simultaneously examine social, political, spiritual/religious contexts, and this furthers our understanding of the meanings and complexity of human experience in contemporary society.

PEOPLE STORIES

In my work I try to develop a critical perspective on these multiple meanings of "American" and "artistic culture" by examining the symbols, practices, histories that contribute to cultural experience. By keeping afloat these "working ideas," we also engage in discussions that discover linkages and tensions between vernacular and elite culture as well as diverse and multiple cultural identities and affiliations.

I divide this work into two tracks of cultural studies inquiry:

1. Cultural studies as the discipline, discourse, rhetoric, intellectual rigor of "reading texts" and the interpretation, deconstruction, and analysis of human practices struggling within the agency of power, expression, identity formation, and national history.
2. The study of culture more as human expression, which tends to value the human expressive side and places emphasis on creative agency as it honors peoples' cultural rituals.

The most rewarding exploration always is the study of people—their customs, navigation of images, beliefs, and cultural artifacts and practices created to underline those experiences. This is where my passion lives. Culture is created and represented somewhere in between the space of human social constructs (laws, systems of government, religious and cultural rites), contact we make in society, and our daily existence. Culture then is the proof that somebody has been doing some living down here.

So museums (as the storerooms for cultural objects), concert halls (as spaces of public cultural ritual), music/cultural movements (i.e., Hip Hop, Soul, and social protest) are examples of people working and living to be in accordance with the zeitgeist (social spirit) of their times. Author Albert Murray has also written, "The artist (writer) never ceases being concerned with human fulfillment . . . they provide the most adequate frame of reference for coming to terms with contemporary experience."[8]

Popular culture and arts are so important and compelling because they are where people are expressing in vibrant, innovative ways their uncompromising willingness to be alive. It is within these forms that people celebrate the victories of being human. In these ways common culture (vernacular, popular) becomes the "most reporting" entity and representative of the broadest range of human expression for cultural mining. It's important that we critically measure the world in which we find ourselves living and that we explore some shared values in our observations of our cultural experiences. And within these transcriptions, in this lens, in these sites, we consider "working ideas," we can reveal ourselves, our beliefs, and hopes; and we come to these truths through participation within the culture we create in society in particular historical moments. While no theory of explanation in particular comes from this way of looking at culture, there is at least a wrestling with meanings of human expression in time. There is the discovery of people stories, of who did what to whom; their reactions, celebrations, and representations of this identity; cries and tangible responses; some artifacts; some other whats; some more reasons; a where; some hows; a when; and maybe a why.

·6·

Mobilization and Cultural Creation: The Rise of African American Consciousness and an Interpretation of African American History and Culture (1990)

There are many ways to examine, interpret, and then theorize African American history and culture. Social, political, economic, religious, and aesthetic probes are necessary regardless of research design because of the multitude of perspectives, data, and concepts embedded in African American existence. It is difficult to talk about African American life apart from these categorical interpretations. Writers who approach the subject may use different sets of questions to address African American life, but it seems the main objective remains constant; to show the distinctiveness of African American culture.

What is it about African American culture and history that sets it apart as a unique phenomenon? Vincent Harding, in *There Is a River: The Black Struggle for Freedom in America*, describes his historical probe as a quest for meaning. In the opening pages of his work he asks the following questions:

> Why did it happen? Why were we chosen to be chosen, if we were? How in the midst of such death and suffering could we find so much strength to love, so much determination to live, fight on and be free? In the permanent and grueling exile, how could a people dance and create songs and art, fashion institutions of hope, bear so many Children of beauty?[1]

Harding attempts to examine African American history to uncover records of past generations, and to find meaning that will illuminate the proper paths toward the future. As a historian and theologian, he designates "the Black struggle for freedom" as the locus of cultural meaning.

In *The Black Family in Slave and Freedom, 1750–1925*, Herbert G. Gutman suggests that African American culture grows out of resistance, and he identifies resistance as the characteristic element that shapes African American history and culture. Gutman's research centers around the slave family, and later the free African American family, as the agent which transmits cultural norms and values.

Some writers and interpreters cite the development of the African American church as the source of the most substantial account of African American history and culture. Gayraud S. Wilmore, in *Black Religion and Black Radicalism*, writes:

Black Americans want to know, and indeed must know, more about who they were and who they are if they are serious about who they will become. Black religion has been a critical component of the American passage from slavery to freedom. Their religion was the organizing principle around which their life was structured. Their church was their school, their forum, their political arena, their social club, their art gallery, their conservatory of music.[2]

While Eugene D. Genovese was not primarily concerned with African American cultural development, *The Political Economy of Slavery* touches upon slave life and its impact on southern mentality. He writes:

I begin with the hypothesis that so intense a struggle of moral values implies a struggle of world views and that so intense a struggle of world views implies a struggle of worlds of rival social classes or societies dominated by rival social classes. In investigating the hypothesis I have rejected the currently fashionable interpretation of slavery as simply a system of extra-economic compulsion designed to sweat a surplus out of Black labor. Slavery was such a system but it was much more. It supported a plantation system that must be understood as an integrated social system, and it made this community the center of Southern life. It extruded a class of slave holders with a special ideology and psychology and the political and economic power to impose their values on society as a whole. Slavery may have been immoral to the world at large, but for these men it increasingly came to be seen as the very foundation of a proper social order and therefore the essence of morality in human relationships.[3]

With such a powerful interpretation of the social context for Black and White relationships, we may ask, "What was the African American response to such a social order?" In James Mellon's *Bullwhip Days: The Slaves Remember*, he writes: "Indeed whoever would understand the black community in America today must seek to understand not only the conditions of slavery in which that community was born, but also the experiences of racism, for it was racism that gave American slavery its distinctive character."[4]

Mellon edits numerous slave accounts within which an ex-slave says, "If you want Negro history, you will have to get it from someone who wore the shoe, and by and by, one from the other, you will get a book."[5]

Some writers have chosen to analyze cultural creations of African Americans to interpret the meaning of their culture and history. In *The Spirituals and the Blues: An Interpretation*, James Cone writes:

I want to examine the spirituals and the blues as cultural expressions of black people, having prime significance for their people. . . . Black music is unity music. It shapes and defines black being and creates cultural structures for black expression. . . . Through music, black slaves ritualized their existence and gave to their lives a dimension of promise and new reality that could not be contained in human theologies and philosophies.[6]

The work of these six writers reveals the multifaceted nature of African American cultural and historical interpretation. A multidisciplinary approach to this subject provides the most thorough interpretation. We begin to see how cultural norms and values are formed and maintained by talking within social, political, economic, religious, or aesthetic categories.

Within the context of mobilization and cultural creation, the origin of African American consciousness, there are several factors that help guide our interpretation of African American historical and cultural development:

1. African Americans came into slavery with a rich African cultural heritage known either by direct experience or by oral and cultural transmission—what DuBois calls "social heredity." Many of these cultural values continue to have a profound effect upon the way African American history and culture evolve.
2. Multidisciplinary probes including methods of social, political, economic, religious, and aesthetic sciences are necessary to examine African American history and culture.
3. A resistant spirit that includes constant growth, constructions of meaning, and redefinition of existence in a new world characterize African American history.

Approached in this way, the deep truths about African American culture and history surface and can be interpreted within the many parameters of the Black experience. In short, as Gutman suggests, Black resistance to total White domination in America produced many personalities, institutions, cultural creations, and an African American identity. The following discussion focuses on a few early African American movements to reveal the "grassroots" thought and motivation behind the creation of a distinct and viable African American cultural history.

Two subject categories serve as the matrix from which the interpretations spring. The first is "World Expansion: The American Fantasy and White Superiority." The second is "The Great Tradition of Black Resistance and Mobilization: Religion, Law, and Art (Music)."

WORLD EXPANSION: THE AMERICAN FANTASY AND WHITE SUPERIORITY

The European acquisition of power and desire for worldwide colonization produced an insatiable world market. Following the Renaissance, the commercial revolution, and the concept of the "new man," the American fantasy of a "new spirit" developed. These are all pieces of the process that spawned the type of social philosophy Genovese suggests. The exploitation of Black labor and Black life became the enterprise through which American desires and goals were achieved. Black labor became the means for worldwide economic growth in the "new age." John Hope Franklin writes: "If Negroes helped to raise the curtain on the drama of economic life in the new world they were to play an even more important part in the exploitation of its resources. Once fastened to a lifetime status of slavery, they became an integral part of the economic life of the old and of the new world."[7]

Slave labor produced a social order which, for centuries to come, placed Whites and Blacks in a master/slave, superior/inferior relationship. Many of the wounds suffered under the American system of slavery have yet to heal. African American mobilization and cultural creations must be understood within the context of this social fabric. As servants/slaves for life, stripped of all dignity and sense of human worth, African Americans were forced to carve out new meanings for themselves.

Blackness symbolized inferior status and was disdained as racism became the dominant mind-set in colonial America. A racist mind-set remains tightly woven in the United States social fabric even as we move toward the twenty-first century. DuBois's prophetic notion of the color line as the blight of the twentieth century is fulfilled. The need for resistance against the oppressive American social order requires that African Americans continue to draw deep from the well of humanity to produce a will to survive.

These issues dramatize the fact that African American social and political mobilization and artistic creations, for the most part, developed from a resistance to a social order that was designed by Whites to completely dominate Black life. This order, what Harding describes as "White fantasy," gave rise to Black solidarity that resulted in African American social and political movements as well as African American literature, dance, and song. James Cone describes the multiple layers of Black spirituals: "Black music is also social and political. It is social because it is black and thus articulates the separateness of the black community. It is an artistic rebellion against the humiliating deadness of western culture. . . . Through song a new political consciousness is continuously created, one antithetical to the laws of white society."[8]

These "laws" were written to legalize White oppression on moral, social, economic, and religious grounds. Racist anthropological theories and selected biblical references became the "proof" that the White world, specifically White Americans, needed to "morally" assert White superiority and "justify" the enslavement of Black people. The social fabric of American life continues to rest on factors of economics and race. One of our most famous "Founding Fathers," Thomas Jefferson, expressed it this way:

> To our reproach it must be said that though for a century and a half we have had under our eyes the races of the red and black men . . . I advance it as suspicion only that the blacks whether originally a distinct race or made distinct by time and circumstance are inferior to whites in both the mind and the body. The improvement of blacks in body and mind, in the first instance of their mixture with the whites has been observed by everyone and proves that their inferiority is not the effect merely of their condition in life.[9]

THE GREAT TRADITION OF BLACK RESISTANCE AND MOBILIZATION: RELIGION, LAW, AND ART (MUSIC)

Religion, law, and art are the determinants of culture. African Americans constructed a distinct culture out of resistance to the particular and peculiar American social order. Religious perspectives, art, and an adopted social stance created a method to challenge the existing order. I want to look at these larger cultural determinants and the African American consciousness that arose in the beginning of the late eighteenth century and continued throughout the nineteenth and twentieth centuries.

Religion

African American religious or spiritual responses to slavery, slave revolts, and the rise of independent Black churches provide powerful examples of the role of resistance in the creation of African American consciousness. As Wilmore writes:

> An exceedingly elastic but tenacious thread binds together the contributive and developmental factors of black religion in the United States as one distinctive social phenomenon. It is the thread of what may be called, if properly defined, "black radicalism." It [black religion] has been equally concerned with the yearning of a despised and subjugated people for freedom from the religious, economic, social, and political domination that whites exercised over blacks since the beginning of the slave trade.[10]

Religious organizations and the biblical theme of a justice-seeking God provided African Americans with a foundational principle for many of their movements and for their art. At this point I would like to draw attention to Black mobilization in social, religious, political, and artistic responses to slavery.

Slave Revolts

Blacks resisted slavery through physical revolts, as documents from eighteenth-century African American intellectual discussions reveal. A tradition of violent resistance exists in African American history, contrary to the concept of the docile, master-loving slave. I would like to briefly discuss three particular slave revolts. They were the initial stage of a deliberate surge of African American cultural creation and consciousness.

Africans who found themselves caught in the snare of slavery were acutely aware of the degree of savage and inhuman acts perpetuated against them under the American system. Although the institution of slavery itself was not foreign to Africans, European and American "New World" concepts of slaves as chattel strongly contradicted African notions of servitude. Historians Mary Francis Berry and John W. Blassingame report that for slaves in Africa: "There is little doubt that the ordinary domestic slaves which formed by far the most numerous class had, as in ancient Egypt, happier lives than many of the wage earning slaves in the modern civilized world. They had few anxieties, lived usually well with their master, and their physical wants in the warm climate were not many."[11]

Charles K. Meeks found among writings from the Hausa, Fulani, Yoruba, and Nupe peoples that the fate of the African slave was significantly different from the American experience. Meeks writes about life for African slaves: "Their lot was by no means hard. They were not usually overworked and enjoyed a considerable measure of freedom. They could and did, in fact, frequently rise to obtain the highest positions of the state."[12]

Racism was not a tenet of African slavery, and therefore African slavery did not contain contrived suggestions of inferiority.

African culture figured greatly in the lives of slaves in America. Berry and Blassingame explain, "Inspired by their African fore-fathers, American-born slaves engaged continuously during the nineteenth century in conspiracies, rebellions, and attempts to escape from bondage."[13] These revolts and forms of resistance demanded the liberation and elevation of the entire race.

Revolts were numerous. Reports as early as 1712 reveal that 25 to 30 slaves in New York City, armed with clubs and knives, attacked Whites and burned buildings.[14] Whites burned, beat, beheaded, hanged, castrated, amputated tongues, shattered limbs, and retaliated against Black people in other brutal ways. Despite these perils, slave revolts continued on rural colonial farms and plantations both in the South and in the islands.

Toussaint-Louverture led the famous revolt in the French-ruled island of Haiti. His actions provided an example of strong, sensible, Black leadership as the revolt effectively overthrew the Haitian slavery system. This uprising also symbolized a potential "Negro problem" in the Western hemisphere. Revolts were positive proof that Blacks were unwilling to succumb to slavery as their destiny in the Americas.

> Up Afric Up, the land is free. It sees no slave to despot bow.
> Our cry is liberty—On: Strike for God and vengeance now.
> Fly, tyrant, fly, or stay and die. No chains to bear, no scourge we fear. We conquer or perish now.[15]

With the spirit of Jeffersonian democracy and the Haitian and French revolutions of the 1790s, it is impossible to ignore the impact of these revolts for Blacks everywhere. Physical aggressions play a significant role in African American mobilization, consciousness, and cultural creations.

What has been called a "radical interpretation" of Christianity turned the pious Black Christian into a rebellious, liberty-seeking warrior. Christianity, along with the "long memory" of African ethics, provided the unique justice-seeking philosophy that supported a radical liberation thrust. Such was the case of three incredible personalities whose carefully planned revolts occurred at the turn of the eighteenth century.

Gabriel Prosser, known as Black Sampson, was an intellectually gifted man who was also a diligent student of the Bible. A slave himself, Prosser believed he was chosen by God to organize a massive revolt with thousands of slaves. Prosser's plan was to kill Whites, seize ammunition and the state treasury, set up a separate territory, and demand the statewide liberation of Black people. The revolt, which was to take place during the summer of 1800, may be the first well-planned strategic slave uprising in American history. It was foiled, however, by a severe storm and slaves who revealed the conspiracy to their masters. On October 17, 1800, Gabriel Prosser, along with 34 other slaves, was executed.

The Denmark Vessey conspiracy was another example of conscious resistance. Vessey's proposed revolt was planned in South Carolina in 1822. Like Prosser before him and, later, Nat Turner, Vessey saw himself as a leader of his people. Vessey purchased his own freedom after spending his childhood as a slave. He was a carpenter, and, like many Black leaders, was steeped in Bible studies. He believed the Bible showed examples of an oppressed people who rose up to claim their independence.

Vessey was also a member of the Hamstead Methodist Church, one of the Black churches that eventually broke away from the White denomination. Baptist and Methodist denominations allowed more autonomous control of congregations and were the most sincere evangelizing groups to approach and embrace enslaved Africans. Baptist and Methodist styles of worship were also much more acceptable to new Black converts because Baptists and Methodists were "spirit filled and Holy Ghost led." The church also served additional purposes. Vessey and other conspirators used the church service as an opportunity to meet and map out the revolt. Their plan was to gather some 3,000 to 9,000 slaves for an attack that would begin at Charleston and extend approximately 80 miles into the state. This revolt was foiled by a "loyal" slave who revealed the plan to his master. Vessey and 37 slaves were executed.

In 1831, Nat Turner led the most successful American slave revolt. Turner believed he was a prophet appointed by God to lead his people to freedom. (Important parallels between Sunday school lessons and the real-life drama experienced by oppressed Blacks in America seemed to go unnoticed by White theologians.) Turner described visions of great bloody conflicts between Black and White forces. When the time was appropriate, Turner, armed with a hatchet, an ax, his intellectual gifts, and his power as a preacher, led a group of men through South Carolina. Turner and his men killed 57 Whites within a 20-mile area of the Boykins District in South Hampton. The White community quickly passed monumental amounts of legislation to restrict the rights of slaves to assemble, preach, read, or write, as Whites attempted to ensure against further revolts.

This radical form of Black mobilization was replaced by less violent but equally determined institutionalized efforts. Working within the American legal framework, intellectual exchange and empowered writing figured into efforts to obliterate slavery and radically change the social structure of American life. Published speeches and literature of the nineteenth-century free Black intelligentsia display a crystallized African American consciousness and form a powerful mass of human voices.

African Americans began to interpret their own history, reflect more critically on their place in the world, and determine their own destiny. Their religion was solid and significant and they talked about it. Their art was essential for their survival and they sang about it. Nineteenth century Black writers began to publish their own laws through numerous pamphlets, books, newspaper articles, and declarations of purpose. These cultural creations serve as a framework to interpret African American culture and history, and the documents written by an elite faction of the total Black population prove the existence of a clearly defined African American culture.

The Rise of the Independent Black Church

The Black church in America stands as the oldest African American institution and is worthy of historical and cultural investigation. The Black church indisputably contains many African retentions and is the most viable cultural, educational, political, religious, and social center in African American life. Like the rise of the slave revolts, the rise of the independent Black church can be attributed to both Black resistance to White domination and Black solidarity.

Enslaved Africans initiated their own services according to the amount of freedom afforded them on the plantation. White observers saw that African Americans had a distinct way of "religiousizing." Comparisons between the African American religious culture and the forms of religion that developed on the island plantations reveal important similarities and suggest the tenacious nature of African cultural aspects. In the South, Black worship describes both a physical gathering and a cultural/psychological phenomenon. The Black worship service had the potential to become a political Black "war-ship" service that threatened White domination. These ceremonies were shrouded in secrecy because of laws and regulations that stemmed from events like Nat Turner's revolt.

Free Blacks in the North did not escape the cultural, social, and political problems even in a slightly more independent community. These problems, in conjunction with the rise of an African American consciousness, precipitated the emergence of separate religious communities. A group of free Blacks in Philadelphia, for instance, created the Free African Society, the African Methodist Episcopal Church (AME), and the St. Thomas African Methodist Episcopal Church of Philadelphia in response to White domination, discrimination, and degradation.

Richard Allen, a former slave who purchased his own freedom, is a central figure in the evolution of the Black church. Allen was compelled to preach after his conversion to Christianity. He settled in Philadelphia in 1786 and was invited to preach at St. George's Methodist Church to a segregated congregation. One day, because of a slight violation of the rules that separated Whites and Blacks within the church, Richard Allen, Absolom Jones, and several other church members were physically removed. An intolerable history of discrimination against Black parishioners at St. George's ended that day. Allen and others left the church never to return.

In 1787, Black parishioners formed the Free African Society, a benevolent organization which fed Whites as well as Blacks. Later, in 1794, Allen and his parishioners built Bethel African Methodist Church. Absolom Jones, because of his desire to break away from the Methodist domination, founded St. Thomas African American Episcopal Church. Other free Black congregations established their own independence as well. African Americans from Pennsylvania, Maryland, Delaware, and New Jersey came together in 1816 to formalize the first national independent Black denomination, the African Methodist Episcopal (AMB) Church. Richard Allen became the church's first bishop.

The Law and African American Consciousness

African American history and cultural movements evolved from a whirlwind of complex and involved social, political, and economic circumstances. All parts of the Western world experienced political and social change; African American culture did not develop in a vacuum. Like the influence of the French Revolution in the 1790s on Haitian-enslaved Africans, the American Revolution affected African Americans in thought and action. Thousands of African Americans fought in the war for American independence. These Blacks acquired their freedom and helped to establish free Black communities in both the South and the North.

While the liberation of their brothers and sisters in the South remained crucial, free communities were interested in immediate social advances and the acquisition of the constitutional privileges guaranteed them as Americans. For example, the African Union Society was formed on November 10, 1780. This organization, along with the Free African Society, became increasingly important and had an impact on the formation of African American ideology. As Robert Harris describes, these organizations "offered some stability for their members in a hostile society by providing a cushion against misfortune with sickness, disability benefits, burial insurance and apprenticeships. They encouraged the education of black youths by starting and supporting schools."[16]

While free Blacks attempted to establish a cultural identity as Americans of color, the concept of emigration challenged the destiny of Blacks in America. The American Colonization Society (ACS) was formed in 1816 by White philanthropists to return all people of African descent to Africa. Some Blacks saw the value of emigration as well. Almost a decade earlier, Black shipowner Paul Cuffe had successfully transported several African Americans to Africa. But one month after the ACS was founded, some three thousand free Blacks met at Bethel Church in Philadelphia to denounce the ACS and its intentions. African Americans believed that their primary goal was to liberate all enslaved Africans. Their second aim was to elevate the race in America to enjoy both full rights as citizens and equal participants in the formation of American society. Colonization was not the solution to America's "unwanted boarders problem."

In 1830, a Black community in Cincinnati suffered a rash of violent acts committed by Whites. The first African American convention met in Philadelphia, the largest free Black community in the nation, in response to these attacks. Richard Allen, president of a subgroup called the American Society of Free Persons of Color, claimed that Blacks were born in America, enriched it, and, as a result, were American in custom, habit, and mannerisms. This statement signifies the origin of a strong African American identity and cultural consciousness. From this point forward, African Americans continued to create cultural structures that gave support to their communities, and, through scholarship and literature, enlarged the concept of African American identity.

David Walker's *Appeal to the Colored Citizens of the World*, published in 1830, stands out as one of the most important documents in all of American history. Walker's work is one of the most concise and compelling indictments against American society to date. The appeal dispelled any notions of the United States as a "conscious-free" racist society. Walker's work inspired many later Black leaders, including Frederick Douglass and Martin Delany. Delany published *The Condition, Elevation, Emigration, and Destiny of the Colored People in the United States* in 1852.

An African American cultural consciousness was developed, documented, and dispersed. Frederick Douglass and Harvard-trained physician, politician, editor, and businessman Martin

Delany, preachers such as Sojourner Truth, James W. C. Pennington, historian William Wells Brown, scientist Benjamin Banneker, and poet and prophetess Phyllis Wheatly all came forward to concretize an African American identity. These historical figures represent an identifiable African American cultural consciousness that was created to liberate and elevate Black people.

Cultural Creation, Music

Music is one of the most visible and influential cultural creations of African American existence. Black music is art in the sense that it is, of course, the manifestation of the skillful use of the imagination to create objects of human expression. But for our interest, like all Black creations, art was closely tied to the hardship of African American experience. We must consider the unique aesthetics of Black musical expression. African American music is tied to Africa in artistic quality and cultural function. In its initial stages, African American music expressed emotion and frustration as well as hope in a higher power, a God who was always among the people. It was religious music and, as James Cone suggests, it was social and political.

An aesthetic probe into African American music reveals more about its social and psychological implications than its philosophical meanings. The music is direct expression that is pure, concrete, includes religious affirmation or social protest, and is sometimes music that simply entertains. African American social and religious music from the 1700s through the late 1800s can be interpreted as existence art organized around social circumstance. The social element, more than any other aesthetic reason, provides us with a functional definition. Beauty must initially be found in the sincerity of the song that symbolizes inner expressions and yearnings which are the root of any artistic creation. Black art is concrete expression.

> O freedom, O freedom
> O freedom over me. And before I'll be a slave,
> I'll be buried in my grave
> And go home to my Lord and be Free.[17]

The African American form of the folk song, the reconstructed European hymnal, the field or work songs, the jigs, the Spirituals, the Blues and instrumental art pieces like fiddle, banjo, and guitar improvisations are all culturally tied to the African aesthetic/social meaning of art. Music in Africa is a concrete expression of every aspect of African community life. The griot/composer/poet, the priest, the mother, the worker, and the children all use the "African song" as a constant form of human expression and sharing. In *The Music of Africa*, J. H. Kwabena Kenatia writes:

> The treatment of the song as a form of speech utterance arises not only from stylistic considerations or from consciousness of the analogous features of speech and music; it is also inspired by the importance of the song as an avenue of verbal communication, a medium for creative verbal expression which can reflect personal and social experience. . . . [Songs] may deal with everyday life or with traditions, beliefs and customs of the society.[18]

The African-aesthetic base of Black art remains in American art. This point is crucial. Much of African American music, especially the Spirituals and the interpersonal Blues or folk songs, can be characterized by the simultaneous saturation of religious and social experience in the artistic expression. This gives Black style a depth and sincerity which, for lack of a better word, is "soul." Any discussion of the aesthetic quality and meaning of Black music must consider the art as the expression of both the social context from an African American perspective, and a rich, indelible African heritage. In this situation African Americans created, in essence, cultural extensions of Africa by restructuring and integrating European religious concepts and new musical sounds to express their experiences.

CONCLUSION

The discussion of these issues brings to light my understanding of cultural creation and consciousness and attempts to view African American history and culture from a multidisciplinary perspective. Within the matrix of European intentions for world expansion and the resulting American dream, Blacks began a consistent and determined resistance against White domination. An overview of the growth of an African American cultural consciousness is impossible without social, political, religious, and ethnological considerations.

The degree of African retentions which still exists in African American culture shows how Black response to social conditions necessitated the conscious creation of Black mobilization and other cultural structures. Further study would incorporate the role of the African American family in the struggle to emancipate and elevate enslaved members. Out of this immediate family struggle came the creation of an African American culture defined by religious expression, song, and literature. African Americans were also determined to formulate a public philosophy based on the principles found in a restructured constitution and the God-ordained liberties afforded to all created souls. African American history and culture is fascinating because of its incredible richness and complexity. My interpretations only scratch the surface of the vast amount of information that needs to be considered. A quest for meaning, an analysis of social structure, a search for family values, an encounter with religion, a political and economic probe, an experience of heart and song, a journey into the minds and hearts of an incredibly beautiful and strong people are all necessary to rewrite a story that has been barely told.

The Undeniable Groove: Black Rhythm in Artistic Expression (1992)

They always keep exquisite time and tune and no words seem hard for them to adapt to their tunes . . . so that they can sing a long meter tune without any difficulty . . . with the most perfect time and rarely without any discord.

—Francis Anne Kemble[1]

The unmistakable and most distinguishing art qualifier or identifiable handle of Black musical art making is its rhythmic complexity and vitality. Certainly there are many harmonic, sequential or cadence (turn arounds) conventions, licks and breaks that have been created by Black artists in the African Diaspora. But worldwide, and particularly within the last fifty years, Black rhythmic conception has dominated aesthetic conventions clearly in popular forms of music. These conventions have had a major effect on music that has been composed throughout the world including traditional West African music, African pop, the music of the Caribbean, and both South American and Latin American music, Reggae, and the African American creations in the States, the Spirituals and Blues, Jazz forms (Swing, Bebop, Cool), Rhythm and Blues, Funk, and certainly Hip Hop and Rap forms. Also included in this family is contemporary concert music by Black composers.

My aim and purpose is to speak as a composer offering suggestions on how to interpret Black composed works from an aesthetic/cultural theoretical framework. I will do this by using some of Henry Louis Gates's literary observations, West African spiritual aesthetic sensibilities and some African American notions of form, style, and feel. I tie all of these forms of expression to their common philosophical grounding: rhythmic expression. I am also trying to initiate a user-friendly aesthetic dialogue which attempts to speak about Black rhythm and its vitality, and how one goes about using "it" to create works of art as well. Hopefully, some serviceable suggestions can be generated which can inform dialogue about the nature of contemporary Black rhythm in both vocal and instrumental composed art forms. This dialogue will center around certain pieces of Black composed works and projects that have come about as the result of this "grappling" with the Black rhythm aesthetic: T. J. Anderson's "Themes of M.B. Tolson," my own "Spiritual Songs for Tenor and Cello," and some reflections on Queen Latifah's "Listen 2 Me," from the *Black Reign* CD on Motown Records.

"Each literary tradition, at least implicitly, contains within it an argument for how it can be read."[2]

Essay originally appeared in *"This Is How We Flow": Rhythm in Black Cultures*, edited by Angela M. S. Nelson, University of South Carolina Press, 1999.

If Gates's assumption is true, then there is no need to speak of any new theory for how Black art making is done, how it should be perceived, or what constitutes its aesthetic life. Whether we are speaking of setting text to music, composing a new work within the stylistic families of Black musical art, or of trying to get a handle on the meanings of its expressive power or simply talking about the artistic experience, the notion of "rhythmic life" is a primary issue. I am defining rhythm as the science of coordinated movement in sound, but this extends outward to include all creative works, thought, and performance that come as a result of Black artistic expression. This larger concept of "rhythmic life or life force" includes music, poetry, mythology, dance, and visual expressions of living (painting, sculpture). Black life and expression have RHYTHM. This used to bother me because it is exactly this idea that Europeans and White America would use to debase the intellectual and aesthetic value of Black art and style, reducing Black artistic quality to an innate ability to "keep good time." Rhythm, in my mind, means coordinated movement at many levels; physical, spiritual, symbolic, literal, and intellectual. I must return to my own "homeland" which is rich and fertile. I want to show evidence of this rich and fertile science or life force by examining its ideological roots and, as mentioned earlier, examine musical examples in the literature which help to emphasize these points.

IDEOLOGICAL ROOTS AND PARADIGM SHIFTS

Duke Ellington made this popular philosophy palatable and fashionable, "It don't mean a thing if it ain't got that swing." Well, "that swing" is what I call the Undeniable Groove. The ideological and cultural roots of this rhythmic base are a West African conception. A. M. Jones, in *African Rhythm*, writes, "Rhythm is to Africa what harmony is to the European, and it is within the complex interweaving of contrasting rhythmic patterns that he finds his greatest aesthetic satisfaction."[3]

Western notions of rhythm in composed works define it as secondary or as a subordinate element that usually functions to link notes and harmony together. Time is thought to commence from the beginning at the start of a downbeat. African notions of rhythm are very different. There is a completely different aesthetic viewpoint and meaning in place for perception, creation, and performance of artistic expression. John Miller Chernoff writes:

> Africans are concerned with sound and movement, space and time, the deepest modalities of perception. Foremost is the dynamic tension of the multiple rhythms and the cohesive power of their relationships. This involves the subtle perfection of rhythmic form through precision of performance, complexity and organization and control of gestural timing.[4]

Unlike a typical, classical seventeenth-century European order of musical design, in traditional Black design, rhythm is the determining factor, the controlling element in composition or creative expression. Therefore, a paradigm shift away from Eurocentric notions of rhythm, form, text setting, and performance practices needs to be recognized. Again, each culture produces its own rules for the implementation of artistic structure. And these rules work independently with, while critically "peepin'," the old traditions to make sure they are in line with the new modes of thinking and living and creating art forms.

Hungarian composer Zoltan Kodaly, in his *Confession* (1962), wrote that music should never be contrary to the natural melody trend of a language and should never be diametrically opposed to the character of one's native cultural expression. At the turn of the century, the critics complained that Stravinsky had replaced the expressive power of harmony with motor power and argued that he destroyed sentiment and subjective emotions. In a sense, then, critics claimed that Stravinsky's art, along with other avant-gardes, destroyed traditional notions of pleasing and beautiful music. In a progressive Black aesthetic, again on all levels, beauty is in the rhythm, the groove. The groove is moved to the forefront. This urgency of objective meaning in expression, and the immediacy of the perception of the direct aural experience, shifts us away from the European romantic paradigm. This "rude treatment" of expression, this urgency, and "soul" as some have called it, is what we mean by "life force" and vitality. This is now an aesthetic qualifier for artistic meaning.

TEXT AND DOUBLE MEANING IN BLACK ART

Another aesthetic suggestion and observation for Black art in terms of dealing with literary forms, poetry, stories, myths, and love lyrics (Blues, R&B) is of course its expressive liveliness in terms of rhythmic phrase construction (an issue to which I will return), but also its double face, or what Gates called "double-voiced text" or Black texts of being. These two components of Black expression, rhythmic vitality, and multiple meanings, are what gives Black art forms their elasticity and depth.

Black music has a long-standing tradition as an art form of rebellion and cultural creation, and these two characteristics are in many cases inseparable in the work. Many Black works created in the African Diaspora have double meanings, codes of insurrection, messages of spiritual freedom or political liberty, love songs of the beauty and the pathos of love, called Blues-songs, and these dualities characterize the depth of the Black text.

This duality, in addition, helps to propel the music that is created to carry the text. These double folds of meaning, coupled with a unique approach, or syncopated phrase execution, all work to validate the claim that Black expression is artistically distinctive and that "rhythmic expression" is its most salient feature.

> Many Thousand Gone
>> No Mo auction block for me, no mo, no mo no mo
>> No mo drivers lash for me
>> No mo peck o' corn for me
>> Many thousand gone
> Didn't My Lord Deliver Daniel?
>> I set my foot on the gospel ship, and the ship it began to sail
>> It landed me over on Canaan's shore, and I'll never come back no more[5]

The play on words with mixed-bag eschatologies such as "Swing Low," "Wade in the Water," "Great Day," "Freedom Train A-Comin,'" and "Steal Away," from the African American Spiritual canon, are great examples of art traditions which worked within the expressive rhythmic paradigms discussed earlier. In the past, musicology might have dismissed these examples as simplistic, or refer to them as "vacuous religious moaning." A more careful examination reveals that these songs are indeed structured poetic text with consciously constructed codes for insurrection and escape. Since slavery, Black ways of talking and expression have served Black people as "coded private yet communal rituals." Upon hearing a Spiritual, the Blues, or modern Rap, there is a reverberation of meaning, a duality that reveals there is always more than what the word says on the surface. This rhythm of meaning is another aspect that gives Black art its particular value, what I call life force or vitality.

ESU "EMCEE" ELEGBARA: THE MYTHOLOGICAL
ROOT OF THE RAPPER

As we consider the rhythmic vitality of Black texts, and this idea of the rhythm of meaning, this duality, we should consider one of the most compelling of newer forms of Black expression, namely, Henry Louis Gates Jr., in *Signifying Monkey: A Theory of African American Literary Criticism*, suggests that "the middle passage did not obliterate significant artistic, political, nor metaphysical systems in black belief." Gates identifies a mythical figure in West African culture, Esu Elegbara, a double-voiced master of the spoken word, both spiritual and profane, a link between the gods and humanity. This figure was one who had the power of the spoken word, who became in his own conceit a trickster, a master of deceptive languages, and a master of stylish expression.

I would offer as another suggestion for the interpretation of Black texts, and in particular, more popular forms of the modern rapper, that somewhere, as Gates himself hints, there are vestiges of Esu Elegbara within the expressive, oral, and written consciousness of Black text writers. Black people in Cuba, Brazil, Miami, and Spanish Harlem all make references to this mythical character. Robert Farris Thompson, in Flash of the Spirit, notes that Esu Elegbara, "became one of the most important images in the Black Atlantic world." Despite my own suspicion of the artistic merit of many Rap products, I can now see that the trickster, gangsta, hood-wearing, crotch-grabbing, hustling, jive-talking, double-meaning, self-titled poet, lover of women, slick, stylish, ego-bearing, macho-minded figure known as a rapper might very well be our old friend Esu Elegbara in disguise. These associations between Black American literature and oral traditions to Esu Elegbara are compelling.

I am talking about traditions, styles, conventions, canon, and performance practices. In addition, I am suggesting that consideration be given to the whole of Black experience, the middle passage, and the cultural memory of African spiritual aesthetic and performance practices to provide a foundation for performing, creating, and understanding Black expressions in music. Rap as an art form viewed within this context exemplifies the point that there are linkages to all sorts of similar roots which help to tie traditional and contemporary Black music to common grounds. African conceptions of beingness and expression, again and again, provide the philosophical/cultural grounding.

TEXT AND MUSIC

I have always been interested in the result of music. It has been said that my approach to setting language is not traditional in terms of the way American and English composers set text. I see speech as rhythm. I mean that's what Black speech is all about. There is a certain vitality in language, particularly in Black speech and that's what I want to capture in my music. (T. J. Anderson, contemporary composer)[6]

It is clear from this statement that Black speech, and in particular, the rhythm and vitality of it generates an aesthetic and therefore musical interest from which works of art have come. This is the case in popular forms such as Rap, and in concert works by Black composers as well. Consistent stress patterns, additive rhythms, and phrase constructions heard in instrumental music are many times derived from the treatment of speech patterns in vocal expression.

The work that brings particular light to some of these aesthetic and cultural suggestions for examining Black musical art works is the piece, "Variations on a Theme by M. B. Tolson," by composer T. J. Anderson. The work, composed in 1969, is scored for soprano, alto saxophone, trumpet, trombone, piano, violin, and cello. The most intriguing and inventive aspect of this piece is its rhythmic inventions. Secondly, it clearly stands firm in the traditional Black arts traditions, fusing the Spirituals, Blues, Bebop, and Swing with European treatments of dissonance and Viennese notions of displacement of melody and *sprechstimme*. Of note also is the use of double-voiced texts of African proverbs and a Blues street text.

The excerpt I want to focus upon is Anderson's treatment of the Blues text which reads: "Come back baby, come back. I need your gravy, I'm weak and wavy, Skidrow bound, talk of the town, and I don't mean maybe." This lyric reflects the Black literary criteria for text and vernacular: slang (baby), metaphoric comparisons (gravy and sex), street rhyme, signifying (stating something explicitly to mean something implicitly), and the duality of the bittersweetness in adult love relationships as heard in many Blues lyrics. The final portion of the work is built on 12-bar phrases like Blues structure and the voice spins out the one line in different permutations, lengthening and shortening words in all sorts of different rhythmic variations. This creates at once a hearing of the entire phrase as well as placing rhythmic emphasis on certain words creating a texture of motivic cells with the instruments and syllabic repetitions of portions of the text.

In Anderson's work we have an example of a Western-schooled composer extending unique African American styles and traditions into the traditional European setting while simultaneously expanding the Black traditions to include a European avant-garde aesthetic. The pitch organization of the work is generated from free associations and is heard in variations organized in motivic cells which are displaced pointillistically.

These motivic variations are heard in rapid successions in one, pairs, and groups of instruments, and then again in tutti explosions. Anderson constantly shifts his orchestration function from interdependence to solo, to voice against ensemble, to create a rhythmic texture that gives life to a seemingly hopeless and helpless plea in the text. The rhythmic variations and the interesting vocal treatment of the text with half-spoken, half-sung glides and harsh rhythmic breaks in selected syllables, the motivic cells and counterpoint and exchange rhythmically between the voice and the ensemble, are delightfully incomprehensible, and are perhaps the most striking features of Anderson's work. "Themes of M. B. Tolson" is an unrecognized masterpiece in twentieth century chamber, vocal literature. The work stands firmly in African American traditions as well as exemplifies the best in Black style, conventions, aesthetic norms, and rhythmic vitality.

"SPIRITUAL SONGS FOR TENOR AND CELLO"

"Spiritual Songs for Tenor and Cello" by William Banfield is an example of the composer "revisiting the homeland" and recasting traditional African American Spirituals in new contemporary languages. The work has been criticized as well for "destroying traditional and sentimental religious values." The work is simply a late-twentieth-century exploration of traditional Black folklore, reworking and recasting the music in order to explore the powerful potential of pain, despair, and the profundity of hope and eschatological vision inherent, and critically unexplored, in most Spirituals.

The Spirituals of Black folk are some of the best examples of American folk philosophy; they are as profound as anything yet written. Over and above and under the adventurous treatment of music and text, and the profundity of depth and despair which fosters unshakable faith and joy, is once again the Undeniable Groove which dresses the work and gives it its audible life force. A look at the text reveals again some of the literary aesthetic qualities such as duality, spiritual depth, and reflection as well as odd phrase structures which confound traditional text meter configurations.

Were You There
    Were you there when they crucified my Lord?
    Were you there when they nailed him to the tree?
    Were you there when the sun refused to shine?
    Oh, Oh, sometimes it causes me to tremble
Were you there when they crucified my Lord?
    Hold On
    Keep yo' han' on de plow, Hold on!
    If you wanna get to heaven, let me tell you how
    Jus' keep yo' hand on the gospel plow.
    If that plow stays in yo' hand
    It'll land you straight in da promised land
    Keep yo' hand on da plow and hold on.
Nora said, Ya lost yo' track,
    Can't plow straight and keep looking back
    Keep yo' hand on the plow and hold on
    Mary had a golden chain, every link was in my Jesus' name
    Keep on climin' don't you tire
    Every rung goes higher and higher
    Keep yo' hand on the plow and hold on

"Spiritual Songs for Tenor and Cello" opens with the spiritual "Were You There?" In traditional settings this piece is usually heard as a solemn hymn. Here to the shock of the audience it is cast in very dissonant, disruptive music. The tenor lines and cello accompaniment are set in nontonal relationships, clearly dissonant, harking only referential to the original melody and harmony. Here there is the attempt to set up a painful and despair-filled landscape, ending in a very reflective and bitter cello cadence.

Although another aspect of this piece is the slow rhythmic jar that is set up in the relationship between the two voices, clearly, in "Hold On," the cello line is modeled after contemporary Funk-Groove bass lines one might hear from Larry Graham or Marcus Miller. The rhythmic vitality both in the cello line and the tenor's treatment of the text and melody can be described as "Funk Spiritual" if such a thing can exist. The entire vocal melody is not only disjunct and syncopated throughout, it is set in rhythmic counterpoint to a consistent Black backbeat in the cello. This rhythmic texture projects a two-dimensional pulse where the notion of one and downbeats are at times imperceptible. Then, midway in the composition, rhythmic characters of both instruments are reversed where the tenor voice is the anchor for the verse and the cello is cast in rhythmic syncopation against the tenor, off setting the listener's sense of the downbeat.

Again, the play here on rhythmic and philosophical concept is that even though the surface may be bumpy, and the waters may roll rough, nevertheless, hold on. The multiple meanings of spiritual reflection and social and political agitation and protest can be seen side by side. Even the function of the piece of art has multiple uses and meanings and supports my contention of the way rhythmic conception plays out in totality in Black art.

THE NEW POPULAR MUSIC AESTHETIC: HIP HOP
CULTURE AND THE QUEEN'S BLACK REIGN

There are many reasons to investigate Hip Hop and to link Rap and Black concert music to this concept of "rhythmic life." Besides the fact that it is clearly the most provocative musical art form of the last decade of the twentieth century, the real meaning of this new cultural activity is found among the "folks" where the operative meanings (language and behavior) are used, created, and worked out daily. There are a lot of social, political, and new, postmodern aesthetics at work in "da hood" where urban youth breathe and work it out. Just as in the Hippie generation of the 1960s (Rock and Roll), or the British youth in the 1970's (Punk, Slam), sociologically there is no difference. This illustrates a paradigm shift wherein old notions of rhythm and Black movement as the "simpleminded, natural behavior" of "Negroes" can be broken.

Rhythmic movement in this late-twentieth-century art form is the self-conscious mode of intellectual and creative expression. Coupled with this fact is the need to tie Hip Hop cultural expression with all creative Black expression within the Diaspora. Despite its ugly commercial exploits, and its sometimes harsh language, Hip Hop truly stands in the same camp as all other "welcomed" branches of the family of Black arts traditions. The emergence of new language forms (Hip Hop jargon) and modes of expression (both in music and movement, dance, and poetry) can be seen. Language, movement, and new aesthetic sensibilities create musical form, structure, syntax, and style. These elements are based upon the "rhythmic way" in which another generation of young Black people "speak."

TEXTUAL ANALYSIS

While some of the greatest writers of Black literature and critical theory such as Zora Neale Hurston, Ralph Ellison, Langston Hughes, Lorraine Hansberry, Richard Wright, James Baldwin, Leroi Jones (Amiri Baraka), Harold Cruse, Toni Morrison, and Maya Angelou might scoff at the following literary analysis of the work "Listen 2 Me" by Queen Latifah, it nevertheless illustrates best many of the assertions I have made for literary, rhythmic, and musical meaning in contemporary, progressive popular Black music today. I have devised symbols and indicators to place handles on the meaning and function of portions of the lyrics in "Listen 2 Me."

In the rhythmic play of speaking voices in the work, there are three principle speakers, which are "CV," which stands for community voices; "JR," for the Jamaican rapper; and "QL," which stands for Queen Latifah, principle griot.

"Listen 2 Me"

QL: Yeah Queen Latifah in the house, back for 1992, and 1993, on through the decade, come onnnnn.

CV: Listen to me, hear me now, listen to me (4x)

JR: Well in Jersey they're listening to me. The people uptown are listening to me. The people up in Brooklyn are listening to me. The people in Jamaica are listening to me.

QL: Well it's a party over here, a party over there, and in every nook and cranny, it's a party everywhere. And that you should have known when I walked through the 'do, I'm pumped I got the flava', I'm pumped I got the flow. Before you even try ta dis me, let's get something clear, there ain't no fair between me, and you want the atmosphere. Hail to the Queen and the Sire, I'm lightin' fires. Your style is whacked as two flat tires. It will only take a second for me ta just wreck it. Smoother than my body butt naked, I don't have to prove shiiiiii., just keep doing hits, and Niggas be all on my two tits.

And if you think this is odd, I'm telling that after every single rhyme I thank God, for giving me the talent to make your head nod, Tony Dufat's (her producer) down, gotta keep him going round, Listen 2 me now!

QL: . . . Cause it's the move for making the Hip-Hop song, 'ya should have known it was on. The places I've been, the people I've seen, and everywhere I go its, "give it to 'em queen." Cause Hip-Hop is for real, I'm dealing with the truth. Cause all over the world it's aggravated youth. So every time I grab the mic you know that I can rock it, so I can have some fun and put some money in my pocket. You can always know the time, just recognize the sign. Can't nobody put a padlock on yo' mind. Listen to me now.

Here in this musical work of the Hip Hop genre, Queen Latifah plays out two roles I see in most Rap, or Hip Hop dramas. She is the M.C., master of the event, making the party happen, dissin' and dimmin' on the rest of the "sorry-ass crews." She also functions as Esu Elegbara, griot and rapper, bearer of cultural, social, and political truths. The main point of "Listen 2 Me" is this: You can always know that this is the time (knowledge of self) just recognize the sign (the emergence of the Hip Hop groove). From the African notion that the spirit will descend with a good song, in postmodern spiritual secularism, there is no one except yourself who can lock up your mind. The lyrics seem to suggest, listen to me now, or, in other words, "WAKE UP!"

To many, this may seem simpleminded and vacuous, but to those within the cultural ritual, these meanings are premium in experience because they give life. The rhythm dictates worldview and taste, sensibilities and values. The "sign" brings affirmation, self-worth, liberation, dignity in Blackness, and new subcultural identity. The music, the beat, the vibe, the message, the dance move, the rhyme, the queen is here. Heyyyy! In Hip Hop culture, the rhythm, the flow, the flavor and style are, as with traditional West African cultural/ritual constructs, synonymous with God, the initiator of life. Even if the rappers don't know or acknowledge this themselves, they are trapped in the unavoidable web of cultural osmosis and transfer. Movement, then, is like God Spirit and represents vitality and life force.

The significant handles and suggestions for interpretative meaning are present in this song's lyrics. Notions of double meanings in text, the importance and place of a philosophy of rhythm as essential (the flow), the trickster-poet who is master of the spoken word, the rhyme, the flavor (style), and the reason, all for the people are present and have considerable meaning.

CONCLUSION

I have attempted to bring these works, concepts, and assertions into a meaningful dialogue and have suggested they are all tied to the life force for Black creative and intellectual creation, rhythm. By discussing these works and concepts within a specific cultural/aesthetic/theoretical framework, I wanted to recognize the deeper and more meaningful aspects which are often overlooked. Within the Diaspora, Black artists, philosophers, educators, intellectuals, poets, dancers, inventors, scientists, and singers have continued to forge meaning within multiple contexts of expression from Blues poems to symphonies, from literary works to Hip Hop rhymes. The key to understanding and appreciating these instances of beautiful expression is found within the embracing arms of Black creative expression. These works simply say:

Touch me, embrace the rhythm of my expression and you will be moved by the sincerity of my motion, the depth of my emotion, the intelligence in my choices, and the spirit and voice of God in my convictions. Rhythm, the ground of my being, is wide open to every kind of human expression. What I bring to you is the ultimate understanding. . . . the Undeniable Groove.[7]

· 8 ·

Aesthetics for a "Teaching Theory": Meanings in Black Music Practice and History

It has been stated that the blues were a cry of the black man's soul under the oppression of the white. But let us make no mistake; when a Negro sings the blues, it is not to give way to sadness, it is rather to free himself of it. . . . but rather express a confidence, a tonic sense of vitality.

—Hugues Panassie[1]

THE WORLD WE LIVE AND READ

One of the discussions within educational circles today is the growing interest again in contemporary popular culture as an impulse which matters for educational practice. The argument is that we are in a new era and many of the old models and cultural sites need to be dusted out and revamped. References are being made to media studies, advertising, the creative use of digital technology in film and video, the growing pervasiveness of celebrities who speak for us on matters of importance from milk, politics, and policy to the best information systems, and forces us to, as they say, "recognize." Popular culture rhetoric is everywhere! Cross- and interdisciplinary approaches give teachers the tools to be able to articulate what's happening. There are some who do this intuitively but there is a need to have more discourse to equip educators to incorporate and interpret these things. This is painful, because so much of our grounding keeps us locked and this is discomforting to let go. There is a new philosophy needed and our young people won't hear all of the old patterns. Contemporary culture is at least grounded in a worldview that a majority of our society reads and understands.

In his film *Representation and the Media*, Stuart Hall focuses on the politics of image and culture representation and encourages a more active role in thinking through the implications of what is communicated through culture. He encourages that these questions, and this "interrogation of culture" help us to play an important role in gaining knowledge and control over what we are fed and decidedly shaped by.

With the convergence of impulses in entertainment, business, information technology, and media, these times are pervasive and cannot be ignored. The uses of this megacultural phenomenon, contemporary culture, beyond our critique perhaps can be pointed to as a compelling moment when creative outlooks are being taken seriously in the world. Those who are involved in teaching are constantly looking for ways to bring examples of creative personalities and movements to the classroom experience, to link young people with the relevant impulses, socially, educationally, politically helping them to understand shifts in the worlds they enter and exit through. Impacting students with ways to process and think about sustaining focus,

89

work, life commitments is one of our great challenges in humanities disciplines' evolution, curriculum enhancement and revision, and it's just plain good sense wisdom to share. The way of the future for education is a dynamic look at contemporary culture, these convergences, and the use of cultural studies questions to focus on the higher and lower frequencies in society. The "inescapable web of mutuality" Dr. King spoke on frighteningly takes a hold of our throats, fears, and pocketbooks. Better know the world we all live in!

Creating in the world is a way of believing and "working the world." Artistic movements from Hip Hop, Civil Rights, Bebop, labor movements, Harlem Renaissance, to impressionism, all are aligned ideologies, creative identities, and mechanized movements that have meant and mean something significant is brewing in the lives of people throughout time. In this way culture always reflects great movements where people did what mattered.

Teaching provides illustrations and great measure of excellence in our history, and productive focus is what educators revel in. It's what we believe in, where our passions lie, as a way of understanding life. Black music again in this way is an incredibly powerful educational model that I depend upon for teaching in contemporary society, because the inventiveness and the musical innovation of artists show how people rise up, create, excel, and live.

I had a pastor who always told us, "Know what you believe and why you believe it." I always held onto this. What is the philosophical and expressive, artistic logic in what we believe? In this way we ask what is the Black aesthetic, the ways that speak and reflect ideas about music making and how that is worked out in the interpreting of culture; we use this as a model for ways to understand life and "work in the world." Our attempt to address these questions is seen here through the lens of music practice, history, and education. In particular Black popular music has always been a forward-leaping forum as a contemporary cultural movement of ideas, from Blues poetry and rhyme to Rap and beyond. Its always in pursuit of the now narrative, if we listen closely and critically.

One of the most frustrating aspects of dealing with contemporary culture is its constant and rapid change. Every time one attempts to hold onto it for a moment to see what it is, let alone comment on it, it moves and changes. But you can't sustain tradition without "calling it out," loving it, and watching how it grows and changes. As educators we have to sit down at the table and look at the implications of culture in order to explore and share. The idea that you have to contain living things in pages (a jar) in order to appreciate them is a bad one. In terms of beginning an educational discussion of the meanings and workings of an aesthetic, there have been so many great writings on or about Black music practice and history. At some senseless point I even tried to name some of the most important books about Black music culture. As a starting reference, here are some "must reads" in absolutely no certain order of importance. In my own journeys these are some of the most important books written on Black music culture. I'm sure many more could be added.

- *Blues People*, Amiri Baraka
- *The Souls of Black Folks*, W. E. B. Dubois
- *African Rhythm and African Sensibilities*, John Miller Chernoff
- *Rhythm and Resistance*, Ray Pratt
- *The Death of Rhythm and Blues*, Nelson George
- *Hip Hop America*, Nelson George
- *The Music of African Americans*, Eileen Southern
- *Music, Society, Education*, Christopher Small
- *The Spirituals and the Blues*, James Cone

- *Stomping the Blues*, Albert Murray
- *Black Music and Some Highly Gifted People*, James Trotter
- *The Crisis of the Negro Intellectual*, Harold Cruse
- *The Power of Black Music*, Sam Floyd
- *To Be or Not to Bop*, Dizzy Gillespie
- *The Autobiography of Miles Davis*, Miles Davis and Quincy Troupe
- *A Change Is Gonna Come*, Craig Werner
- *This Is How We Flow*, Angela Nelson
- *Music Is My Mistress*, Duke Ellington
- *The Forge and the Flame*, John Lovell
- *Fight the Power: Rap, Race, and Reality*, Chuck D
- *Race Music: Black Music from Bebop to Hip Hop*, Guthrie Ramsey
- *One Nation under the Groove*, Gerald Early
- *We'll Understand It Better By and By*, edited by Bernice Johnson Reagon
- *Noise and Spirit: The Religious Implications of Rap and Hip Hop*, edited by Anthony Pinn
- *Black Noise*, Tricia Rose
- *Landscapes in Color: Conversations with Black American Composers*, William C. Banfield (Yes, I am aware that this is my own book. But, honest, it contains the best collection yet of Black contemporary composers talking about Black music process, history, and performance experience.)

THE MEANING OF ARTS AND MUSIC

I don't claim to be a writer, but I do have ideas I like to write down. You have to allow the music to find you that makes you lose your mind so that you gain your soul. Music and art are about soul moving and gaining. Being creative by mirroring our human experience is like responding to a whisper from the spirit saying, "This is your lighted path to walk and speak on, walk and share in this way." This way of sharing has to come with a certain amount of a desire to share inner feeling. That's the way art works to inspire passion within people first. So much of what the West teaches is that we think, therefore it is. The idea of waiting "to become" is rarely highlighted as a way to be. If one waits, listens, observes, hears a song, is arrested by a painting, the result of this most uplifting experience is incalculable. We gain from our insides being shaken up not only by what comes articulated in words, but by, as I always say, "not watching my mouth but my feet for the pounding on the ground." People movements are invariably founded upon acts and ideas; that's how we evaluate meaning being affected.

Philosopher/aesthetician Suzanne K. Langer writes, "Because the forms of human feeling are more congruent with musical form than with the forms of spoken language, music can reveal the nature of feelings with a detail and truth that language cannot approach."[2] Many believe that the activity of artists constitutes the creation and execution of a body of expressive works which contain a language of emotions, sensibilities, and creative impulse, which have "meanings" in forms understood and communicable. In other words this "closed language" of and by the artist has specific meanings that are congruent to the realm of human experience, emotion, and feeling.

The expressive products of the arts transcend the individual artist and as well connect to a broader range of human experiences and conditions. These may be triumph, sorrow, great happiness, fear, wonder and excitement, passion, anger and rage, praise or intense contemplation. In this way, there is something in creative expression that is important and very meaningful to human understanding and being. If we factor in the growing complexity of the twenty-first-century problems of race, class, sexual psychology, and sociology, artistic creation (as well as what constitutes its emotional character and presentation) is increasingly becoming a powerful tool as an indicator of societal stability or instability. The importance then of musical expression in our lives is paramount from the angle of its beauty and emotional, spiritual, and psychological power—but further, we respond to the artist as a social agent who is inextricably bound to cultural or societal evolution.

Artists have always had equations for creativity and are sensitive to where they are contextually, in the present. There is also concern about the beyond, pushing on, commenting on, and illuminating where we may be headed. The other thing that should never be taken out of the equation for creativity is to be where people are. Progressive art must be committed to where people are. These things taken together with a host of tastes, perspectives, styles, and individual genius give us a grasp or hold and understanding on artists and creativity in our modern age.

In his work *Music, Society, Education*, Christopher Small writes:

> Artistic activity, properly understood can provide not only a way out of this impasse in musical appreciation (in our traditional training, the fear of the encounter with new musical experience), but also an approach to the restructuring of education and perhaps the whole society. Simply because the artist sets his/her own goals and works with the whole self, reason, intuition, the most ruthless self-criticism and realistic assessment of a situation, freely, without external compulsion and with love.[3]

Now if we believe that what an artist does has some validity in that it communicates something of value, next someone may ask, What is the artist "saying"? Is it literal, and does it mean to be literal? Is it an informed statement, or totally free expression? Was this supposed to reflect what I believe is beautiful or lovely? Is the ugly I see, feel, hear some definition of beauty according to the artist? Does the artist care what I care, or see, or hear, or understand? Of course these are the problems of aesthetics which have been argued over for at least a hundred years, but what is significant here is that the absorption in the artwork or experience does illicit these kinds of reactions, unlike staring at a rock. There is something in the experience of artistic exchange, artist to art piece, and art piece to observer. Whatever it communicates, it is something which connects to human sensibilities, is intangible, but yet materializes in all kinds of unforeseeable actions. This is why music is thought be so "dangerous," subversive sometimes. I don't think, for example, America really understood freedom as anything other than what freedoms were gained due to the people's struggles and demand for them. Those demands for freedom are what America means by freedom. Those demands have been for and by the people, and it is within this context, this web of meaning, that American democracy was spun. Many have pointed, for example, to the earliest, American–soil–produced freedom songs, the Spirituals. Who could miss the meaning of a line like "Didn't my Lord deliver Daniel? / And why not every man?" That meaning and subsequent actions transformed this country.

In the movie *Contact*, the real drama in the plot rests on this very simple idea. None at first could interpret or make sense of the data sent from another planet, but the lack of comprehension was not at all the issue. What was of importance to the principle characters was that something was attempting to be communicated, and that brought the two worlds together.

Art has important meaning to us as humans because when we experience it in the form of dance, visuals, language, drama, and music we instinctively respond with a knowingness which is above constructed principles. It is our reaction, our innate human spirit that yearns to be embraced, engaged, and connected with. An absence of artistic reflections in our world deprives us of a fundamental mode of human living and being which, anthropologically understood, reveals histories of peoples, prior to modern technologies, who poured who they were or where their people were into art left for interpretation, fulfillment, and record. Does a note left standing in 2010 really tell us anything significant about who we were in 2005?

A JOB DESCRIPTION FOR ARTISTS

Poet Maya Angelou reminds us in one of her poems that hope doesn't take away problems but lifts us above them. I like the agency involved in hoping. In this way the poet becomes an architect of words and ideas that allow us to move from the dream into reality. If you are an artist you want your job description to read: "Wanted, one who creates to lift people and to explore inner experience and celebrate the joy of living." This is a genetic wiring and I'm convinced of it. Next to creating music, many spend time thinking about how artists take in human experiences, life, and culture and how their take on these things helps people to see again themselves in ways they wanted to but didn't have the words for. This is a big job.

Art provides people with spaces of reflection or experience to breath again, to find their ground. Because everyday life often locks you into manufactured schedules and routines, the arts can slap, inspire, and seduce you back again into a human zone, as it were. Arts fill up the empty spaces we have in life; or when there is too much clutter in your life, art experience can knock the clutter away so that you can feel, see yourself, and dream again. Art is the yell of the ugly, or at the ugly, in order to overcome the fear of it.

Art reminds us that there is a dialogue between this concrete reality, ourselves, and the meaning of existence if we follow its seduction to dream, reflect, which then leads to a critical judgment.

Being an artist, one is connected to a unified effort, a community throughout time and across peoples that shapes human history in ways of marked significance. So the arts are an important part of this continuum that sustains societal balance and progression. This balance occurs because the arts place emphasis on so many aspects of human experiences, emotional, psychological, intellectual, which transcend historical and cultural particularities. Through the living modes of texture, sound, movement, and color this work is an indicator of human pulses. If you're an artist, you're a beat master.

When I contemplate the power of artists' work, I'm blown away by the role these individuals play, but it saddens me when this work is dismissed or mistaken as lightweight fluff. I try to stay focused on taking a biography of the parts of artists' work in our culture: (1) what artists do, what they create; (2) how people respond to what artists create, how their lives are affected by their participation in art; (3) how the artists and their work have come about in culture, how these products and interactions have been made possible, mainstreamed, and disseminated.

THE EDUCATING POINT: WINDOWS OF THEORY (WAYS OF TALKING ABOUT)

John Coltrane was quoted as saying, "The main thing for a musician is to give a listener a picture of the wonderful things he senses in the world."[4] The educating point of Black music is that it has grown as art, allowing people to see a world that's beautiful despite the ugly picture life sometimes paints with you in it. There is a lot more being brought to the table in regard to education and the relevance of various expressive forms. This music is about impact, inspiration, protest, and power; staying "on the beat and in the groove"; and having the guts, the craft, and the creative voice to say it effectively, your way, and to move somebody with that "saying," that flow. This is a much more compelling way to engage creative thinking. We are seduced by discourses that arouse passion in people, thinking about the meaning of their engagement in this life. Many times I find myself more at home in a room with a group of people who are turned onto and tuned into what music does for people and means to people, those who believe that music is more than music. It means more than that; it counts for more than that. Duke Ellington, when asked about his music process, said, "this [playing the piano], this isn't making music, this is dreaming, dreaming is what I am doing."[5]

A QUASI-QUALITATIVE STUDY (CASE STUDY)

I have been in residence at Central High in St. Paul Minnesota from 2002 to 2004, teaching music and music and the humanities, conducting the big band and orchestra. Central High is a global village. Never in my life have I seen a wider collective of African American, Euro-American, Asian American, Asian, Latino, West African, West Indian, and Indian people in one mix! These students listen and live in contemporary American popular music. On occasion I brought together my university and high school classes into a cross-generational, cross-class (freshman in high school to seniors in the university) mix, which provided me with a rich barometer on the meanings and issues brewing among young American people. A most revealing sharing were the discussions with high school students about the cultural connection between the art and literature movement of the Harlem Renaissance and the Hip Hop movement currently. Hip Hop here was used as an overall category inclusive of this generation's identities, those born between 1980 and 2004, and whether they listened to Missy Elliot or Avril Lavigne. A scenario was given: as we look at the Harlem Renaissance and Hip Hop movement, what are the impact and implications on culture? Students in Ms. Rebecca Bauer's Literature of the Harlem Renaissance classes reviewed and read the writing and lives of figures from Langston Hughes to Zora Neal Hurston. I came in with the musical movements of the social protest 1960s and Motown and correlating meanings, goals of the Harlem generation, again comparing these with the untutored poetry of the Hip Hop movement. I suggested that we could perhaps see Alain Locke with his 1925 writing, *The New Negro as One*, "coining the phrase" of the movement, a visionary supporter. I suggested Russell Simmons could be viewed similarly as one "coining the phrases" of the Hip Hop generation, mechanizing, generating, and bankrolling culture.

Looking at Locke's map and the movement of "race men and women," the goals seem to be

1. Uplifting the race;
2. Documenting, commenting on, and creating the culture;
3. Calling out and critiquing American society (particularly the younger generation of artists, beginning with Hughes's manifesto *The Negro Artist and the Racial Mountain*).

Looking at the twelve/thirteen-year run of the Harlem Renaissance (1920–1933) and the now twenty-five-year-old stretch of Hip Hop (1979–2004), I asked, what similarities could be made between these two cultural movements? The students responded that this Hip Hop generation

1. Voices the modern concerns of the world today more realistically;
2. Demands to be listened to;
3. Is interested in the betterment of the world of its parents, which it acknowledges it can't change and reject, but with which it deserves the right to express frustrations;
4. Uses its popular culture as a way to better the world by bringing more people and issues out, and more aggressively;
5. Wants to be taken seriously and, through its popular culture, powerfully demands a voice in the culture;
6. Creates a culture that is intimidating because of its width, breadth, diversity, and more "in your face" realism, which better reflects and equips it for the world today.

One student (a Euro-American) I remember shared that as a way of breaking her father open to "our issues" she made him listen to Tupac's "Changes." She noticed that although he first resisted, after experiencing Tupac's words, style, and convictions, he had more respect for her generation's music and issues.

This sharing and exploration for me was extremely rewarding as a musician and educator. I was able to take away, despite my suspicions of problematic imagery, and pop music's sometimes lack of music substance(s) and practice, some further indications of contemporary popular music being engaging and as relevant as any other generation's music as a link to "its culture in time." Although some of the responses are clearly the same as any younger generation to the generation of parents, there are some new concerns and social dynamics that make these times markably different, and thus responses are of course different. (See chapter 10.) The assumption that is made is that this generation is getting less from the music, and while the music is sometimes, "less than," the engagement in and connection with its narratives is far greater today. Perhaps this is due to the increased role of the media in appropriating and projecting popular music and icons from youth culture onto an adult global marketplace. Nevertheless, the sharing with students is immeasurable.

SOME MODEL SPECIFICS

Music culture is the example of how people have come through the use of their art to achieve what they dream of, the freedom to be alive and to inspire. If as a teacher you could look at a music, and without being a musician see constructs for order, moments of reflection, examples of mobilizing a team into action, examples of an effective group interaction and interplay, and expression of individual accomplishment, or pure genius, what kind of music would you show students? I always hear about classical music being used as one of the best illustrations—in culture, sound, aesthetic, and method of construction—of human achievement to be inspired by and to model. A couple of million dollars in research have been poured into the empty claims about intellectual advancement that happens to babies even in a womb, hearing Mozart through the ears of a pregnant mother. And while any study that advances art as well-being is "all good," few studies are financed and propagated as "fact" related to the relevance for the culture and intelligence of Black artistry, ever! On the other hand, we must resist the ignorant mythologized assumptions that Black people stand for everything diverse, harmonious, and politically correct for all times. I am reminded of a call I received from a woman who wanted me to speak to a community and, I quote, "to talk about safari culture, in the continent of Africa, to teach diversity and the African way of life as it relates to teaching children through stories, music, and dance." Teaching with Black and/or popular music culture as a model does in my experience provide numerous and multiple windows for all sorts of things educationally.

SOCIAL/CULTURAL RELEVANCE

1. The historical/cultural development of American society can be seen through the emergence of every form of American popular music. (Spirituals, Country, Blues, Rock and Roll, Hip Hop)
2. Musicians as popular priests are a model for performance and the use of art for meaning and spiritual conviction. (Thomas Dorsey, the father of Gospel music; John Coltrane's "A Love Supreme")
3. American vernacular wisdom poetry can be found in the text of most Spirituals or Blues songs.
4. Artistry with connectedness and meaning is expressive for "people use"; music has a role in linking with people's "lived in" lives. (Bob Marley; "Celebrate good times, come on" from Kool and the Gang's "Celebration")

PERFORMANCE PRACTICES

1. One performance practice is to construct and play on a musical form and "spin" it in different ways by looking at Blues construction and performance: I, IV, V/A–A–B. This is constant but at each cycle a different twist of the melody, rhythm, and logic of the melody or improvised verse occurs which must remain consciously constant and consciously changing. This is an interesting way to base music on change and relevancy in music structure and performance.
2. Group interplay and interdependence constitute another practice, as seen in big bands from Count Basie to Sun Ra.
3. There is a rapid growth of music and creative, inventive morphing of forms and styles in our culture (Spirituals, Blues, Ragtime, Jazz (early, Swing, Bebop, Cool, Free, Hard Bop, Jazz-Rock), Gospel, R&B, Rock and Roll, Disco, Hip Hop).
4. Creative artistry, innovation, virtuosity, and individual self-expression are evident within the structure of a form (Robert Johnson, Sister Rosetta Tharpe, Miles Davis, Charlie Parker, Art Tatum, Thelonious Monk, Sarah Vaughn, Ornette Coleman, Jimi Hendrix, Stanley Jordan).

THE COMPELLING BLACK NARRATIVE: WHY?

There are several themes from cultural studies frameworks which I think are important in Black musical studies:

A. Music as an expression of time, place, and spaces (personal and communal), a kind of transport into inner dimensions of the participants
B. Music as individual and collective empowerment
C. Music as a cultural/ethnic voice

How can we forget James Brown's "Say It Loud, I'm Black and I'm Proud" or Miss Ross's "I'm coming out, I want the world to know, I gotta let it show"? Note the active transcendence of the work, which moved in several communities for affirmation. Who's coming out?

Culture then as a study should be focused toward the realm of its ability to empower, deepen, and enlarge human experiences among many people within a society. Within the scope of the larger questions relating to our study of culture(s), the study of American cultural history and expression is a search for places where identity and nationhood are being formulated, authenticated, ritualized, and represented. The exploration of these various expressions is what culture and cultural study are all about.

For me, Black music culture makes very real the claim that this literature, text, as it were, is the most salient example of the African philosophical framework and worldview I raised earlier that music is the appropriate framework through which life experiences must be examined and celebrated. Many of these questions are raised, mused about, sung, and riffed on by creative artists.

Teaching Black music culture provides students of many stripes and interests with a very powerful model for interpreting contemporary as well as historical social phenomena relative to class, gender, politics, spiritual expression, and identity. This sharing traces the formation of Black musical culture, which simultaneously influences and becomes one of the most important markers of our national identity. I focus on the interdisciplinary nature of music as a teaching subject within the humanities using the themes in cultural studies and the idea of identity formation to broaden artistic notions of functionality.

If we are to understand cultural studies as an academic discipline that began as a search for the subjective inner voice, focusing on particularly "the marginalized and the powerlessness of the least," I pose the following question in our historical context: When did the powerless speak for themselves and question the power of suffocating institutions in their own authoritative voices? If this group has a place in claiming a legitimate authority or agency, Black Americans seem to be a very fitting control group. The stream of consciousness, the artifact that expresses the banner of critical inquiry, rage, and existential angst is Black music. In its articulation, even the larger cultural accommodations, productions, and exploitations become a product of extremely important dimensions within the cultural studies playground. I'm reminded of one of the first old slave Spiritual songs, "Oh Freedom": "Freedom over me! When I am free! An' be-fo' I'd be a slave I'll be buried in my grave an' go home to my Lord and be free." Then there is "Many Thousand Gone": "No mo' auction block for me, no mo' driver's lash for me, no mo' peck a corn for me . . . many thousand gone . . . Steal away, steal away. I ain't got long to be here." And there is also insurrection with coded plans, as in "Swing Low Sweet Chariot": "Swing low, swing low sweet chariot [the Underground Railroad] coming for to carry me home." In these cases, each slave song contains double meanings, cultural coding, and messages of antiestablishment sentiment, along with messages of hope and spiritual, physical, and political freedom and empowerment. Following the songs in this way seems to characterize the meaning and depth of so many Black Spirituals.

I find this emphasis in cultural studies to deal with the hegemonic and suffocating effects of our society (itself a larger "culture" and therefore needing critique) empowering, at present.

In its search for meaning within lived conditions as heard in popular culture, cultural studies finds resonant voices of expression and is ready-made for a critical recognition and celebration of Black popular and sacred music. I find the Spirituals, Blues, Bebop (the quintessential first American artistic, aesthetic-social, musical revolution), Soul music of the 1960s and 1970s, and, of course, Rap and Hip Hop cultures to be compelling as examples of people stories in critical resistance and conscious communal affirmation. Or, in other words, they call down of the old African ancestral Holy Ghost to purge away the "hegemonic demonic."

These songs, discourses in melody and styling, ask questions from the inner experience: "How long, oh Lord? And when I get to heaven, I'm gon' walk all over God's Kingdom," "R.E.S.P.E.C.T. Find out what it means to me," and "Say it loud. I'm Black and I'm proud!" In my teaching, this is why I'm comfortable spinning this large historical framework in cultural studies. Because of the traditional African notion of music being the "appropriate framework" through which a community (society) mediates its total involvement in life, popular music has provided a set of eyeglasses which can view aesthetic, cultural, and sociopolitical development simultaneously.

A study of this music enriches the classroom experience and highlights significant movements in American history usually treated in other contexts and studies. I tell my students that speaking creatively is a way to regain ownership of who you are. This reclaiming is particularly significant if who you are has been caught up and tangled in a sticky web of history, race, economics, class struggle, and identity crisis. Sound like a common problem? It is. I always focus again upon the work and ideas of Black American artistic expression and attempt to lock these discussions within a historical framework as the musings of artists in connection to their social environment, inextricably bound to communities across the country and time.

These are other critical questions to be addressed: the what, who, when, where, how, and why.

- How can we define Black music as an important cultural phenomenon?
- What are some of the philosophical frameworks that can be appropriated from this cultural study?
- What are the causative factors (migrations, social, political, religious) that led to the development of the various kinds of Black music (Spirituals, Blues, Bebop, Gospel, R&B, Rock and Roll, and Hip Hop)?
- What does the development of Black music tell us about American society (i.e., socially, culturally, in terms of its evolution)?
- What are some of the most powerful musical movements or artists who provide great examples of "meaningful art"?
- What are some of the great lessons that we learn from the study of music, artists, and movements?

Looking at it this way, I say, our collective goal is to examine and to "weave a narrative" in order to learn something meaningful and memorable about the art and lives of artists as well as the impact these expressive creations have had upon American cultural history and identity. This deepens our understanding and appreciation of aspects of the art forms, which are unique but also universal in expression and meaning. Again this way of opening the wider lens reduces the perception and minimization of the cultural product as mere "popular commodity."

So, this is the emphasis I try to put on seeing music from a larger place, by first examining its historical/social/spiritual roots and then letting students review American aesthetic and cultural sensibilities through other sets of eyeglasses, such as race, culture, gender, and music as mass commerce and commodity.

That is, putting contemporary music into a cultural "sounding" emphasizes its values from these larger contexts, not merely as entertainment or diversion. As stated earlier, many times artists exorcise demons of social despair and transport folks by simply being there and being aware of joy, pain, triumph, imagination, and spirit—because they operate the vehicle, the music, the art. If there is any voice in these times that cuts across our social, racial, sexual, political, and ethnic divides, it is the crosscurrents of contemporary musical artists. And by beginning with the creation and development of Black American music, students get a lot out of this and are very moved by the music. Overall, they gain a deeper understanding of navigating and exploring their own cultural spaces.

SOME OTHER DIRECTIONS

My friend Dr. Kyra Guant expressed to me her ideas in teaching Black music as an opportunity to "play with the aesthetics of Black style." This means a sound and aural experience in learning. You have to be able to create a communal environment of sharing and exchanging to think musically in body with another person. She shared with me in conversation that she is intrigued with looking at how DJs cut records and spin, and that this is a model for how young people see themselves, work themselves, and navigate identity culturally, and socially, and physically in a multivoiced, layered environment. Sampling here is a way of perceiving and then dealing in the world, a patchwork of identity.

There are three social-personal themes in Black popular culture that I see going on: authenticity, imaging, and identity. This idea, the search for the inside story, the view from "the inside (*reel*) real," "spun with" on reels containing the substance of the folk, is what again is driving expressive culture. Clearly this is a postmodern adaptation. (You go girlfriend and tell 'em like it is.) Black identity has been manipulated in the public place for so long, including naming and renaming (slave names on the auction block, "Black," "nigger," "colored," "Afro-American"), that authenticity, image, and identity have become powerful ways of reclaiming the self. You can really see this in Hip Hop rhetoric and styling.

One of the major psychic battles Black people have faced is confronting the deafening and blinding barrage of images that uphold other people's worth while simultaneously exploiting, degrading, and suffocating Black identity and worth. So especially, identity and image become major themes in Black life and artistic work. "I am somebody," "You all that and some," "You go girl." Again, the artist recaptures and identifies the identity of him- or herself in art.

This then translates to transcendence and invites other identity searchers in. We learned this lesson from Rock and Roll. The music was a place for assigning an identity and subscribing to an identity apart from your parents. As Quincy Jones put it in his autobiography,

> Black music was the substance, the metaphor for getting out of the place I was in. You can't even imagine the impact that jazz musicians had back then. We were constantly looking for identity. We identified with Black musicians. They had dignity, intelligence, fun and they were accomplished. That's what we wanted to be like and spend the rest of our lives in, that.[6]

Are the contemporary searches for identity satisfied by the images of artists and the values expressed in the art today?

Teaching people in our society that being creative and taking time to explore one's inner voice and thought has great rewards, but that is as well the great challenge, mainly because this larger culture, mainstream, has reduced the importance of creative arts to mere entertainment or specialty interests. In contemporary culture, the majority of the emphasis is on training for success, for gaining access to money and power in business, information technology, sales, service, and finance. But training in music, art, dance, and drama allows one to search for meaning, inspiration, spiritual impulse; and this is the great example of human experience and excellence. Young people feel they are a more integral part of their success story if they are allowed to bring to a product a piece of who they are, what their story is. I think despite our capitalistic surges, people always return to the basic humanistic codes. That is what is apparent in the lure and continual draw of the popular culture rituals in music.

American music, especially the forms of Jazz, Folk, and contemporary popular creative works, places more value on creativity and human expression through experience, concrete, authentic, and pure. Music as a discipline allows for and demands the opening of creative spaces, moves us back to individuality and self-critical expression. If artists proceed in these ways, which I believe they do, society sings along. In the raising up of all these individual creative voices we have a choir expressing and creating multiple experiences of human "sounding."

The work of a musician is tied into and around creative investigation. Nothing is more important in the life of an artist than the work space of the artistic mind. What is this sound, what is it made up of, how should it be expressed, what are the standards so far, what can I bring to this? These kinds of questions, apart from what the lyric says, or how funky the groove is, or how effective this passage will be, are what artists grapple with.

And lastly as this relates to a teaching theory of music, the potential for human agency, empowerment, cultural structuring with meaning and community cohesion—this is what Black music teaches us as we utilize its meaning(s), history, and creative languages. This is the business of educating in our culture. It's our map.

· 9 ·

Keepin' It Real: Arts and Humanizing Processes (1999)

As a musician I tell you that if you were to suppress fanaticism, crime, evil, the supernatural, there would no longer be the need to write one note.

—George Bizet[1]

I'd like to think that when I sing a song, I can let you know all about the kicks I've gotten over the years, without actually saying a word about it.

—Ray Charles[2]

You create the way you have to in order to give, that's life itself, and someone will say it is the product of knowing, but it has nothing to do with knowing, it has to do with giving.

—Franz Kline[3]

You can have the world in five seconds. . . . Just click and go!

—Media One and AT&T[4]

As we look to enter a new millennium we are also witnessing a great and grave technological, informational, sense-titillation race to some world out there with unlimited access to a utopia of push-button "quick knowledge." We are also nearing societal breakdown as this relates to everyday human relations. These facts should be apparent in this society's unprecedented unchecked fascination with violence, quick success, psychic readings, network television programming, Hollywood's narrow culture-shaping imagery, visionless and hate-filled politicking, and music and visual images with no seemingly usable message or meaning. While this race is masked in user-friendly, media-hyped commodities such as information technology and what should be understood as a friend, popular culture, the underpinning punch is the decline of our capacity to be humane while we are being programmatically desensitized by the rush of entertaining imagery and shallow slogans. We are becoming intoxicated and complacent with the ease of convenience consumerism. This convenience consumerism, media "hype ya'," can be seen crossing into every arena we find ourselves engaged in, and as an artist I am concerned. I believe we are fast losing our capacity for human understanding and compassion. We are losing our civility, our human spiritual selves, and in a fast way selling our soul to too many self-inflicted evils. Remember "You can have the world in five seconds. . . . Just click and go"?

We have in a sense a charge, a rehumanizing mission to keep us and help us be more sensitive within the scope of daily human interaction. I am not suggesting that TV and the movies, the Internet, Wall Street, and Capital Hill rhetoric, or even Rap music and MTV, are causing the problems. These are reflections of our damages as well.

There is no reason why contemporary technological advances and popular cultural creations should not be pervasive tools in societal shaping. But it is important to maintain a very critical stance and uphold the primacy of human values before we are bought and sold on materialistic or commercial or fad ideology. I think we have to continue to be critical, as well as skeptical, and keep a watch on who we are becoming in this time.

Education that creatively tackles this challenge, by embracing contemporary cultures (media technology, popular culture, information technology, Internet) and cultivating an informed appreciation and analysis creates a necessary balance which ensures evolving to and learning from contemporary expression in our culture. As well such a balance safeguards us from the inclination to be "swept under and over" with the great and grave races.

To be more specific, the quote "You can have the world in five seconds" is from a television ad showing young people fascinated with software engaging them with "worlds of knowledge" at an alarming speed. So many themes of our culture revolve around speed, control, getting ahead by any means accessible, and, of course, "getting paid." One of our biggest challenges as I see it is to "keep it real," as younger people say, and temper the great and grave race to this postmodern modernity with a continued renewal and commitment of our capacities to stay humanized. I like what Cal Thomas, a syndicated columnist, said recently, "Great horrors do not occur overnight, nor do they develop in a vacuum. They [our horrors] begin with small compromises unnoticed by most people. They advance on a wave of apathy, subtle appeals to selfishness and a loss of God-consciousness."[5]

THE HUMANITIES

As an educator and artist my interest is a focus on our need to underline the importance of the humanities as a study and humanizing activity within educational institutions, which then connect to commonplace communities. More specifically my interest is the arts and cultural and ethnic studies. This great race of ours is unfolding during an unprecedented time of great social, class, and race relations complexities. For me these are the human issues and where our time should be spent. As scholar and writer Henry Louis Gates Jr. writes, "Ours is a late twentieth-century world profoundly fissured by nationality, ethnicity, race, class and gender. And the only way to transcend those divisions, to forge, for once, a civic culture that respects both differences and commonalties is through education that seeks to comprehend the diversity of human culture."[6] The continued critical examination and expression of contemporary tangible and symbolic manifestations of our shared cultures can be one very meaningful road to our renewed commitment to a humanizing process through arts and education.

Perhaps I am just an old romantic dreamer who wishes for the cultural heroes during the late sixties and seventies, when revolutionary social movement leaders and especially artists created music, dance, poetry, and theater which were filled with messages of mission and meaning for communities. This was also a period of some of the most well-crafted, musically written and performed popular music in our history. There has clearly been a decline in recent years. Marvin Gaye, in "What's Goin' On," sang, "Mama, mama, there's too many of you dying. You know we've got to find a way, to get some love in here today."[7] If we are in fact witnessing in this great and grave race a decline in human spiritual values, an honest, critical, societal assessment is necessary in recommitting ourselves to be on watch and keep afloat a human value platform that does critique and temper the all-too-intoxicating winds of the new millennium advances.

For me I choose to commit to the revolution with my work in the field as an educator and artist creating courses and creative works which dance with yet question the great and grave race. So, studies and inquires that combine contemporary culture with literature, history, philosophy, religion, and social sciences equip us to create a "map" or engineer new roads and bridges for human travel in terms of interpersonal interaction and cultural/social appreciation and understanding. In terms of musical creations, one might look at the work of Bob Marley, Richard Wagner, Aretha Franklin, John Cage, Clara Schuman, or even Prince, and investigate not only the product for its artistic merit, but the impetus behind the inspiration, and its context. I am also interested in how the artistic product connects with human experience, its impact and result—both the positives and negatives. I am attempting to keep myself focused on developing persuasive arguments in support of creative engagement as an artist and aspiring scholar to the end of illuminating and exploring artists and artistic products/processes as these relate to their interaction with contemporary social and spiritual phenomena. In this way we use the investigation of artists and artistic product to examine concept and theory, history and social action, aesthetic contemplation, process and product, and human spiritual transformation. The combined studies and investigation of contemporary cultural phenomena, peoples, and histories within the American experience provide us all with a rich and meaningful exchange which ensures our successful participation as responsible and sensitive citizens, as well as human achievement and "sense-ability."

Again as an informative tool, creative works engage us at so many levels; taken seriously and reflectively they are all about the capacity for humans to imagine, hope, reflect, then move to make tangible and real human achievement. Artistic expression is one's own creative process, yet it transcends and connects ultimately with others. Music, in my way of thinking, simply put is tone organized to tell human stories, and the principal building materials of music are our emotional, psychological, physical, and mental experiences. I continue to embrace the notion that music, literature, visuals, and dance are interwoven and integrated expressions of the same representations. This is what gives artistic expression its beauty, charm, wit, its power, its meaning. Arts are always, always commentary on our attempt to understand and appreciate human activity. Again, while this is mainly an artistic viewpoint, the concept of what has been referred to as "artistic knowing" or "artistic forms of knowledge" provides us with a broader understanding, a critical perspective and process for engaging contemporary culture and traditional educational pursuits holistically.

RESEARCH AND THEORY

There has been a lot of research on and talk about the educational value of the arts and humanities and their pervasiveness in the development and shaping of societal thinking, and certainly the workings within the academy. The study and analysis of the humanities and the arts are thought to be activities which are the embodiment of human imagination, the record of human achievement, an important record of intellectual processing and refined reflection and action that distinguishes us as human. Our connection as humans is remade every time we hear a song, see a painting or a dance, or hear a story. In this way the human imagination and spirit is constantly reawakened, revitalized, energized, refined, and inspired. The breakthrough research on learning by Howard Gardener, a research psychologist and author of numerous books including *Frames of Mind*, *The Theory of Multiple Intelligences*, and *Creating Minds*, shows that humans evolve and grow by learning through multiple languages (intelligences). Within the various humanities studies—music, literature, art, dance—students examine integrated ways of accessing reality. The U.S. Congress in the Goals 2000: Educate America Act of 1994 declared that the study of arts serves national interests in education. Shortly after, some 46 states declared their recognition of this and commitment to adopt standards that included arts education. In 1996, the U.S. Department of Education reported on the need to do research and development on the study of creativity as an appropriate developmental experience for youth. The 2000 education budget was increased some 600 million dollars for educational commitments and partnerships to educate communities with "enriching" activities in education. Music and the arts are now seen as equal components to the "core" curriculum.

For our purposes, as this relates to connecting contemporary societal phenomena, a recent report survey conducted by the Institute for Civil Society (1998) showed in overwhelming results that young Americans embrace creativity and contemporary creative pursuits and see these activities as "central to their lives and futures." It was noted that the creative process, whether done individually or collaboratively, greatly "stimulated interests in themselves and the ability to participate productively in society."[8] Popular culture was seen as the most influential macrocultural expression young people are consistently drawn to. Over 90 percent regarded movies as a top priority, providing a great example of creative ventures that are uniquely imaginative and connected most with impressions of self-identity. Many young people are of the opinion that instead of thinking negatively on this, we must " learn to listen to" this and see it as an opportunity for new critical, exploratory, and integrative methods to be used for educating contemporary students. All of this again underlines the need for us to see creative activity in education as crucial to our efforts to humanize our world and sensitize it in order to more effectively participate as citizens.

Scholars in religion and cultural criticism have moved to more critical examinations of American popular product. In the book *The Theology of American Popular Music*, Michael Eric Dyson argues that artists

> wrestle existentially and artistically with disenabling forms of degradation, disempowering forms of devaluation, obstacle ridden forms of other-ness, and disparaging forms of difference. Thus, their artistic production heralds unexamined but crucial resources for the contestation of disempowerment, marginality and difference, and that these forms of artistic expression are resistant not reactionary, and that furthermore they exhibit a unique, post-modern brand of spiritual consciousness synonymous with religious expression.[9]

Here we can see the validity in examining popular, vernacular, common, ethnic, or folk traditions that reveal, in essence, the souls of the folk, the *geist* of the *volk*. Education focused on the humanities and creative engagement moves us closer to this goal.

In *Arts Education and Human Development*, Howard Gardner argues that

> artistic forms of knowledge and expression are sequential, more holistic and organic. . . . From the first artistic encounters one gains a sense of the nature of creating and reflecting and continues to evolve throughout someone's life. . . . This growth involves the deepening of this knowledge and an attainment of higher levels of understanding rather than the simple accumulation of more facts,

more skills, or more bodies of language. . . . This is the attainment of qualitatively different forms of knowing.[10]

Christopher Small's revelatory and prophetic work of 1980, *Music, Society, Education*, places a crucial importance on the arts as a "transformative expression," "as the arts are able to dramatize that every voice, every sound is of equal importance with every other, yet gains it full significance only in relationships with other sounds. Artists catch ideas and visions that are crystallized in metaphorical form."[11] He puts forward the idea that arts education and creative activity placed in the hands of individuals allows the possibility of a "potential society" to happen and deepens our appreciation of the human Spirit, and offers the potential for transforming young people from consumers of culture to creators of it. "The artist sets her or his goal and works with self reason, intuition, the most ruthless self criticism and realistic assessment of a situation freely without external compulsion and, with love."[12]

The author sees art, education, and society all inextricably bound with contemporary and cultural expression as exhibited by "creative artists" as a necessary prelude to change and reform of education and ultimately the entire society.

MUSIC AND THE ARTS

The challenge in music and the arts is to be able to illustrate to students, regardless of their chosen academic major, the practical application of the conception of creative expression. The Blues, Jazz, and American stage work, among other expressive forms, are indigenous cultural forms which can be used to critique, enrich, and expand our understanding of what the arts do. Further, as mentioned earlier, one can examine the role of an artist with spiritual and political ideas as well as cultural practices, and exemplify the arts' universal transcendent nature, and particularly American expression and its persuasiveness in shaping the cultural identity recognized throughout the world.

Principles gained from these creative constructions, such as democracy, pluralism, eclecticism, and free expression within structure, are concepts inextricably bound to contemporary art and literature. The creation of Spirituals and the Blues, for example, perpetuated a cultural identity, a political/spiritual/social identity, that was life affirming. These experiences and the cultural apparatus they formed became crucial to the shaping of American art, law, economic theory, political platforms, and so on. Not long after the people's protests were heard in song, which inspired the masses, legislation begin to reshape America's social design. Similar movements can be seen in the protest Folk/Rock, Civil Rights, and social/art consciousness movements of the sixties leading into the seventies. In this way, music illustrates the nature of human relationships and shows the profound connection between creative construction and social discourse.

Art has important meaning in our world, because when we experience it in the form of dance, visuals, language, and music we instinctively respond with knowingness which is above constructed principles. It is our reaction, our innate human Spirit, that yearns to be embraced, engaged, and connected with. An absence of artistic reflections in our world deprives us of a fundamental mode of human living and being, which anthropologically understood reveals histories of peoples, prior to modern technologies, who poured who they were into art left for interpretation, fulfillment, and record. We must be careful not to lose sight of these primary staples of human activity and purpose. Creative expression, in the forms of artistic work(s), is our record of humanity and one of marked significance.

HAVING THE WORLD IN FIVE SECONDS

There exists a false idea and ill-informed rationale that we can arm the young of society for future successes without developing a critical distance of appreciation, discipline, and rationale for ethics in accessing this modern utopia of resources. There is a very utilitarian and pragmatic thing going on when one opens a book, thumbs through, discovers, and underlines. This time spent discovering oneself is an investment in something that is not so easily disposable. It seems we are in a race to get access to volumes of thickly pasted thin data, fast.

Again, I am not at all suggesting that we are not at a great advantage with our technologies as well, but I am singing a call to alarm that we advance sensitively, cautiously, keeping in the race, but in it at a long-term jogger's pace. This space for retrospection, analysis, and reflection is where the humanities keep young preparing minds in touch with the inner, spiritual, creative, and human-valued world.

Back to our friend, the seductive commercial message "You can have the world in five seconds." Again our task is to accept the charge of the humanities and arts and educate vigorously and passionately, in a way to ensure a balance of contemporary intellectual curiosity with human value and creativity. Obviously one cannot possibly have the world in five seconds, nor even begin to appropriate and appreciate its diversity, complexity, richness, and beauty without taking the time to critically process its meaning and explore its human value based on millions of years of development. And again, if we are not careful and critical, we can be, little by little, as the technologies place in our hands "certain powers," given over to such eases. And I'm sure folks, without being too preachy, we are losing something too fast, very fast. Education has to be continually retooled to think about creative ways to match the proliferation of media messages of consumer rave and rage somewhere in partnership with contemporary culture, providing both enterprises with the savvy of balancing success and values—having "sense-ability."

I was moved by the cautionary comment of a wise senator in the end-of-the-century Clinton impeachment trial: "In our race to win, win, win, we have no memory or concern to uphold our legacies and mandates for human compassion." I am further reminded of the criticism of my most critical composition professor, American composer, now deceased, William Albright. As I raced to create all kinds of new music, he commented, "Bill, you have an ocean of music but it's puddle(s) shallow." I never forgot that. Artistic knowing, I believe is the revolutionary charge to temper the great and grave race and be committed to providing the activities of humanizing and "keeping it real."

The Rub: Markets, Morals, Theology, and the Making of Music in Contemporary Popular Culture

(Russell Simmons, Biggie Smalls, Mary J. Blige, 2002)

The genius of Black people is, that you ain't seen rap coming. We keep reinventing our-selves through our expressions. The reality is the different styles that young people invent are an attempt to mark their own particular environments with the style they are accus-tomed to. And style is an attempt to put your stamp on your existence. . . . Black people keep inventing and re-inventing, asserting and re-asserting so that we can mark our own existence through the prism of style and give some sense weightiness of our existence. But we should not resist the edifying character of Hip Hop Culture as a tool of aesthetic, economic and social expression for young people.

—Michael Eric Dyson[1]

IN SEARCH OF THEOLOGICAL MAPS WITHIN HIP HOP MUSIC

*R*einventing of self through artistic expressions, marking existence and all the while selling records is a complex formula. This is an intricate relationship between artistic desire and goals, communal expectations, and the larger market demand. At the opening of a segment special celebrating 20 years of Hip Hop on MTV, a long list of Hip Hop artists come on and give a litany of their beliefs and hopes for what Hip Hop is: a dance . . . a way of talking . . . freedom . . . a form of poetry . . . my culture . . . my womb . . . the mothership . . . the voice of America. Hip Hop artists, Dr. Dre, L. L. Cool J, Missy Elliot, Ice Cube, DMX, Nellie, P. Diddy, were here celebrating the mostly good and plenty of this wide world popular phenomenon. What's most impressive is what we are getting from contemporary hip hoppers is a passion and a belief in the music culture itself. We have not seen this from a group of popular musicians who speak for a whole generation since the seventies. As one host put it, "No other music speaks more directly and profoundly to young people all over the world."

It is useless to try to negate the profound influence and impact of Hip Hop culture: its music, artists, and its ideology and spirit. One has to come to the conclusion that above the fray of the madness of the opiate popular cultural form, media hype, and Hollywood's seduc-tive imagery machines, there is something extremely powerful and meaningful in this music, and it's appeal at deeper levels is telling. Anything of depth and with meaning in culture has

Essay originally appeared in *Noise and Spirit: The Religious and Spiritual Sensibilities of Rap Music*, edited by Anthony Pinn, New York University Press, 2003.

such power because of sustainability. It sticks. Hip Hop culture has been a music and musical cultural form with us for twenty-five years strong and counting, and like the Blues born on record some fifty years before, Hip Hop is becoming a foundation for most contemporary popular music, from Rap to Rock and contemporary Jazz impulses in between. This is market.

As with all Black arts from the Spirituals to the Blues to Gospel, Big Band, Bebop, Rock, Reggae, Soul, Funk to contemporary R&B, Hip Hop is attached to this family and bears the mark of African functionality, musical, cultural, social, and spiritual roots. This is the very basis of Black culture and Black American music forms. This is Morality.

We are all witnesses to the potential and power of popular culture and its role in shaping who we have become to a large degree, post-1970. Popular culture in its various shapes is the most influential human-driven agency in contemporary society. While we wait, the church in its various denominational divides hardly moves toward its prophetic self. Yet, Paul Tillich in his *Theology of Culture* many years back concerned himself with the relevance of "hearing" voices from outside the walls of the institution that were relevant and worthy of our attention.[2] Herein lies the rub.

Artists in the past have "called up" spiritual, intellectual, and aesthetic power to represent authentic and vivid examples of human need and meaning. They have reflected and projected prophetic musical musings, which have moved us in times to consider who we were and were fast becoming. Given the last hundred years of extraordinary musical/historical movements, artistry and social revolutions (the Jazz Age, Harlem Renaissance, Bebop, social protest and social action in the sixties/early seventies, Hip Hop, MTV, and the Internet), how are artists in popular forms continuing in the Black arts prophetic vein and moving us to self-reflective listening and action? Hip Hop music culture does provide a viable road map for where contemporary music culture is, and is heading. Hip Hop culture does as well, like so many of its cousin forms in Black popular music that provide a road map down paths for certain kinds of truth and this alone is relevant territory for social, cultural, and theological interest and inquiry. But given the stream and spray of influences from contemporary commercial markets and ideologies (what sells), does such moral vision and hope for artistry to speak in this way even make sense today?

Contained in this essay are these questions and reflections in no particular sequence: given our contemporary need to be relevant, musical, and commercially viable, does a religious sensibility or a moral commitment strike a dissonant chord among this generation, this society and these contemporary markets? What effect will such rubs between commercial market needs and a growing necessity for a moral conscious culture have upon the artistry of contemporary popular culture?

I want to pose these questions and explore some historical examples of how Black musical forms have maintained a balance in addressing their relationship to being commercial (market), community and socially accountable (morality), and maintaining artistic integrity (musical). I want to proceed by:

1. Pointing to necessary links in Black music, aesthetically, historically, socially/theologically;
2. Seeing Hip Hop as a historical cultural form;
3. Defining a possible Black music theological perspective;
4. Suggesting some ways to examine Black contemporary culture by providing some examples from the field that serve as models.

In the final analysis, I would like to simply examine some possible road maps for relevant inquiry for contemporary society pointed to by Black popular and Hip Hop culture and music, despite its potential to be suffocated and pulled continually downward into vacuous marketability.

There are several journeys that need to be taken:

A. To discover Hip Hop's own value base, and to search for meaning in the artists' messages, a theology of Hip Hop and popular music culture.
B. The task to appreciate deeper meanings and relevance and to place Hip Hop in the realm of art as a significant form.
C. Another task on the journey would be to find the crossroads of action, process, and revelation. As Paul Gilroy pointed out in *The Black Atlantic*, C. L. R. James's powerful notion that within expressive culture it is, "the musicians who are presented as living symbols of the value of self activity."[3] Within these explorations, the musical, theological, and cultural relevance become clearer in helping to establish in the final journey some helpful maps found in contemporary popular music culture and times.

DISCONNECTED DISCOURSES: THE RELEVANCE OF THEOLOGICAL INQUIRY IN POPULAR CULTURAL FORMS IN MUSIC

The Depth of Music's integration into almost all of the various aspects of African social life is an indication that music helps to provide an appropriate framework through which people may relate to each other when they pursue activities they judge to be important and commonplace.

—Jon Miller Chernoff[4]

In this day of confusion, we must find the root of the problem in order to solve it. The problem is the lack of truth and communication among man and woman. The word of music is one of the strongest means of communication on the planet. The message is Peace, Love, Wisdom, Understanding and Unity.

—Kenneth Gamble[5]

Yo Hip Hop is a way of life. It ain't a fad, it ain't a trend. Not for those of us who are true to it. It's reflected in our slang, in our walk, and our stance. In our dress and our attitude. Hip Hop has a history, origin and a set of principles. . . . It's our way to release tension, to let out frustration that young people face in the world today. . . . It has evolved to represent what is happening now, the reality of street life. . . . Hip Hop is the Lifestyle, the philosophy and even the religion, if I may. It will remain for some of us as the raw essence of life.

—Guru[6]

A release valve, cry for help, CNN for the youth, rap, and rage are terms we don't normally include in our discussions relative to theological reflection or inquiry. Yet each of those terms (used in the marketplace, various magazines and articles to describe Rap) actually relates very easily with the spiritual ideas of prayer, redemption, gospel, the word, and revelation. The theological quest for exploring and hearing the work of contemporary artists is both compelling and important. Sometimes seen as disconnected discourses, the dialogue between theology and popular culture deserves more serious time and attention toward examining, decoding, and interpreting. Theological inquiry of this type is absolutely essential.

Theological inquiry is the probe through which we ask questions about the spiritual or religious nature of things, meaning, content, delivery, and intent. Popular culture and expression are so important and compelling because this is where people are expressing in vibrant, innovative ways their uncompromising willingness to be alive. My own definition of theology is the conscious thinking, asking, probing, and activity which circles around illumination of the human condition and in that revelation, enlightenment can come. I had a theology professor in divinity school whose definition for theology was "anything that illuminates the people and moves them beyond." That always stuck with me. Maintaining a balance between market forces or demand and artistic or moral integrity is the great rub among artists within many disciplines. And yet we find that the most compelling artists of today are finding themselves many times swimming in an ocean of market sensibilities which too often seem in conflict with art that moves us along and illuminates our paths.

But it is within these forms that people celebrate the victories of being human. Contemporary popular music, Rap and Hip Hop culture, are the places it seems, specifically within the framework of Black American cultural mapping, that we find the makings of relevant, rich theological "matters." As an ideology and cultural movement, it teeters on the edges of socially defined religiosity, at least in terms of an identifiable cultural system defined by a need to be in touch with a community. Anthony Pinn in his *Why Lord? Suffering and Evil in Black Theology*, effectively argues for "a hard labor, a strong and aggressive inquiry which must have the capacity to appreciate and respond to the hard facts of African American life."[7]

His nitty-gritty hermeneutics is a deeper understanding of Black religious thought and its various discussions on the matter of the problem of evil. He speaks of a "guiding criterion" as the presentation of Black life, couched in "black expressivity and linguistic creativity, a concrete orientation in which the raw natural facts are of importance."[8] Any exploration of cultural activity must happen from the inside where the participants set the rules for engagement and expression which underlie Pinn's point. While I am not suggesting Hip Hop is some kind of church service where spiritual anointing is sought, some idea of shared community is in fact relevant here and that is why an artist could speak of a musical movement as a womb.

Paul Tillich speaks to this in a chapter called "Aspects of a Religious Analysis of Culture" from his *Theology of Culture*. He writes,

> Religion is the substance of culture, culture is a form of religion . . . in the most intimate movement of the soul, (this) is culturally formed. In order to fulfill his destiny, man must be in possession of creative powers, analogous to those previously attributed to God and so creativity becomes a human quality. . . . Some may have the strength to take anxiety and meaninglessness courageously upon themselves and live creatively, expressing the predicament of the most sensitive people in our time in cultural production. The great works of visual arts, of music, of poetry, literature, architecture, dance, philosophy, show in their style both the encounters with non-being, and the strength which can stand this encounter and shape it creatively. This makes the protesting element in contemporary culture theologically significant . . . based on man's encounter with reality used for the needs of daily life and for the expression and communication of our ultimate concern.[9]

Tillich's claim is also that religion is our ultimate concern. He goes on, "Anxiety and despair about existence itself induces millions of people to look out for any kind of healing that promises success" (50).

The role of culture in providing places where folks find healing and explanations for direction in their lives is paramount, especially as we turn to the functionality of Rap as an expressive form. I think this is what Tricia Rose as well gets at in terms of the nature and function of Hip Hop music to move among the folk who yearn for revelation. She writes, "Rap music and hip-hop culture are cultural, political, and commercial forms, and for many young people they are the primary cultural and linguistic windows on the world."[10] In another place she writes,

> Rap music brings together a tangle of some of the most complex social, cultural and political issues in contemporary American society. Rap's contradictory articulations are not signs of absent intellectual clarity, they are a common feature of community and popular cultural dialogues. Cultural expression that prioritizes black voices from the margins of urban America. . . . They speak with the voice of personal experience, taking on the identity of the observer or narrator.[11]

In this search there is a point of human inquiry and a place of human activity contained in the music. It is at the crossroads of these two points where music, culture, social progress, morality, and market demand meet. This point actually is at the core dialectic (sacred/social) that has been in Black music performance since the Spirituals morphed into the Blues (Charlie Patton) and race records morphed into Gospel music (Thomas Dorsey, Sister Rosetta Tharpe). When these musical forms which embodied the questions, interests, artistic explorations, and sacred/social aspirations became marketable, the rub emerged. Early rural Blues singers were itinerant preachers, simultaneously as is the West African griot who with song gives myth, wisdom, family history, insults, jokes, and artistic virtuosity. The lines are continually crossed. As the father of Delta Blues tradition Charlie Patton sang about love interests and morals, he rapped and preached over his Blues licks substituting words for runs and runs for words ("you gon' need a lawyer when you come around . . . King Jesus is his name"). When this product gets recorded and becomes a sellable item, it creates the demand and interests in style, song, musical, and moral reasoning. These questions from the artist's position are usually inextricably bound together and just happen to be a part of the cultural dialogue.

WORD AND REVELATION

One way to perhaps gain further meaning in this cultural dialogue from a moralistic point of view is to rely upon unmediated truth, that which is not powered by man's authority, petitions, or actions but appears despite man's futile attempt to reach God. Revelation, our truth(s), happens where human action, living, and waiting occurs and is evident and illuminative because peoples' lives were changed. This business of changing lives is a reality and why so many people are moved by the music, artistry, and inner motivation. The belief in oneself that artists illicit from their audiences and fans, the general public is real. Consequently, the role of the artist often is to speak outside of reserved places of religious languages (in the general public) and this perhaps may not inhibit a revelation of sorts. Truth appears because we took a look there and what drew us was the yell and the scream. One has to ask what does this form of creative expression, contemporary popular and Hip Hop music tell us about the human condition that the news, CNN, a preacher, a teacher, a theology, or market demographic cannot? There is an understanding that music moves people and speaks to certain dimensions of the deeper, in-wards that many times our rhetoric cannot reach. Popular culture has always provided young people with their platforms.

QUESTIONS AND CONDITIONS RAISED
BY HIP HOP CULTURE

1. The reporting of today's young Black males' relentless search for an identity place, a major anchor for our humanity in a contemporary society.
2. It explains and explores the difficulty and frustration in living in a world defined by materiality and having nothing but a burning desire to gain access to material wealth because the market forces say that's what we must become driven by. Much of the music becomes their fight back.
3. It explores the complex relationships that emerge among seemingly young, disadvantaged, angry, and disillusioned citizens, men and women left with the bleak consequences of the everyday, in plain speech that is understood in the "peoples'" languages and popularized.
4. It explores the emptiness and reality of rejections from home, school, police, society, community, and a church that has a lack of adequate responses to contemporary youth needs.

These are some of the places where there is fire and smoke among contemporary young people. Without artistic and compelling viewpoints we would simply not hear and watch the fire burn silently. Contemporary music is not doing the theology, but these are road maps of inquiry and analysis from the ground that allow us to do theology and to work on ways to hear through the fire to move people along and help illuminate the way. What we are needing to do is to irradiate the blockages and despite its sometimes-ugly trappings, the morality at least in terms of initiating the search, comes through Hip Hop and popular culture. Like its cousin forms before it, contemporary musical expressions identify real sore points in our social constructs. The moral implication rests on the response and actions of citizens to hear the clamor and the ring among its fellows and to act. Popular culture opens the doors to communication and addresses you as "potential neighbor" and it is in this function that it helps to balance the pull between morality and market interests.

BROADER SPIRITUAL DIMENSIONS
OF BLACK MUSIC PRACTICE

Music and the arts rely upon inner subjective experiences and are the outgrowth and reflection of the musician's conscious thinking about those realities in relation to the world. As author Albert Murray has written, "The author (writer) never ceases being concerned with human fulfillment . . . they provide the most adequate frame of reference for coming to terms with contemporary experience."[12] Likewise, Dr. Bernice Johnson Reagon of Sweet Honey in the Rock writes:

> I think that I have always found it important to sing. Because once I became involved in the Civil Rights Movement I found the way I wanted to Live. I wanted to live being clear, and articulate as an artist about what I thought about the world, my people and the society we are living in and helping to shape. If we are a socially conscious people, and if a point of view, a system of principals and values are going to affect the space we live in, it will be most effective if we "put it out there." We can't talk about living in a time when we're losing ground, and losing young people. You lose ground, when you don't hold it.[13]

The history of American popular music owes many of its expressive, structural, and stylistic formulations to great artists creating within our newly created language and indigenous music forms, which merged together African American sacred and folk traditions. Music such as the Blues, Spirituals and Jazz, and Euro/American religious and folk ballad songs form a larger tradition called "American Popular Music." Rap and Hip Hop culture are shaped within the very same trajectory, and despite its current commercial exploits, before the child turned so ugly, it was nurtured in the soil of a community which emphasized some core values, most of which are now foreign to Hip Hop's current commercial attributes. And the music put it out there. The music creates a value system of our soul places, values about what we want and hope for in life, values about our identities, values about our love relationships, values about our ethnic/cultural names, and values about the notion that I am somebody and I have an experience that is worthy.

Neil Postman, from his book *Amusing Ourselves to Death*, states:

> Our conversations about nature and about ourselves are conducted in whatever languages we find it possible to and convenient to employ. We do not see nature or intelligence or human motivation or ideology as it is but only as our languages are. And our languages are our media. Our media are our metaphors. Our metaphors create the content of our culture.[14]

If this is so, seeing musical expressions as a metaphor for a kind of theological probe is helpful. Especially if getting to the music allows us to get closer to the people who are screaming or celebrating aspects of life. My work as an artist and educator has been focused on looking at music and artistry, particularly in Black popular music and interpreting this work as essential to spiritualizing the world. My premise has been that the music, the lyrics, the performance as ritual, albeit a televised, video medium, becomes a participant and carrier of important statements of our being, our human conditioning which is relevant and essential. The trick has been how to transpose our everyday veiled understanding of this activity as entertainment and to see it unveiled as meaning-full. So, there is a kind of theology which is essentially decoding and interpreting the work of artistry, which I love. Part of this is understanding that in many cultures music marks thinking, reflection, prayer, and conscious human activity. Music is carried by chosen and trained, spirit led and artistically gifted individuals in every society.

In some Brazilian traditional native tribes, they even kidnap the village composers for the worth of their songs. At home our own American artists from Louis Armstrong to Mahalia Jackson, Janet Jackson, and Tupac, all have been given by the public and then negotiated with by the record industry, a certain space of worship in our lives.

These are our popular priests. It is relatively easy to see this connection and the movement of ideas, emotions, and sensibilities moved to action when you consider music that was connected to these three players; the artists, the audiences (society), and the industry (market). I don't think they are always on the same page, but when intention, need, and musical artistry link up, there are important impulses that resonate and produce an engaged and sensitized society, and I believe as do many artists that these are driven by singing and performing musicians. Here is the Theology of Music.

The word itself, religion is simply from the Latin word *religare*, meaning to tie back together. Music is a public expression, a ritual, as some have said, a quest to find meaning in community, song, and performance. It is easy to see the early examples of musician's workings at Woodstock in 1969 when our society had accepted the place and space of musicians, and young people declared their pulpits and saw them as priests. And while some critique can be made of motives, behavior, and suspect ritualistic manifestations, the fact remains that there was a cultural synergy laced with a committed meaning of which we must conclude is significant.

Since then, every ten years or so, a generation of young people adopt and/or create a musical/cultural, even spiritual, identity represented through artistry. And, more importantly more so than it being countermainstream culture, it is a committed, grounded, and some would even argue "faith" that covers their "ultimate concerns." This is where we find ourselves again with Hip Hop. Hip Hop culture is connected to a four-hundred-year musical/cultural development and popular culture since Mammie Smith's "Crazy Blues" set the rules of how images and messages get constructed. We have to look beyond the interests of commodity and grapple with what aspects of an ultimate concern are being manifested.

One of the main roles that music artistry has in our culture is its ability to give a shape, a voice to ideas and things that everyday people feel and have but see music as empowering them to be it. These deeper dimensions, sometimes unspoken but a real reality, get at a kind of spiritual, inner experience that music is the carrier of. The philosopher Susan Langer said something that has always stuck in my mind, "the forms of music are more congruent with human expression than other forms of communication because they speak with . . . a detail that language cannot approach."[15] In her thinking music was the language of our emotions. Spirit, deeper inner ideas, do not live in the realm of spoken thought. Even the apostle Paul speaks about the true things of God sounding like foolishness to the wise. In the Greek tradition, Plato demanded censorship of certain musical modes to "protect" citizens from demoralizing emotions.

There is no lack of protests from every adult generation since Plato, fearing the work of popular artistry in music. White suburban parents in the late 1950s and 1960s rallied publicly that White American children should not be allowed to listen to Black American music. That of course was ignored especially when the industry found it profitable, so much so they invested in White artists to make it alright, palatable, and fashionable to gravitate toward popular music icons singing out of that Spiritual-Blues impulse, to steal a Cornel West term. Brittany Spears and the Back Street Boys are industry profit makeups that every generation produces the need for. This began with Black artistry in the marketplace. Unfortunately in this music-image formula music and morals have gotten extracted out. But in minds and practices of those Black artists in the early days of rural Blues, to Gospel to the Gospel laced R&B groups, to Soul and even Hip Hop, there exists little difference between what music expresses in a spiritual, social, romantic, or religious function and sentiment. The old saying among Black musicians is that the only difference between a Gospel song and an R&B song is the singer changes "Jesus" to "Baby."

Music is the "appropriate framework," as John Miller Chernoff has pointed out, through which identity, values, community expression, and teaching are mediated through musical artistry and participation.[16] Again the African saying, "The Spirit will descend with a Good song" comes to mind. This means that when the whole community is "feelin' it," dealing with it in song, when the care and concern of our worth is being realized, God(s) give blessing on that and descend among the people. This kind of spiritual ritual in the Black public domain is evident in the Civil Rights period where song, as Bernice Johnson Reagon pointed out, moved the people to righteous activity, and gave them not only a song to believe in but principles, values, and a way of life that cut across civic, religious, interpersonal, and aesthetic places. This is music theology.

Music in our society, our culture functions as a form of moving expression that shapes the practices of everyday life. So persuasive is this expression, that every generation "logs" onto the program, the artists hold onto the spiritual and deeper dimensions of human relevance, the expressive core values no matter how diluted it is in the industry. It is near impossible to play convincing music without this deeper performance dimension. And this is precisely why people respond so passionately, actually spiritually instinctive way. These values which are essential for folks in any society impact our understanding of who we are. I don't know of a religious experience more sustaining than a musical one. This is music theology and where I spend my time, sometimes squeezing the meaning into a clear glass that people can see and drink and taste. The challenge of the ongoing front is to rescue Hip Hop and R&B artists from the commercial exploits of a market driven industry and maintain a critical and tough love approach as artists, parents, teachers, and community leaders. A challenge that left unattended to can only continue to allow the further demise of these powerful art forms, Black popular music and Hip Hop.

MEANING IN THE MARKETPLACE: BLACK MUSIC AS SIGNIFICANT CULTURAL FORM

In his *African Music, a Peoples Art*, Francis Bebey writes that, "Music is an integral part of African life from cradle to the grave and that it covers the widest possible range of expression including spoken language and all manner of natural sounds."[17] *Griot* is a term used throughout West African society to designate a professional musician. Music is at the heart of all the griot's activities and is yet a further proof of the vital part one plays in African life.[18] Griots speak of

> the history of the people, wisdom of the philosophers, corporate ethics and generosity of spirit, thought provoking riddles. . . . The virtuoso talents of the griot command universal admiration.
>
> This virtuosity is the culmination of long years of study and hard work under the tuition of a teacher. . . . They are looked upon as . . . the inventors of melodies, poem and rhythms and their role is essential to ceremonies, that are the combination of philosophy, mythology, technique and art.[19]

He writes elsewhere, "The African musician is an artist who dedicates himself to the service of the community at large."[20]

Hip Hop music, in terms of musical performance function, is very closely tied to the roots of all Black music in the Diaspora, be it Europe, the West Indies, New York, or New Orleans. The line of artistic/cultural evolution is very clear: griot, plantation fiddler, slave preacher, Blues singer, preacher who sings, last poets (Black arts movement), and finally rappers. The function or role of Rap's performance and delivery style bears family marks resembling every kind of Black music doing. Even the line, "It don't mean a thing if it ain't got that swing,"[21] is the same as, "It don't go if it ain't got that flow" (a contemporary Rap line).

We should not forget Congo Square, the eighteenth-century "public designated" place where enslaved Africans were allowed and encouraged to practice traditional West African performance practices, known as the "Ring Shout," and has come to be mo' better as the "Soul Train line." African retentions are prevalent in every Black style that has developed in the American public marketplace. Secondly, the griot as an artist, is studied and dedicated and an important carrier of traditions of marked significance. Hip Hop and contemporary popular artists are modern day griots, albeit sometimes misguided.

MARKET FORCES

As a market force within popular culture Rap became big practice among youth and turned into big money once again for the profit opportunist industry. We learned this lesson from Rock and Roll. The music again is a place for assigning an identity and ascribing to an identity that is culturally defined, that then gets marketed and commodified. A *New York Times* writer reported,

> Rap like most everything from the Blues to alternative rock before it has been officially embraced by those who originally ostracized it, avariciously consumed by those from whom it sought independence. White young people (who make up 80% of hip hop sales) are listening to and using elements of rap not for theft but because they relate to it, because the music is a legitimate part of their cultural heritage. Black and White fans are flipping back and forth between the local rock and rap radio stations, simply in search of the best song.[22]

This is the rub. There is in fact a search and a need for meaning in the marketplace, even among youth. The market sells a product that appeals to an inner call and identity of consumers. But this is where the concern and responsibility of the industry stops. At this point I believe it is the artists' job to provide meaning in the marketplace. In his book *Life and Def, Sex, Drugs, Money + God*, record mogul Russell Simmons addresses in plain speech his responses to the navigation around and through the rub between meaning and market forces. Russell seems to end up in his autobiography saying that the record industry is a multipronged business that only responds to core audiences. The core audience in response to the industry products (which are created to satisfy audience impulses) is in search for identification with that product which suits needs. Being true to that core audience, he argues, is the first rule for an artist wishing to be successful. He writes, "To me, Hip Hop is modern mainstream youth urban American culture."[23] His companies he believes have always stayed true to a core audience and their interests. Even the slightest recollection of youth urges from the Jazz Age through to Elvis and the Beatles reveals that morality has not been what has driven youth to the marketplace in search of culture. But there has been a search for something. Russell argues that culture is the construction of image, and that image is contained in music, film, fashion, magazines, television, comedy, and politics. He writes, "My whole career has been about cultivating understanding and expanding this core audience for Hip Hop culture and watching the impact ripple out into the mainstream."[24]

At age 44, Russell has been moving toward a spirituality that seems to have come from maturity, but as well listening to that core need. From clothes and comedy he has recently moved to MTV Poetry Slams, with an emphasis on spiritual, inner values, and culture. Could the noise from the culture have called attention to the fire, and thereby produced a change in his own attitude on how to address the needs of the core youth audience? The answer to one of the questions dealing with where is the resolution to the dilemma of market versus morality is: there is no resolution. The market is not interested in morality but marketability and materiality. It exists to provide a forum for making sellable commodities and popular artists and their products are hugely profitable. There have always been artists who struggled happily with this rub and the dilemma of creating work that sustains a core audience while making music that illuminates and moves people beyond.

What generally tends to happen is that popular artists grow up and their interests and core audience change. This is why in order to stay alive, the record industry is always out looking for some new, young face to exploit. The public's need for more substantial human value-based music will always outweigh temporary excesses in empty entertainment and fascination with exploiting youth.

The role of the artist in the marketplace is to, by conscious construction, allow their gifts to find and speak to a core audience for the purpose of moving people with and to joy, and to lift, even entertain (which in a traditional use is good and meaningful). It is the responsibility of the artist to command the marketplace. The battle is on.

A JOURNEY FOR MUSIC, ART, AND THE VALUE OF SELF-ACTIVITY

Music gives pleasure. Our music gives joy. Our music is about awakening the Spirit. When joy comes to call, no one can ignore the message.

—Marvin Gaye[25]

Carlos Santana on his 1999 *Supernatural* CD refers to a writing by Gabrielle Roth which states, "Many of my favorite shamans are rock stars. They probably don't even know they're shamans but they know how to get to ecstasy and back, and they know how to take others with them. They may not have a license but they know how to drive."[26] In his notes he thanks all his musicians with similar gratitude for their "songs which capture our mission to spread hope, peace, love, light and the joy to the heart of the listener." On Paula Cole's 1999 release called *Amen*, in a song entitled, "God Is Watching" she states, "God is watching us play our Ghetto wars. God is watching us play our games. God is waiting for us to overcome. God is waiting for us to just love one another." Another example of a popular priestess is Lauryn Hill, who on her "Superstar" from the 1998 release *The Mis-Education of Lauryn Hill* states, "Come on baby light my fire. Everything you drop is so tired. Music is supposed to inspire how come we aren't getting any higher? Now tell me your philosophy on exactly what the artist should be? Should they become someone with prosperity and no concept of reality?"[27]

Artists through their musing provide a space for people to be moved, touched, and inspired through song. Rapper and Hip Hop producer, now elder cultural statesman, Chuck D, in his completely informative and insightful autobiography, *Fight the Power, Rap, Race and Reality*, makes his case very clear: "Educating through music is what I was meant to do." But there is a rampant street or market ideology that says education is knowledge of self and keeping it real is the marker of authenticity. Many have played it too close for comfort in regards to aligning themselves with the role of keeping it real as a service to youth. Gangster Rap while many claim provided a real set of eyeglasses into the darker and more true dimension of urban struggle, lost more here than gained. Unfortunately in an attempt to live in a keeping-it-real facade and appeal to a market force, the carriers of Hip Hop rhetoric (Vibe, Source, MTV, BET) have in some ways added to a diminished intelligent portrayal of the art form. Too often it is reduced to the market trappings of styling and high profiling with no serious content. Brothers be vibin' to the beat with a flexible neck and nothing upstairs in the head.

The tragic Hip Hop news piece that served as a vivid portrayal of dramatic irony and a sad reminder of how fragile life is, was Tupac and Notorious B.I.G.'s rise and tragic deaths. Two great artists and beautiful souls, lost. Much has been written and agonized over Hip Hop's roost coming home depicting violence and bringing on violence. But, Biggie's "Juicy," one of many of his works left behind to teach us, as a song and video piece is so very powerful in what it conveys using the theme of overcoming adversity to push toward, "the positive."

"JUICY" (NOTORIOUS B.I.G.)

This record is dedicated to all the teachers who told me I'd never amount to anything. It's for all my peoples in the struggle. . . . You never thought Hip Hop would take it this far. . . . You know very well who you are, they won't hold you down, reach for the stars. . . . You had a goal, don't know just how many, cause you're the only one who went from good to plenty. . . . Considered a fool cause I dropped out of school, stereotype of a Black male misunderstood. . . . Can't write off, I like the way I live, case I went from negative to positive.[28]

This video and song are good examples of how Biggie tries to show a positive change in the life of a "bad boy," a transformation through Hip Hop from rags to riches, doing well (materially) by becoming a Rap star. The video is full of imagery with plenty of friends (crew), possessions, and fun. Despite its obvious immersion in a full range of material idolatry, the message that comes through to Biggie fans is that you can make a change in your life, and, it's for the good of the whole crew. The visual is filled with all his crew, hanging out at a pool party, and actually is quite mild in comparison to party and thug hanging visuals that have come even since this nineties video. And while there are numerous video and Rap pieces that are far more positive in terms of imagery and message, the spirit of this record and video is pure uplift and I think this is the deeper message that rings through. So that even playing it close to the edge, toying with the images of market materialism, the producers still come off with a Rap video that projects a very positive and uplifting picture of the potential of youth in urban culture, its desire and values.

"NO MORE DRAMA" (MARY J. BLIGE)

Mary J. Blige, called the Hip Hop queen, has been described by many serious musicians and insiders in contemporary popular music as "Mary who is just so real." In this description they are referring to her intense sincerity. This quality, whether a belief system or dramatized in the emotion of song performance, is the single most arresting quality of popular music arts and where much of the Hip Hop community lay their trust in terms of accepted value systems.

"It feels so good when you let go of all the drama in your life. Now you're free from all the pain, Free from all the games, Free from all the stress, to find your happiness, I don't know, only God knows where the story ends for me, but I know where the story begins for me, It's up to us to choose whether we win or lose. And I choose to win."[29]

The songwriting team of Harris and Lewis (Jimmy Jam, Terry Lewis of multimillion-dollar Janet Jackson pop formulas) chose to sample appropriate portions of the theme from the TV drama *The Young and the Restless*. And while the lyrics and her compelling vocal version would be enough, contemporary music always moves on at least four fronts simultaneously as a promotional market tool: recorded song, promotional pieces (radio, media, print), tour, and video. The entire video focuses on Mary in a violent and physically abusive relationship, and the visual underscores a young woman at the end of her wits and pushed to her limit as she declares, "No more drama."

The power of artistry to make plain by singing the deeper realties of our existence and to illuminate at once simultaneously literally thousands of individual life stories, is popular culture and the songwriters' greatest gift in terms of creating art that moves people and allows their humanity to be affirmed.

The point here in short is that there are numerous examples of artists whose musical poetry and action provide examples of consciously spun, plotted maps for cultural/social travel. In these maps are wisdom, real and revelation waiting to be cast. These works and workings are extremely visible symbols and performance text, which are being taken seriously by a significant segment of our society. Our inquiries, our theological probes, our missions for morality in the market must take this public expression into account when assessing the impact and effect upon popular music and its rub with market.

CONCLUSION

Once I realized that I'm a voice that people listen to, I realized I had to fill my voice with something of substance. Through rap music I've seen people all over the world magnetized to thoughts and ideas. My goal is to be used as a dispatcher of information.

—Chuck D[30]

In the event of my demise when my heart can beat no more I hope I die for a principle or a belief that I had lived for. I will die before my time because I feel the shadow of death. So much I wanted to accomplish before I reached my death. I have come to grips with the possibility and wiped the last tear from my eyes. I loved all who were positive. In the Event of My demise.

—Tupac[31]

Our times desperately need to be in touch with the practices of the past, which linked performance values rooted in musical excellence that helped secure our culture against crisis. It is at this point that the quality of the music, our aesthetics, philosophies, performances, that the hope for a better life will be recognizably distanced from the bleak emptiness of vacuous contemporary life and market demands. The Soul era stands out as a period in Black artistry where the music communicated a general philosophy of refusal to accept the undesirable and a determination to both illuminate despair and create a better future. "A Change Is Gonna Come" (Sam Cooke/Otis Redding), "Wake Up Everybody" (Harold Melvin and the Bluenotes), "Higher Ground" (Stevie Wonder), "What's Going On" (Marvin Gaye), "Yes We Can" (Pointer Sisters), "Ain't No Stopping Us Now" (McFadden and Whitehead), "I Will Survive" (Gloria Gaynor) are titles which suggest again a comfortable alignment of strong moral and community commitment and great commercial artistry. This has not gone away. The entire wave from the new R&B movement out of Philly with Jill Scott, the Roots, Erykah Badu, Musiq SoulChild, and others are examples where Hip Hop style and old school talent and sentiment in the marketplace have collided again among a number of new record industry acts. Cornel West has written, the future of our artistry may hang on the quality of the response to our contemporary social challenges depending on not just the talents, but moral visions, social analyses, political strategies which highlight personal dignity.[32] Toni Morrison's beautiful discussion of our great Black music literature sums it up best: "a sustaining force, which healed, nurtures and translates Black experience into above all else, art. My parallel as a writer is Black music because all the strategies are there. . . . It makes you hungry, it slaps, it embraces, music is the mirror that gives necessary clarity . . . and literature ought to do the same thing."[33]

There are still numerous examples of music output that moves within the Black popular music traditions while managing market and morality. Black artistry is so greatly steeped in the tradition of telling human stories for the purpose of uplifting by examining the pain, and working ways through to wholeness. Singing and performing are just one strategy employed by creative artists to manage the madness and provide joy and a lifted spirit in the face of the consequences of the everyday.

By doing this, again as Paul Gilroy suggested, we can continue to present our lives and our arts, our communities, our nation as living symbols of the value of self-activity, and the hope in maintaining until revelation comes, yet another day.

The more positive rhetoric from the Hip Hop griots is self-knowledge, speaking the truth, keeping it real, giving a shout out for my peeps, and it's all good, baby baby. These are all significant markers for meaning, performance practices with an emphasis on revelation, dislodging negativity and moving the ritual participant toward enlightenment. In this way Black popular music, and Hip Hop culture, truly becomes relevant for theological inquiry, and as well sounds off as a particular kind of mapping for contemporary times.

Truthfully, in every age from biblical Jerusalem to the Enlightenment, through to the search to define modernism in the twentieth century beyond the meaning of September 11, we are simply squeezing the jagged-edged trigger to not explain away, but to just be in exploration, in the meanwhile waiting for God's revelations, and loving the griots who while telling stories, initiate the waiting period. That's good theology: artists' continuous search for moral reasoning in a market-driven age.

Black Artistic Invisibility: A Black Composer Talking 'bout Taking Care of the Souls of Black Folks While Losing Much Ground Fast

(Delivered at the University of Pennsylvania, 2002)

> The ultimate effectiveness (power) of any group of people is the degree to which they have as awareness of who they are and respect for themselves. The instruments that facilitate this development is education, cultural images and celebrations that build a shared aesthetic, role models and the projection of cultural heroes and heroines.
>
> —Na'im Akbar[1]

> I am an invisible man. No, I am not a spook like those who haunted Edgar Allan Poe; nor am I one of your Hollywood-movie ectoplasms. I am a man of substance, of flesh and bone, fiber and liquids—and I might even be said to possess a mind. I am invisible, understand, simply because people refuse to see me.
>
> —Ralph Ellison[2]

INTRO THEME: THE BLACK COMPOSER AS INVISIBLE

*D*ear reader; I am a Black American composer and I am invisible. I am perceived I think like a ghost passing in a memorable melody, heard rarely and never seen. I wanted to share a composer's take and journey on defining an aspect of a Black artistic tradition, its representation and identity in twenty-first-century expression. If we examine the state of scholarship about African American culture in traditional music disciplines, we find that too often the academy consistently obscures the beauty, complexity, and variety of Black life and artistic expression. By doing this the academy misses an opportunity to have an encompassing and relevant discourse related to the study of Black music, folk, and life, in total. Basically there is sumptin' going on that allows us to ignore and thus dismiss the variety and diversity heard and taught within the whole of Black artistry. I like to think of this as the cultural politics of misrepresentation. I am as well concerned with a definition of Black musical value and our current generational divides on this issue. I want to erase the invisibility of Black composers, the men and women who are our "Black Beethovens."

In this age of P. Diddy, Jay-Z, and Beyonce, I want to introduce into the scholarly discourse, into the loop of representations, this identity and expression which has been central to Black American composers since William Grant Still wrote, in 1930, the "Afro-American Symphony" based on the Blues.

Mainstream American media has dismissed important creative, cultural/social/spiritual aspects of Black artistic expressive culture and following that lead as well are the educational, cultural institutions that arm our society with relevant and lasting impressions of what is valued and what is preserved. This devaluation leads to not only the suffocation of major portions of Black culture, but as a counterproductive ploy, investments are made into the commodification of negative cultural imagery and overblown pop teen "celebri-dom." The dark clouds of cultural chaos and the ever present potential of the invisibility of our own diversity in music is underscored in the fact that for the most part in mainstream America, the only music that is now accepted as defining a Black modern cultural aesthetic, is Hip Hop. I listen and enjoy Hip Hop music. I love the form and the forum for engaging ideas. But in our current suffocation, our current drowning as Rome is definitely on fire, too much of popular culture in this way is doing more damage than good. Unfortunately because idea inspiring messages and strong healthy doses with images of Black productivity are missing, the possibilities of empowering values inherent in contemporary expression are muted.

> Writing the book confirmed ideas that had been rolling around in my head for years . . . how to measure this world in which we find ourselves, where we are not at all happy, but clearly able to understand and hopefully, one day transform. How to measure my own learning and experience and to set out a system of evaluation, weights and meaning. . . . This is the history . . . this is your history, my history and the history of the people . . . the Music, this is our history.[3]

So the question now is, how are we measuring ourselves and are the cultural forms engaged in expressing, celebrating, and critiquing culture in ways that continue to help navigate our survival as in the past and give us hope and joy in our living frames? If we are measuring our world only in terms of Hip Hop and Destiny's Children, we are in trouble. I have a friend who speaks of BET as our televised Festival of Ignorance, a sexual minstrel show where Black males are being constructed as the commodity of anger and Black females in too many videos are diminished further as an image of a slut, sex-driven, power access thirsty babe for leisure use for the crew.

No other voice or use. I'm convinced that Black people and scholars are as much of the problem as anyone else in this cultural phenomenon. Mostly because we don't speak out and educate. I respect Tricia Rose's *Black Noise*,[4] but after seeing her recently, I am convinced she is saddened by the diminished potential of what could have been a major cultural marker in our expressive evolution forward. For all of my big brother Michael Eric Dyson's powerful portrayal and advocacy for the use of Hip Hop as an aesthetic tool for young Black people, our popular music art forms need retooling. So, instead of complaining I wanted to offer a few alternative models, places, and movements in our culture, heroes, and heroines of Black music culture; Black American composers, their work and their worlds.

I am reminded of the seriousness we gave again to Black women writers after seeing the Oprah book club. As well hearing spoken word and freestyle poetry after SLAM with Saul Williams, we got "literate again." Our reconsideration of our dance forms as a cultural expression of note with Savion Glover and George Wolfe's "Bring on the Noise" helped us to see dance as an expressive historical/cultural form and narrative. We will need of course launching forums supported by Black engaged scholarship to take a serious look at the work of Black composers and other forgotten and overlooked Black art forms as a part of the packaging of our cultural rituals, intellectual artistic canon(s), our literature in poetic and musical form.

This is my goal as a Black artist in the academy. Along with a camp of colleagues representing at least three generations of artists, we are creating the spaces and making the works of a Black music canon in modern serious Black music. I don't like labeling music, but this is a movement that includes Jazz, operas, contemporary instrumental music, ballet and symphonies.

We got some Black Beethovens living up in here, and what's most sad is y'all don't even know it!

BRIDGE: THE POLITICS OF MISREPRESENTATION

The Negro is a natural musician. He will learn to play on an instrument more quickly than a White man. They may not know one note from the other, yet their ears catch the strains of any floating air, and they represent it by imitation. Inferior to the White race in reason and intellect, they have more imagination, more lively feelings and a more expressive manner. With their imagination they clothe in rude poetry the incidents of their lowly life and set them to simple melodies. Blessed power of music. It is a beautiful gift of God to this oppressed race to lighten their sorrows in the house of their bondage.

—"Songs of the Black," *Dwight's Journal of Music*, 1856[5]

If it were left up to academic discourse as seen in the above, we would continually be reduced by a shallow and limited analysis offered as "the fact" of our creative work. Recently, I read a *New York Times* article complaining that Hip Hop singer Mary J. Blige needed to become angry again in order to reach her best as an artist. They don't want us to be doing anything but . . . "clothing our rude poetry in the incidents of our lowly lives."

As I see it one of the most valuable battles, movements to watch on the music/cultural front is in the field of new concert music composition. The players in this game are Black American composers and the performing/commissioning concert music venues (symphony, chamber, opera). For many Black composers our historical/cultural sensibilities are always clashing with mainstream schooling; that is, with what we want to write, how we are organizing contemporary musical materials, and the historical-cultural narrative for libretto, scripts are not rooted in the traditional formula. Black composers writing in the academy and concert performance industry is in itself the embodiment of cultural warfare. Because we use the Blues in complex forms, we use melodic, rhythmically complex formulas, disjunctive 12-pitch tone rows, but we too express our romance and rage through 100 instrumental voices.

These works are heard in 100 concert halls a year across America, but y'all ain't there. Black American composers have been synthesizing Black expression and experience in these powerful representations for at least 100 years in American music literature.

There are numerous recording labels carrying this important work: Albany, Videmus/Visionary, Tel Arc, Columbia, Koch, Collins Classics, New World, CRI.

My role models are T. J. Anderson, my teacher, who served as one of the Atlanta symphonies first Black composers in residence. Also, my dear friends Patrice Rushen and David Baker and many others who place culture, experience, and craft in a blender and serve up works that are some of the best examples of the successful contemporary multiethnic perspective in arts culture. The embodiment of the politics of culture(s) and representation are best exemplified in the music processes and products of contemporary Black American composers. These works are extremely rich, relevant and provide multiple sources for study in music, literature, cultural studies and Black music history, which reflect a rich past and project the potentiality of a strong future in Black musical artistry, in total.

Composers of African descent from Chevalier de St. George's writing in pre-Beethovenian times to Francis Johnson in the early nineteenth century, to James Reece Europe at the top of the twentieth and Tania Leon a contemporary twenty-first century example, have been involved in one of the bloodiest battles in Western aesthetic construction and thought. They have done this by bringing the meaning of vernacular culture, ideas, and identity to bear on the meaning of being an architect of Western art form. Upon the waters of Western expression, these ethnic boats that carry vernacular music, culture, and identity hold crew, mission, and captain in place and have succeeded in "crossing over." In doing so Black composers have created one of the best examples of truly innovative Black music, rarely heard.

Two books recently published which document this work: published in 2001, the *International Encyclopedia of Black Composers*, Fitzroy Press, produced by Center for Black Music Research, CBMR (Sam Floyd). As well, my own *Landscapes in Color: Conversations with Black American Composers*, Scarecrow Press, 2003. This book explores the life and work of contemporary living Black American composers working across the United States.

Landscapes in Color is a rare collection of insights by contemporary Black musical artists and one of the most diverse with a broad view of Black music making. The composers speak from such a wide variety of backgrounds on American music and culture. These days we usually just hear about Black music from rappers, producers, and artists in R&B, Gospel, or Jazz. So much of who we are has come from musical artists and so their work is extremely important as well to gauge where we are headed. The book serves several purposes related to our central question and the idea of finding the core of twenty-first-century expression and representations of Black American music culture. Sources like these:

- Serve as an important and rich commentary on American music making and its development from the perspective of Black music makers.
- Composers are talking about their musical making process and the development of their musical careers, narratives, and inside stories.
- Challenge, make certain charges to the way we teach, look at and consume music in our culture.
- Present very powerful alternative views, which are transformative to the way we have learned about American artistry. (Namely, that White artists were the only ones creating worthwhile important works.)

The writing as well contains discussion between myself and 40 of the leading Black American composers of our day. Many of these people our readers are very familiar with, for example:

Composer Ysaye Barnwell (member of Legendary and Sweet Honey in the Rock) talking about the essential functional character of music making in the world. Bobby McFerrin talking about creative responsibility. Patrice Rushen, in many ways the model for a Janet Jackson, Alicia Keys, Norah Jones and one of the most influential women in the L.A. music scene, taking a stab at the lack of personal accountability that rappers have when they speak. Anthony Davis, composer of the opera *Malcolm X*, talking about Jazz redefining the direction of symphonies and operatic tradition in America. Great drummer Tony Williams talking about life as a young musician working with Miles Davis or the old great Jester Hairston, composer of "Amen," talking about how the Spirituals changed American social sensibility, seeing this happen as early as the 1920s in his long professional life.

These perspectives are far reaching insights about music making, music education, the record and performing industry, and the transformative role of art in our culture. The work of Tania Leon, Daniel Romain (New York), Donal Fox (Boston), Julius P. Williams, Jonathon Holland (Berklee School of Music, Boston), Alvin Singleton (Atlanta), Regina Harris Bioacchi (Chicago), Lettie Beckon Alston (Michigan), George Lewis, Anthony Davis (University of Southern California, San Diego), Stephen Newby (Seattle) along with Billy Childs, Patrice Rushen (Los Angeles), Jeffery Mumford (Oberlin College, Ohio), Gary Powell Nash (Fisk, Tuskegee), Roger Dickerson (New Orleans), Anthony Kelley (Duke University), William Banfield (University of St. Thomas, St. Paul, Minnesota) are examples of contemporary Black composers of this generation creating in various places all around the country.

One of the main deterrents to present-day successes for young people is the lack of inspirational models of excellence, image, and identity. When there is less of that kind of talking, which is exactly what we face in popular music culture today, our society becomes bereft of places where young people especially get nurturing. Black artists of this caliber are a real shot in the arm and their examples and music are so powerful.

DEVELOPMENT SECTION: THE PROBLEM OF A CLASH IN GENERATIONAL VALUES AND MARKETS

Every generation out of relative obscurity must discover their mission, fulfill it or betray it.

—Frantz Fanon, *Wretched of the Earth*[6]

If this generation does nothing, they are not our future, they are our fate.

—Maulana Kerenga[7]

I recently participated in a conference on the state of Black scholarship and the arts. Black studies programs that began after the Civil Rights era in the early seventies are celebrating 25- and 30-year anniversaries. And they are asking just this question, where is Black America, the Black academy, arts institutions and communities in leadership? Just as important is the question how is Blackness represented and evolving in the global environment? This wider lens is the result of our recognition of the ways that, "African Diaspora experiences and traditions have functioned on a global scale and resonated within the spaces of a variety of international projects."

In most of these discussions the focus is on: the critical examination of the human, cultural, social, political, economic, and historical factors that have created and shaped the African American and African Diaspora experiences post-1970. The main point in agreement is the degree to which Black artists have taken up the torch to be instruments of change. It is clear that a more progressive and informed generation preceded us who were the models of this kind of activism. So how do we encourage and not just attack due to possible generational, even class differences, a new generation with seemingly stark differences of cultural values?

The Hip Hop underground is the most socially and politically active generation since the long death and silence of the Black community which fell asleep throughout the eighties.

Grand Master Flash reminded us, "It's like a jungle sometimes it makes me wonder how I keep from going under."[8] The relevancy of more contemporary underground Hip Hop and Rap scores big in this discussion.

But to be honest though, this is a "teaching moment" where it is crucial that we all instill forward direction by both celebrating and critiquing contemporary culture.

I enjoyed recently exchanges I had at a similar conference in St. Louis aimed directly at the role of Black theater in addressing a lack of diverse artistic hearings in our culture. Cultural critic-historian Gerald Early, well known as cultural commentator on recent PBS specials such as Ken Burns's *Jazz, I'll Make Me a World* and others, commented on the fact that art always has engagement in the world. Art is politics in that anyone who does a work of art defends a certain set of values. Early reminded us of the history of Black audiences, that despite commodification and commercialism, we were an audience who could always see beyond bad politics and empty rhetoric and still be moved powerfully inwardly and externally. So, I guess there is still hope even in our current flood of suffocating popular images and music that on the current surface seem bleak with possibility.

All the playwrights and directors who attended the St. Louis gathering like the University of Pennsylvania event spoke of an eternally understood and practiced notion, that Black art has maintained many of its dynamic characteristics and still remaining intact is the power of the rhythm in speech and its soul motion the Blues aesthetic. The players in this dialogue, playwrights, director and composer, began then to speak of collaboration and the processes of envisioning new Black artistic movements that allow seeing ourselves trusting, sharing, and working in a variety of capacities attempting to reveal "truth."

RECAP: SOME HISTORY, EXTENSIONS OF THE TRADITION, AND ARGUMENTS FOR THE MUSIC OF BLACK COMPOSERS

Bohemian composer Anton Dvorak, while living here in the United States, stated in 1893: "I am satisfied that the future music of this country must be founded upon what are called the Negro melodies. They are American. They are the folk songs of America and your composers must turn to them. . . . I discover in them all that is needed for a great and noble school of music." In 1912, James Reece Europe, composer, bandleader, and conductor of New York's Clef Club Orchestra, stated, "As composers, no matter what else you might think, we [Black composers] have created an orchestral language that is unique and distinctive and lends itself to the peculiar compositions of our race."

In the discipline of composition and concert music, Black American composers have in recent years provided many examples of what I have called, "extensions of the tradition." These composers and their traditions are the result, the call and response if you will, to the prophetic words of Anton Dvorak.

Black American creative thinkers in the concert tradition are both vindicating past blocked voices and forging new musical practices. Contemporary black composers are gradually becoming a real presence on the American concert music scenes.

This is important I think because the music so wonderfully reflects much of what we already accept as our own musical culture. But we didn't come to accept all this music as American and worthy overnight. Black music innovators such as James Reece Europe (1881–1919) who experimented with the 100-plus All Black Clef Club Orchestra included five pianos, ten drum sets, mandolins, harp-guitar, banjo, cello, and brass. The band work of Francis Johnson, Scott Joplin's *Treemonisha*, or Sister Rosetta Tharpe's eclecticisms are early-twentith-century experiments which were pioneering. Fletcher Henderson's orchestrations and pathbreaking arrangements which set the pattern for the American Big Band Jazz, or as mentioned earlier, William Grant Still's evocative and innovative early fusing of rural Blues and the orchestra producing his *Afro-American Symphony* in 1930. These were all experiments as trailblazing as anything in American music by our White counterpoints such as by Ives, Cowell, Varese, and Cage, though almost never recognized.

As tradition bearers, the generations who succeeded these innovators work back and forth between a great range of traditions: African American vernacular, West Africa and Western European Classical/Romantic and avant-garde traditions. And all this pluralistic, boundary crossing innovation occurs within the matrix of contemporary American music.

CODA: A CLASH IN CULTURAL VALUES IN MUSIC?

When you have a Black artist who attempts to make art, that art should be an expression of one's culture, gifting, and be a product as well of the time, individual tastes, and craft. But in order to be heard, many times a Black composer's work is relegated to the Black History Month program when the work truly deserves to simply be on a concert program on any month. Many people are unaware of the whole of the process and politics of being a Black composer, and I mean hearing about the problems, process, and actually hearing the product.

I have been extremely blessed, fortunate, and have a big enough mouth to have been given a great number of opportunities to grow and develop as an actual composer. I mean I really am commissioned to write symphonies, concertos, operas, ballets and to write music for the opening of bridges, museums, and libraries. I know this must be rare. After I completed my eighth symphony, many of my friends began to get worried, as several of the European composers died after their eighth or ninth symphonies. But for a Black composer writing in the academy and concert performance industry is in itself the embodiment of cultural warfare, and certainly Black cultural representation and identity is one of the exchanges most salient points.

You may ask, what are some of the central issues that rise up in this exchange, this clash that provides us with some understanding of an embodiment of the politics of culture and representing Blackness? When a young person decides they want to be a composer, that choice is wrought with a whole battery of restrictions, strictures, and terrain that must be navigated within traditional art venues and it's especially tricky for a Black person. My musical hero was Jimi Hendrix. My mother and father took me regularly to hear the Detroit Symphony. My mother told me, "One day that orchestra is going to play your music." So, I logically thought I would write music for Jimi Hendrix to play with the orchestra. As it turned out, some thirty years later the Detroit Symphony did play my music, but not before a long series of identity crises which I am still repairing from. Here are eight political "mine and mind fields":

- Finding the opportunity to do one's art (A Jazz player can go play somewhere where the musician can see and be seen among peers. Where does the Black composer go?)
- Liberation of Voice (In concert music you can't always have just your own voice like Ellington or Macy Gray because it must be mediated through the thick aesthetic of conventions of traditional concert music instruments, methods. This can limit what you can say, and how you say it.)

- Audience (Who's listening?)
- Acceptance and placement (I used to say, "We are choking at the neck of a big white goose who we expect to falsely hatch golden brown eggs.")
- Documentation (Who cares? Record companies . . . history books . . . curriculum writers?)
- Workplace, job (How many Black composers did you have for your theory/composition teacher? The old boys' network still exists. I was the first Black man to graduate with a doctorate in composition in 1992 from the University of Michigan. Why aren't more young Black scholars in the fields of composition, musicology, theory, and conducting encouraged and supported to pursue the academy?)
- Language dilemma: tone row or Blues scale (If you sound slightly Black, you might not be called back. Or if you don't "sound Black," you may be asked to flatten some of your thirds.)
- Disruption of the Western cultural formula (A Black composer? What and where is that? Here there is double backlash from both sides, White and Black, because of the behavioral/social/cultural codes entrenched deeply in the identity formation of both communities.)

I should mention, that being a composer, an artist is tough, tough work for anybody green, blue, or fuchsia. But the Black artists' challenges in a classical art world dwarfs our White contemporaries' issues by legions.

CADENCE

My suggestion is to ignore and fight the misrepresentation and past limited acknowledgment of Black artistry and seek out the music products of contemporary Black American composers. For educational, observation, and study, you can see the richness in the whole dynamic from performance practices to the embodiment of our cultural heritages, and the best examples of the amalgamation of western European practice and vernacular culture. It's all there in the work, processes, and product of Black American composers.

Here for cultural study and references are the politics of embodying culture and the tangles of representing and defining Black art in our contemporary culture. In all this perhaps we are trying to make the institution do something it was not meant to do? Again, I always say, "We are at the neck of a big white goose trying to make it lay a golden brown egg." And implicit in this is the reevaluation of cultural and national values. There is much to gain from this view and engagement.

The task for us here will still be the challenge in addressing how to tap into the current generation's sensibilities that are forward, but critique that which is shackles and chains. We have to have enough love and courage to roll up the sleeves and commit to educating and art-ucating in a way that maintains those powerful and needed foundations in arts. This must be parallel to positive, productive Black movement in the world socially, artistically, and spiritually. We must be up to this task or we perish and go down, empty. Our cultural critiques, explorations and vision(s) keep us filled and overflowing, thusly fulfilling our missions and ensuring our future.

The instruments that will facilitate a rich future will be by employing a knowledge to a full range of Black peoples' expressions, images, and ideas. This is how we take care of the Souls of Black folk in the twenty-first century.

You Call That Music! Hip Hop
(with Libby Larsen, Alexs Pate, Russell Simmons)

(This text is taken from my Minnesota Public Radio show,
Music and Power, recorded September to November 2003.)

CURRENT HIP HOP MUSIC

*J*ust the other day at a restaurant I overheard a suburban gentleman talking with a table of friends. He was going on and on about how in his day musicians really played about—and sang about—something, and how this Rap and Hip Hop trash is a cultural travesty. He named the Temptations, Sam and Dave, Marvin Gaye, Gladys Knight. "Now that was music! What have they done to it?!" he pounded on the table.

We've got to ask: Why is it so difficult for this gentleman, and so many others, to embrace this music? Is it so bad or so unmusical or so threatening, that most of us just can't get with it? Franz Fanon, in his *The Wretched of the Earth*, said, "Each generation out of relative obscurity must discover their mission, fulfill it or betray it."[1]

Since those glorious days in the 1960s and 1970s—the days of Marvin and Gladys—we've had at least three major movements led by young artists who've risen up to claim ownership of the new territories of music. We've had Punk, Metal, Grunge, Alternative Rock (Nirvana), but Hip Hop is the big one. In no other musical movement are the relationships between music and power, and art and identity with lyrics of powerful protest and social rage more clearly evident. And, while in its early stages some 25 years ago, many of us absolutely believed and hoped that this music would be over soon, we're now grappling with what to make both good and bad of this powerful, pervasive and long-standing musical form.

And so, in this essay we'll ask: Can we value Hip Hop as music? What are the artists trying to say? Is the language repulsive, the imagery damaging and dangerous? What's the cultural meaning of this music's incredible international market punch? And we'll look again at Franz Fanon's claim to see if the Hip Hop generation has found its cultural mission—and fulfilled it.

But first, let's get up to speed and define what "Hip Hop" means, learn where it began, and follow the shape of its history. Consider this a short course with Dr. Bill: a kind of Hip Hop 101.

We're going to have to clarify a few things and a few terms. Like, what's the difference between Rap and Hip Hop? You see, Rap is the verbal performance and Hip Hop is the larger music/culture and style.

Actually, there's much more to Rap and Hip Hop than just catchy rhymes and rhythms. After almost two decades as a part of American culture, Hip Hop has spurred a huge recording empire with hundreds of artists and thousands of records and billions of sales. In an article a few years back, writer Christopher John Farley made the claim that Hip Hop has "transformed American culture."[2] That's a pretty powerful statement, if it's true. It's clear when listening that there is in the minds of the artists a delineation of the terms, conditions, meanings, and directions in the forum of Hip Hop.

It's the fall of 1979, and the first glimpse we get of Hip Hop culture is heard in the now famous line, "I said a hip, hop, the hippie, the hipidipit, hiphop hopit, you don't stop." You remember, the first Rap record of marked success was "Rapper's Delight," by the New York–based Sugar Hill Gang.

GRIOT MUSIC

But the real roots of Hip Hop go back much further. From comic narratives on record, to Black R&B, to Gospel DJs in the South—all the way back to the slave preacher and the West African culture bearer, the griot. In fact, musicologists and historians have always noted African-based orality as one of the world's great performance practices.

You can trace the love of wordplay and rhymes up to the present through Mohammed Ali, the last poets of the Civil Rights and Black arts movements, Gil Scott Heron, to little Black girls rhyming to their jump rope games on urban sidewalks across America.

Rapping in the Black community was nothing new. But as the recorded history of Hip Hop goes, it all began really with the innovations that went on at neighborhood block parties, in the early 1970s, particularly in the Bronx.

In 1971, when an enterprising and gifted recent Jamaican immigrant named Kool Herc, nicknamed Hercules because of his really loud sound system, began his style of spinning records for parties, he did something new.

This was the Disco era—dancing at parties was the thing. Remember "clubbing?" Well, the neighborhood parties in Black communities were more homegrown.

Anyway, Kool Herc's innovations were twofold. First, instead of using the Disco tunes that were current, he used more funky R&B from the 1960s—like the James Brown songs he'd favored from his days in Jamaica deejaying. Second, in many of those records there was "the break." The break was the place in the record where the singing stopped, and just the drumbeat was left. Well, Kool Herc figured he'd use this opportunity to "rap" to the crowd. And he used two turntables playing the same record back and forth to prolong the break. The two together would drive the audience into a frenzy and the break becomes a marked moment in music history.

Enter B Boys, a dance crew who specialized in steps, moves, and flips that become known as, you guessed it, "Break Dancing." Remember that? Well soon there was a need for a DJ, breakers, and an emcee as well. Other early rappers introduced other techniques into the game, such as the innovation of a high school DJ named Joseph Sandler, known as Grand Master Flash who was an electronic whiz kid. Grand Master Flash created a special switch box/mixer that allowed him to cue up a record in his headphones so that he could accurately switch between multiple records and select specific breaks. He turned this into great skill way before CDs and digital technology were common. So a ritual is born. A ritual with the multiple roles of the DJ, the emcee, and the dancers. And this ritual flowered into a self-contained culture that includes visual art, clothes, and a very rich vocabulary in addition to its music Hip Hop. And by the early 1980s, Hip Hop has become the next big youth entertainment movement, following the Folk, Rock, and social protest songs of the 1960s and 1970s. And as usual this new music, along with its language and visual symbols, was quickly absorbed into the international marketplace. Today, the number one youth music in most parts of the world is, unquestionably, Hip Hop. That's power.

But what's interesting about the rise of the rappers as central cultural figures is the attention that was paid to what they were saying, not simply to their skills as party-meisters. With all the hype, it's easy to forget a very important aspect of the Hip Hop movement—the community of activism. The posses of DJs, rappers, and dancers were "gang size," literally, the size of a gang. And in some cases they were actual gangs. But the twist here is that many of these gangs tapped into the communal function of Hip Hop culture as a way to use the messages to promote collective activism. Groups like Afrikka Baambata and his Zulu Nation created manifestos that strove for "unity in our community," and wove themes into their works such as knowledge, wisdom, freedom, peace, unity, love, and respect. You can't miss the social relevance of the 1982 hit by Grand Master Flash aptly titled, "The Message."

"Don't push me cause I'm close to the edge. I'm trying not to lose my head. It's like a jungle sometimes. It makes me wonder how I keep from going under."[3]

I think today, in most commercial hearings, this element of Rap, the important message within a very popular form is what we tend to forget about. Coming right out of the Civil Rights and war protest eras, Hip Hop's roots are powerfully planted in social consciousness.

Rap is seeing the same kind of commodification (meaning the watering down, homogenization of) that we saw in the teens and twenties of the twentieth century with the Blues: a music begins with rural people. Then, somebody records it. At first, as the music becomes popular, small New York club bands of Black musicians play it, but then along comes F. Scott Fitzgerald and company and it becomes this youthful frenzy—the "Jazz Age." Paul Whiteman and Benny Goodman become the kings of Jazz and Swing. The commodity becomes big, big business.

R&B race records of the 1940s the same thing. Somebody records it, a DJ plays it, again, young people go crazy, we get Rock and Roll, and Elvis is born and in 1957 he hits the charts.

Now, speed forward twenty years to 1977, Black neighborhood party music, somebody hears, codifies it, it becomes a national craze. Enter Eminem and by the late 1990s we have yet another American music idol. Get the picture. Pretty powerful stuff.

One of the power tricks in cultural criticism that's played is to reduce the relevance of a particular movement, thing, or person by claiming in print that it has no history, shows no craft or invention, lacks refinement, and carries no intellectual weight. The histories of many kinds of popular music include such critical dismissals by the gatekeepers. Jazz was at first "jungle music" and would destroy the values of young Americans. There was similar outrage over R&B, and soon after with Rock 'n' Roll.

The other day on a radio show I heard a host talking about Rap, sampling, and DJ scratching as "collage assimilance." It's amazing how the cultural media denigrates, designates, disseminates, commodifies, and then justifies—in the name of cultural evolution and modernity.

Equally amusing is Allan Bloom's logic, from his *The Closing of the American Mind*, where he writes,

> Picture a 13-year-old boy sitting in the living room of his family home doing his math assignment
> wearing his Walkman or watching MTV. He has been provided with the comfort and leisure by

the most productive economy ever known to mankind. And how does this progress culminate? A child whose body throbs with orgasmic rhythms . . . whose feelings are made articulate in hymns to the joys of killing parents, and whose ambition is to win fame and wealth imitating a drag queen who makes music. In short, a non-stop commercially-prepackaged masturbational fantasy.[4]

Heavy, Allan and oh so off base.

Now as a young musician on my way to college music school I remember what I was thinking in 1979. I was thinking that this childish jibber this "Rap" by New York music wanna-bes would go away. And I said, "That's not music!"

Well, I was wrong. I've had to mature and listen up, and as a musician I can honestly say, "There's music going on there and a lot of it!" So let me play DJ Dr. B for awhile and go through some of my own favorites.

1. Sugar Hill Gang: "Rapper's Delight" (1979)
2. Grand Master Flash: "The Message" (1982)
3. Run DMC: "You be Illin'" (1986)
4. Public Enemy: "Fear of a Black Planet" (1990)

For my ears this is the start, in the early 1980s, of hearing words, a narrative that draws you in. That's "the Rap effect," with the most persuasive and important aspect of this music up-front, its message direct. Rapped straight at the issues and at you, the listener.

5. D.J. Jazzy Jeff and the Fresh Prince: "Parents Just Don't Understand" (1988)
6. Hammer, "Too Legit to Quit" (1991)

By now, moving into the 1990s, Rap in the larger context of Hip Hop is a category in the record bins, and a major force in the national music scene. With examples like "Parents Just Don't Understand," Hip Hop is now totally accepted as pop commercial music.

But musicians and crafty producers are not just sampling other music, they're conceptualizing rhythms, harmonies, riffs, turnarounds, and hooks aided by some of the hottest production technology in the business. Musical initiative becomes an equal creative partner to "the Rap" in Hip Hop music. So for us musicians, hearing artists like Teddy Riley and D'Angelo in the 1990s infuse a musician's sensibility into Hip Hop, well, we started to take notice of the fact that this music was competing not just commercially, but musically. So Rap and Hip Hop in the 1990s sound great. Also, these artists have now morphed from being a part of an underground movement to being mainstream celebrities. Will Smith and the Hammer will definitely go down in history as two of the biggest entertainers in American history. They were rappers first. You simply cannot miss, diss, or dismiss them. That's power!

Hammer's "Too Legit to Quit," well, that says it all, doesn't it! Hip Hop has legitimized itself using its own rhetorical form. The music has created its own rules and challenges the rest of the music business to keep up!

7. NWA, "Straight Outa Compton"

But another variety of Rap/Hip Hop emerged in the late 1980s–early 1990s and caused huge controversy: "Gangsta Rap."

Now, to be honest, like most folks, I was completely repulsed by what at its surface level seemed to be a completely unnecessary glorification of violence. But again, I was wrong. "You are now about to witness the strength of street knowledge" was the epochal manifesto in NWA's "Straight Outa Compton" from 1988. ("Get it, Niggas with attitude!") An FBI official wrote a letter to the record label saying, "Music plays a significant role in society, and I wanted you to be aware of the FBI's position relative to this song and its message." This happened two years before the Rodney King incident and signaled in a way a useful and prophetic use of Rap as a kind of, in Chuck D's words, "CNN for the urban community." A rude, crude, direct, and alarming music/speech had become for the first time in American history a commercially available way to engage the public.

The Parental Advisory stickers now on many CDs was the result. Again, that's power. Now, when I hear "Straight Outa Compton," I respect it as something very important. I respect it as art. It positioned itself to live out its own rhetoric, it set a standard for the performance practice of rapping, and it was truly relevant to a generation that began to expect its music to "keep it real."

Of course, Gangsta Rap got commodified and grew to be a poison. In addition to a performance standard, it unfortunately also set a standard for the use of abusive language and degrading imagery. And I think it's fair to blame their industry that profits from these records.

But, I do think we have to keep Gangsta Rap in perspective. Its narratives clearly demonstrate the poignancy and relevance of the community activist nature of popular music in America. For this reason, we can't dismiss this part of the Hip Hop phenomenon.

8. "Express Yourself," by NWA

You can't ignore the powerful style, the connection to the old R&B tradition, the centrality of the idea of expressing your own ideas, and the fact that those ideas are linked not to violence, but to First Amendment rights. The concept of authenticity and originality is a big part of art, and the concept of the power of reality giving voice to the concerns of the community is important. No teacher in America would miss the beat of this message, yet so much of this aspect of the music has been lost in the fuss about lyrical content. I think we need to reevaluate these messages. There is much to salvage.

9. Arrested Development: "Tennessee" (1992)

When this record hit, I remember being a doctoral candidate in music composition at the University of Michigan. Some friends wanted to give me a break from being locked up in a room and made me go out dancing. This record, "Tennessee" by Arrested Development, came on and I lost my musical mind. I was blown away with the lyricism, the flow (that's the Hip Hop term or the metric logic and timing of the rhyme scheme). I was taken by the performance of the rapper, the leader of Arrested Development, Speech. And I listened to the message. This record brought it all together for me: music, performance, meaning. Rap and Hip Hop culture could now be grasped by a doctoral music student!!

I know it may sound silly to you, but it took me 12 years of growing up with this form as a musician, as a Black musician, to begin to hear it as real music. Okay, that may tell you something about me, but I think it tells you more about the strength, vitality, and ultimately the legitimacy of this musical form in our culture. Tricia Rose, the scholar who as well was moved during her formative school years, wrote one of the best books on Hip Hop culture, *Black Noise.*

10. En Vogue and Salt-N-Pepa: "Whatta Man" (1993)

By now, I'm a professor in Afro-American Studies at Indiana University teaching Black music. What happens when you take the hottest R&B female singing group, En Vogue, and couple them with the number one female Hip Hop group, Salt-N-Pepper? Well, you've created the greatest sexual liberation banner song since Aretha Franklin's "Respect." But here we have the women proclaiming respect for men. Big tune and huge cultural statement!

11. Coolio: "Gangstas Paradise" (1995)

With this 1995 record by Coolio, "Gangsta's Paradise," we've crossed into media partnerships with Hollywood. Like its predecessors from the 1991 film, *New Jack City,* Coolio's work is the sound track feature of the movie *Dangerous Minds.* Clothes and perfume follow. And in 2001, MTV produced *Carmen: A Hip Hop Opera,* adapted from the great masterpiece by Bizet. All of these cultural stuffings now define the game. That's some cultural criss-crossing for ya! For me, Coolio's "Gangsta's Paradise" is poetic, riveting, psychologically engaging, a programmatic rendering that connected immediately with the movie's story line. And his sound is so menacing, I'm now drawn into Hip Hop as a powerful performance medium, as good, perhaps, as any other kind of art song. You see, one rapper can pull off a better performance than another, and that's the classic qualification given by the cultural police for legitimacy.

12. D'Angelo: "Brown Sugar"

D'Angelo's "Brown Sugar," while not a Rap record or artist per se, is the concretization of Hip Hop and urban contemporary R&B. And Rock artists following the Beastie Boys example weren't far behind in falling into the Hip Hop fray. The music is all meshed together now. R&B artists don't just want to sing, they're "flowing" now, using Hip Hop styles, the two inextricably bound.

I love Tupac's "Brenda's Got a Baby." In Tupac's obvious role as message giver to the community make this the compelling issue of the work. The other thing for me is that I as a musician can hear this as music because of the vocal accompaniment. Rap aligning itself commercially with musical, sometimes old-school music conception, and that has an effect on how it's put together like a contemporary musical form.

13. The Roots: "The Spark and Dynamite"

"Yo, the feet that I walk with, the ears that I hear with, the eyes that I see with . . . hey we got a doctorate in cold rocking it" (that's we be edumacated in telling da truth on the microphone).

Now this is a Rap band with legitimate musicians who, like Public Enemy, has gained respect as one of the few groups to sustain its following by staying close to the idea of Rap and Hip Hop—and the idea of giving an important message.

14. The 2001 recording by Rap artist Jay-Z, on MTV Unplugged with the Roots, plus strings, represents the commitment of Hip Hop artists to work with other musicians. I can't miss the fluidity, craft, and execution of the performance practice in Jay-Z's work, as a performing artist.
15. Miles Davis: "Doo-Bop" (1992)

Now for the musician's justification: to have the greatest Jazz master of all time, Miles Davis, embrace Hip Hop and leave its creative markings on his last album says it all. So when Roy Hargrove, one of the leading young lions of Jazz, comes with his Hip Hop/Jazz CD *Hard Groove*, an obvious connection is made and the obvious mark of Hip Hop artistry has been made on Jazz culture, still thought to be the "great art" of the Black tradition.

With the impact in 2003/2004 of the positive messages of Talib Kweli's "Get By" or Black Eyed Peas' "Where Is the Love," along with the other efforts by 50 Cent, Jay-Z, OutKast, a dead Tupac, Ja Rule, Missy Elliot, Snoop Dogg, one can see Rap has diversified, grown up, and become an industry player in the music world.

When I hear all this music, poetry, music recording technology, when I take in the images and commercial force of Hip Hop, I can't miss the musical implications of this movement. Hip Hop is clearly one of the most important musical movements to rise up in the twentieth century.

THE FUTURE OF BLACK MUSIC: HIP HOP?

I attended the 2002 BET awards show in Los Angeles as an NPR reporter looking at the behind-the-scenes work of music director Patrice Rushen. I guess I was interested in how these big award shows are put together, and, by now, Hip Hop has taken over. I mean, most of the show was driven by Hip Hop artists, despite the fact that the music director and her musicians were some of the most respected players of instruments in the L.A. scene. Patrice went on to be the musical director of the 2004 Grammies. I asked her were there any differences artistically between what she witnessed in 2002 and her observations in 2004. She was hopeful. She was seeing more variety reflected.

> This is a transitional year and the concerns have been raised. In the past these shows were slanted towards who sells more records. Ninety categories are not even televised. Things like art design, the best children's record are this year being given more of their proper due. I see a real concerted effort to rebalance, reevaluate what messages are being sent. The consciousness is more apparent. This year the pretelecast awards are done with a live band and concert performance with Diane Reeves and Nicholas Payton, jazz artists, who themselves have been nominated. This year represents a new consciousness about what we want to present and give credit to without sacrificing excellence. My hope is that I am even being seen as more, because I am allowed to talk to the artists not just as a "hired gun" but as an artist who can "school them." This will foster a lot of what we are hoping will begin to happen in Black popular music again. (March 2004)[5]

There is still quite a strong reaction among "old-school" musicians about exactly what's going on in the music industry today. As drummer Ndugu Chancelor commented, "Now we're dealing with track artists and Pro Tools artists who have to be supported by computer systems. It's a different ball game now, it's different. This is a genre of music that's not supported by musicians at all, but by programming. This makes for a different thing."[6]

Yes, Hip Hop and popular music making is a very different kind of music making today, and some people like the guy I mentioned earlier, pounding on the table and claiming, "It's a travesty!" may not see it going anywhere. But this is exactly what every generation has thought of the music of the following generation. Remember, Swing musicians called the next development in Jazz, Bebop, "noise."

If you can believe this, one of our nation's most important classical music composers, Libby Larsen, now serving as a special assigned chair of education and technology at the Library of Congress, has actually transcribed, that is taking down note for note, rhythm by rhythm, Nelly. Yes Nelly's *Nellyville*, so that it can be read by so-called trained musicians.

Libby's been touring the country teaching music educators how to, "come alive" by learning about rappers' innovative rhythmic creations. She argues that traditional music education in America is at least 50 years behind the times, and if it doesn't pay attention to Rap and Hip Hop, it'll never catch up to where most young people in school are today. Now that's pretty powerful!

I asked her when did she become aware of Hip Hop music as music?

> My daughter, who was 14 played it for me. I was to give a speech at the Texas Music educator's convention. I was interested in how we teach beat and rhythm in music education and she played Hip Hop for me. She played Nelly and said she wanted me to listen to it with, my "music ears." As I listened I was made extraordinarily aware of what is happening to music in America. I used to believe that melody is something you can whistle, but melody in rap is rhythmic melody. But the rhythm is so very complicated, supported many times by a simpler harmony so you can appreciate the intricacies of it. In fact we are going about the business now of redefining what we mean by melody, meter and form is. Rap in particular is incredibly intricate.[7]

This begins to give our form another view.

Another scholar looking at Hip Hop is Alexs Pate of the University of Minnesota. He teaches a course called In the Heat of the Beat: The Poetry of Rap. His concern is more with the word with Rap as literature. I asked him several questions:

1. How do students respond, and what do they find, after examining this music as an intellectual inquiry?
2. How do they come to terms with the conflicting ideas of, on the one hand, artistic speech, knowledge, art, and, on the other hand, the sometimes problematic and crude language and images of the music?
3. What's your opinion of the value of the art form?
4. Can Rap be considered literature?

Alexs responded:

> What I try to do is get students to respond to rap as word, and to its social cultural implications, to consider the literary and artistic quality. We must be cognizant of the way art has always functioned in society. Art has always incorporated obscenities, unforgiving images these things are natural to art. As any good discerning reader you have to be able to read through the plethora of work and begin to identify qualitative issues criteria that allows you to find the meaning and implications. I am always directing students towards thoughtful intense reading. That doesn't mean I am not going to find obscenities, or that the images won't upset me or challenge me. When I think of the Black poets who influenced me, a lot of that poetry wasn't pretty. The more meaningful Hip

Hop is certainly muted by the more popular beat driven rap. But that's just a popular category of it that's played on BET. That doesn't define the art form. When you evaluate literature you don't go to the worst, you go to the best to define it.[8]

One of the most articulate scholars about Hip Hop culture is Michael Eric Dyson of the University of Pennsylvania who's currently teaching a full year on Rap artist Tupac. In a recent speech, Michael said,

The reality is that the different styles that young people invent are attempts to mark their own particular environments. Style is an attempt to put your stamp on your existence. Young Black people keep inventing and re-inventing, asserting and re-asserting, so that they can mark existence through the prism of style and give some sense of weightiness to their existence. We should not resist the edifying character of Hip Hop culture as a tool of aesthetic, economic and social expression for today's young people.[9]

IMAGES, MESSAGES, AND WORDS THAT DESTROY VALUES

Many have argued that the dominance of Hip Hop has greatly diminished the positive value and impact music once had in the 1960s, 1970s, and early 1980s. Some have even gone as far as to blame the decay of American moral fiber directly on, as we noted in the Bloom criticism, Rap and Hip Hop. In his 1993 television show, *Both Sides*, Jessie Jackson took on the question.

In an episode called "That Type of Rap," Reverend Jackson asked whether Rap was polluting the minds of young Americans, or whether it was just another form of artistic expression. A 19-year-old that year was sentenced for killing a state trooper and claimed, "Rap music made me do it." At that time Rap accounted for 10 percent of the 7.8-billion-dollar recording industry. There was a huge groundswell against violent or "Gangsta" Rap, especially from the Black church community.

As well, the issue was raised of the negative portrayal of women, and the constant use of the B word. Jesse Jackson asked, "Where is the redemptive dimension, the defensive element which traditionally created resistance to oppression?" On this program one guest went so far as to compare the power of Rap to the propaganda campaign of the Hitler regime which led to the Holocaust, raising the question of the role of the record industry (Time/Warner) for promoting violence (*Cop Killer*). Congress also raised these questions to the industry and the media. Can we blame Rap for violence? What's the responsibility of rappers to curb their violent messages, if it's thought that the content of their music can lead to destruction and violence?

And none of us can forget the news of the deaths of Tupac Shakur and Biggie Small. Rap performance ideology had taken its rhetoric too close to the edge, when the end result of a market-mechanized East Coast–West Coast dual ended with the death and silencing of two of the most respected artists of the entire genre. And what do we make of the extreme success of a rapper who claims to be the most authentic because he survived nine gunshot wounds? This kind of "keeping-it-real" authenticity translates into real market power and increased sales.

I mean, Jessie James, Al Capone, the Godfather, Jimmy Hoffa, and now the modern-day gangsta rapper—they all fit all too neatly into our American thug/hero formula.

But there have been an equal number of very powerful responses to these questions. One of the most persuasive and important of these has come from one of the architects of Hip Hop culture, megamogul Russell Simmons, owner of Def Jam Records, Phatt Farm Clothes, producer of the blockbuster film *The Nutty Professor*.

In a recent appearance on the public radio program *Fresh Air*, Mr. Simmons defends the stories and images behind the music. We learned from Libby Larsen that Hip Hop has musical value and from author Alexs Pate that Rap at its best is literature. Russell Simmons is the man who helped to establish Hip Hop in mainstream globally. He created the legendary show *Def Comedy Jam*, and his *Def Poetry Jam* is now an HBO show. His 2001 memoir, *Life and Death: Sex, Drugs, Money and God*, articulates the entire commercial development of this movement. I call Russell the Alain Locke of contemporary art movement, Hip Hop. In doing my MPR show, Russell agreed to speak to me about his interpretation of the value and meaning and relevance of hip Hop. True to his way of doing business, he called me for an interview on his cell phone, just leaving a Hip Hop political forum.

> Rap is about disenfranchised poor people. And these people have become leaders in mainstream American culture, and relevant to all those voiceless people. And 80% of those who buy this music are not Black. And that's what makes it so relevant, because people who are driving in their cars in Beverly Hills understanding the plight of people in Compton. People who live in trailer parks are connecting to the same energy and know that they have the same issues and poverty conditions of people who are living in the urban area, in the projects. Now the connection is made between all young people in America and they are listening and understanding the plight of the poor, and that is a big deal that will change America to be more sensitive to the suffering people in our country. I'm just a front in these cases. Puffy ran to raise one million dollars for music education. Jay Z has a scholarship fund, he's registering voters. Hip Hop summit registered 11,000 voters (New York). In the Detroit, Hip Hop Summit people came out with paper and pen in hand to empower their community. They are doing a lot of good. The Hip Hop community is responsible and powerful, more known in the minds of youth in the world than President Bush, or Condoleezza Rice. Their ideas about empowerment is as known and respected as Howard Dean's or the politicians. In the first Hip Hop summit with Jay Z, Puffy and Mariah Carey, thousands of people came out and the majority put back millions of dollars into the education budget. They are rallying their strength to do good in their communities. They are thinking about higher elevation and consciousness. It's the truth if you listen to it. Hip Hop poetry is truth because people connect to truth. Truth always sells. Hip Hop is the most honest, with most integrity of any commercial art form being distributed today.[10]

There's no doubt about it. Despite all the talk, criticism, and commercial hype, Hip Hop music is a huge global force from New York to Tokyo, to Brazil to Africa. There are estimates that five billion dollars are made a year from the music, the advertising, the clothes, and the merchandising. This is one sure way to measure its cultural force and power in the West, and Hip Hop culture has become one of this country's leading exports, literally changing the way businesses across the planet are selling their products. Take these artists for example: Missy Elliot, megamillions; Jay-Z, Damon Dash, Burke with their Roc-A-Fella Enterprises worth 300 million; Master P, 500 million; P. Diddy, another 500 million; and Russell Simmons's half a billion. After Snoop Dogg's line, "With my mind on my money and my money on my mind," or P. Diddy's, "Its all about the Benjamins baby," one doesn't have to wonder what all the "Bling Bling" is about.

Hip Hop today is big business. It's gained street likeability, and branding in the marketplace, and has become an incredible power in contemporary culture. Considering Hip Hop's pervasive presence, there's no way to escape its meaning and impact in the world today. As

Queen Latifah stated in her *Black Reign* album, "Cause hip-hop is for real. . . . I'm dealing with the truth, cause all over the world, it's aggravated youth. . . . You can always know the time, just recognize the sign, can't nobody put a padlock on your mind."

Remember Franz Fanon and his statement about each generation needing to fulfill its cultural mission? One of art and culture's primary functions in society is to allow people to dream and create visible, viable, and real cultural agency. Musical expression is a place for social criticism and rage, but it also helps us find the strength to make a better way. As a musical force in American culture, I think Hip Hop has found its cultural mission over its 25 years of existence. It's evolving just as Jazz has evolved over 60 years to contain so many different styles. I can now see Hip Hop as being big, bad, and beautiful enough to provide the space for that kind of depth of music and meaning.

Albert Murray wrote that, "The artist (writer) never ceases being concerned with human fulfillment . . . they provide the most adequate frame of reference for coming to terms with contemporary experience."[11] Some days I still cling to my old "trained" musician ways and feel that too much of the music of this generation are derivative. But Hip Hop culture is powering so many of our contemporary music impulses that to miss this is to be walking around with your head jammed down in a hole.

Hip Hop artistry, love it or hate it, is a pervasive cultural force that has significantly marked our society.

· 13 ·

An Essay on Hip Hop and Popular Music Culture as One Road Map in Jazz Education's Future Directions (2003)

Yo Hip Hop is a Way of Life. It ain't a fad, it ain't a trend. Not for those of us who are true to it. It's reflected in our slang, in our walk, our dress, and our stance. In our dress and our attitude. Hip Hop has a history, origin and a set of principles. . . . Hip Hop is the Lifestyle, the philosophy and even the religion, if I may. It will remain for some of us as the raw essence of life.

—Guru[1]

Musicians came up with Bebop to challenge the narrow minded museum-like character of jazz. . . . We keep reinventing ourselves through our expressions. The reality is the different styles that young people invent are an attempt to mark their own particular environments with the style they are accustomed to. And style is an attempt to put your stamp on your existence. . . . But we should not resist the edifying character of Hip Hop Culture as a tool of aesthetic, economic and social expression for young people.

—Michael Eric Dyson[2]

THE CHARGE

As Jazz educators, the statement from the Dyson quote above, "to challenge the narrow minded museum-like character of jazz," hits us all pretty directly. But whether it was Thomas Dorsey's pepping up the church music with Blues changes and feels from his days being the musical director with Ma Rainey, or the fusion of Bebop into mainstream big band culture in the 1940s, or Rock and Soul in the Hard Bop era of the post–1950s, American music has always been a cross section of different musical impulses colliding, borrowing, inspiring, and infusing styles and approaches. And there has always been a rub between the market demands of popular culture and the tastes of artistry. In this essay I'd like to pose some questions: Can Jazz education, culture, and art find spaces and places to play in and gain musical and aesthetic insights, new performance codes, new parameters for form and invention from its distant cousin Hip Hop? Given our contemporary need to be relevant, musical, and commercially viable, does a contemporary popular artistic sensibility strike a dissonant chord among Jazz educators? What effect will such rubs between commercial market needs and a growing necessity for a contemporary and forward-looking Jazz culture response have upon the artistry of

140

contemporary Jazz education? I want to pose these questions and explore some historical examples by pointing to necessary historical, aesthetic links and consider Hip Hop's own artistic value base. Perhaps somewhere buried in this stream of commercial expression there are models for expression, form, and musical construction and instruction.

SOME HISTORY MARKERS

Caravan, Manteca, and Cubana Bop were cross-cultural/stylistic examples of blends that have made lasting marks on the culture of Jazz without diminishing its musical values and artistic codes. In many ways Hip Hop's musical framing was already successfully integrated into Jazz culture years ago, and Miles's *Do-Bop* is only one successful example. A variety of contemporary Jazz artists, such as Pat Matheny (*We Live Here*, 1995), Branford Marsalis (*Music Evolution, Buck Shot La Fonque*, 1997), Erykah Badu (*Baduizm*, 1997), John Scofield (*A Go Go*, 1998), Don Byron (*An Existential Dred*, 1998), Jill Scott (*Who Is Jill Scott*, 2000), Roy Hardgrove, (*Hardgroove*, 2003), have leaned successfully in this direction. The record bins have endless examples of Jazz carried with Hip Hop framing that make the point artistically. Jazz music has made the next organic pairing, its next inner-cultural revolution, a kind of a Be-Hop, as I call it. The sound, color of Jill Scott's and Ms. Badu's voices as well as the contemporary phrasing and settings in these examples scream of Billie Holiday's lyrical and stylistic treatments. And how many great soloists in the day took their notes from singers? Hip Hop culture and contemporary musical impulses imported from MTV, VH1, and BET may cause "upset stomach" in the art and culture mind-set of traditional Jazz educators. Yet this is par for the course, as in every era the emergence of the grassroots, the more rough and silly conventions and aspects of the common vernacular culture, were ignored and dismissed by the status quo, the establishment, the academy. Where would Bebop be without Gillespie's "Oop Pop a Da" and others? This was a way of catching and framing a music-syllabic phrase which was revolution within the culture.

All arts impulses benefit from constant study, appreciation, and critique, and sometimes a closer look at cultural congruency is helpful. On a recent recording project, I worked with Grammy-award-winning producer Michael Powell; we were listening to playbacks which included performances by Patrice Rushen, Don Byron, Billy Childs, Sounds of Blackness, Nelson Rangell, and Mark Ledford. As I was listening to the diversity of styles it struck me how many contemporary musical impulses inform Jazz music today, and Hip Hop is all over us! At the opening of a segment special celebrating 20 years of Hip Hop on MTV, a long list of Hip Hop artists came on and gave a litany of their beliefs and hopes for what Hip Hop is. They spoke of the music as: a dance . . . a way of talking . . . freedom . . . form of poetry. . . . my culture . . . my womb . . . the mothership . . . the voice of America. Hip Hop artists including Dr. Dre, L. L. Cool J, Missy Elliot, Ice Cube, Eminem, DMX, Nellie, P. Diddy were here celebrating the mostly good and plenty of this worldwide popular phenomenon. What's most impressive is that we are getting from contemporary hip hoppers a passion and a belief in the music culture itself, as evidenced in the opening quote from Hip Hop artist Guru. We have not seen this from a group of popular musicians who speak for a whole generation since the seventies. And not since the beboppers have we had a group of insiders who articulated the music's artistic, social, and commercial value.

As one host put it, "No other music speaks more directly and profoundly to young people all over the world." It is useless to try to negate the profound influence and impact of Hip Hop culture: its music, artists, and its ideology and spirit. One has to come to the conclusion that above the fray of the madness of the opiate popular cultural form, media hype, and Hollywood's seductive imagery machines, there is something extremely powerful and meaningful in this music, and its appeal at deeper levels is telling. Anything of depth and with meaning in culture has such power because of sustainability. It sticks. Hip Hop culture has been a music and musical cultural form with us for 25 years strong and counting, and like the Blues born on record some 50 years before, Hip Hop is becoming a foundation for most contemporary popular music from Rap to Rock and contemporary Jazz impulses in between.

As with all the forms, from the Spirituals to the Blues to Gospel, Big Band, Bebop, Rock, Reggae, Soul, Funk, to contemporary R&B, Hip Hop is attached to this family and bears the mark of African functionality, musical, cultural, social, and spiritual roots. This is the very basis of Black culture and Black American music forms. We are all witnesses to the potential and power of popular culture and its role in shaping who we have become to a large degree post-1970. Popular culture in its various shapes is the most influential human-driven agency in contemporary society. Artists in the past have "called up" spiritual, intellectual, and aesthetic power to represent authentic and vivid examples of human need and meaning. They have reflected and projected prophetic musical musings, which have moved us at times to consider who we were and were fast becoming. Hip Hop music culture is providing as style a viable road map for where contemporary Jazz music culture is, and is heading. Hip Hop culture, like so many of its cousin forms in popular music, provides a road map down paths for certain kinds of musical truths, and this alone is relevant territory for inquiry.

It's not that there are shortages of relevant examples and projects going on, there is just not enough talk from educators about contemporary popular music and the recognition of its performance materials for Jazz. The work of contemporary Gospel artist Kirk Franklin, the Thomas A. Dorsey of the twenty-first century, is ripe in the cross sections of Gospel, Jazz, and Hip Hop. There's no way to miss the harmonizations, "riffing," and swing so prevalent in these "live" recordings. Better get it in your soul! But given the stream and spray of influences from contemporary commercial markets and ideologies (what sells), does such an inclusive vision make sense for traditional Jazz education today?

My goal is to simply speak, perhaps de-demonize Hip Hop and contemporary popular and mass culture impulses, suggest a view of them in another or the same cultural/aesthetic framing as Jazz culture, and look at a few useful musical applications for Jazz education.

For example, a suburban Jazz band teacher or college Jazz instructor could come into the classroom and play a CD of the Roots or Mary J. Blige and have a serious instructive conversation about phrasing, energy, commitment to the art, and one's responsibility to say something. Or if a Jazz course would be inclusive of Miles's *Do-Bop* or Tribe Called Quest, Talib Kweli, Mos Def, or Common as being influenced by and influencing the "canon," this could truly be another beginning to chart some new expressive territories in Jazz education. And I do realize I am taking some jumps into a zone in which I will be called into question by colleagues for a number of reasons, but a move forward artistically as an impulse and educational resource is where the common people sit as well, and not always just in the academy, fingering through the new Jazz education textbook.

BROADER DIMENSIONS OF POPULAR MUSIC PRACTICE

The history of American popular music owes many of its expressive, structural, and stylistic formulations to great artists creating within our newly created language and indigenous music forms, which merged together African American sacred and folk traditions. Music such as the Blues, Spirituals, and Jazz, and Euro-American religious and folk ballad songs form a larger tradition called "American popular music." Hip Hop culture is shaped within the very same trajectory, and despite its current commercial exploits it was first nurtured in the soil of a community which emphasized some core values, most of which are foreign to current commercial attributes. Music creates a value system of our soul places, values about what we want and hope for in life, values about our identities, values about our love relationships, values about our ethnic/cultural names, and values about the notion that I am somebody and I have an experience that is worthy. But most importantly, there is a musical style, syntax, a groove, a phrase flow that is rich and dynamic and applicable to Jazz and that is as comfortable and common as the notion of swing. And this is the dialogue Jazz education could be having within contemporary popular music surges.

One of the main roles that music artistry has in our culture is its ability to give a shape, a voice to ideas and things that everyday people feel and dream of. There is no lack of protests from every adult generation since Plato, fearing the work of popular artistry in music for arousing those dreams and other creative, experimental surges in society. Dizzy and Bird were harshly criticized for their radical shake-up of performance conventions. And while I am not suggesting Hip Hop artists are in exactly the same arenas artistically, there is a very real historical continuity with radical accents, new phrase construction, new aesthetic conventions, and the emergence of a new generation of creators who adopted some standard conventions and rejected others in favor of establishing their own voices. Remember, White suburban parents in the late 1950s and 1960s protested publicly that American children should not be allowed to listen to Black American music for the same reasons. That of course was ignored, especially when the industry found it profitable, so much so that they invested in artists to make it palatable and fashionable to gravitate toward popular music icons singing out of that Spiritual-Blues impulse (Cornel West). Brittany Spears and the Back Street Boys are industry profit makeups that every generation produces the need for. This all began with Black artistry in the marketplace, and both streams, popular R&B and the more Jazz-driven traditions, are popular market products and share the same commercial trajectories. Unfortunately, in today's "music-image" formulas, music, morals, and especially forward-reaching creative artistry have gotten extracted out. But in the minds and practices of those artists—in the early days of Rural Blues, to Gospel, to the Gospel-laced R&B groups, to Soul and even early Hip Hop—there exist all of these expressive parameters: what music expresses in a cultural, spiritual, social, and artistic framework. I think an "academic-classroom only" kind of outlook begs for some of this understanding to be injected into our philosophies and pedagogy, and popular artists tend to keep these ideas active as performers and carriers of contemporary musical culture.

SIGNIFICANT CULTURAL FORM AND MARKET FORCE

Hip Hop music, in terms of musical performance function, is very closely tied to the roots of all Black music in the Diaspora, be it Europe, the West Indies, New York, or New Orleans. The line of artistic/cultural evolution is very clear: griot, plantation fiddler, slave preacher, Blues singer, preacher who sings, last poets (Black arts movement), and finally rappers.

The function or role of Rap's performance and delivery style bears family marks resembling every kind of music doing in the tradition. Even the line "It don't mean a thing if it ain't got that swing" (Ellington, 1932) is the same as "It don't go if it ain't got that flow" (a contemporary Rap idea).

In his *African Music: A People's Art*, Francis Bebey writes that "Music is an integral part of African life from cradle to the grave and that it covers the widest possible range of expression including spoken language and all manner of natural sounds."[3] "Griot" is a term used throughout West African society to designate a professional musician, culture bearer, and artist. Music is at the heart of all the griot's activities and is yet further proof of the vital part one plays in African life. Griots speak of,

> the history of the people, wisdom of the philosophers, corporate ethics and generosity of spirit, thought provoking riddles. . . . The virtuoso talents of the griot command universal admiration. . . . They are looked upon as . . . the inventors of melodies, poem and rhythms and their role is essential to ceremonies that are the combination of philosophy, mythology, technique and art.[4]

I have argued that somewhere in the unconscious creative soul these ideas have always been a part of popular music making in American culture.

As a market force within popular culture, Rap and Hip Hop have became big practice among youth and turned into big money once again for the profit opportunist industry. A *New York Times* writer reported,

> Rap like most everything from the Blues to alternative rock before it has been officially embraced by those who originally ostracized it, avariciously consumed by those from whom it sought independence. White young people (who make up 80% of hip hop sales) are listening to and using elements of rap not for theft but because they relate to it, because the music is a legitimate part of their cultural heritage. Black and White fans are flipping back and forth between the local rock and rap radio stations, simply in search of the best song.[5]

This economic barometer (sorry) is an indication that there is a significant musical impulse in our time which cannot be ignored simply based on market culture demand.

In his book *Life and Def, Sex, Drugs, Money and God*, record mogul Russell Simmons addresses in plain speech his responses to the navigation around and through the rub between music making and market forces. Russell seems to end up in his autobiography saying that the record industry is a multipronged business that only responds to core audiences. The core audience in response to the industry products (which are created to satisfy audience impulses) is in a search for identification with that product which suits needs. Being true to that core audience, Simmons states, is the first rule for an artist wishing to be successful. He writes, "To me, Hip Hop is modern mainstream youth urban American culture."[6] Russell argues that culture is the construction of image, and that image is contained in music, film, fashion, magazines, television, comedy, and politics. He continues, "My whole career has been about cultivating understanding and expanding this core audience for Hip Hop culture and watching the impact ripple out into the mainstream."[7]

SOME MUSICAL MAPS

Hip Hop is a clear example of West African retentions, as much as the Blues from the Delta. It is almost a mirror tradition of the roots. And this is only important in terms of the passing on of art (rites), the role of griot, and the reason anybody does music in the first place: to communicate expressive ideas and human experience. Hip Hop is a necessary link between the Blues, Jazz, Bop, avant-garde aesthetics exhibited in Ornette or the AACM of past, Steve Coleman's experiments and the next newer and fresh products of Jazz art. The relaxed grooves of Erykah Badu's phrasing and the intricacies of syllabic intonations of a Jay-Z are examples of models for application from popular music forms which may be useful for Jazz pedagogy. The emergence of new forms (Hip Hop jargon) and modes of expression (both in music and movement, dance, and poetry) can be seen as infusing Jazz phrase construction, language, movement, and new aesthetic sensibilities to create possibilities for musical form, structure, syntax, and style.

In terms of musical attributes the most important of these are: (1) the radical shifts of musical phrase and pulse conception; (2) Hip Hop's unbound elasticity and adaptability to other popular arts traditions (spoken word, dance, film); (3) rhythm and pacing. Like any other generation we are finding younger musicians coming out with all kinds of patching of forms, sonorities, loops. The multiple venues and access that younger musicians have today to technology and its ability to (while most of us look at it undermining the traditional long-range-orientated, discipline-developing apprenticeships) place powerful creative options in their hands should make the point. This generation is defining their own standards for creative surges, their own heroes and their aesthetics and methods of learning (i.e., sampling, patching loops, and sequencing). I too scratch my head, but we are as well amazed with the innovations and creative spirit that popular culture in the last ten years or so has helped to spur. This kind of music dynamism creates expressive and inventive platforms for solo invention and the compositional terrain is rich as well.

These are the kinds of lessons Jazz has already learned from its cousin vernacular forms at significant points of Jazz stagnation and purism. The exchanges happened when Chicago social energy took over New Orleans flow, when Sister Rosetta Tharpe and Thomas Dorsey stole back church music from Jazz and claimed it as Gospel, when interesting notes and jagged rhythms were preferred by boppers, when Ornette said, "the shape of things to come," when Blakey and Mingus said, "Think it's time to go back to church," and when Miles saw Jimi Hendrix and Sly and said, "Bye." Every time it changed, traditional Jazz culture dug deeper into Black folk vernacular and in that dig came up and out with its fuller self, reinvented and maintaining in the end integrity. I don't doubt that will continue. Hip Hop conception has persuaded Jazz soloists from Miles Davis to John Scofield, Regina Carter, and Kenny Garret to slow down tempos and dig deep into the contemporary pocket of "the groove" and refashion their innovative approaches to the pulse and flow of Hip Hop and rappers' speaking. Hip Hop music culture seemingly has had no fear of attaching itself to other musical perspectives that have been willing to "listen." If we take a look at Jazz innovation from Louis Armstrong's modernization of modern time conception to Ellington's, as well as concert music composer William Grant Still's, devotion to fashioning their art in the Blues, Hip Hop as well can be wrapped around and throughout Jazz culture in spirit, form, rhythmic conception, and sonic reconfigurations.

CONCLUSION

The positive rhetoric from the Hip Hop griots is self-knowledge, speaking the truth, keeping it real, giving a shout out for my peeps, and it's all good, baby baby. The single most important music attribute from Hip Hop in my mind—and it is as clear as "It don't mean a thing if it ain't got that swing"—is the musical performance philosophy that Hip Hop musicians and poets ascribe to for great performance. In Hip Hop expressive culture, the high performance qualifier is, "You got ta flow." I remember so vividly Frank Foster's 2001 sharing at IAJE in Long Beach, California, of what Count Basie told him as good arranging advice, "Keep it simple kid, and make it swing." Hip Hop is a musical style (25 years old) and approach to rhythm and phrasing as illustrative as Cool seemed to be to Bebop, showing it to slow down, or what Hard Bop's reliance on Gospel and Soul appeared to Cool to be saying: "fire up again." In all these cases Jazz never stops being Jazz but only moves up and out a notch. Every great tradition flowers from a simple seed and blossoms into a tree with a variety of shapes, petal colors, and textures. Hip Hop is a musical/cultural expression within our Jazz musical culture and it is ripe for such philosophical, pedagogical, and creative adaptations. Perhaps an in-depth listening provides many directions for Jazz educators to consider.

· 14 ·

The Sass and the Cool: Sarah and Miles; Tribute to the Staples of the Black Aesthetic (1990)

I don't feel like a big star. I just feel like me. Plain Sarah Vaughan.

—Sarah Vaughan

I know what I've done for music, but don't call me a legend, just call me Miles Davis.

—Miles Davis

These two statements were made by Sarah Vaughan and Miles Davis who consistently avoided any reference to themselves in their music and accomplishments. Their expressions and their personas, however, provide us with one kind of description for their art; sassy and cool. Vaughan and Davis have made incredible contributions to the output, or canon, of American Black music. We can speak of their creative contributions, even their styles and attitudes towards music making as staples of the Black aesthetic. These staples have incredible artistic merit. As a tribute to Vaughan and Davis, this writing examines what it means to be Black and sassy, what it means to be Black and cool. This is not an analysis of their music in content and form. I am interested in how to perceive and measure the artistic expressions and accomplishments of Sarah Vaughan and Miles Davis.

THE BLACK AESTHETIC: THE SASS AND THE COOL

When I talk about the Black aesthetic, I am simply searching for ways to look at and describe what constitutes Black art, "more specifically, Black music. I deal with the what, why, who, and the what happens when of Black music. I deal with what Black artists think about when doing their art and the end results of what we perceive, hear, and experience the artistic expression "to be." The philosophy of Black aesthetics is the philosophy of "Black art doing." As part of the tribute to Sarah and Miles, I want to say that their approaches and their individual "voices" have become landmarks within the recognizable attributes of Black art. Their music, their approaches, their styles, and their selves are staples of Black art. I think we can get a lot of descriptive mileage out of "the Sass and the Cool," in reference to both style and the outcome of the music. The Sass and the Cool cannot be dismissed as trite. They are powerful and picturesque ways of referring to their modes of expressiveness. As Amiri Baraka once wrote: "Black music is essentially the expression of an attitude, or a collection of attitudes, about the

147

world. . . . The music is the result of the attitude, the stance. The notes mean something, and the something is, regardless of the stylistic considerations, part of the black psyche as it dictates the various forms of black culture." Sarah Vaughan was affectionately nicknamed "Sassy" by pianist John Malach in 1945. Webster's defines sassy as "pert, open, and bold," from the Latin word "apertus," which means open, free, forward, stylish, and lively. A 1961 *Ebony* article described Vaughan as indifferent to social approval, cold and aloof, often unfriendly, curt, and defensive. Both her style and musical manner have been described as daring, expressive, sensibly sophisticated, rich, beautifully controlled, possessing the ability to change or inflect the melody at will. Ella Fitzgerald called Sarah Vaughan the greatest singing talent in the world.

There seems to be an interesting correlation between the description of Vaughan's personal characteristics and her musical ones. Sarah Vaughan had one of the most beautiful and rich vocal sounds ever heard in modern recording. Her technical ability was impeccable. Sarah moved when she sang. She swirled, and had an inviting, sensual intrigue in her performance practice. This has a direct effect on the way the air is distributed in her breathing and phrasing, this affects vocal sound execution and tone. Her indifference, daringness, expressiveness, sensible sophistication, freeness, and lively and stylish trimming, her "sass," are identifiable musical attributes. All of these translate into style, artistic merit, and recognizable character and are effective ways to discuss Black art expressiveness.

Webster's defines cool as "not excited, calm, unruffled, nonchalant, indifferent, self-assured, composed." In a *New York Times Magazine,* Baraka says about Davis, "Miles is my ultimate cultural hero; artist, cool man, bad dude, hipster clear as daylight and funky as a revolution." Miles has been described as capricious, bitter, undependable, shy, sensitive, warm, witty, as public enigma number one, and even as the prince of darkness. The late Miles Davis remains one of the most influential musical personalities in modern society as a bandleader, stylist, and composer. Besides Leonard Bernstein, Elvis Presley, and Michael Jackson, Davis has had no equal in public personal appeal and notoriety. Ask anyone born before 1970 if they've ever heard of Miles Davis and you will probably hear that he was a "mean looking, cool talking, spacey-like trumpet jazz dude."

Cool in reference to Davis easily translates to a description of his persona, approach to musical expression, and even refers literally to a school of players known as, "the Cool School." Davis even created a staple sound effect, the stemless harmon mute, heard first in 1954. To hear this sound today conjures up visions of Davis, or someone else who is "cool," leaning back, playing into a microphone. A 1959 recording, "The Birth of the Cool," has now become the staple sound for the Cool School of Jazz. This sound is described as part of a style which de-emphasizes the ragged, angular approach to boppers, and opts for an even and smooth playing approach. As with the description of sass, the concept of cool is both an aesthetic description and an approach which dictates how music is conceived and crafted.

The creators of cool, Miles Davis, Gil Evans, Gerry Mulligan, John Lewis, and George Russel, were attempting to create a performance and compositional approach that would be a contemporary reaction to Bop, the style Miles helped to create a decade before. They played consciously with a lighter tone, and their mental approach to playing and composing was less agitated, more at ease and flowing, more lyrical, more cool. Davis arranged the rehearsals and sold the band/music concept (which consisted of two trumpets, French horn and tuba, alto sax and rhythm section) to Columbia Records in 1948. The recording became known as, "Birth of the Cool."

In his autobiography, Davis explains the cool as, "sweetness, humanity, hummable music that shakes people's ears a little softer than Bird and Dizzy did. The 'Birth of the Cool' came from Black musical roots. It came from Duke Ellington."[1] Davis speaks of Ellington's musical conception as, "putting his own personality on certain chords."[2] Again, cool translates easily here as aesthetic terminology with concrete musical meaning that affects structure and sound. The idea of the "voice or the face" of the musical artist also appears here. The idea of "being who I am" as a musical approach produces an attitude or grows out of one. Artistically this is meritorious. This is a staple established by Vaughan and Davis. As Davis wrote, "I just didn't play those licks that I knew I couldn't play because I realized early on that I had my own voice. . . . I was playing my own music. . . . I was finding my own voice and that's what I was mainly interested in. . . . See music is about [being] stylish."[3]

My point is to establish a context for meaning, to validate my assertion that sass and cool provide one way to talk about Sarah and Miles and the staples of style they established. Unfortunately, in the academy, Eurocentric Western thought reduces too much of the best music into neat, tightly wrapped, and narrowly defined analytical packages. That is okay when one wants to construct a building or leave something behind in a museum. But the best examples of Black art live, walk, breathe, and have something to say about how people move in this world. Black art is a consistent testament of Black humanity and concrete reality. Speaking about music making in these cultural and/or stylistic attitude terms cannot be dismissed as trite or nonintellectual. Sass and cool are aesthetic sensibilities that contribute to the creative process and are recognized as part of the pedagogy, part of the performance practice, and are essential for technique and music analysis.

The sass and the cool are necessary mental approaches which make the technical and the artistic execution of Black art making meaningful. Attitude is a prerequisite for effective and authentic Black art. Today you can't rap 'bout something, or to someone, 'less you mad 'bout something. "Gotta Get It in Your Soul," "It Don't Mean a Thing if It Ain't Got That Swing," "Say It Loud I'm Black and I'm Proud," and "Who Stole the Soul?" are all artistic titles of songs composed by Black artists who clearly recognized the essential aesthetic staples of their art and culture. These nontechnical colorful descriptions have a lot to do with how music gets made.

Black artists have no problem understanding their meaning in context. I'm reminded of a comment Wynton Marsalis made to a conductor about the phrasing of a line. Marsalis said, "That phrase is not hip enough." He meant that the musical idea did not fall right, the expression was flat without any artistic or human expression that could have brought out its best music potential. The "voice" and "face," what I call the artist's identifiable sound, are attributes that give artistic expression character and substance. Today's menagerie of new artists who are cranked out daily by the record industry are generally conceptual duplicates of "acts" on other record labels. This "zoo of musical chaos" is concocted by the misguided discretion of A&R directors (I call them apples and raspberry people because, in too many cases, what they do has little or nothing to do with making music at all). Many of these "acts" overdramatize the "attitude" but have little musical substance or anything worthwhile to say. This is evident in many of today's little Doo-wop 'n' love "kiddie vocal acts" and the vulgar "let's kill each other" theme Rap groups who have no character, no voice, no face, in essence, they have little artistic value.

These two qualifiers, the artistic attitude, the sass and the cool, and the identifiable character of the artist, the voice and the face, are what make Sarah Vaughan and Miles Davis models for what I mean when I speak of staples of the Black aesthetic.

SARAH VAUGHAN: BIOGRAPHY

Billy Eckstine said, "The sound of Sarah Vaughan, you love it when you hear it. It belongs to her." Sarah Vaughan died of lung cancer on Tuesday, April 3, 1990. She joined an ever-expanding heavenly band that now includes Miles Davis, Sammy Davis Jr., Leonard Bernstein, Aaron Copeland, Art Blakey, Dexter Gordon, Jaco Pastorius, Emily Remler, Count Basie, Benny Goodman, Duke Ellington, Artie Shaw, and Marvin Gaye.

Sarah Vaughan was born in Newark, New Jersey, on March 27, 1924, six years later than Ella Fitzgerald and nine years later than Billie Holiday. Sarah received her training, like so many Black artists, from the old Negro Conservatory on Mt. Calvary Holy Ghost/Jesus Temple Blvd., USA, known to the locals as Mt. Zion Baptist Church of New Jersey. She sang in the choir and began her career as a pianist and organist as a child. In 1942, she won ten dollars and a week's worth of additional appearances in a vocal competition at the Apollo Theater in Harlem. Billy Eckstine heard Vaughan during one of those appearances and encouraged her to audition for bandleader Earl Hines. She was hired as one of the principle singers and secondary pianists. In 1944, she joined Billy Eckstine's band that included Charlie Parker, Dizzy Gillespie, Art Blakey, and for two weeks, the 18-year-old Miles Davis. Sarah Vaughan was really born into the industry as a Bebop singer, by all practical definitions, and is therefore considered the voice of the modern Jazz era. During the early part of her career she sang with Dexter Gordon, Art Blakey, Fats Navarro, and, of course, the Boppers, the group she credits for having taught her so much about the art form.

By the 1950s, Sarah Vaughan was widely respected among the musicians as "a great exponent of new Jazz," and was described as a "singer who sang as an instrumentalist." Sarah signed her first recording contract in 1946 with Musicraft Records. George Treadwell, who was also her first manager, is credited with having given her the advice that catapulted her into commercial success; she needed to change her appearance. One critic commented that Vaughan had a broad, ski lift-like nose and was nothing to look at. She was subsequently given a cosmetic makeover and a new wardrobe. The balance of artistry and commercial success is a tricky proposition, but Sarah Vaughan, throughout her career, even during the time of her illness, maintained her "voice of face" and her artistic integrity. (One of her last recordings was on Quincy Jones's *Back on the Block*.)

Two major recording contracts, one with Columbia in 1949–1954, and one with Mercury in 1954–1959, kept Vaughan in the spotlight. Most of these recordings were done with a studio orchestra, but Mercury allowed her to pursue live Jazz recording with combos on a subsidiary label. Wynton Marsalis now has the same type of contractual arrangement with Columbia Records.

Sarah Vaughan was a song stylist, a balladist of incredible breadth and quality. There is no other vocal sound like hers, so expressive, so fluid. Her lower register was passionate and rich, and she could also move swiftly, taking advantage of her two-and-one-half-octave range with ease. Besides leaving a legacy of "qualitative sass," she created a technical standard of vocal execution for popular singing that opened the door for a Whitney Houston or an Anita Baker. These are just some of the staples Sarah Vaughan left for others to cherish and emulate.

MILES DAVIS: BIOGRAPHY

Miles was born Miles Dewey Davis II, on May 26, 1926, in Alton, Illinois. He died on September 28, 1991. Davis grew up in an upper-middle-class family. Davis's father was a dentist who, along with his wife, had high hopes for all the Davis children. His parents encouraged Miles Davis to excel. "Uncle Johnny," a close family friend, presented nine-year-old Davis with his first trumpet. Miles Davis took music very seriously. In his autobiography, Davis recalls the excitement he felt listening to the old radio show *Harlem Rhythms*, which regularly featured the music of Louis Armstrong, Lionel Hampton, Bessie Smith, and Duke Ellington. Davis also attributes his musical curiosity to his many visits with his grandfather in Arkansas and remembers the power of the down-home church Gospels and rural Blues. These early impressions helped him conceptualize the sound of his own music.

When he was 13, Davis's father gave him a new trumpet. With this instrument Davis began to study seriously with Mr. Buchanan, his high school band director. He continued with another teacher, a German named Gustav who was the first trumpet player in the St. Louis Symphony. With these experiences, plus the opportunity to play in a fine high school band, Davis began to venture out into the professional scene in St. Louis. He gained a local reputation as an up-and-coming trumpet player, which was no small task because of the city's tradition of producing excellent trumpet players. Clark Terry, for example, was just a few years older than Miles Davis.

In 1944, Billy Eckstine's band came to St. Louis and invited Davis to sit in for an absent trumpet player. Charlie Parker, Dizzy Gillespie, Art Blakey, and Sarah Vaughan all played in the band at that time. Davis, after playing with them, made up his mind that he had to be with Parker and Gillespie. Davis came up with a plan to get to New York. Against his mother's wishes but with his father's support, young Miles Davis left for New York to attend the Julliard School of Music. Davis spent his money and his nights roaming the streets of New York primarily in search of Charlie Parker.

Although Coleman Hawkins encouraged Davis to pursue his studies rather than Parker, Hawkins told Davis where Parker could be found, at the Heatwave Club on 145th Street in Harlem. Miles went there and desperate because he could not find him, stepped outside. There in the night Davis heard a voice say, "Hey Miles, I heard you been looking for me." It was Charlie Parker. Over the next few years Davis learned from both Parker and Dizzy Gillespie, two great mentors who, in Miles Davis's words were his "main influences and teachers." Davis spent his days at Julliard and his nights in the Harlem clubs with Parker. Davis says, "we were all trying to get our masters degrees and Ph.D.s from Minton's University of Bebop under the tutelage of professors Bird and Diz." School could no longer hold his interest and Davis, after a semester and a half, left Julliard to begin his career as Miles Davis, the legend.

A person's level of achievement is measured by the effect their humanity or artistry has on others. A positive effect is a true yardstick to measure accomplishment. Miles Davis's impact and influence upon other artists is probably his greatest achievement. He was one of the music world's greatest teachers in the history of Western music making. Miles Davis has inspired and worked with a number of artists including Teddy Riley, Kenny Garret, Marcus Miller, Prince, Darryle Jones, Branford Marsalis, Wynton Marsalis, Mike Stern, Al Foster, John McLaughlin, Dave Holland, Joseph Zawinul, Chick Corea, Jack Dejonette, Lenny White, Wayne Shorter, Herbie Hancock, Ron Carter, Tony Williams, John Coltrane, Cannonball Adderley, Sonny Rollins, Horace Silver, Tommy Flanigan, Quincy Jones, Paul Chambers, Philly Jo Jones, Bill Evans, John Lewis, and Gerry Mulligan. These men went on to make "face" contributions in the music industry; many of them became legends like their mentor and master teacher, music conceptualist, trumpet stylist, and all around "sir bad dude," Miles

Davis. This is a testament to his genius, contributions, and magnitude as a great American artist.

I have attempted to create a context by which Sarah Vaughan, Miles Davis, and the African American aesthetic concepts of musical approach, the Sass and the Cool, can be consciously examined as artistic performance philosophy and theory. Their artistic contributions and the force of their aesthetic and historical contributions must be recognized in Western art making. Sarah Vaughan and Miles Davis are royal subjects in the kingdom of Black creative arts, but they cannot be surpassed in the old, stale kingdom of Eurocentric aesthetic theory and history. I think they do well to sit there within that realm as queen and king as people shout "Long live the Queen, 'Sassy Sarah,' and long live the King, 'Cool Ass' Miles!" They are truly two of the most important staples of African American artistic expression. Thank you Sarah, and Miles, man, stay cool.

Poetry, Blues, Rhetoric, and Prayer for the Complacent: Wearing Afros in Late 199?

(January 1993)

$\mathcal{N}$ow that the world is surely falling apart, it cannot be said in enough wayz that these must be the END TIMZ. The countdown has begun, and we bear witness and weep. Social chaos in race and class, war and threats of war in every quarter, violence multiplied by violence plus deadly disease, families devastated and divided as our earth crumbles, shakes, and burns.

I don't think King could see this in his dream, and upon seeing it Malcolm would wake from his nightmare. With eyebrows raised, we scratch our heads, poke down lips, situation SERIOUS! Approaching the new century, we will walk into new dark shadows with fear and curiosity. Must one really retreat to a quiet peaceful zone for safety and peace of mind?

Children kill children, death by senseless murder is given out by these who wear this destruction as a badge of honor, the right proof of "Who I is." The songwriters and the movie script sketchers, as production effect, project a staple for success, the Gansta' of Death, hero fo' da peoples, what up dog? Black folk are destroyed by a lack of knowledge and exploitive industries and the media that views them as "the despised onez, and the onez responsible." And some weasel named Murray ignorantly turns a bell upside down and asks them to take pride in their "inferior clan." Church and politics, government and industry are filled and fueled by scandal. It's hard today!

I'm doing well, and I travel in circles where people are not so badly affected, but the effects of this crumbling society touches them too. Nobody escapes the craze from the concrete jungle and many are trapped within the hedges of suburban unspeakables. Everybody is concerned, yet unconnected, and there are too few alternatives to the downslide slip.

I have reached a very sad state of mind, a complacency I know is selfish, dismal, and defeatist. I sometimz scream out, "Let 'em kill themselves, it was their choices. I chose well!"

I weep in shame and pray, "God Black Mother of us all, create within me a desire, a love for my world, these timez and these desperate communities, and a hope for a change in our sad state of affairs." But youth is no longer on my side, that is, youthful naïveté and optimism.

I'm then complacent to enjoy the privileges of my accomplishments, and the cushions of my awards, while I see my sistas and brothers less fortunate wallow, as I think I see it, in their "own mess." I sit here writing, facing snowcapped mountains, while visiting, being well put up, contemplating the affairs of "otherz." How sad! I am no use to any community in such a way of thinking. But I'm caught between a deserved pride in my hard work and sacrifices, and a God-given humanity which demands responsibility for my brother. The art I create, the book I sketch, the lectures I give, and the reflections I ponder are for select audiences, elite almost, but far too many of my own will never benefit from their own product. Oh Franz, my Black skin and this wretched white mask! This is the awful dilemma that so many of my friends face, as we search for our inevitable call for meaning and purpose. The White institutions we serve drink us dry, fry us burned, and exploit our gifts to designed selfish ends while holding up in our sweat-drenched faces their own peoples' accomplishments as "far superior." I wonder were we all poisoned in our pursuits of academic excellence and artistic refinement?

While these dayz in the late-1990s Black Americans are facing some of the worst battles in our entire 400-year-plus period, "certain of us" are advancing to unbelievable places, surpassing our White counterparts, nothing new, just the flavor of it is more bitter now. This because while the juices of our accomplishments are "berry-er," our conscious is strained by cousins, uncles, brothers, and sisters in jail, doped out, babied up, in a mind craze, and in turmoil and painz beyond belief and help. My God, what do we make of such discrepancies in our present historical track, in our social design?

No one, no preacher, not even Cornel West, not Jesse, silent these days, nor the poet of grace Maya, no politician, no Rap artist has any suggestion that leads us to enact a realistic, informed, and sensitive process for recovery! Oh brother DuBois, the souls of these Black folk are becoming Blacker than you warned of! This is where we are wearing Afros in 199?

Black pride? "Mariah Careyism" carries quite a cost! As for a Black man, a shot of four o'clock Oprahism! What do we do with Michael Jackson? Sad. O. J. Simpson, Mike Tyson, Tupac Shakur, Ben Chavis, implied woes or weaved injustices? Sadder! Our Black artists, Black institutions, politicians, preachers, our shiningest pride?!

It's sad that I retreat into a mind-set of complacency and detachment, where I sit so comfortable assessing the case of the misguided, blaming the uninformed, and intellectually sneering at White males because I know "the history."

Perhaps, those of us who sit so comfortably can begin to band together, use our gifts and resources and lift up a unified vision-filled prayer, release and dismantle the rhetoric, create a powerful poetic (meaning meaningful plan), and change the key of our Blues-songs to tonalities that operate in registers of meaningful changes. Then, and then only, can our complacency justify our pursuits for peace of mind and make "real" our present accomplishments as we pick out our Afros in 199?

3
TWO INTERVIEWS WITH THE AUTHOR

· *16* ·

The Work: Illuminating the Way and
Moving the People Beyond (1997)

AN INTERVIEW OF WILLIAM BANFIELD
BY BRIAN C. BROWN

Brian C. Brown: What vision do you bring in your involvement as an artist/educator?

William Banfield: As the holder of an endowed chair in Arts and Humanities, I am aware that this is a post that was set up at my university to have scholars and artists within the academy encourage interdisciplinary studies. It was set up to teach courses within the humanities, whether it be in literature and English, or sociology, or music, or whatever. One of the principles of the endowed chair is that person would generate courses and initiatives that link the humanities in an interdisciplinary fashion.

That's one of the things that I've always been involved with, both as an undergraduate and in my master's program, as well as the work that I began to do at the University of Michigan with my studies there. In the past I have had to struggle with interdisciplinary studies because it wasn't a part of the psyche and the mechanism of the traditional college at the time. I was discouraged. But it is quite prophetic and timely that such a studies initiative is now a part of the thinking of the academy as we are trying to get people and students to think more about integrated knowledge and integrated experiences. So that someone taking a course in political science needs to look at how art works or the media works within that, and that person is more informed and has a more balanced perspective.

This approach to arts and education resonated with all the things I believe about education and educational initiatives connecting with artists and artists' role in society. I mean that was my master's thesis area. It was actually a master's in theology. I looked at Richard Wagner and the politics of Wagnerian opera and his understanding of philosophy from Schopenhauer and Nietzsche, and about the great human soul, and artistic attempts to struggle existentially with self and social meaning. And so, as an interdisciplinary study that master's helped me prepare for that.

I taught in Religion and Near Eastern Studies at the University of Michigan. And at IU (Indiana University) I taught in African American Studies and Music which are interdisciplinary programs.

Here at my university (The University of St. Thomas) we initiated an American Cultural Studies program. I proposed it along with 12 faculty members as a minor in the study of American cultural experience as it relates to music, literature, and the arts and contemporary experience. To accompany that we conducted a symposium on American Cultural Studies which received enthusiastic support from the National Endowment in the Humanities. I invited cultural critic Henry Louis Gates and musicologist Susan McClary to come and help inaugurate the program. I am serving as director of American Cultural Studies. We proposed bringing together some 30 courses which were courses that were already on the books, and now are under the rubric of "American Cultural Studies."

This includes four courses I developed with colleagues: The Theology of American Popular Music; Black American Music: A Historical Survey; Consuming Ideologies: Music and Rhetoric in Popular Culture; and Introduction to American Cultural Studies. These are the courses I teach, in addition to composition.

BCB: You often speak of the power of collaboration. And you certainly have had an impact on your students. But have your students influenced you in your own composing, in your own music?

WB: Sure, most definitely. And working with students one-to-one in composition and creative construction really allows you to get beyond the books to a kind of real spiritual exchange, especially in composition. Because what music is, is the concretized understanding of someone's thinking, someone's reasoning, and someone's emotive makeup. I mean this is what I believe music is. Some people believe music is a scale that you manipulate. Well, I think most artists and most musicians believe that music is a creative force, it's a creative ideology, it moves and has its own way, but it also works within the psyche of the artist. It's their world and their expression.

So that alone necessitates, in a kind of an exchange when you are teaching composition, a real personal discussion about what that musical note means and how to organize that in a way that expresses both what the student is feeling and seeing and how that makes sense. My job as a teacher is to have them make that creativity make sense in a structure.

So, you are talking about a real engaged enterprise when you are talking about composition. Absolutely those students influence me because they tell me what they are thinking. And then it teaches me and it challenges me to rise up yet another level to get to what I need to say to encourage them to move toward what their dream is. And everybody is different. There are no two or three composers who write and have the same experience. So, every time I have the chance to sit down with someone for 14 or 15 weeks, it gives me an opportunity to exchange with that person. So, that's why I think teaching like that is very taxing in a good way. It takes a lot of energy. You can't just go in and prepare and then leave because it continues to live with you each day. And so, when they're writing, I'm kind of writing and responding to that. So that's very instructive to me.

BCB: You have taught a course titled "The Theology of American Popular Music." Mass media would have us believe that these are two contrasting ideas, that there can't be a religious or spiritual influence in popular music. How do you reconcile that notion with your students?

WB: I do that in many ways. First we go back to the basics of the foundations of music. There are certain principles within the Western notion, but I move from two angles, both the western European notion of history and philosophy and also the African notion of being and philosophy. And when the students see that popular music is the marriage of both of those ideologies, and if you look at it from both the angle of their spiritual implications in both of those traditions, they come away understanding very clearly that popular music is the result of both and a modification of what might be a spiritual quest for that Blues singer, or that Gospel singer, or even in some cases the Rock and Roll singer, and certainly the Jazz performer.

And so, they are able to see that. We start with the whole Greek notion of music being able to affect human thought and behavior. And that's why there were so many rules against it because people would hear the music and they would become ecstatic and there was this thing that the powers "to be" could never control. You see, that tells you right there that it's (music) about something that's transcendent, that there is something beyond. That's why music is so powerful.

So when that's used for good purposes it's very easy to see how one can have an understanding that their role as a creative agent has to do with connections with things that are beyond the finite toward the infinite. And I think that's where the philosophical understanding of it comes from the West.

When you look at cultures in the larger world beyond Europe, like Africa and other cultures, they understand music primarily to be the connection between the individual speaking and the Theos. And in African theology the whole notion is: we think therefore we are, as opposed to: I think therefore I am. So everything I do relates to my community and it has no reason, no meaning, unless that community is connected to the Theos. So there you see the connection between community alliances and the individual being a respected and an understood connection with that community, and that God gives blessings to that.

There is an African saying that says, "The spirit will descend with a good song." And what that means is that God is connected to that experience when the song is good because the song is good aesthetically when it relates to and is a reflection of the community in total. That's why in the Black church when the spirit hits there is ecstasy. And that's part of the religious experience. Because the music helps to usher that in.

When we get to the western European tradition, because of the way history has gone, that element gets left out. So that in order to hear the true voice of God, supposedly one would sit there in quiet contemplation. But if you go back to the Scriptures, it says make a joyful noise before the Lord. And so, you see that these two things always go hand in hand.

In short, what happens in popular music is that the songs that became a part of the popular mainstream were songs that grew out of the camp revival meetings. These were spiritual revival meetings and these were the hymns from Europe. These Africans had their own read on this and they gave it a kind of stylistic spin, and the reporters and the Europeans were saying, "The Africans slaves are going on and 'carrying on' in ways which are beyond what these hymns are about."

And the whole commodification of popular music began with these Black folks doing different things with this western European music and so we get the Spirituals, we get the Blues, Ragtime, and Jazz and all popular music, whether its Country and Western or Rock 'n' Roll, it gets its aesthetic spin from that. And many artists have maintained that "spiritual" connection. They are saying, "What I do is a part of my spirituality." And so, though it may come in a popular form, if you look beneath that, you will find these kinds of convictions that they have. And so, the course tries to look at both of those things. And then you look at what religion is and what theology is. Theology is the logos (knowledge) about the works and the thoughts of humans about the Theos. So any time anybody is doing that it becomes relevant for theological discourse. And certainly when an artist is seen, even if they are yelling out at God in their song, it is relevant for theological examination.

BCB: You have mentioned in the past that the composer's duty is to reflect their society. How do you do that personally in your music?

WB: That has been an easier thing for me because those things were always a part of my training. And when I went to divinity school, that was what I set out to do. Then I went to West Africa and I saw that concern for one's society was always a part of the traditional African experience. So that again energized me. Then through studies of people like Wagner and all kinds of people like Messiaen and those folks, that gave me the justification from the European notion.

I think of myself as an artist using imagination, care, and excitement about people and life, to craft and construct works which connect and corroborate with, underline or make commentary on, things we all experience. There is a conscious effort to immerse myself in the navigation of what it is to be spirit and joy-filled, anxious, excited, awestruck and taken by, Black, American, born in 1961, and from Detroit. All of these things and a gazillion ideas, experiences, people, travels, and common lines from the texts of life, compel me to write. I believe music making is one of the great forms of a certain kind of literature we have. I define literature in this sense: composers—creative music makers—are the authors of narratives, novels, and the poetry many recite in their inner worlds each day. We bring concrete sound to those unspoken narratives, and the music is a combination of all the literature we read from poetry to film, to Alvin Ailey dance movement, to every Rap, rhyme, song, Blues or opera we take in. Music, from rough, vernacular Blues, to symphony, is a text of marked significance which embodies the experiences of human conditions.

My music is a synchronization of all those perspectives and I try to create my own voice in that. I have opportunities to always write music that I think comes from the heart and inspires people toward beauty or sometimes toward more critical societal reflection. But certainly, I want somebody to walk away and feel like, "Wow, that music really said something, really moved me." And if it moves people, then it's doing the work of a spiritual nature because people are being moved beyond where they are.

I had a theology professor, Gordon Kaufman, and, while he was very radical, I asked him what theology should do. And he always would say, "Theology's job is to illuminate the way and move people on." And I always remembered that as something I need to be doing and so I always considered my music to be theologically based; as long as it did that, it illuminated them in some way and it moved people on. And so that's what I try to do.

BCB: In a recent interview you mentioned that the academy has done a lot of damage to the creative artist. Could you comment on that?

WB: I tried to say that from an experiential perspective. Having gone through the academy at New England Conservatory, then Boston University and the University of Michigan, then teaching at both Michigan and Indiana University, I am speaking from the perspective of an artist, having gone through these programs and seeing that in fact the academy, while it has done a tremendous job to codify conventions and histories, has done a lot of damage to creative artistic spirit. Because it is an institution, it is not designed to foster creativity. But it should be sympathetic and should inspire people to be creative.

We lose that when we get in our board meetings and we get in our pedagogical, institutional kinds of ideologies and political and stylistic approaches. It does damage to the students. So, there needs to be a balance in courses, particularly in the arts, that deal with history and theory. But then move theory and history toward conception, creativity, concept and proper application.

The students aren't going out so that they can sit in their room and memorize the theories they learn. They are supposed to use these theories as examples of how things were constructed.

In order to allow them to step out on a foundation so they can be free and liberated from these theories, any great artist you look at may start with a theory then move on to self-expression. We don't deal with that, particularly in music; we stay with the theoretical and say that you have to understand this and do this in order to be musical. That's not correct. You're musical first, you're artistic first, you're creative first, you're human first, and then you learn these things to help govern these things and put them in a framework so that people can appreciate your creativity.

There is a saying that my teacher used to say: "Any man or woman in the shower can be creative, but the composer knows what to do with that creativity." I think there needs to be a balance. The institution should be set up with a balance of courses. So, what I hope to do as an educator within the curriculum of music and the humanities offerings is provide an understanding of what a creative artist does in addition to memorizing their theory.

I like my role as an artist who educates, because it allows me to engage with students outside of music, beyond the agenda of whatever they do. That's the role of the humanities right now, to humanize the institution or as the students say, "Keep it real."

BCB: Growing up in Detroit, what were your musical influences?

WB: In the case of a lot of African American households, it is a very eclectic kind of thing. And I say this having gone through this and having talked to a lot of folks in the arts about what their influences were. Our house was full of Beethoven and Ellington, Pavarotti and Al Green. There was this wonderful mix of all these things. My parents would take me to the symphony. And my church, which was a huge, progressive Black church, would do the anthems and the Bach and Beethoven, but they also had a Gospel choir, too. That's what African American ideology is all about. It is about this great amalgamation of these perspectives, both American Western and those things that are part of the retention from African life and culture. And is a part of the shaping an African American identity.

And so, the outcome of that is, in many cases, unlike what the media projects, which is what I fight against, is this one narrow vision of what culture is all about. It's really about all these many influences. That's what I had around my house. We had Dinah Washington and we had some Beverly Sills singing some Broadway thing. So, this was what influenced me early on. I mean, Jimi Hendrix was a big influence. But then, when I was in high school I wanted to be just like both Ellington and Johannes Brahms running around in Vienna trying to find himself. Then when I got into school and saw how hip these European avant-garde composers were, I was then influenced by Stravinsky and what he was doing in mixing cultures. And there were also guitarists. So, there are a number of performing artists: Andres Segovia as well as Jimi Hendrix and Wes Montgomery. So, those things influenced me from all angles. Definitely Ellington and definitely Stravinsky, but definitely Leonard Bernstein, too. He was a big influence on me. I had a chance to meet him and he encouraged me before he passed away to continue mixing African American idioms within symphonic and American musical mediums and conventions. Bernstein encouraged me to create something that was absolutely unique in terms of my own voice but absolutely American. And that would be a contribution that I could make to this culture musically. And I am continuing to try to do that. So, he was a very big influence on my thinking.

BCB: You are involved in so many different projects. What is the common draw for you? In other words, what pulls all of your interests together?

WB: Creative activity. Absolutely. I think I was just born to be creative. This has been a real problem. It's a joy now because I'm older and I can walk away from some of the criticism and some of the challenges that I have because I have been blessed to have done a lot at (I guess I'm still young) a young age, so it allows me to have a little freedom and not to be intimidated by some of the opposition we all go through. But certainly when you are involved in a lot of things you get more opposition. To whom much is given, much is required, as the saying goes. And so you take those things in stride. No matter what, the bottom line is creativity.

I remember an undergraduate English teacher who said, "I'm convinced that what you are doing has merit, but I really don't read what you write." And so, I was always trying even to a fault, to be creative in the way I pulled things together. Even my writing was very creative in a problematic way for the English professor. So creativity is the bottom line. As long as I'm being creative, I try to keep myself happy in that regard.

BCB: In your talk titled "Creating Opera from Multiple Traditions," you reference the end of the century. How is the year 2000 going to influence your music?

WB: Well, only in the sense that since we are living through it, it serves as a historical marking for us. All the work that I'm presently involved in (teaching, essays, operas, piano concerto, symphony, Jazz performance works) have all become my first large-scale expressions of the millennium. These works express in my mind the best things I felt that I absorbed during our last months of the twentieth century. I wanted my works to be a great pairing, a comfortable and effective bringing together of the best of what I took in mentally, spiritually, and musically. The millennium mark was for me an attempt, at least in some principle, to move out and ahead. Everything's not going to change anytime soon, but this realization that I was moving to a new period was very real in my creative thinking.

And, there should be a change from the perspective that things are "new," that we are "moving along." Every group of artists addressed this at every new century. It's not that one date is supposed to change everything. But certainly people should be thinking that 100 years is a pretty good time to test something out. If it isn't working within a hundred years, let's try something else. You know, I think that's a fair rule. So, from that angle, I think everybody is thinking about doing some different things. And I think that's fair.

And I think that's a good thing to do. The world's not going to change that much in the years following 2000. But how this relates to art is that it gives you a good chance to look at the last 100 years to see what we've done and what conventions have come up. What kinds of approaches we've used; how the public has addressed these things; how have we done in education; what are we doing in our creative avenues and institutions. What have we done? What things can we do that are new? And what should we be implementing now? So it's a great opportunity for us to re-address all those things and I'm addressing it musically and culturally, as so many artificial barriers and categories have now been brought down and our cultural, stylistic and national sensibilities are converging. The breakdown of the barriers in art between what's classical and what's popular, and what's high and what's low is happening. We're trying to break that down a little bit because in the classical arts, that is in "art" music, the standard is high, which it should be. But unfortunately, the high standard breeds a kind of exclusivity that is problematic. And what should happen with high culture is it should invite everybody in to reach for the high goal.

The high goal is not something that should be limited to those who have only the preparation or only the influence to reach that. I mean, the high goal is something that everybody should have access to. So, in the case of a symphony orchestra, the person who donates $5,000 or $10,000 to the orchestra should most definitely be there. But what about that kid who never had a chance to hear that. Well, in my case, when I heard the orchestra, I said "Wow! Just think of how many Jimi Hendrix tunes I can write now!"

I saw this as an opportunity for my songs to be played by the symphony orchestra. So then I tried to get the skills necessary so that my music could be spoken through the voice of the violin or the trumpet or whatever. So, that's really the way it should be. But if I were never exposed to that, I would never have known. One of my high school teachers had a doctorate. And so I said, "Doctorate in music? What is that?" And he explained that to me. He explained theory and history and culture and then I wanted a doctorate in music so I could do my music "better."

So that's one of the walls that we hope the contemporary artist is able to break down. If you come hear my symphony, you're going to hear American influences of the Blues and Jazz, as well as popular music, things you wouldn't have heard in Beethoven. But Beethoven was doing the popular music of his day, which we don't talk about. That's not classical music. He stole music from the peasants in the traditional sense of how they meant it, from the common folk who were in the street. Their songs were then put in Beethoven's symphonies. So, that's what I think we need to be doing with symphony orchestra and opera. That is, using the "stuff" of our times to tell the stories.

My mom went to see Ellington when she was 14 or 15 or so. And he came out at the beginning of the set and said, "And what would you like to hear this evening, little lady?" And so consequently what I did about a year or two ago, I wrote a big band piece for a big band orchestra. And the name of the piece is "And what would you like to hear, little lady?" And it's taken from that experience my mother had as a child when Ellington asked her what would she like to hear.

BCB: For you, what is the creative "mark," the staple of creative excellence of the twentieth century?

WB: Jazz as a musical movement of culture, style, and as a language. Jazz is one of the most important creative movements in the history of mankind. That is not verbiage. That is not overstated. I can say that as someone who not only loves the music, but also as someone who has studied and can speak with authority in that regard. That of all human artistic movements, the spiritual, intellectual, cultural, political, and musical movements, it is one of the most important.

One thing that we haven't done in the traditional academy is study Jazz music fully as a cultural movement. If you look at the lines of Charlie Parker, you are going to find the lines that are equally as intricate as Bach lines. Bebop worked on this notion of outlining very intricate chords without even stating the chords. They were stated through the melody. So contrapuntally it's the same kind of technique that Bach and so many of the western European composers used to outline their tunes.

As a matter of fact, Charlie Parker had never heard Bach's music until very late in his life. He once said to somebody at a party (and that person told a good friend and teacher of mine), "Why didn't you guys tell me about this guy Bach?" And then he started to study it. But he had already set down a very intricate pattern in his compositions that was based on this contrapuntal creation of this line which defined and outlined a very intricate sonorities. So, from that angle, it's such a technical art form. But at the same time it's a very liberating art form and very much involved with the human expression. It's the best of both worlds. It has taken on universal kinds of meanings. And that's why it's a great movement, not only in the art form but in what it says. What Jazz has done for the American culture is that it has become our staple around the world. And so, it's unfortunate that it's not studied with the kind of critical issues and questions that should be addressed to it in the academy.

· 17 ·

An Interview with William Banfield
(James P. Johnson, Duke Ellington, Anthony Braxton, and the AACM) by Alan Baker, Minnesota Public Radio, March 2003

This interview was conducted as part of "American Mavericks" by Minnesota Public Radio. You can find out more at: musicmavericks.org.

Alan Baker: What connections can we make with James P. Johnson, Duke Ellington, and other developments in early Jazz?

William Banfield: What I think we're talking about is tracking the development of orchestrated or enlarged Jazz or Black music forms. From Spirituals to Blues to Rag to the concert things we see now in these larger orchestra pieces that utilize Jazz practice tradition and are heard in larger forms and ensembles.

This notion of orchestrated Jazz has an incredible and wonderful history, so by the time James P. Johnson is doing his piano and clarinet concertos, and we're familiar with Gershwin and certainly Ellington, you see people who are taking risks and experimenting with ad hoc instrumentation. This all started very early on, actually, as musicians began to pull together performance practices from the Spirituals or Blues (to chicken bones even). Rhythmic ideas of pulling these things together. We see this going on. Also, we have to mention Scott Joplin who was also doing early experimentation. We are talking about the late nineteenth century. It's already a practice in place and being notated by Scott Joplin and others in the Ragtime period, and by the late nineteenth century we have all the musicians in New Orleans who were attempting to do the same thing. They were bringing Spirituals, Blues, European band music, and performing in smaller ensembles with mixed instrumentation so that the musicians have the capacity to do all kinds of things, to improvise as well as do things from the score.

So James P. Johnson and Gershwin, who are starting to dream about this thing in the '20s, have really remade a tradition that's already going on. That's what's really important.

One of the pioneers in this effort is James Reese Europe, who in May of 1912 performed at Carnegie Hall with his Clef Club Symphony Orchestra. If you listen to the orchestration in that enterprise alone, 125 Black musicians doing an ad hoc instrumentation using mandolins, banjos, five trap sets, ten pianos. Basically, he said what he was attempting to develop a kind of symphony music that, no matter what you might think, it's different and distinctive. It lends itself to particular compositions of the race. Already, he's talking about how the music has to match the instrumentation, and, if you do it, you have to do it with a different kind of instrumentation. He was a pioneer in this effort, and we're talking about Carnegie Hall in 1912! By the time Paul Whiteman comes on the scene, and Benny Goodman, and George Gershwin, and all those that follow including James P. Johnson, they are already modeling what James Reese was doing in the early part of the century.

As a child, James P. Johnson is also watching his parents play. They are doing ring-shout dances, Spirituals, and Blues at the piano at home. Johnson is a child prodigy who is born with perfect pitch. Not only is he hearing everything, he's also watching the putting together of all these performance practices. Very early on, this is a part of how he sees the world musically. When he and Gershwin are dreaming about taking Black popular forms, the Spirituals, the Blues, the Ragtime, and putting them in larger orchestrated forms, they are dreaming about this in the '20s and making these piano rolls, and they both decide to do this. The interesting thing about this is that George always had a friendship with musicians and colleagues in Harlem.

When Ellington and Johnson are doing this in Harlem, all of these guys are in New York and Gershwin is there too. William C. Handy has written a book and he is orchestrating the Blues while this is going on. George Gershwin is a wonderful part of this discussion. Both of these gentlemen attempt to do this. Gershwin gets the credit for it and his works are great, but at the same time he becomes a great inspiration and a continual inspiration for James P. Johnson who then is able to initiate his pieces later on. We're talking about his Jazz piano concerto from 1934; we're talking about his clarinet concerto in 1942. This is his dream to bring those vernacular forms to the concert stage and to orchestrate them for larger works and forms. He is able to do that. He does musicals and ballets. His opera in 1942 is a collaboration between him and Langston Hughes. Earlier this year, we had the premiere of this piece in Michigan that had been sitting for a long time.

AB: We don't think about James P. Johnson's name first, but it seems like he was a very significant player in the community. Talk a little bit about his significance historically.

WB: James P. Johnson is considered the "Father of Stride Piano." That's how you've publicly come to know him. That's only one aspect of his work. He had these other aspirations from his parents and also from hanging out in Harlem at the time and really being impressed by what's called the "Race Men" ideology. There were great thinkers starting with Martin Delany. Then in 1903, we get W. E. B. DuBois's *The Souls of Black Folks*. There is a Black intelligentsia that are writing about upholding the race and expanding the forms that Black folks are using in literature and in music.

That inspires James P. Johnson. He is in Harlem and doing the Harlem Renaissance, doing the Jazz Age and so he is a part of all of this. The most popular way we come to know him is as the "Father of Stride Piano." It is this very virtuosic piano approach that is the next leg and arm of Ragtime. This is how we come to know him. At the same time, he's writing music with his mentor Fats Waller, and he is also a songwriter. He's also accompanying Bessie Smith and Ethel Waters. He's writing musicals and then hanging out with Gershwin. The idea is that he's going to take these forms, and "You and I, Gershwin, are going to write these large orchestrated pieces for symphony orchestra or large ensemble and then I'm going to take these ragtime piano pieces and these blues pieces and these show tunes and take it to the next level on the concert hall."

Gershwin was able to do this and James P. Johnson was able to do it. He continued to study as well: contemporary harmony and counterpoint and theory. He was making those applications as well in addition to studying orchestration. By the late '30s and '40s, this is when the other larger pieces are beginning to emerge: his "Harlem Symphony" in 1932, a piano concerto in 1934, a clarinet concerto in 1942, and so we see that he is able to work consistently up to his death.

AB: Tell me a little about what we are hearing in the "Harlem Symphony" and in the confluence of all that music that comes out in the larger forms.

WB: What you are hearing is a well-developed Ragtime style. Vestiges of Black church music, certainly the Blues, and you are also hearing a lot of popular music traditions that you would hear in the minstrel show, in the vaudeville and Tin Pan Alley traditions. He's mixing all of that together. He's also aware of the classical form. There are some of those traditional forms that are being spun out.

You are hearing all of these things together and at the time it was "experimental." It was new. Now it seems very common to us. These gentlemen were true trailblazers to bring all of these forms together, and at a time when the country was still divided on how to value the vernacular forms. By the time we get to Duke Ellington, his attempt is to do the same thing. He gets the critical acclaim for it in 1943. The critics are confused and they say, "We don't understand what he is doing." Gershwin, James P. Johnson, and Duke Ellington, when you look at that period, then you get to see what it is they are doing. They were trying to shake out this interest between what was "popular" and what was "classical." That's the formula that we are still trying to shake out.

AB: Talk about the premiere of "Black, Brown, and Beige" and that struggle in Ellington's music.

WB: "Black, Brown and Beige" in 1943 was a media event at Carnegie Hall because it was well publicized in popular print, it was well attended by the leading critics in art circles and his supporters at the time, and Duke Ellington had a number of successes internationally. There were a lot of things written about the work of Duke Ellington. We have a major star here at age 44. The critics could like him. It was okay to like Duke Ellington. So the concert was very much appreciated and highly written about. The critics had a problem with "Black, Brown and Beige" because of the premise that this was a tone poem that would somehow pull together the entire history of the African American. It was an interesting idea to do musically, but many of the critics had a problem being able to pull it together. They saw it more as a wonderful vehicle for several Jazz tunes. The synthesis of this larger form with the Jazz energy, they really didn't understand this. Paul Bowles wrote that it was an "impossible synthesis" and that these two styles are on different wavelengths. The classical mind-set is on a different wavelength than the Jazz or popular music, and that people would walk away confused. That's what people noticed, that they were sure they liked everything that was going on, but there were various ways to interpret that. "There were good moments here and there, but 'Black, Brown and Beige' we didn't quite get." When you listen to it now, the many recordings of it now, it was quite an adventuresome piece. It was quite beautifully done, but just like "The Rite of Spring," people didn't get it. It's the same thing.

We may get into trouble for comparing the "Black, Brown and Beige" premiere to "The Rite of Spring." But the same consciousness is there. What we are doing is breaking into some new territory. Audiences are not sure what that is because they have not heard it. The artist is left with trying to pull together these things, and be true to his own voice, and be true to tradition, and at the same time move ahead. This is difficult.

AB: Do you think that the breaking of those rules made people uneasy? They didn't know how to absorb it? Do you think that because of the notoriety that preceded the concert, do you think that they weren't prepared for it?

WB: I think that with any artist, when the popular culture sets a formula for that artist, that's what people want. When the artist decides to continue to grow, which is what Ellington was doing this whole time, people have a problem with that. They say, "No, we like that good thing that you do." This is something we see played out even today. When an artist decides to try to change a little bit, his or her core audience doesn't follow them down the path very often. This is the case with Ellington. It continued to be a problem as he tried to expand these forms. They were telling him, "No! This is what you should be doing." To a large degree he did that, but then we have recordings where he plays with John Coltrane, where he's hanging out and trying to get a sense of things. In the same way, he's not as forward or fast as Miles Davis, but certainly he is expanding the form. He experimented with the sounds within it by having players play violin or taking the orchestration and spinning it a different way. He was constantly experimenting from the very beginning. There is this interesting innovation going on with Ellington all of the time, even if his audience is not aware of his conscious attempt to innovate and go beyond the borders.

AB: Do you think that is because he is successful at maintaining his voice no matter what the forces employed.

WB: Absolutely. I think his voice is always there. That's a part of the thing that defines Ellington. The voice includes experimentation. Artists have a way of voicing and writing tunes. They have a particular palette that you come to know as their voice. That doesn't change. All the way up to the '60s and middle '70s. You still hear the Ellington voice, but he's trying to spin that voice. Every artist is always inspired and influenced by the other cultural forces that are around him or her. When Ellington is playing it safe and just doing what the people want, he's also concerned about social issues, particularly of Black folks. Sometimes people didn't want him to go there. He always was committed to that. He thought that his music was the way Black peoples' experiences were viewed and how those were explored and how those were growing.

He always stayed true to the folks. That's something that's beautiful about Ellington's work. Even though you hear it up on the stage, you still hear Black culture expanded and put on the concert stage. These folks didn't want you to lose the essence or the essentials of the culture in the music. They are just saying that it, too, can have this expanded form and be heard in these various ways.

AB: I'm assuming there was plenty of resistance from musical insiders who were giving concerts. Politically, talk a little about his struggles to keep his voice and make those statements in venues that may not have been welcoming.

WB: I'm not going to address that because it's well documented and I don't want to cite anything. *The Duke Ellington Reader*, edited by Mark Tucker, has many of the correspondences, but mostly the critical reviews and also has a lot of Ellington's own articles where he would talk about his music and works in music journals. You can see in his public discourse in the press that there were some questions where he stepped outside of what is his accepted role. Oftentimes, you can see this going back and forth. He was true to his plan from the very beginning.

He was attempting to provide people with entertainment, but it was enlightened entertainment. We use the word "entertainment" to mean just that: It's to make people feel good, but it's also to move people in various ways. I think that's what Ellington was always doing with his forms all the way from the '20s up to his death. You see it in the larger suites that he began to record. Those were an attempt to bring all kinds of North African music forms in, and so you see him dealing with this all the way through his life.

Now, when you get to Anthony Braxton, the AACM (Association for the Advancement of Creative Musicians), we also have a real attempt here to experiment. I think Anthony Braxton is the Black version of Schönberg or Babbitt. This is the Black intellectual avant-garde. They brought Black vernacular culture to the experimental framework. It's a different formula here. They are reconstituting forms and traditions. We were talking about James P. Johnson and Ellington who went to Black vernacular, but what's interesting about the Chicago movement in the '60s was the fact that they also went to social dynamics of Black folks. There was an incredible bursting open of new kinds of expressive modes. Political venues were being looked at. The establishment was being shot down, as it were. That's institutions of education, politics, and economics as well as musical institutions. That means the symphony orchestra and western European mechanisms. These were being shouted at. This is not only the Black avant-garde, but also the European avant-garde.

White American avant-garde was attempting to reconfigure music in different ways. The Chicago music looked to Africa. They saw in the way in which African music was organized, there was a spirituality of Africa, the notion of music as ritual. You aren't just doing something for the concert stage, but are really engaged with the audience. These were some of the other things that shaped the music and the movement.

Black social cause, American social cause. You have the avant-garde that's going on in both of these circles. Black traditional music circles and Jazz performers and traditional concert music performers are also breaking in new areas.

So there is a wonderful mix there. "Free Jazz," which came with Ornette Coleman's album in 1961, is an attempt to turn Jazz on its head again and just have no changes. Play exactly what the energy dictates in terms of the performers playing of the instruments. What does that tell us about where we are going to go as opposed to a score? This is kind of a radical thing. With this side of concert music, you had aleatoric practices, free associations. You had atonality and serialism going on. All of these forces together begin to converge and I think that the AACM and this group of musicians really brought all of this together in some very wonderful ways. Anthony Braxton becomes a central composer in that movement.

This whole Chicago movement was also trying to move away from the European notion of a sole composer, that there was a communal music that was important. It was important because that was central to the kind of social politics that were going on with the Civil Rights movement, which then got mechanized a little later on. You see how it's all moving together. They were also bent on playing original music and helping each other facilitate one another's music. They had the founding of the AACM on May 8; they drew up the papers in 1965. This ensemble and this political and musical group tried to keep all of these principles in place and they trained younger musicians in this way.

They did clinics, performances, and concerts where these musicians upheld the principles and ideas of the AACM.

TRITONE SUBSTITUTION: MUSICIANS IN TUNE AND IN TIME

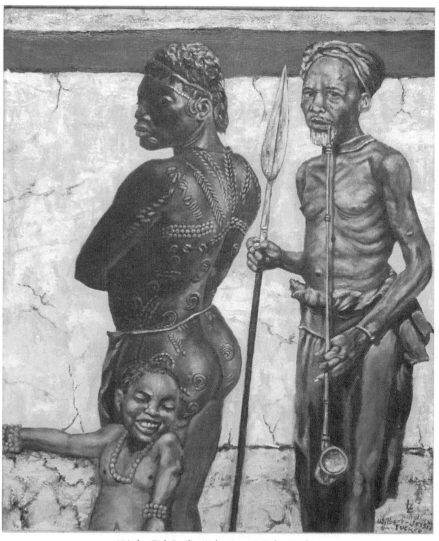

"Little Girl Smiling" by James Zeke Tucker

Radio Programs Introduction

I have hosted four radio programs, and the most recent aired from an NPR station, WCAL from St. Olaf College in Northfield, Minnesota, and MPR, Minnesota Public Radio. The program was called *Essays of Note*. I conceived of a program that would allow me to dig into and explore a wide variety of subjects related to musical artistry. The shows ranged from how we listen to music to asking, Whatever happened to Soul music? I mixed George Clinton with Schubert, explored the meaning of rhythm across traditions, and compared the orchestration techniques of a string quartet to that of a Bebop front line with tenor and trumpet. As well I covered artists from Chevalier de St. Georges Bologne, writing in the mid-1700s, to Quincy Jones, composer Libby Larsen to Sun Ra. *Essays of Note* was wide and wild! But it made it plain that contemporary artists are quite deliberately breaking down the walls and categorical divides that separate great music. I asked, "What is our responsibility to grasp the full expression of the culture of our times?" Here are some of the best of the show's essays, text only and no music.

· 19 ·

Q: The Music of Composer Quincy Jones

> Music was the one thing I could control. It was the one thing that offered me my freedom. When I played music my nightmares ended. My family problems disappeared. I didn't have to search for answers. The answers lay no further than in the bell of my trumpet and my scrawled penciled scores.
>
> —Quincy Jones[1]

*W*ho would you say is recognized as the most successful musician in the music industry? No, its not Strauss, nor Stravinsky, not even Leonard Bernstein, or Michael Jackson. The most successful person in the music industry is the composer Quincy Jones. "Quincy Jones?" you might say. "But isn't he a TV film scorer, or pop music producer, or film producer and big band director, or didn't he produce the Academy Awards last year or didn't he compose the music for the Summer Olympics?" You get my point. Quincy Jones the composer is one of the most successful all-around musicians of our time. One of the great masters of American music of all kinds, he never has stopped being his first dream, a composer.

> There was a tiny stage in a room with an old upright piano. I tinkled on it for a moment. That's where I began to find peace. I was eleven. Each note seemed to fill up another empty space I felt inside. Each tone touched a part of me that nothing else could touch. When I plunked those notes and laid down those first chords, I found trust, and began to learn how to hope and cope. The search for just the right piano notes soothed me. I'd found true love and nurturing. I'd found music. I'd found my mother.[2]

In this essay on Quincy Jones I want to share with you not only his music and doings from his life, but as well themes about music from his words released more recently in his autobiography, called *Q*.

Born in Chicago 1933, and later moving as a young child to Seattle, Quincy Jones has been involved as a composer, musician, producer, conductor, and film scorer making music for over 50 years. His record as a musician is unparalleled. No musician has penetrated the multiple industries as have Quincy Jones. As a child prodigy he backed up Billie Holiday, toured on the road with Lionel Hampton, began arranging and conducting the orchestras for Sarah Vaughn, Frank Sinatra, and Count Basie. And Quincy has always been a composer. Nadia Boulanger, the great "composers' teacher" who taught and influenced everybody from Aaron Copland, Milhaud, Messiaen, and Walter Piston, said two of the most influential musicians she ever knew were Stravinsky and Quincy Jones.

In France, I could envision my past, present and future as an artist and as a Black man. I took a wider view of the human condition that extended to both art and life and later helped me to take stock of global markets. I became comfortable as a citizen of the world. Studying at the American School of Music at Fontainebleau, Nadia Boulanger told me, "Sensation, feeling, belief, attachment and knowledge. That's what every artist strives for. The type of music is immaterial when you are aiming for those qualities."[3]

Known widely as well as a composer of popular TV show themes like *Ironside, Sanford and Son*, and *The Bill Cosby Show*, he also was the composer for such pathbreaking films as *The Pawnbroker, In Cold Blood, In the Heat of the Night*, and *The Color Purple*.

For me, I had always looked up to Quincy Jones as a great hero and composer. Just like you know a Ravel orchestration or the rhythmic and harmonic density of Stravinsky, there is also a distinctive composer's sound of Quincy Jones. Note the flugal, flute doubles, and treatment of the crafty inner line writing, tasty and economic use of voicing in the brass and woodwind writing, all of which have become Quincy Jones compositional staples.

Quincy Jones, like many musicians, ended up searching for work and quenching his desire to arrange in New York in the 1950s. On the road with the biggest entertaining recording/touring band in the country, Lionel Hampton, he had by 18 written and recorded his first large ensemble arrangements. In 1955 at the age of 22, Jones was asked by Dizzy Gillespie and the State Department to direct a touring Jazz orchestra to represent the United States in Europe. He traveled the world as a young conductor earning experience and sharpening his ear. He was thereafter appointed vice president of A&R at Mercury records, just in his early thirties and in charge of, in his words, "big orchestras and sweet divas." "Arranging is difficult work, but at its best it's like painting. The final product is beautiful to hear, a tapestry of different colors and textures and densities, a blend of experience, architecture, soul and science."[4]

As a producer and recording artist he has earned, count them: 76 Grammy Award nominations. He has earned 14 Grammys, including Best Instrumental Arrangement, Best Cast Album, Producer of the Year, and Album of the Year. He produced *Thriller* with Michael Jackson which went on to become the biggest selling album in music history. As well, he has been awarded the American Music Award, an Academy Award, Emmy, Presidential Arts and Humanities Award, and 15 honorary doctorates including: Howard, UCLA, New York, and Harvard Universities.

A hard school advocate of American popular music forms, he recently said, "American music is a life force. It's the music that the entire world has adopted as the voice of their Soul." Quincy Jones's most impassioned work, that which he lives for, is orchestration and composing. He is one of our most important American composers and musicians having brought together techniques and conventions out of western European, Blues, American song, Latin and world music, Jazz and Bebop, Rhythm and Blues, Soul to Hip Hop. Like Louis Armstrong, Aaron Copland, Leonard Bernstein before him, he is one of the most influential figures in music and the model of a truly great American musical artist.

· 20 ·

Mozart's Afro Cousin: Joseph, the Chevalier de St. Georges

$\mathcal{O}$f all the composers and musicians I've studied and admired, none of them are as fascinating and multilayered in their daily life practice as Black French classical composer Joseph Chevalier de St. Georges Bologne. Chevalier is an "opera story in the making. Born in 1745, Guadeloupe, West Indies, to a French nobleman and a Black West Indian, he was a very famous French musician of his day whose talents, accomplishments, and life are legend. In this essay, we will explore the work of this eighteenth-century composer, violinist, and conductor. Here is a man that was the French fencing champion at 17, a military officer in the French Revolution, a skater, target shooter, boxer, dancer, swimmer, violinist, composer, and conductor. Yet, we don't really hear much about this classical musician, Renaissance man, the absolute forerunner to the Paul Robesons of the twentieth century.

Chevalier was a composer whose portrait prints painted by American artist Mather Brown sold by the hundreds in London; he composed eleven symphonies, three operas, many comedies, a dozen string quartets, ten violin concerti, songs and arias, piano and violin sonatas; he snubbed Mozart his junior in Paris, conducted the most well-known Paris orchestra, and was influential in establishing the foundations for European classical tradition, and yet we today hardly hear of his work. A sketch of his career runs something like this: After years of study from his youth onward as a violinist, in 1769 following an invitation by his teacher, the famous French musician Francois Gossec, he joined the string section of the Concert des Amateurs, the most famous orchestra in Paris. In 1772 he became principal director of it. In 1773 he premiered, as performer, two of his violin concertos. In 1773 he published a first set of string quartets and by 1775 he had published 11 violin concertos after making his orchestra the most successful orchestra in Paris. He was invited to take over as the director of the Paris Opera but refused due to complaints from several leading ladies. Actually his first opera *Ernestine* was produced in 1777 and followed with another in 1778. Over the next twelve years he wrote four more opera-comedies.

I find his music from an artistic standpoint to be well crafted, reflecting solidly the forms and styles we have come to now term, classical. Chevalier's music is full bodied with character, rhythmic and melodic wit, contrapuntally engaging, very lyrical and imaginative. He was clearly in command of the forms of the day, as mentioned earlier along with his teacher and a group of innovative French artists were leading the way to help establish classical forms. You can hear this especially in the string quartets, which Joseph and this French school excelled in.

Joseph never forgot that he was Black, which is extraordinary given the historical circumstances as he lived during the height of slavery. He actually put together a band of Black West

Indians which he trained, conducted, and showcased. The ensemble became a leading attraction at Versailles.

During his life, in addition to his music work as well as numerous military posts, he directed the theater for the Duke of Orleans, Orchestrede la Loge Olympique, and the Cercle de L'harmonie. As one writer wrote, observing Chevalier near the end of his young life, "The famous Saint Georges could be seen conducting, leaving nothing to be desired as to the choice of pieces and superiority of execution."

A noted German poet, patriot, and friend wrote of his death, "On that day, they talked about nothing else. In all the theaters, promenades, cafes and gardens, in the streets they stopped to exchange the news, his name echoed in all the papers. . . . He was the perfect Frenchman, he was the Voltaire of equitation, music, dancing. . . . The French will admire him eternally." Chevalier St. Georges died from ulcers in 1799 at the age of 54.

21

James P. Johnson's Stride

I wanted to take a moment to focus in on the piano music of a special composer. When you hear Chopin, and you know it's Chopin, you really get the sense that Chopin the composer was a pianist. It's piano music we identify and hear as being from a composer who plays the instrument. The music is an outgrowth of what the composer really does as a musician. That is distinctly different I think from a composer who writes a piece to be played on an instrument that one simply assigns the music to be played on. In this essay, I want to focus on one of the most distinctive pianist/composers of American music culture, the piano work of James P. Johnson. Born in New Brunswick, New Jersey, in 1889, pianist James P. Johnson first learned piano from his mother after watching from the stairs numerous family gatherings where his parents hosted friends and family for meals that often included floor shows, Gospel songs, dances, and instrumental renditions on the piano. The unique "Stride Piano" style that Johnson was called the father of included the earlier forms of Ragtime, Southern rural dances, folk tunes, classical piano and the compositional styles, and approaches including early-twentieth-century popular song.

This type of piano playing and composition was not, as Ragtime was, for the everyday amateur. In fact, much of the Stride Piano school was formed by topflight New York pianists who sought to use the form as a showcase for piano virtuosity. By the time Johnson was in his early thirties, he was called the greatest Black pianist in New York by the leading musicians. James P. Johnson worked alongside George Gershwin writing for the Aeolian Piano Roll Company. During this time Johnson shared his dream with Gershwin to base works on traditional Black themes and styles and elevate them to the "concert stage." Gershwin clearly took this idea, literally, to the "concert stage."

What's clear in Johnson's conception is that melodic, harmonic sequences and theme development is not happenstance, but are clearly worked out and consciously developed as a part of the whole piano composition, despite its seemingly cavalier and effortless performance.

> Let me make a general observation. The test of first-rate intelligence is the ability to hold two opposing ideas in the mind at the same time, and still retain the ability to function. One should be able to see that things are hopeless and yet be determined to make them otherwise. To see the improbable, the implausible, often the impossible come true. Life was something you dominated if you were any good. Only in 1920 did the veil finally fall, the Jazz Age was in flower.[1]

So writes F. Scott Fitzgerald in *The Jazz Age.*

This is the era that James P. Johnson and young artists who lived in New York were swept into and Johnson's music epitomized the spirit of optimism and boldness so sought after as the virtue of the younger generation. And for a Black artist, the music helped to keep in mind the implausible and the possible, that's what Jazz is, its negotiation of "the changes."

During a later period in his life he studied composition, counterpoint, and orchestration, and out of this interest came his most ambitious works. One work he orchestrated was for large ensemble; it's entitled "Yamekrarw: A Negro Rhapsody," written in 1927. This work echoed his dream and aspiration to take reshaped folk tunes and share these in the concert world. Following in 1932 was his *Harlem Symphony: A Piano Concerto* and *Clarinet Concerto* in 1942.

After performances of his stage shows, several large concert works and work with singers and small ensembles, James P. Johnson who died in 1951 from a stroke, left an incredible body of compositions and recordings.

James P. Johnson was a pioneer who not only cemented an American piano music in our history, but was a path breaker in his dream to meld styles and tradition for the music of the future, our present.

22

Just Make Music: The Music of Douglas Ewart

I had the honor of speaking to Frank Foster, Count Basie's great arranger. He shared a bit of wise counsel he had received from the old master. "Swing that music and keep it simple kid." This got me thinking about how we sometimes in our fuss to do music, we too often forget about some of the basics of any great music. Even the old adage of classical music to cultivate "a succession of agreeable sounds," is grounded in the idea that music is a language of sounds and that musicians are sound organizers, and that sound comes to us in infinite ways. In this essay, the music of a musician who not only fashions his works by organizing sound, he as well makes the instruments that make the sounds: Douglas Ewart. Douglas Ewart, a native of Chicago and a member of the influential AACM school (Association for the Advancement of Creative Musicians), has been creating bamboo flutes and an array of musical instruments for over 25 years. Pieces from his *Bamboo Meditations at Banff* are just one example of how he makes music.

Douglas Ewart was born in Kingston, Jamaica, in 1946, and began at the early age of ten exploring the world of sound around him and designing his own instruments. He immigrated to the States in 1963. In the early seventies he began to study composition, saxophone, and clarinet at the Association for Creative Musicians School of Music in Chicago. This group, the AACM, created one of the most forward looking movements in contemporary music, spawning such innovators as Anthony Braxton, Joseph Jarman and the Art Ensemble of Chicago, and others. His work, "Red Hills," an Ewart composition, features his Clarinet Choir consisting of greats Don Byron, Anthony Braxton, Edward Wilkerson, Roscoe Mitchell, and Henry Threadgill. And get this, the ensemble includes E-flat bass and contra bass clarinets, E-flat soprano clarinet, E-flat contra alto clarinet, B-flat soprano clarinet, and E-flat alto clarinet. We should listen for instead of distinct melody, the hypnotic rhythm, the density of horn colors, and the interdependence of the ensemble to create a variety of expressive sounds.

The work, "Migration of Whales," again finds Ewart on B-flat bass clarinet joining his Clarinet Choir. But listen to the assured direction of this melody amid the dark tones and dissonance of the sonorities. For me, there is still beauty and melodic clarity despite such first seemingly clouded environments.

Ewart's *Ewartology* opens with an instrument he invented called the "Ewartphone," which he describes as a B-natural instrument with a B-flat tenor mouthpiece. In the Charles Mingus tradition of the testifying at the Wednesday night prayer meeting, Douglas draws upon the rich Spiritual-Blues tradition of the Black Southern rural church. But listen to the gorgeous, rich, and "weird tones" of this instrument. Notice as well how the other clarinets and bass in the ensemble join in just like a church testimonial. There are even ensemble players who vocalize and hum resonantly in the background. Ewart states for him as a musician, he is always looking for that unheard sound. Douglas Ewart's music resounds to us as a voice from our musical past, as well as sounds from our great-expected future. I hope you have enjoyed making music with Douglas Ewart.

23

Regina Carter

I remember well: it was 1980. I was a college sophomore at the New England Conservatory of Music in Boston. There in the venerable Jordan Hall in rehearsal was Regina Carter, sitting there playing Beethoven with the orchestra on a purple Barcus Berry electric violin. It seems even then that things with the violin would be different. Some twenty years later, Regina Carter has emerged as the most recognized and prominent voice in the Jazz violin world. In October of 2001 she had her debut with the Minnesota Orchestra and in 2003 with the Detroit Symphony.

In this essay, we will spend a few moments in music with violinist Regina Carter.

I actually remember Regina coming to my band rehearsal in the eighth grade. She was already a legend in her hometown, playing at age 14 with the chart topping R&B group Brainstorm and opening up for Michael Jackson. A native Detroiter, she is the product of the Susuki method and the public school system. After schooling at the New England Conservatory, Rochester University, living, studying, and performing in Europe for a few years, and numerous recordings and performances with the likes of Steve Torre, Wynton Marsalis and the Lincoln Center Orchestra, and Cassandra Wilson, she has become the voice of Jazz violin, much in the same way Stephan Gripelli and Jean-Luc Ponty had in the decades before her.

A difficult feat for sure, violin on the radio other than an excerpt from a classical concerto is rare. Even more rare is the violin wrapped in more progressive popular terrain as Hip Hop or smooth, contemporary Jazz. Carter does all these styles, and it is typical of musicians of this generation whose work is marked by boundary crossing at a moments notice. Critic Greg Tate has written of Carter,

> Beyond the hard and fast rules of modern music, various schools and cliques are artists who would better be described as musicians who play jazz rather than strictly jazz musicians. On Regina Carter's records she might be heard using ideas from Chaka Khan, to Billie Holiday, intermixing her rhythms with an African djembe drummer or the modern music of composer Mark Helias.[1]

What I'm noticing is that the contemporary young violinists in classical circles and education listen to Regina Carter. Hard to believe that that scene on the stage of Jordan Hall first evoked doubts about her acceptance into the mainstream violin world.

We too often take for granted the many ways in which musicians in this culture and time of expected innovation are stretching boundaries and constantly recharting territories. Carter is an artist who is pointing, painting, and playing the way forward for this century's new artists.

Ms. Rushen, Our All-Keys Player

*W*hen I think about diversification in a music career, someone like a Richard Wagner comes to mind: conductor, an impressario-like music promoter, or a Leonard Bernstein, with conducting, composing, performing, doing musicals and TV shows, and teaching; or a Quincy Jones, with movie scores and hit records. There is another, a lady, and her name is Patrice Rushen. We first came to know her as a young piano wizard in the Pop/Jazz world, but Ms. Rushen too has become synonymous with the term "triple-threat"; that is, the musician who does it all. I'd like to share a few of Ms. Rushen's workings over the last 20 years.

At age 17, she was presented at the Monterey Jazz Festival and after leaving college at the University of Southern California (USC). Before Janet Jackson, Britney Spears, Alicia Keyes, Norah Jones, there was a talented singer, pianist, dancer, and multi-instrumentalist making videos, as a "real" musician. But her true love was composition. As a piano student entering the preparatory program at the USC at age three, she later graduated from USC as a composition major.

Patrice Rushen has emerged as a composer, arranger, movie scorer, producer, and musical director having written, played, and conducted for Frank Sinatra, Prince, Janet Jackson, and Sheena Easton, to name just a few. Recently Ms. Rushen won awards and recognition from ASCAP for her recent sound track hit which was the year's most successful sound track composition for the movie *Men in Black*. Other film scoring credits include the hugely popular film *Waiting to Exhale*, Robert Townsend's *Hollywood Shuffle*, and two full-length HBO movies. Ms. Rushen served as composer in residence this year with the Detroit Symphony, and last year NPR aired internationally her premiere performance of a new piano concerto with the Grand Rapids Symphony. She was the music director for the 2004 Grammys.

Rushen has established herself as one of the most versatile performing artists, composers, producers, as well as one of the leading women in the industry. Having been nominated for Grammys and being a musical orchestra director for the Emmys, as well as being a musical director for someone like Janet Jackson, she has covered every kind of music as she has said, from Bach to Boyz II Men. She has as well served as the Thelonius Monk Institute's first artistic director, and as an educator has lectured across the country at universities and colleges, and performed for the Yamaha Corporation as a piano clinician.

Many of us were first exposed to Ms. Rushen as we danced to "Forget Me Nots" 1982. Imagine the great irony and joy from us old-siders who remember it from then to hear it now remade in video as Will Smith rapped, danced, and chased down aliens in *Men in Black*. And the irony of it becoming Ms. Rushen's most successful work, some 20 years later?

Like the American composers before her such as Leonard Bernstein, Henry Mancini, and Quincy Jones, in the work *When I Found You*, you can really hear the multiple influences of popular song, her classical training, and Jazz influences. And I know you've heard me say this before, but the artists of our day find it difficult not to immerse themselves in landscapes that contemporary music making is providing. She has said in numerous interviews when asked how does she do so many things, she eloquently and honestly states, "When I went into music, nobody told me it had to be one kind of music that made me a musician. So, since I never knew the difference, I will continue to make music in the many ways I have learned how." I'm finding it a commonplace among students and practitioners alike that our music(s) are happily becoming wider and wider. I'm glad that artists like Ms. Rushen's exquisite work give us all the comfort and license to, as she said, to "go there."

Billy Childs: The World Where I Live

$\mathcal{M}$y ultimate goal is to create original musical environments which, like real-life human drama, are unpredictable yet inevitable. However, the pursuit of originality is especially challenging in today's corporate driven age where conformity is usually more rewarded than innovation." These are words of contemporary composer Billy Childs. In addition to being a Jazz pianist who has influenced and inspired even such masters as Herbie Hancock and George Duke, who also experimented with multiple forms traversing styles, Childs is becoming a serious voice in the contemporary classical field of composition. In this essay, I would simply like to feature some of the work of this composer from his symphony to chamber, to jazz, to New Age leader. We want to travel through the world where Billy Childs lives.

Born in L.A. 1957, Billy Childs was trained in the preparatory department at the University of Southern California, later completing studies in composition, and went on to record with such legendary artists as J. J. Johnson, Freddie Hubbard, Branford Marsalis, and Chick Corea. Recording six albums on Windham Hill, GRP, Schanachie, and Collins Classics, his works have been performed by the Los Angeles Philharmonic, his piano concerto at the Monterey Jazz Festival, and large symphony for voice and orchestra, *Distant Land*, recorded on TelArc with the Akron Symphony.

While he claims influences from everybody from Bach, Stravinsky, and Hindemith, he credits piano master Keith Jarret as having the lasting mark on his creative development of bridging the divide between concert piano, American Jazz, symphonic, and concert work.

During a time when composers are given more and more choices, venues, audiences, and markets to play in, it's great to come across voices that make use of the multiple opportunities in fresh ways. Billy Childs's work in my mind travels back and forth across the categorical lines without sacrificing originality and voice. We could simply listen to two different discographies, or tracks of his work: Billy Childs the influential Jazz pianist composer, or Billy Childs the contemporary composer.

It has been said of Billy Childs's work, "Billy Childs is an artist of infinite resources. Childs has with each new recording forged new paths for himself and his listeners."[1] I hear in theses pieces the lessening of the stubborn rubs between Jazz/Rock, the rhythmic and harmonic complexities in the language of someone like a Mycoy Tyner, and the orchestral sweep of a masterful orchestrator like Ravel. Of particular influence is the work of another composer boundary-crosser, Chick Corea.

The latest works by Billy Childs were recently released as the luscious background surrounding Grammy Award–winning vocalist Diane Reaves. Here without overstepping the role, I still hear all the nuances of his voice, craft, but exceptional sensitivity as an arranger. I think this underlines the point, of composers today effectively navigating a tremendous amount musical, stylistic, and industry territories.

Our listening journey, in the words of Mr. Childs, is "to view music as a metaphor of the time and place in which we all live." From his many examples of orchestral and chamber pieces which push the edges of music, Billy Childs's music world is where our world should be. That is, where ideas are the manifestation, the result of everything we are influenced by. His world is large, and we are enlarged by it.

What Makes a Piece of Music for You? (Hale Smith)

$\mathcal{A}$s I have been listening and enjoying a lot of music recently, there have been those pieces, musical pieces, which will not leave me. This caused me to think a little bit about my own experience with music as a listener. It also made me wonder about others' listening experiences. I have been wondering about pieces that have been hanging onto my soul and my inner ears. Music that changes me. The more I began to think about this, the more questions about listening experiences begin to come up. For example: What drives you or calls you to a piece? What keeps you there? What new things does one discover about a piece, or about yourself? What brings us back again?

For me, I'm finding that the pieces that keep me coming back are works that serve as a kind of transport that brings me to an experience with the work within my own head while listening. So, in this essay, I want to address the question "What makes a piece of music for you?"

For most of us the musical component of the work draws us in and keeps us. The melody, harmony, the catchy rhythms, lyrics, the performance or ensemble, the story line or subject. Though we hear all kinds of music, it is that one musical piece that just sticks with us. Why?

There is a work that transfixes me, it pierces me every time I hear it: Hale Smith's *Toussaint L'Ouverture 1803*, for voices, then piano. I say voices and then piano because all of a sudden after I've bought into it being an alluring a cappella work, he drops in the piano. And this one surprise element, so elegantly placed, holds me for the duration of the piece.

After thinking about it, there are about five things that make Hale Smith's piece work for me as music:

1. Its ability to transport. I'm taken somewhere every time I hear this piece.
2. The piece leaves you with so many questions about how it moves surprisingly from phrase to phrase. And in waiting for the answer when listening, you find yourself. You discover new things. The more you hear it, the more you like it. I think that is what's giving me joy in listening to this piece.
3. The event for me is the piano entrance about halfway into the work. The piano then stays with the voices and just increases the beauty of the music as it unravels.
4. The other thing I want you to hear is all the shifting sonorities; they move so skillfully from ugly to gorgeous. The first few times I heard this piece I couldn't sit still long enough to dislike the harmonies because they always fall into such luscious resolutions that are beautiful.
5. Lastly, the piece is just interesting and sustains that line of interest, with breaks and entrances and silences from beginning to end, that makes me want to listen.

Toussaint L'Ouverture 1803 was written in 1977 to celebrate the historic figure François-Dominique Toussaint-Louverture, the principle leader of the Haitian slave revolt of 1791. Smith writes that his life as a liberator made him a symbol in the struggle for equality for peoples all over the world. A self-taught military genius, under his leadership he ended British and French rule on the island of Hispaniola, now the Dominican Republic.

Listen to this ending phrase with the words: "So when the Spring sends out her first thin fingers, he turns upon his cot, and coughs and dies." There is an ugly, dark, elegant beauty about this piece that continues to stick with me. And these kinds of in, out, turn right, turn left twists are what draws me back to it, as I listen on a ride with each new hearing.

While I am an admirer of many kinds of music and enjoy all kinds of listening experiences, the Hale Smith work *Toussaint L'Ouverture 1803* is so very powerful that it drives me every time I hear it. I appreciate the fact that musical works have the ability to grab hold of the many ears we have as listeners. So, the answer for me to the question, "What makes a piece music for you?" The work is music when it ceases to be silent in my memory and sings loudly beyond my hearing, sings loudly in my head, my inner ears. It doesn't go away but lives with me.

Where Do the Musical Geniuses Go? (Jaco Pastorius)

I'd be willing to work forever and forever if I were permitted to write only such music as I want to write and can write . . . what I myself think is good."[1] Wolfgang Amadeus Mozart was born 1756 and died at the age of 35. We remember him and his music which lives on. And, we remember him as a genius, an artist of extraordinary powers in musical ability. He died and was buried short of any honor bestowed to great people. On this essay of note, I'd like to share with you the music and work of another genius, Jaco Pastorius. He was born 1951 and died 1987, found dead, tragic and senseless. He was 36 years old. Jaco, like Mozart would probably have been willing to work at his music forever too. Where do the geniuses go?

Jaco Pastorius was born in Norristown, Pennsylvania, but he grew up in Fort Lauderdale, Florida. He was simply one of the most innovative, original, and revolutionary artists of the twentieth century. Known as the world's greatest electric bass player, he was respected and sought after throughout the music industry and set new standards for bass playing still unmatched today. And here, the terms "electric" and "bass" should not discourage us from serious attention. His playing exhibited the kind of original virtuostic genius that is by sound alone unforgettable. He left numerous recordings, compositions, and performances that show there is little logic in the early loss of this kind of gift. Never had the bass directed the melody, harmony, and overall spirit of a work like Jaco's bass lines and musical conceptions.

On the Charlie Parker tune, "Donna Lee," and he too, Yardbird Parker, was another kind of genius performer who died senselessly at 34, Jaco's interpretation and performance is simply from another planet. Before this kind of approach, there was no other model of performance on the instrument with this kind of fluidity, melodic beauty, and harmonic breadth and power. Listening to this performance, you can hear every chord change, and melodic and musical invention converging at a moment, simultaneously.

Jaco became as well a most important contributor to the band Weather Report, one of the most respected performing ensembles in Jazz.

Jaco was the son of a well-respected musician who left Pennsylvania with his family and settled in Florida. By age 13, Jaco had mastered the drums, guitar, and began to turn to piano and then electric bass. By his late teens he had absorbed most of the contemporary playing approaches and incorporated traditional Jazz, Rock, R&B, and classical conception into his languages. By the time he was in this twenties he had performed with such greats as Carla Bley, Pat Matheney, Joni Mitchell, and of course Joe Zawinul and sax/composer great Wayne Shorter, whom he joined with Weather Report.

Probably Jaco's most recorded and performed composition is *The Voice of a Secret*. Heard and realized by his Word of Mouth Orchestra, I think this is one of the great melodies. It is simple, memorable, and musical, but is constructed with the complexity of a great musical mind. Mozart was like that.

Another of his outstanding works is "Liberty City." It is difficult to miss the convergence of bass wizardry woven simultaneously with melodic and harmonic richness. But this music all grows out of the musical presence of Jaco and his bass playing. I've always appreciated and been floored by Jaco as a virtuoso performer whose work is so brilliant, technically and conceptually ahead of his time. Few artists revolutionize the sound and capabilities of an instrument, and as well fashion music conception to grow out of that playing so that a recognizable musical voice and approach emerge. It is extremely hard to come up with something new in art. Perhaps Picasso, Varez, John Cage, and Thelonious Monk come close to sharing this mantle.

Charlie Parker at 35, Mozart at 35, and Jaco passing as well too early at 36, short of the dreams to play on forever and ever. Although these artists have left for us at least an impression of their artistry that will live on and on. But one has to wonder: Why did they die so young and where then do the geniuses go?

5

MODULATIONS: TALKS WITH AND ON CONTEMPORARY ARTISTS

"Keep Your Head Up" by Tara Ann Banfield

The Music Kept Us from Being Paralyzed:
A Talk with Bernice Johnson Reagon

MARCH 11, 2000, MINNEAPOLIS

WB: What is your take on the role of artists in society?

BJR: I made a very conscious choice about what my role would be as a musician. I was not working in a vacuum. I actually chose to link myself up with an older function of music and I had to choose because, growing up in Southwest Georgia, I experienced and participated with music in school, on the playground, and in church. Coming through high school and college I began to deal more seriously with the kinds of thinking related to what we think of as "fine arts." Here, I was involved with learning music that I had not learned at my mother's knee so to speak. I was a student studying music in a department dedicated to the understanding and transmission of music on all levels: from listening and appreciating to mastering the performance of music and becoming involved in the practice of concretizing. I was very aware of African American popular music, as I moved through my teenage period the genre that we swung with was Rhythm and Blues. I enjoyed music as a consumer, listening to radio, dancing to the popular hits, knowing everything I could find out about my favorite stars, and singing those songs that were within my range with local groups we organized. At the same time the commercialization and commodification of music began to have an impact on the music we experienced as church music. Again, through radio and live performance shows, we found our favorite singers and songs, and bought sheet music and formed local choirs to perform that music.

As I think about it, both of these commercial systems benefited from accessibility beyond purchase, there was a way in which even as we held our favorite artist with great respect, we always understood that the greatest compliment to them was to make their signature songs our own. The greatest hits were not out of reach for us and mastering them did not involve being a music major in an educational institution.

None of these earlier experiences prepared me for what I discovered going into the Civil Rights movement where I saw music naming my position, and naming a position where I was countering a position I had previously held. Living within the African American Southwest Georgia community meant that I was also living within a segregated society and that my safety and well-being was assured in direct relationship to my willingness to operating within the boundaries drawn for Black people by that society. We were socialized to try and stay out of trouble. We had to figure out how to achieve and be the best we could be as a Black person with some promise and not get wiped out by racism. Charting that course with us were teachers and parents and elders who really loved us and tried to show us how to weave our way. Breaking partnership with that path and saying, "I want to be a part of another stream," I began to question and become involved in frontally attacking the whole thing. Then I discovered there was music in that new position, music that served it, energized it, and became an instrument to creating and maintaining that position. That was new for me. Surprisingly, most of this music was not new music, most of it was music I had already learned and embraced from other music, sometimes doing it exactly as I had learned it and sometimes shifting it so that is was very contemporary. And always during this time singing and creating the songs with those who had also stepped across the line, out of the safety zone alongside me.

Once I got out of jail for civil disobedience during the 1961 Albany, Georgia, mass demonstrations, briefly, I tried to go back into the old patterns. In December 1961, I was suspended from Albany State and then got a scholarship from Spelman College and went into the music department. I was not able to function in the music department, although I formed a transformative relationship with Dr. Willis Laurence James, who was chairmen of the department and director of the Spelman Glee Club. Dr. James was trained as a violinist and loved the European musical traditions; he also loved the folk traditions created by African Americans and saw our culture as creating virtuosity that was unparalleled by any culture. It was a unique experience to find a Western-trained musician who had not tucked his own cultural music treasures on a lower shelf. I left school to work full-time in the Civil Rights movement as a Freedom Singer. I also got married, had two children, went back to Spelman to complete my bachelor's degree, this time with a major in history where for the first time, under Dr. Vincent Harding, I was allowed to do some of my research using song lyrics as historical data alongside conventional archival documents. I was actually moving out of the conventional path of studying and performing music and trying to discover a way to study music that had some relationship to what I had discovered being on the front line in the Civil Rights movement. I continued to move in that direction and began to think of it as a kind of oral community people history. Moving my studies to Howard University as a graduate student in history, I was also reading ethnomusicology, anthropology, and folklore. I made a decision that I really didn't want to go into any field where music was dealt with as an end product to be analyzed and performed without understanding why it came into being, what it served as an element within a cultural historical moment or period. I needed to go into fields where scholars were being trained in the practice of reconstructing history and then I could find what music had to do with creation or support and the telling of those stories.

While at Howard in history, I also worked in the music department under Dr. Vada Easter Butcher, who headed the Project in Ethnic Music, which included music created by Black community–based and –trained musicians as music very important to academic study.

At the same time, in search for a part-time position to supplement my stipend, I became vocal director of the D.C. Black Repertoire Company, working under Vantile Whitfield, the artistic director of a new theater founded by Robert Hooks to train a new generation of talented African Americans for careers in theater, film, and television. In this role I suddenly became involved in teaching music forms that I had grown up with. There were songs I had learned in school, on the playground, at home, in church that were well suited for some of the works we were doing at the theater. I had never really taught these songs to anyone, and certainly never tried to teach them to singers outside of that particular culture. All of these actors were African American, but it was 1971–1972 and they were all urban. There were one or two who had backgrounds and styles of singers that reached back before the 1950s. As I began the work, I had to work out a way to reconstruct a sound out of voices that had never been bent and woven in the way we grew up singing in Southwest Georgia. The process of working out how to teach songs and sounds for the theater also provided me with the infrastructure to be a composer. I had to take apart what I heard in my head and contend with people who didn't hear it. That process gave me a composer's language. I began to experiment with using this sound with original works.

Some of the strongest singers in my workshop began to talk to me about forming a group and going to the concert stage with the music I was using in my workshop. In theater, the play dictates what music might be needed: children's songs, work songs, funeral songs, train whistles, wind, Blues, etc., so I wondered what concert format was available for a repertoire that mirrored life. I had done an album in 1965 produced by Father Robert Hunter entitled *Sounds of Thunder*. The program consisted of some of my favorite songs. When I sent them to a booking agent to see if I could get work as a musician, she had responded saying that I had to make a decision of what kind of singer I wanted to be. Did I want to be a Blues singer, Folk, Jazz singer, Gospel? She pointed out that all of those genres were represented on the album, and the music business was not organized that way. My workshop members were asking me to revisit something that had already been a source of rejection, and initially I ignored their suggestion. But they did not drop it and I decided that the least I could do was to see if something would come of it. I decided to go ahead and Sweet Honey in the Rock was the result.

One of the central things that guides my work with Sweet Honey is the relationship I found in how ritual Black church served the people who came into it. People who went to church went to get something from that experience. In order to get it, they had to participate in creating it. There was no such thing as coming, sitting down in your seat, and having something come to you from the stage. You had to come with a need and understand that what you got out of the experience would be determined by how open you were to receiving and giving. From the time I was a child I understood that people went to church to create something they could use to feed and nurture them and make it possible for them to get through the next step of their lives. And without any real conscious work, this was definitely the way I saw music working in the Civil Rights movement. There were those times when we were moving in new ways, and going against everything we had been taught that might keep us safe, and as we moved forward, terrified, and possibly facing real physical danger, we used the songs and the singing. It never stopped a bullet or a jailing, or kept you from losing your job or being suspended from school, but music kept you from being paralyzed, it kept you moving. Without consciously drawing from these experiences as I moved into the Sweet Honey work, I offered who I had become. In looking back, I know now that I was looking for a concert format approach that offered our contemporary audiences a similar experience. And so it is, that to this day, people come to a Sweet Honey performance bringing all that they are, looking for something, reaching for something, and they more often than not tell us that they take away something new and more to assist them as they move through their next day. Sweet Honey in the Rock has successfully operated well beyond performance at the level of entertainment. Our ticket sales have remained steady through recessions. We have been blessed to continue when other concerts are canceled for low sales. We serve a constituency where our audience members buy Sweet Honey tickets in a different category of importance than they have their entertainment funds. It's something they need to do in order to do what they have to do. We have built a constituency because we actually, in the guise of being concert singers, are doing something very similar to the cultural ritual I experienced growing up; it has to do with what you create to keep the balance in your life. So when I think of the function of what Sweet Honey does, and what I do by myself, I feel it is a contemporary expression of what I saw as I grew up as a Black child in the South.

WB: I wanted to ask you to comment on the context that has changed here a bit. We are up against some new data, sensibilities, some new things that shape our cultural responses. Black folks, America, the larger cultural global questions, and access to all this. Can music still plug in somewhere and provide a balance for young people who can go to so much other stuff? How do we combat, or embrace, or meet the needs of where we are today?

BJR: My models are always small and very clear. When you work on a big scale there is always a perversion of the model. There is trash that shows up, because you can't maintain consistent integrity at all the stages of a global scale. My work is on a small scale because I tend to put things together in new ways and I want to do it in a way so that someone else can use the model. In my work as a scholar and in my Sweet Honey work, there are contemporary models for contemporary challenges. We have taken our work internationally and have tested what we do all over the world, and with younger audiences, older, White, Black, gay, lesbian, differently labled, always mixed. Each concert is a different gathering, in D.C., San Francisco, Chicago, Boston, different configurations, an open invitation to a local community to gather in the name of affirmation, change, and the love of great music.

Changes in music are often driven by what is happening within the society. Soul music was the direct result of the Civil Rights movement. During the movement, the church is the place that often hosted the local organizing, and the church literally left the buildings and went into the world, into the street, into jail. With the music of Ray Charles, you get the sound of the church moving into the world. Anyone who talks about Ray Charles or Aretha Franklin and does not talk about the Civil Rights movement is not having an appropriate discussion about what Soul is as a musical form. You can't have one without the other.

Consider the freedom songs we used in the movement from young people's music, we used more Ray Charles songs than any other popular musician. There is often a relationship between what people are doing in their daily lives and what their popular commercial artists are creating to sell to us as products. What you have with the Civil Rights movement is something that comes out of the community that dominates not only the community voice but also the national voice. Popular Black music culture of that day drew upon that, and if you look at dance, visual arts, literature, and the spoken word, you will find the same thing.

What you have today is art again reflecting reality and the oppressive role of the music industry. When you look at the challenges of the African American community, the AIDS crisis, violence, joblessness—there are some of today's popular artists echoing that devastation. And I am careful to say some artists in this case because too often I am asked to speak on Rap and Hip Hop as if these forms have no redeeming value. For the record, Sweet Honey in the Rock have two poets who loved these forms and performing their compositions on a number of different subjects has become an important part of our work.

I always suggest that music must be selected, not simply by genre, but by whether it is a part of affirmation, meditation, nurturing, creating energy, standing for your rights. . . . There are examples, too many for my taste, where what we are offered feels like a simplified amplified echo of devastation without a call for change or hope. The music industry now moves in on African American youth music culture earlier and differently than it used to. Moving into that sector of our culture at puberty, where there is often a brief excursion into challenges verbal and physical, where young people "dis and dime," or as we called it when I was that age, "playing the dozens," on each other. The question is not does it exist but what do you do with an industry that exploits that transitional life and culture sector and sells it as a commodity? What does that do in terms of distorting the culture? Why is it that the music industry has been allowed to sell the cesspool of our culture to the world? What does the commodification of trash do to the talented people who would move on to other things as other generations have done, were it not for the chase of the money?

The kind of expression that denigrates women, and radiates no hope, and reflects depravity exists in all cultures, but not in the living room of our lives. What happens to the young talented wordsmiths who do this as a part of a puberty ritual and their need to extend and explore their creativity? We do have to ask what the impact of an industry that responds to profit has on the natural trajectory of the maturation of cultural expression. What happens to an artist who sells a million records in the early stages who begins to hear other things because she is creative? But, if it sells a million records is there an investment from her industry partners to her development and maturation as an artist, or is she held hostage to her first success? You see that I have lots of questions here, but no big answers.

I often suggest that people look at Stevie Wonder's early work, and you can see how his work changed as he lived and matured. We are not having much success in seeing our young artists having that kind of trajectory with today's industry. If you look at somebody like Malcolm X, as a major force in the transformation of African American culture, today he is bigger and more accessible than he was when we were right there with him. It is important to look at the impact of the industry on some of the potentiality of young people. If they had lived longer lives (Tupac, Biggie Smalls), one would hope that they would have changed many times before they died. If you are a musician or a poet, if you develop, you are not going to operate out of the same content and sound for more than ten years! Again, Stevie Wonder's work provides an important and incredible lesson, that is, of watching someone who is not destroyed by operating within the commercial genre. Prince is an example of an artist who has taken a hard stand to own himself and his work. The truth is he is a composer who composes at a certain rhythm that was in total conflict with the way his company operated. Recording companies control when you put something out and their sense of timing might not have anything to do with your creative rhythm. And in this case, Prince's name was not his to own, so for a while he did not have a name. This is a contemporary struggle that is very compelling to me. Prince's struggle is to his right to be an artist and to find ways to have his work heard as a composer. I found it appalling that so many stories about his struggle made fun of his absence of a name instead of telling the harder more painful story of his struggle to maintain his integrity as an artist. The transmission of Prince's music is not through paper scores, but through audio recordings, he needs access to the air to be heard.

Sweet Honey never knows where we are being a link. We don't know where, when, and who we are going to touch, or how or if we will be a hookup or be a foundation for someone who is looking for something. It is our work to offer as best we can, with integrity, a singing voice of reason, of love, of joy, of respect, acknowledging the need to stand and struggle for change and transformation. We have done this for now over 30 years and we have been carried and supported by those who let us know how important it is that we are here.

Four Talks on Artistic Responsibility (Bobby McFerrin, Ysaye Barnwell, Billy Taylor, Patrice Rushen)

$\mathcal{O}$ne of the things that is on a lot of people's minds is the idea of artistic responsibility in the public marketplace. If all the fury over the Timberlake/Janet Jackson performance during the halftime show of Superbowl 2004 taught us (or them) anything, it is that our culture has now become aware of the poisonous possibilities of irresponsible imaging, marketing, and music making. Music is too powerful a force to take for granted, especially these days when people's investments and trust are manipulated, and rhetoric in the public place, politics, and policy sap over us heavy and deep with lightweight self-serving emptiness. Our society is vulnerable and eager to "fall in love" with a soothing, comforting something, and these days that means arresting magnetism. Popular artists have the stage right now, and everyone is looking and hearing. So, as they say, what you say ain't no joke. It's serious!

I have spent the last ten years or so talking with artists, educators, and focused student groups about artistic responsibility and the role of musicians in shaping our lives, healing us, and moving us along. In these four reflections by Bobby McFerrin, Ysaye Barnwell, Dr. Billy Taylor, and Patrice Rushen, the artists from various generations and perspectives deal with public perceptions, image, and meaning. From a public forum Civil Rights perspective (Ysaye Barnwell, Sweet Honey in the Rock), to contemporary "rubs" (2004 Grammy Awards and Image Awards music director, Patrice Rushen), four friends in the industry speak here with me about the issues related to artistic responsibility.

BOBBY MCFERRIN ON ARTISTIC RESPONSIBILITY

William Banfield: Bobby, should we be concerned about the role or image of popular musicians today?

Bobby McFerrin: Nothing, nothing, nothing is insignificant. Nothing at all. Everything that happens bears witness to what is going on. I can certainly understand that rappers, for example, are reporting what is happening in their neighborhoods. That is true. But also, I have thought about teaching a course on what I would call "creative responsibility." It would simply be to get other creative people together to talk about the influences and the impact that our art has on society, because you can't tell me that it does not. Certainly, yes, we have the freedom to do what we want, but should we use that freedom all the time, when you think that your art is displayed in a public place, where kids may hear or see it? I would simply like to just get these artists to stop and think, two or three times down the line, about the piece that they are working on. I think the argument that they are just reporting what is happening in the neighborhood is valid, but they can also report on other stuff that is happening in the neighborhood—the grandmothers that raised them, the papas who are working to feed their kids—they can report on those things, too. They don't have to just report on the violence, the gangs, the drugs. That ain't the only thing that is going on.

I had no expectations for "Don't Worry, Be Happy." In fact, when I was working on my record that song wasn't even part of the plan. I was struggling with another tune, and I couldn't come up with anything. "Don't Worry, Be Happy" was this phrase I had seen on a poster. Lots of times when I am trying to memorize something, if I am trying to memorize a Bible verse, I sing it, make a song out of it. The tune "Discipline" came out that way [sings "Discipline"]. So I sat down, and I wrote the lyrics to "Don't Worry, Be Happy." It took me 45 minutes to write the lyrics, and I think within an hour it was recorded. I had no expectations for the song whatsoever. I was just writing a song. I had no idea that the song was going to do that well. I think it was just the times.

I understand that we are a whole ball of mixed-up stuff. The song has two phrases—"be happy" and "don't worry." The "be happy" is always out there, but the "don't worry" part gets overlooked a lot. We worry about too many things. We think too much about the ills of the world and what have you. Jesus says in Matthew, "Don't worry about your life, don't worry about it." He is not saying don't be concerned about the ills of the world but that you should do what you can from day to day. You should keep yourself focused on simply helping your brother who is sitting next to you. You can change yourself and work with your family. You can work with the people who are with you. I don't know if I was really trying to say anything with that song, except don't live under a cloud.

PATRICE RUSHEN ON ARTISTIC RESPONSIBILITY

William Banfield: Patrice, do you have any reaction to what rappers are saying in their songs?

Patrice Rushen: I find it unfortunate that the glorification of a certain aspect of that kind of life, growing up that way, has now been, it has taken the place of the ones who were speaking their minds about their situations. I do have some problems with the music industry conveniently and systematically, I feel, financing it without balancing it with the other things that are happening. When you look at it, racism is alive and the kids are young and they don't particularly understand it, and some of them maybe never will. This is a voice that they have, this is a way they do things, there are some of them who are making money. That's all they see. I think using rap as a means of expressing their life conditions and wanting to put it out there in the form of the music they can relate to stopped a long time ago. It is an industry now where it is about doing that and doing it a certain way in order to make money.

I am not condemning that, but I am saying that there is no balance. There are other people out here doing something else, too, and that was always a part of our music too. There was always R&B, and there was Jazz and there was Gospel and there was the support, and there were radio stations playing all of it so that you got that there was a palette of Black music out there as opposed to what we have now. I don't know about Indiana or Detroit, but out here, we don't really have an R&B station. They play oldies or they play Rap.

WB: What would it take, from your standpoint, to get us back to that? To be able to combine those worlds of the kinds of wonderful energies and progressive stuff that is happening in Hip Hop to mix it with the kinds of things we always had. Is it going to happen or do you see it going completely downhill?

PR: I hope it is going to happen. I think that it will happen because I think that usually happens when people look back, and rappers are having to do that because they are sampling all of the music that was done in the 1960s, '70s, '80s, even in the '90s, it is sending them back to find grooves. Their vocabulary was limited and so it is sending them back to find grooves that may be a little bit more unique. They are starting to include melodies again. I think what happens when you look backwards sometimes you start to realize the importance of how that music was put together, that it requires a certain amount of skill and discipline. They are very creative in the way they use stuff. They are using my stuff, sometimes I hear it and it's like, "What?" They are very creative but they don't know how to put it together. They are going to find out how to put it together because they are going to run out of things to sample. They are already up to me, they are already sampling music from the '80s. I have heard Michael Jackson's music sampled. Some of that is music of the '90s. It is about learning how to put it all together and I think it is going to bring them closer to those of us who know and give us a chance to expose them to more of what is happening and how that music was put together.

It is about learning music. I am looking for that to happen. I asked a well-known rapper to participate on my new CD—I asked two and one told me, "I don't do R&B." I told him, "You know that hit record you have out now, it's actually 20 years old, it is actually Sly Stone." I knew he couldn't hear me right then, but I told him and I tried to be as loving as I could because I knew he didn't understand. I said, "If you adopt the industry separateness with your feeling and your attitude towards music that you are using, you are setting yourself up to have a very short career. Because when they finish with you, you will have nowhere to go in terms of learning anything that gives you the insurance that you are going to be out here for a while. Your thing is built on someone else's thing. It is not about not doing that, it is about using that to be able to learn how to do it and therefore be that much more of a creative source longer because you know what to do. If we separate ourselves from one another that way, I can't learn from you and you can't learn from me, so what do we accomplish? You had a hit and I had a hit, now what?" He was really cool about it; he said, "Well, I'll take that into consideration, my sister." I said, "Okay, my brother, good luck." His career is history.

The thing that really is upsetting is that it is not out of anything other than the game that has been played and continues to be perpetuated. As long as they don't get that there is a commitment and a discipline that is involved in playing music, just like the discipline and commitment that is involved in playing football, basketball, baseball, karate, dancing, broadcasting, writing. There is a passion that is there beyond just the doing so that you can at some point contribute. That is part of the responsibility too because, like I said before, there is a spiritual connection to people who are touched creatively and have the ability to take what is on the inside and put it out there. That connection to me reeks of responsibility to give it your best and to learn as much as possible and to listen because I think that that creative stuff is a door that opens, that if and when you walk through it, you have a responsibility of leaving something there for the next person to walk through the door. That can be in any kind of way, from the sampling of your compositions, or the body of work that you do, or maybe by walking through that door it turns you on to some aspect of your creativity that involves you being able to pass the word on, like teaching, or some combination of all of that, but you are supposed to make a difference. If it was such that everybody could do it, everybody would be doing it.

The fact that you have been touched that way, I think there is something to that that says you are supposed to do something with this. Behind the scenes, and what is going on with television and all that, until I saw that, I didn't make the connection that I could ever do anything close to that. That was Oliver Nelson. We have got to see each other doing it. That is why when I am doing these television shows now, people come up and they say, "I saw you on TV leading the band." For me, at the time I am doing it, it is a job. I enjoy it very, very much. It is demanding and it calls on me to use a lot of my skills. But another person, another person of color, another Black person, another woman, or whomever, will see me do it and that may be the connection for them.

It worked like that for me. We take it for granted, when we are in school, that the person standing up there in front of the class, we need to be trying to pay attention. If the person happens to be of common ethnicity, that should be even more special to us because the struggle to get to that place is the part we need to learn. That is the part you won't read in the books, and that is the part that you won't get even if you turn in every homework assignment. It's about checking out the person and we don't do that enough.

DR. BILLY TAYLOR ON ARTISTIC RESPONSIBILITY

William Banfield: Do you think an artist has any particular role in society?

Billy Taylor: Of course. I think that an artist not only has a role but a responsibility. We have the attention of a lot of people and it is up to us to say through our art, through any means we can, the things that hopefully we care about. That is the welfare of the community, the welfare of people we care about, the direction the country is going in, any of the things that we as caring human beings would think about. If it is Bosnia, if it is famine in Africa, if it is the plight of women, whatever it is, we should say, "Well, I don't think affirmative action should be discarded because I don't think it is finished working yet," well, that should surface somewhere in our music. Every artist that I know addresses social issues in his or her own way.

Ellington did way back before the term "Black" was fashionable; he wrote "Black Beauty" back in the 1920s. He wrote "Black, Brown and Beige" in the 1940s. Throughout his career he dealt with those kinds of issues. Paul Robeson had his career ruined because he was a super intelligent person who was very caring about what the meaning of democracy was and spoke out in ways that were not acceptable from African Americans in those days. They tried to kill him, literally, by ruining his career. It didn't work, it frustrated him and made him less visible, but the man was so strong and such a wonderful inspiration to those of us who knew him. I didn't know him well. His son and his family lived in the housing project where I used to live with my family and so I used to see Mr. Robeson frequently as he came to visit his grandchildren. I had met him when I had been the accompanist of one of his protégés at Cafe Society. Kenneth Spencer was a wonderful baritone who Paul Robeson supported, and my understanding was that Kenneth was one of his protégés. I don't remember where I got that from, I suppose I assumed from the manner in which they greeted one another and the tremendous deference that Kenneth, who was a wonderful artist in his own right, had to the older artist.

It was just wonderful to hear the two of them talk, just to be in the room with them. They were both very intellectual and socially aware and wonderfully artistic. It was just fascinating to be with them. I didn't even open my mouth; I just sat there and listened. They were talking about things which were beyond my experience. They were wonderful. Any artist of any generation, I believe, should use this kind of artist as an example, to look at the wonderful things that came out of the Harlem Renaissance, when people did have a social conscious and expressed that in their painting and in visual terms, in sculpture, in acting, in film, in every aspect of aesthetic expression that was possible.

So, the short answer is that I believe every musician, in whatever way he or she feels is proper, should do that. I think that ethnicity for me has been something that I have been very conscious of and I have tried to use it based on models that preceded me. People like Duke Ellington, Will Marion Cook, many musicians who were legendary in terms of being able to say, "This is who I am. This is what I look like. This is where I live. This is what I care about. I am different from some other people, but that difference is something of which I am very proud." I was taught that very carefully by people at Dunbar High School, by my family, and by many other people. They didn't just say this to me, they gave me concrete examples.

For instance, when my father took me to see Duke Ellington at the Howard Theater, he pointed out how the Ellington Band looked. He said, "This is a man who is from the city, from Washington, D.C. He has played for prominent heads of Europe and he has done things that very few people who play Jazz have done. You can see the difference between the way he presents his music and the way some other people, who play very well." He said, "I'm not knocking anybody's playing, but look at the difference between him and some of the bands we have seen recently here at the theater. If you are going to play this kind of music, this is one of the things you should bear in mind." My father never wanted me to become a professional musician, he wanted me to become a dentist or something professional in another way, but he was saying even if I was going to do this on an amateur point of view, I needed to bear this in mind. This is a level to which I should aspire. I would go to see Cab Calloway and there he was in tails and looking sharp. Jimmy Lunceford's band would come and all these young guys were sharp. Everybody looks like the epitome of fashion of the day and everyone is well spoken. There were plenty of bands that came and used the vernacular and talked the hip talk of the day and everything. I did that because I wanted to be a hip young guy, but by the same token, I also aspired to this other thing that, in my view, was something that brought another level of listener to you.

DR. YSAYE BARNWELL ON ARTISTIC RESPONSIBILITY

William Banfield: Ysaye, talk to me a bit about the role of the artist, and how you see music at work in our society.

Ysaye Barnwell: I think artists are the storytellers, I think we are the people who pass values from those who have gone before to those who are coming afterwards. I think we articulate things that other people are not able to articulate for themselves. I see this particularly with Sweet Honey. People are constantly saying to us, "I am so glad to hear somebody say this from the stage. This is what I have been feeling and thinking for so long." I think artists keep energy flowing in the universe, I really do. It scares me that budgets for the arts are being cut because kids are not being exposed to that energy in a really healthy and constructive way. I'm scared. I certainly feel that what the young rappers are doing is on a continuum and is not new. I really hope that they know that it is not new. When I do talk to young Rap artists and we get into this, I tell them, all the time, and I start tracing for them, from the griot on, through the minister, all of it. It is a continuum. What they are doing with their music is on a continuum. I don't fault what they are doing, I am nervous and frightened because of the read itself, which says we are in trouble. Our young people are saying these things because we are in trouble. If we had a different view of the world, they would be seeing things differently and using their creative talents in a more positive way. I don't like blaming, that is not constructive for me. I try to figure out where this is coming from. What was going on in society that the Blues evolved? What was going on that Gospel music evolved? What is going on in society that Rap evolved? What is the inspiration, what is it that is propelling our young people into lyrics that are violent, lyrics that are abusive? That is where I try to have conversations with people. I get the question about Rap music all the time in interviews.

I think our entire society is violent and I think that is reflected in the music. I think therefore that they are not only to blame. They are maybe the least to blame because in some ways, I get nervous treading on this territory, but in some ways I feel like they are courageous in putting it out there. It is what is inside and churning over. Putting it out there is probably more constructive than doing it. It is the same thing that happened in Blues. I don't blame the Blues composer because they talk about shooting women, when they talk about shooting their lovers. They talk about a lot of violent things in Blues. What I say is, "What was going on in the society?" For me, when I look at homelessness, when I look at teenagers without jobs and without hope, when I look at people who are being laid off from work, people who are—at Howard University they gave them four hours to empty out their desks and get off the campus. They had a police escort because they knew that if they didn't, somebody was going to go crazy. Well, what happens to young people in the midst of all that? What happens to young people who grow up in a society where everything you hear has to do with war and very little has to do with the making of peace? What do they have to look forward to when monies are being stripped from education? They don't have a computer in their whole school and yet the whole society is moving toward the Internet.

What do they have to look forward to and how does that get acted out? It gets acted out in really abusive and violent ways. Rodney King is not an exception, as we keep seeing over and over again. People are living in buildings that look like they have been bombed out. I don't know where music is heading in the twenty-first century. It is clear to me from looking from an African worldview that music exists because it does something. It never is the art for art's sake kind of phenomenon. If it doesn't make it rain, if it doesn't infuse herbs with a healing spirit, if it doesn't send a fighting energy into weapons that are being forged, then what good is a song?

Quincy Jones asks, "What good is a song if it doesn't inspire, if it has no message to bring? If a song doesn't take you higher, higher, higher, what good is it to sing?" Because of how music is so integrated to every aspect of life activity for African people, I started asking how that applies for Black people. It applies totally. We can see how our music has evolved and at every point that our history has taken another turn, our music has taken another turn. That to me is evidence of music's functionality. Then when you start to look at what the music says and how it was created and how it is used, it is totally clear that we have never dropped that aspect of who we are as African people. For example, when I look at Spirituals, I see the whole history of slavery. Now I have a slightly broader definition of what Spirituals are because I think that they are the whole body of songs written during slavery. I say that because African people didn't make a distinction between sacred and secular. In that sense, the music was very functional. It talked about every single aspect of life activity.

Coming into Sweet Honey, which is a group that evolved from the work of Bernice and the SNIC Freedom Singers. Sweet Honey has that whole tradition of music that is functional. It serves peopie, it passes the values from generation to generation, it is the newspaper when newspapers aren't printing your story. It is the thing that gets played in the birthing rooms, gets played at the funerals, that whole thing. That is what Sweet Honey does in people's lives, so I am told. It certainly is very much a part of how we see the world.

My experience is that Sweet Honey's music primarily, but Black music by and large, seems really to be more universal than almost any other music. My sense is that the music is specific, that Black music is very specific to our situation. Because it is so specific, it addresses what it knows best and in that it becomes totally universal. This is why I think, for example, that people sing Spirituals all over the world. When you say, "Nobody knows the trouble I've seen," people can identify with that even though I am speaking so particularly about myself, that it wouldn't even occur to me that it would include someone who is Indian, or Japanese, or whatever, but they understand that. For example, I wrote a song that says, "There are no mirrors in my Nana's house." One of the lines says, "I never knew my skin was too black, I never knew my nose was too flat, I never knew my clothes didn't fit, I never knew there were things that I'd missed." I am amazed that we can be singing that song and I can see White people crying.

I had a letter from a White male gay a cappella group requesting to sing that song and I was stunned. I called them and told them I was stunned. They said in the letter that the song talked about such unconditional acceptance and love that they found themselves in the song. I said, "You can sing it because you really understand it, but you can't change a single word. You have to sing, 'I never knew my skin was too black and my nose was too flat.' You cannot change that in any way." They agreed to that. My sense is that the more specific you can be about who you are, the more people understand that universally. I think that is what Black music does. It is so personal that it can't be ignored. It just really touches. In that sense I think our music is vulnerable, it is accessible, I don't know how else to describe it.

· 30 ·

Two Articles about Steve Reich (1989)

$\mathcal{T}$hese essays were written between 1989 and 2004 and are in many cases previously published essays I did as a columnist. Here I speak as a musician-journalist commenting on contemporary music culture. The Reich articles are my first public writings as a music critic for the University of Michigan student paper from 1989 to 1992.

STEVE REICH: WHAT IS THE MUSIC OF THE MODERN COMPOSER? (FROM THE *MICHIGAN DAILY*, APRIL 7, 1989)

In this age of Rap, Fusion, New Age, Urban, Gospel, Heavy Metal, and Michael Jackson, one may ask, "What is the music of the modern composer?" For many modern composers, the answer is in an art either deeply rooted in western European tradition, or something well suited for the academic splicing table.

Steve Reich might answer the question thus: "It's 1989."

Reich's music, exemplified on the new Electra Nonesuch release *Different Trains/Electric Counterpoint*, is modern, funky, creative, popular, eclectic, "soulful," and definitely composition.

Reich's music is known to many as minimalism or phrase music. By technique, the composer reduces the musical materials to a simple repetitive phrase or scheme and can generate form and interest by slightly shifting a beat or a note of the harmony. The effect is hypnotic.

On "Different Trains," perceptible process translates to perpetual groove. It cannot be reduced to cool backdrop music for the space cadet, nor to academic specimen music for the "enlightened." Reich's music is alive and vibrant, has meaning, and is experienced like African music, as the celebration of life. (Reich studied Ewe drumming in Ghana.)

"Different Trains," the first piece on the album, is an incredibly intoxicating work. Its immediacy has a lot to do with the fact that both the harmony and rhythms are derived from human speech patterns digitally sampled and played over and over on a tape loop. On the recording, the famous Kronos String Quartet plays music composed by Reich against the pulsating, repetitive voice patterns. This creates an intriguing texture that grabs you both because of its rhythmic vitality and its overall unity. Equally interesting is the fact that Reich uses electronically created train sounds and sirens, adding even more variety to the production.

The second piece on the new release, "Electric Counterpoint," which Reich will perform Saturday, is a piece in three movements for electric guitar and a perfect match of artistry between Reich and gifted guitarist Pat Metheny. The work, a myriad of ten guitar textures and two basses, against which Metheny improvises, is not only rhythmically irresistible, but a gorgeous composition.

Reich's album will soon be heard across the country on any number of contemporary, New Age, Soft Rock, and Jazz stations. But we in Ann Arbor get to witness Reich and his music live Saturday.

ARTIST UNVEILS "REICH MUSIC" (FROM THE *MICHIGAN DAILY*, APRIL 11, 1989)

When I wrote the preview for Steve Reich's concert, I posed the question, "What is the music of the modern composer?" Reich's answer was something like this: "What do you mean? The composer creates the music he/she feels."

Reich's music was heard by a packed house of admirers Saturday night at the Michigan Theater, and they would simply answer the question like this: "Reich music." So, what is Reich music? What is known to us as minimalism (the reduction of musical materials to simple repetitive phrases shifted slightly by rhythmic displacement or subtle additive harmony over a long period) was heard in full form.

Reich's new album features an incredible composition called "Different Trains." The piece uses prerecorded material, and is really an autobiographical documentary on the different experience of being a young Jewish boy traveling back and forth across the United States (New York to California) during the early '40s, and the experience of thousands of Jewish people traveling in Europe during the same time.

The story is told by persons who were a part of Reich's childhood or had similar traveling experiences as Jews in Europe during this time. Although their stories are heard as broken speech fragments, they provide the major themes (the story, rhythm, and harmony) of Reich's composition.

Reich is currently dressing "Different Trains" in a format he calls "music theater/video." In this new format of a piece, Reich sees it being experienced three ways: the stories would be told by the characters projected on a large screen, the musicians would simultaneously play the materials derived from the speech patterns, and the audience would hear the music and experience the drama of the storytelling.

Reich responded that "Different Trains" "dealt with the state of affairs"; it is social art. Reich stated, "Good art lives and dies on the strength of its music, not the validity of its political stance." He cited Wagner as one who wrote music that was politically potent yet also stood as "good art."

Besides the western European traditions, Reich is also heavily influenced by the African American traditional forms, as well as his studies of African drumming and Balinese musical forms.

Did these influences come to bear on the performance Saturday night? Overall, Reich's concert was truly enjoyable and the performances were extraordinary and seemingly flawless (except for the musician who dropped something during the quiet moment in "Sextet").

The concert was opened by a piece called "Clapping Music." It was just that. David Tanenbaum's playing of "Electric Counterpoint" was at first problematic because the early entrances with prerecorded tracks seemed out of sync. But this soon turned into a wonderful and warm mesh of live and taped guitar textures. "Six Pianos" was very intriguing, as we rarely get a chance to hear six pianists play together.

In all the pieces, Reich incorporates much of the musical language we know as common-place in this culture (atonality, Jazz, and traditional). But as all great artists must do, Reich brought his inventiveness to bear upon the language, and we got something called "Reich music." As well, one could clearly hear the influences of other cultural forms.

My only concern is not an attack against Reich's art, but given as an issue for reflection. Reich's composition "Drumming," which was "other cultural"-influenced and brought to the tonal art museum (concert stage), shares with other such works the need to be presented in its cultural context, lest it not be appreciated fully. I share this story told to me by an old African: "The man came to us and told us to put away our religion. And he told us to throw away our art. So he took it to the shores, and told us he threw it in the water. Years later we saw our art in their museums."

Farewell to Lenny: Reflections on a Hero Beloved (1992)

$\mathcal{T}$here are two days that will always be with me. I remember them vividly. One is the day I found out I was one of four composers invited to meet Leonard Bernstein. The other was the day I heard the news of his death.

In the winter of 1988 I received a letter that named me as one of several University of Michigan composers, conductors, and musicologists who were invited to meet with Lenny. The invitation included a concert that Maestro Bernstein would conduct at Hill Auditorium and an after-party at the home of the university president in Ann Arbor. That day I knew that I would finally have a chance to see Leonard Bernstein. Little did I know I would get a chance to know him as a person.

I also remember that other day. On Monday, October 15, 1990, the *New York Times* headline read, "Leonard Bernstein. 72. Music's Monarch Dies." I had been home in Detroit that day and was on my way to Ann Arbor. I was in my car when the announcer said Bernstein was dead. I cried and cried. There was something about that man and his music, there was something in him that was me and what I wanted to become. I was influenced not only by his music, but also by his personality, fire, and passion as a musical being. For me, Lenny was a living Beethoven, a living Ellington. Of all the composers that I love, living or dead, from within my culture or of European heritage, Bernstein moved me the most. I was impressed by him as a personality, composer, conductor, teacher, and as an artist who lived to share his art with people. This seemed evident to me in the very sound of his music. Music seemed to be everything for Lenny. I sensed this simply from his being. As a brilliant conductor, teacher, performer, and aesthetician, Leonard Bernstein was my ideal of the American composer.

His music captures the difficulties and triumphs that characterize the American social landscape. Unlike many composers who take Jazz and European music and attempt to force a marriage, Lenny's interpretations and expressions are authentic. There is something about *West Side Story* that is authentically American. You can hear the cultural war going on between the Sharks and the Jets. In the song "I Like to Be in America," New York Puerto Ricans struggle with issues of cultural preservation and assimilation in America with all the rights and privileges thereof. These all present a kind of majesty of popular culture.

I idolized Leonard Bernstein, so you can imagine the joy I felt to get a chance to see him in person. I couldn't wait. I rehearsed over and over what I would say. Would he be able to listen to my music? Would he encourage me as an up-and-coming young composer? Would he care that I was a Black composer? Would I even get a word in edgewise against the number of bright conductors, composers, and theorists also invited to speak with him?

The long-awaited evening opened with a concert of works conducted by Bernstein that included his own selected works and a Beethoven symphony. He was magnificent. To watch him conduct the orchestra was to watch the baton speak sweetly to the orchestra. That evening all of Bernstein's hand motions and gestures seemed to transfer his every emotion directly to the orchestra players. Bernstein touched his hand to his heart, sighed, leaned backwards, closed his eyes, and caressed the musicians with his direction. There were those who felt Lenny was bombastic and overly dramatic. I think these critics missed the point! Musical expression itself is very dramatic. Musicians who understand this are able to transmit an experience that is alive and real. Leonard Bernstein could breathe life into a sometimes cold, rigid, and familiar Euro-/ Anglo-American musical institution. Bernstein always reminded us that music from the heart was best.

After the concert we headed over to the university president's home to meet Bernstein personally. My friends and colleagues Steven Newby, Denise Ince, Todd Levin, and John Costas and I were all charged by Leonard Bernstein's presence. I had one objective. I wanted to get a picture of him, shake his hand, and tell him how much I appreciated his gifts as an artist.

The president's house was filled with musicians, the press, and, of course, a group of high-society Ann Arborites who were mainly interested in their own snootiness. I never thought among all these people that I would be the "one brother" who could pull Lenny aside and get him to be himself away from the society snoots.

We all patiently awaited his arrival. As he walked past me, my heart seemed to stop about six times. Here he was, short, frail, and old, with snow-white hair but just as lively and elegant as you could imagine. He walked in like he was walking onto a Hollywood movie set, his long cape and turquoise scarf billowed behind him. But something was amiss.

Todd Levin, Stephen Newby, and I got the feeling that Lenny was bored by this atmosphere. We got the bright idea that we (the graduate students) should take him out on the town, what little "town" there is in Ann Arbor. We actually pulled Bernstein to the side, as the press and the Ann Arborites were too busy snooting around to notice, and suggested to him that we leave. His eyes grew big and to our complete surprise he said, "Yes we have to get out of here. I'll call my driver and we'll make the move." We actually got him in his limousine and the four of us drove off toward downtown Ann Arbor! There we were, Banfield, Newby, Levin, and Bernstein.

Lenny was happy because he really wanted to share with us younger composers and graduate students and was not at all interested in hob-snobbing with the president and his crew. In the car Lenny asked Newby and I about our Blackness. He wanted to know how our Blackness was important in our composition. As a composer he was genuinely supportive of our own cultural voices.

We arrived at a local bar and I went in to "prepare the way." I said to the bartender, "Lenny Bernstein is about to come in here. Can you clean a table?" "Yeah, right," was the reply I got from the bartender. "No," I insisted, "it's really true!" When we walked into that bar mouths dropped all over the room. We were a sight to behold; several graduate students walking in with none other than Leonard Bernstein. There we sat, Lenny in the middle and the rest of us gathered around him, asking questions about his life. We asked him about the meaning of art, politics, and culture. We talked about being Black and being Italian. He seemed so genuinely interested in hearing what was on our minds.

For some strange reason Lenny gravitated toward me. He encouraged me to express what he called my Blackness. He said it was beautiful and what made me different. He was not the first to tell me this. I had just returned that year from Tanglewood, where I spent some time with the German composer Hans Henze, who also stressed my ethnicity. Those who are in touch with art in the real sense are also in touch with people in the real sense. People are culture. Culture is people.

Music and art are the expressions of the heart and soul of people. Lenny knew this. When he was ready to leave I walked with him, arm in arm, to his car. I hugged him and told him how much I appreciated him. The black limousine whisked him away. I had the chance to share the meaning of life and art and culture with one of the greatest musical personalities of our time near the end of his life. Farewell Lenny, I shall always love you.

· 32 ·

Ode to a Friend: Michael Powell,
Visionary Producer (1992)

$\mathcal{M}$ichael Powell, Chicago born and Detroit raised, is nationally recognized as one of our leading pop, R&B Black music producers.

His list of artistic projects include the Grammy Award–winning Anita Baker (*Rapture, Giving You the Best That I Got, Compositions*), Jennifer Holiday, Peabo Bryson, Gladys Knight, Patti LaBelle, Karyn White, the Wayans, Jody Watley, and Grover Washington Jr., just to name a few. Powell not only produced these projects, he was also composer and performer on many of the cuts. Powell's contributions greatly enhanced the sound tracks of *Lethal Weapon II* and Bill Cosby's *Leonard, Part 6*. Powell is also an entrepreneur. Oak Park, Michigan, was home to Powell's Vanguard Production Studios, which quickly became one of the nation's premier production studios.

Powell, in my estimation, functions as a composer, producer, and visionary. I certainly remember first hearing the Anita Baker *Rapture* album in 1985. My friends and I, all of us musician songwriters, were pleasantly shocked by the beauty of the work. "Who is this producer?" we all asked. These producers were actually homeboys from Detroit, people I grew up playing with. These guys were on the ground floor in a movement toward a new level of quality and a new awakening in the industry. The leader of this pack, Michael Powell, was, for lack of a better comparison, a "new Berry Gordy."

What made the Anita Baker and subsequent Powell productions visionary was that these were released during a time when the pop market was defined only by high-tech, robotronic, Madonna-like club mix productions. Powell's orchestration, which included all live musicians, was not totally new, but it was certainly fresh and innovative. Up against an industry that defined musical success in dollar signs and numerical sequences as opposed to good, solid music, the qualifiers musicians themselves use to measure a successful project, Powell and company were extremely successful. To be visionary, then, is not simply to possess the ability to create an idea, but to also create a space that gives that idea spark, life, and form.

To be visionary inspires further invention. I believe the first Powell productions created that space for the industry. Like Q Jones, Gamble, and Huff before him, Powell brought music and musicians to the forefront of popular music production. Mike, I love you. I'm glad to be a friend of yours and I thank you for your art.

Michael Powell subsequently produced my album Striking Balance, *2004.*

· 33 ·

His Royal Crowned Prince of Jazz Purists: Times with Wynton Marsalis (1994)

*M*y Wynton Marsalis stories are like anyone else's, colored with what some describe as his arrogant disposition, and spiced with those outlandish remarks about Jazz life as a culture. But, as in any story, there is always the story itself, the person in the story, and most importantly, the story in the person, which is the real deal. In stories, just like in life, it always takes a couple of good "reads" to discover that person who is sometimes hidden within the pages.

Wynton Marsalis, his brother Branford, and Spike Lee are three men whom I admire greatly. Needless to say, my first encounter with Wynton Marsalis is an experience I recall vividly. I was teaching music in an arts program sponsored by the Boston Symphony during the summer of 1987. The program was housed at Tanglewood in Lenox, Massachusetts, and on the weekends we would get free concert passes. The Wynton Marsalis Quintet was one of the featured "popular arts" concerts that year, so I made arrangements to see them. I had never met Marsalis personally and I waited eagerly backstage before the concert, hoping to speak with him.

The show was scheduled to start at 8:00 P.M. By 7:30, everyone in the band was present and in place except for Wynton and drummer Jeff Twain Watts. Eight o'clock came and went and Wynton was nowhere around. At 8:30 he still had not showed. This was a classical concert at the premier concert festival of North America, which ran on serious orchestra union time! Shortly after 9:00 P.M. a white Mercedes glides to a stop at the backstage door. The car door opens. Wynton and Jeff Twain Watts emerge, cool and unruffled. Watts, a schoolmate from Boston, gives me a shake and says, "What's up Banfield? You know Wynton?" Wynton shakes my hand, says, "What's up," and then continues around backstage. He takes out his horn, motions for the guys to go on stage and then, with neither introduction nor explanation, walks out on stage himself. He may not have been on time, but his music certainly was. Without missing a beat he played "Just Friends," an old Jazz standard. The true Jazz expression, the experience, the explanation, the rhetoric, and the grace flow from the horn—Marsalis gave an authentic performance that evening. I was floored.

My next encounter with Wynton Marsalis was a bit more substantial. Wynton held a workshop and lecture at Harvard in the winter of 1988, the same year I finished the last year of graduate studies at Boston University. I attended the workshop and was impressed with his work. I wasn't the only one impressed by him. Camera crews followed him everywhere. He had ascended to the throne of the Crowned Prince of Jazz Purists. The media courted Marsalis as if he had the final word on Jazz meaning and style. Wynton played on that.

His commentary was no less outrageous in person than in all the magazines that quoted him. He explained Black expression for the White kids at Harvard who were in the Jazz band. He said, "You gotta smell the notes when you play them, like you smellin' something nasty. It's real man!" Actually the description seems pretty accurate judging from the expression on a tenor saxophonist's face during a burning solo that suggests the musician is smellin' something "pretty nasty." That's why the music sounds so good.

Marsalis went on to compare the Jazz rhythm section to a car; the drums are the engine, the bass is the wheels, and the piano is the body. He also went on to say that "Miles Davis is not a Jazz musician." This statement was ironic because this was during the time his brother Branford was doing what Wynton called the "sellout thing" with Sting. Wynton himself defined Jazz as "Louis Armstrong." I finally spoke up and said, "Wynton, you are trying to put a choke hold on an art form that has always been a form of expansion and expression." The audience fell silent. Someone should have said "Ouhhhhhhh!" but the silence remained. Marsalis turned away from me, completely ignored my comment, and motioned for the next question. He dissed me.

After the session ended Marsalis came over to me and asked, "You're a fusion cat, aren't you?" I explained to him that I had been in a serious dialogue with his brother DelFeayo and Dr. George Butler regarding a record deal. I asked Wynton if we could talk. We went back to his dressing room and rapped a minute. I was totally moved by the experience and afterward headed for my night gig.

I worked nights at the Hyatt Hotel in Cambridge. My night-owl shift as a room service waiter paid for the days I spent researching and writing my master's thesis. I was paying "out the butt" for my education. Well, there I was in uniform and all behind the front desk, when guess who steps up to check in? Wynton Marsalis, along with Edward Arrendell, his personal manager, caught me in the act of struggling. I mean, this was good honest work, but I didn't want the Crowned Prince of Jazz to see me working in hospitality and food service. I was completely embarrassed. Wynton did not make it any better when he said, "So, this is your real gig." With much pride I said, "No, this is the gig that pays for my real gig."

My next encounter with Wynton Marsalis was in the summer of 1992, after I had become Dr. William Banfield. Marsalis was in Detroit for another workshop, this time at the African American Museum of Life and Culture. Check this. Wynton lectured during the day, I lectured that night. That evening I gave the paper, "Miles Davis/Sarah Vaughan: Staples of the Black Aesthetic." Wynton gave the wonderful quotation that I use in the opening of this book. He said, "Black artists should be about addressing the world in terms of [Black cultural] ascendancy, not pulling it down with values of demise and destruction."

I later called Wynton on the telephone because he was staying with Wesley Skip Norris, a mutual partner and the man who Stanley Crouch refers to on the *Blues Alley* album (1986). I told Marsalis how much I enjoyed his comments at the workshop and I wished him well on his concert performance that evening. Later that night, after the concert at Detroit's Chene Park, the Graystone Jazz Museum held an "afterglow" Jazz session in honor of Marsalis. I was there and was again impressed by Marsalis, who, after playing a full concert, showed up at the afterglow to play with the Young Detroit Lyons until after 1:00 A.M. (People like Legacy, James Carter, Calvin Brooks, and even some of the old guard, like Roy Brooks, came through that night.)

What strikes me so much about Wynton Marsalis is that he almost single-handedly has taken on the role of Jazz priest of our times. (That is not to forget Billy Taylor's pioneering work. Taylor introduced the notion of Jazz as America's classic music.) Marsalis preaches the word of cultural salvation through Jazz artistry. He is committed to this important and challenging office during a time when most Black people equate Jazz with Kenny G. Marsalis did not hesitate to surround himself with those young Detroit lions who fired every possible question about playing toward him. I stood nearby and he turned to me and said, "Bill, if you knew how much playing and smiling I've been doing in the last several weeks . . ." In other words, he was bushed. Yet he refused to leave Detroit's Fox Theater that night until everyone was satisfied with his presence and performance there.

Jazz is the big brother in the family of Black artistic expression. Thanks, Wynton, for what you have done and continue to do to champion one of the greatest American art forms of the twentieth century. Coming up with you around and on the case makes being Black and an artist a high honor. You are more than worthy of a regal title.

Stevie Wonder: He Remembered My Name! (1991)

I had just completed my first record, on my own label, BMagic Records, Boston. I was twenty-two. I thought my record would be a regional hit. I had my friends Najee and Jazz vocalist Carla Cook as featured soloists. Najee had not yet gone national, this was 1984, but he was doing lots of session work and touring with Chaka Khan.

Our record got a Billboard mention, but a regional hit? No such luck. I did receive, however, a call from the financier of the project, who was a real estate investor. This investor asked me, "Bill, how would you like to meet Stevie Wonder? Well," he said, "I have to set up an appointment for you to meet him." He was actually a good friend of Stevie's chief of security and was able to arrange the meeting. He informed me that Stevie was aware only that I was a young musician from Detroit who wished to speak with him and have him hear my music. I couldn't believe it. I was going to get a chance to play my music for Stevie Wonder.

The day finally arrived. Stevie was performing in Boston. I was picked up and escorted back to his dressing room. Before seeing Stevie I was introduced to his brother and also got a chance to hang out with the musicians, who all happened to be homeboys from Detroit. They ushered me into the dressing area. Stevie was in an adjoining room preparing his voice. I could hear as he gargled and sang warm-up scales. I tell my students all the time that, for as long as Stevie has been performing, he still takes time to meditate and prepare his voice before every performance.

I was by now anxious to meet him. But just as I was about to speak with him the doors burst open. A bunch of those stupid reporters and some anchor lady from a local entertainment news program hustled into the room. I knew they were going to ruin it for me. Larry Gittlens, Stevie's trumpet player, pulled me to the side and said, "Little brother, if you want to spend some time with Stevie you are going to have to take charge of this entire room or you'll never get a chance."

What would I say? I stood up and assertively announced that everyone would have to clear the room because I was still not finished with some important business with Mr. Wonder. I informed the news crews that when I finished I would come out and let them in. Well, to my surprise, they all cleared out on the assumption that I was working with Stevie. Hell, I hadn't even seen him yet. Larry just cracked up.

Then the inner door opened and Stevie emerged. I couldn't believe it. Again the perpetual question arose in my mind, "What do I say to . . . ?" We were introduced and Stevie asked to hear my music. I played several pieces, one of which featured singer Lynne Fiddmont Linsey. Stevie asked, "Who is that girl?" I told him and over the years, Lynne went on to become one of Stevie's backup singers. I have since told Lynne that she owes me because I gave her a first audition with Stevie Wonder, free of charge.

My meeting with Stevie was soon interrupted. Those pesky news people pushed in, spoiled the artistic exchange, and stained the experience with a vacuous line of questioning, imposing cameras, lights, microphones, and bad breath. Stevie turned to me and said with sincerity, "Let's get together tomorrow where we can listen and play some music or something, I'll give you a call." I stood there in disbelief. Why would Stevie Wonder make time for me? God is good.

The concert that night was incredible. Stevie did two concerts in Boston and then headed out to New York to Radio City Music Hall for the weekend. I wasn't able to see him immediately afterwards but you better believe I went home and waited all night for his phone call. The call came the next day around 11 A.M. Melvin, Stevie's brother, said, "Bill, Stevie wants to meet with you at 1 P.M. in his suite in the Copley Plaza Hotel." I was now in complete shock. How was I going to proceed and have a conversation with probably one of the world's most beloved artists?

I arrived at his room and Larry escorted me inside. Stevie, dressed in a robe, came out and took a seat. I sat on the floor at his feet. I can't remember much of what was said. I do remember that he encouraged me not to become weary. He said that the music business was a rough road to travel and he told me that although I was talented I had to be ready to endure a lot of stuff and I had to learn to be patient. (I still don't think I've learned to be patient.)

He invited me to stay with his group all day and asked me to come and join them in New York. I was to meet them at Radio City Music Hall. But when I arrived in New York that weekend, with no ticket in hand, standing outside with hundreds of people who were waiting for tickets, I was soon disillusioned about getting a chance to speak with him again. I was in an impossible situation. I tried to push my way through at the side door, where there was yet another crowd waiting for a chance to go in with musician friends. Those of us at this door looked for familiar faces. I knew by this time I had been forgotten and Boston was the only chance I would have to be in Stevie's glorious presence.

Suddenly, one of the band members poked his head out of the door and shouted into the crowd "Is Bill Banfield out here?!" I was dumbfounded. I couldn't believe he remembered my name. I pushed through the crowd once again, proud to have my name. I was escorted backstage and received both a ticket and a backstage pass. Stevie tore up Radio City that night. I heard new technology, new keyboard sounds, a live performance with studio-record quality. Stevie, always on the cutting edge of technology, had the best of everything. The place was jammed full of folks. I have not since seen a concert that was so hot! Of course by this time much of his family, including his children, had made their way to the New York performance, so there was no possible chance for me to see him again. But the memory of that exchange will stay with me forever. Hey, I wonder if Stevie still remembers my name?

His Name Is Prince and He Is What?! (The Artist, Genius, and Meaning of . . .) (1994)

I have a keen interest in the Artist Formerly Known as Prince (he was still known as Prince at the time of this particular dialogue) and his role as an artist in American culture. When I first heard Dr. Banfield's music, I told him that he reminded me of Prince. That statement sparked a series of conversations that finally evolved into the following foray.

—Crystal Keels

William Banfield: How did we get on this Prince thing anyway?

Crystal Keels: It happened during your concert that Sunday.

WB: Yeah?

CK: Yeah, because I sat there and I listened to your work and it seemed to me that you had married so many traditions. It was pretty. I got the same kind of feeling from your symphony that I get from Prince music. That's why, when I saw you, I told you that you reminded me of Prince.

WB: Now that's a first! No one has ever told me that I reminded them of Prince. That's scary. I don't want anybody to listen to my music and make a connection with Prince! But maybe there is something there in your comment that I should appreciate. Maybe there is something there. So what drew you to him anyway?

CK: I started to like Prince when I was in high school. I thought for a long time that I was the only one who liked his work because so many people just dismissed him. He didn't get a lot of airplay on the radio at first. And I told you about how my brother gave me the Prince album because he was repulsed by Prince's naked presence on the cover. My brother was like, "Here take this." I started to read the album covers and found out that Prince did all this work by himself. I could just imagine this person who was so intense sitting in a room somewhere by himself, never coming out, and producing all this stuff. I thought that was really incredible.

WB: Actually, when I first heard about Prince I was equally drawn to him for those same reasons and because he was someone who was our age. We heard about him in about 1979.

Nineteen seventy-nine was when I first heard about him. That was during his first or second album, right? I mean, we look back . . . the first album was *For You*. Nineteen seventy-eight, so I think I must have heard him by then. I remember clearly hearing about this young genius who played 23 instruments and he was only, well, we were about 18 at the time, so they were saying that Prince was 16. Now Prince is three years older than I am, but they were saying he was three years younger. It was part of the media hype at the time, that there was this young genius who played 23 instruments and produced this $100,000 album. That was the largest amount that was given to any one artist for a first signing and that was Prince. So, I was frightened because I thought, we all thought, we were in Boston at the time, and we all thought we were the young up-and-coming and here was this guy in Minneapolis, an unknown who had gotten a $100,000 record deal. We were just . . . I was in awe of him. I remember going across the street and seeing his poster in the window. The poster was actually the front cover of the *Prince* album where he was kind of blue and he was just there. It was just his face and he was naked or something. Not the one on the horse but the second one, I think.

CK: No, it's actually the front side of the horse.

WB: The front side of the horse album.

CK: The winged horse!

WB: The winged horse, yeah. That's how I first heard of him, back in '79.

CK: Well, I have a question and it has to do with the way Prince was received. We can talk about the negative aspects of his work because he is known for his blatant sexual lyrics, etc., etc., but he says he has two sides. Do you see any positive value in what he does?

WB: Only musically, which is important for me, right? I mean, I don't see anything in terms of socially positive aspects, even though I know you want to make a claim of his great philanthropic efforts, and what he does in terms of bringing young people to his concerts, and singing, and giving free concerts and all that. I mean, big deal, that's a nice tax write-off.

CK: Oh, okay.

WB: That's the only way I read it. And that may be kind of a harsh read on his humanity but I think the positive things . . . I think first of all Prince is a genius. I mean, as an artist I've got to appreciate this. This boy is bad, okay? He's slammin'. He's slammin' as a guitarist. He's slammin' as a composer/songwriter, as a lyricist, as an artistic conceptualist. He's slamming as a pianist. His vocal ability is incredible. His range is something unknown. I mean UNKNOWN!!

CK: UNKNOWN!

WB: Hold on to that. We'll come back to that theme. So as a musician, I mean, he's just incredible. I think that too much of serious culture, apart from popular culture, i.e., people in the academy, have not done a serious talk or look at this wonderboy genius, Prince. I think we have to look at him.

The other thing that I think is very positive is his ability to pull all this music together. The boy does Gospel, Jazz, R&B of every sort, and Funk. He quotes James Brown, he quotes Sly Stone, Little Richard, and everybody. He embodies the American Black popular artist in every way. Prince IS the example of that. And so, for all those reasons, as a cultural agent, I absolutely honor him in the supreme sense.

CK: Okay.

WB: But only artistically, so one has to be cautious.

CK: That's interesting. That's interesting because I was going to ask you what you thought his influence is on Black music in general and maybe I can ask you that question in light of the statement you just made. You talk about how he brings all of these things together, but where does he take them?

WB: Well, when he arrived on the scene in the late '70s and early '80s, Prince and his entourage single-handedly changed the sound of popular music. Single-handedly. Just as you can point back to Miles Davis's influence or Charlie Parker's influence, or Duke Ellington's influence, in the same traditional thread, continuum, or track, you can look at Prince as having an absolute influence and, you and I have talked about this, not only in music but also in terms of popular cultural trends and commercial marketing, okay?

CK: Right, right.

WB: He started a new trend of popular music production because he emerged as a solo artist producing music by himself. Even though Stevie Wonder had done it before, by himself, Prince made it the mark of the industry. So, by the time the '80s rolled around, you didn't have a producer or a group of producers who produced a group, i.e., working on the Commodores or whatever. You have one guy, or two guys, producing, doing all of the music by themselves because of technology but also because Prince made that fashionable, I think. And then the Minneapolis sound was all his boys—the Time, and Jimmy Jam, Terry Lewis, he introduced them.

CK: Mazerati, the Family.

WB: Yeah, all those folks, you know. The Family. That was a whole generation, a whole sound. We owe a lot to Prince musically, the industry does. That's a very positive . . . well, I don't want to say positive, it's a very remarkable contribution to musical culture.

CK: Why wouldn't you say positive?

WB: Oh, why are you pushing me there? What was I saying? The positive? Was I supposed to continue with the negative aspects?

CK: Well, I asked you why isn't that positive? His influence? The Minneapolis sound, all of that? His influence on other artists, why isn't that positive?

WB: I think those artistic and conceptual aspects of his presentation are positive.

CK: Okay.

WB: No, I take that back. His musical sharings with us are very positive because he embodies what a great musician should be about in the same way that Wagner was a great musician, that Beethoven was a great musician, that Stravinsky was a great musician, that Ellington was a great musician, and that Charlie Parker and Miles Davis were great musicians. And Schoenberg. They pushed the tradition. They pushed the boundaries and therefore created, with that push, new avenues for artistic expression. So, for those reasons Prince is absolutely someone to be reckoned with. That is musically, artistically.

CK: Okay, so if someone were to say to you that Prince is a modern-day Mozart, and they said that, right, you've heard that before, or that he is a modern-day Beethoven, you wouldn't disagree with that?

WB: Absolutely not. Absolutely not. I mean, in terms of his role as a creator he is comparable. Now, the depth of his work, or its longevity or its ability to sustain in a way that a Beethoven piece or an Ellington piece has, well, that's questionable because we've only been watching Prince now for about 12 or 13 years. It is hard to say at this point. We'll have to see. Like, we look at Ellington now. Here's a man who has created music that will last the next hundred years, the same as Beethoven. Whether Prince will be able to last a hundred years, you know, we have yet to see. Let's talk in about another 25 years. We'll have this conversation again. Let me ask you something.

CK: Well, wait, before we go on, one of the ways I measure the longevity of music . . .

WB: Uh huh.

CK: . . . is if it moves into Muzak.

WB: I see.

CK: If it becomes elevator music.

WB: Ah, ah ha, yeah, gotcha.

CK: He's already done that . . .

WB: Yeah, so what?

CK: . . . with "Purple Rain."

WB: Yeah, you're right.

CK: You get on the elevator and there it is.

WB: Yeah, you are right.

CK: So, his work has become part of our culture. I turn on the TV during the Superbowl and I hear his music, during Superbowl whatever it was, in Minneapolis. I am thinking that he will be one of those artists whose work stands the test of time.

WB: I think you are right. We still have yet to see, but I'm willing to bet you're right about that, especially in terms of American popular culture.

CK: Also, there is the Joffrey Ballet. They have taken his work and they've done it.

WB: Yeah.

CK: I think they've also moved him to another place in our culture. That's something that . . . he was introduced to a whole new audience. His work got a standing ovation.

WB: You were there, huh?

CK. Yeah. It was amazing. People who I never thought would appreciate Prince actually did and I know it was in combination with the dance and all, but the music inspired the dance and the dance inspired the music, so how are you going to separate the two? And these were people older than we are, okay, like, the ballet-going crowd, the "typical" ballet-going crowd. I think I was the only person of color in the room. Well, maybe that's an exaggeration, but he has made that crossover and he has positioned himself in different places in the culture.

WB: Yeah, you're right. Well, you seem to be obviously very supportive of Prince. We've had several conversations about this. How do you explain or interpret his meaning as a social/ political/artistic American phenomenon? I mean, you just said that but let me push that further because you really just answered that. Are you not disturbed by the message or the meanings in his poetry? Let's get right to the deal here.

CK: Okay, in terms of what?

WB: In terms of some of the themes and things that are very explicit in his message. Don't any of them disturb you? We've talked about some of them.

CK: Let's see. Actually, no. His discussion of sex is everywhere.

WB: Prince is sex.

CK: Well, not necessarily because . . . well, yes he is, isn't he? But sex is life and we tend to separate the two. Or at least try to.

WB: Yeah.

CK: And he keeps reminding us, "Hey come on, you know, that's part of life, that's where we come from." He takes the focus, more or less, off of conventional notions of where sex should be. It's like trying to take the beauty of the erotic out of life.

WB: That's very interesting and that's usually the classic defense for him. That it is no different than what we see in any other popular music. But isn't Prince like that times ten?

CK: It is different.

WB: Yeah, it's a bit different. And it's alarming to the point that it may be destructive to the normative sensibility. Now normative, that's a value judgment, of course.

CK: Right.

WB: But I do think that if you talk to ten people you are going to find probably some standard of normative behavior which I think Prince goes beyond. Now, if that is a mark of genius or a great artist then I give him that as an artist. But as a person who also is trying to make a stance ethically and morally about how artistic expression should be couched I think I find Prince a bit on the X-rated side and he pushes a bit the issue of the presentation of sexual behavior in music. You're right, it is a part of it, but he's gone a bit too far.

CK: Well, you are not alone in your feeling. I remember I read an article where Annie Lennox said that he might as well have an orgasm right there on the vinyl because he is able to push his music that far. It is unique. He is unique in that.

WB: Unique as a qualifier of good? Not morally but I mean in terms of . . .

CK: I think it's good.

WB: Yeah.

CK: I think that's part of his work.

WB: You can't separate it.

CK: Yeah.

WB: I mean, like, don't these themes bother you?

CK: His work may be a bit misogynistic.

WB: Yeah.

CK: That bothers me.

WB: Okay but what do you think is the real meaning behind all this religious rhetoric, i.e., "he's coming," "Seven," "God," him being the messiah. What does all this mean?

CK: This is a time in history where people are struggling very hard to find some meaning in their existence and it's gotten harder, I think, because of media images and the number of messages that come in and things falling apart, things like the divorce rate is up and families are disappearing. You get an education but so what? What happens to your life? Why do bad things happen to good people? We talk about things more. Children are exposed to problems in their families whereas we tried to keep that away from them before. We talk about more things, generally, as a culture, and I think what Prince has done with religious notions is the same thing that he has done with different types of music. He pulls from different places and creates a new belief system.

WB: A new belief system. For what reason, though?

CK: That's a good question.

WB: What this belief system is saying is where I have problems. Let's talk about what it's saying, the belief system. The whole notion of him being this dark figure who has this great powerful gift to whose message you ought to listen? He is the messiah? Why don't you come my way? This New Power Generation? I'm the leader of the new revolution, spiritual transcendence through sex, the biracial theme, the abandonment of racial lines, sexual lines, and this whole notion of him being a leader and going his way? This is the new spiritual mode that he's taken? I want to find out if you think there is any meaning behind this, or is this just rhetoric? I mean, is this just a marketing concept or does he really have something in mind with all of this?

CK: That's really hard to pin down because I do believe that there is a marketing aspect. But there is so much more to his blending of both race and gender. There is a whole trend in our culture of people doing that. We can look at Michael Jackson, we can look at Boy George, we can look at the success of the movie *The Crying Game*. It's a time when people are questioning the categories that have been established.

WB: See, that's just it. Not only questioning the categories that have been established but deconstructing the categories, you know, for a new order. And that's okay because I believe society has to continue to push and forge ahead. I mean, that is what modernity is all about. But the problem is that you have to question each new system that, let's say belief system, that is presented or you keep running into situations like, what's my man? Koresh?

CK: Oh, yes.

WB: And before him?

CK: Jimmy Jones.

WB: Jim Jones and what's next? Prince and the New Power Generation leads a musical world astray? Now, I know I'm pushing that and being a little bit ridiculous.

CK: Maybe not, maybe not.

WB: But let's push it for a minute because I think that's what his message implies. That he wants a whole generation of young people to become part of this new generation.

CK: But is that so bad? Look at the old generation.

WB: Crystal, I don't believe that you . . . when we start throwing out some of this stuff . . . let's just look at each one.

CK: Okay. Well, I think that what he's talking about is, and especially if I think of this in terms of Black literary traditions, which I tend to do with him, he . . . take the song, for example, "My Name Is Prince." He has the power to say, "This is who I am." He cannot be pigeonholed into one area because he transcends them all. But he realizes that, as an African American musician, that possibility is there. "Well, he's a Black musician so he's going to do just this." The critics have tried to do this to him. He refuses to have this done to him so he takes control of himself, of his image, and he says, "This is what I am, this is what I do." James Baldwin did the same thing. "I am an artist," was Baldwin's statement, and Prince is the same way.

WB: Yeah.

CK: As a matter of fact, when he did "My Name Is Prince" on the *Arsenio Hall Show* he had actual reviews of his album in his hand and he set them on fire. So his statement was, "Yeah, well, you can try to say that I'm this and I'm that, and you can try to judge my work, but I'm the one who decides what I do."

WB: I have no problems with your support of him as an artist as I stated earlier. You're absolutely right, I put him in the same category as every great musical thinker that has evolved. But now I want to focus; my own interest in dialoguing with you on this particular issue has to do with his moral stance, which I find problematic.

CK: Okay.

WB: Some of the themes are very explicit in his music. Let's take some examples.

CK: So many people are so willing to talk about the "dirt" in his work! And that is what we have talked about before. He is still out there. He's still out there and if he has this big moral problem it's out there. It's not mainstream. People either love him or they hate him and the majority of people hate him because they don't . . . first of all, they see this naked man, or, he used to be naked, but now he shows up with his behind hanging out on MTV and he turns half of the viewers off. People are afraid of him. So, I don't think he necessarily has as much influence as . . .

WB: Influence. Let's talk about influence.

CK: Yes, let's do.

WB: Here we have a man who has consistently produced almost an album a year. He did *For You* in 1978, *Prince* in 1979, *Dirty Mind* in 1980, *Controversy* in 1981, *1999* in '82, *Purple Rain, Around the World in a Day, Parade, Sign o' the Times, Lovesexy, Batman, The Black Album, Graffiti Bridge, Diamonds and Pearls*, and now this new one, *Sex Symbol* . . .

CK: That's what you call it. It hasn't been officially named yet.

WB: I mean, talk about power and influence, not to mention the marketing, the movies, the Paisley Park production studios, and now he has the biggest A&R director deal in the history of the music industry. That's a man of significant influence and power. I have a real fear of that power because what his message is about is so pervasive and influential and so much a part of what I think is the crumbling moral sensibility in American culture right now. He's a power to be reckoned with. A man with that much power who projects the kinds of themes that he does, as I mentioned a few moments ago, is someone to be concerned about.

CK: Your talking about the themes of violence, death . . . ?

WB: Explicit sexuality. That sounds like a real moralist read, explicit sexuality.

CK: Well?

WB: I mean to the point of being pornographic.

CK: Pornography.

WB: I'm not talking about the beauty of sexuality; I'm talking about sexuality to the point of being pornographic. Like, for instance, take the tune "Gett Off," "Twenty-one positions in a one-night stand." That video is about . . . it should be X-rated.

CK: Well, I'll give you that.

WB: Well, except that they have all their clothes on, right?

CK: Right, right.

WB: I mean, this is a huge orgy and he's talking about, "let me bust your behind."

CK: Exactly.

WB: "Turn around baby, let me bust it." I mean, don't you find this problematic for young people?!

CK: Yes! But no more so than the other things that we listen to.

WB: Oh, that is the CLASSIC way out!

CK: Let me tell you, for example, I was at a wedding reception last September and this little girl knew all the words to the song "Baby's Got Back." I was disgusted. I was disgusted. But the one thing I'll say about Prince is, when they came up with this labeling of lyrics and things, he was all for it. He said that he thinks that parents should be able to control what it is their children listen to.

WB: So?

CK: So I think he understands his moral obligation and I think he understands the problems that his work presents.

WB: I see.

CK: But that's how he expresses himself. Now, if Prince approached you, Dr. Banfield, and proposed a musical project, a working relationship, what would you do? How would you react? Say he gave you full control of Paisley Park for a month or two and he came to you and he said, Dr. Banfield, I'd like to open up my facilities to you. I'm available to work with you. Anything you'd like done I will do." How would you react?

WB: I'd take it.

CK: Would you?

WB: Hell yeah. I'm not stupid. We'd have a good time. Me and Prince?

CK: Yes.

WB: Oh man, we'd have a ball! 'Cause I would appeal to his artistic side and I would try to get us both to enter into the world of artistic expression and try to see what it is we could do with the power of his position and with his talent and with his reputation as a musical entrepreneur. My goodness. If I ever had a chance to work with Prince in that regard I would definitely try to. There is one thing that, I think we would both agree, if I ever had the chance to talk with him, I think he would agree with me about the decline of Black popular music artistically. Prince is an artist who keeps the quality of the music at absolutely the highest standard, even in his most minimalist, reductionist music where he is just sampling a loop or just running a groove into the ground for 20 minutes. I mean, it's tastefully done in a way that an artist would do it.

So I think that's one area that, if I ever had the honor to speak with Prince, that would be one area I'm sure we would agree on. And then, if he gave me the opportunity, I would like to go to work in using his power and influence to make a statement about the necessity of bringing the quality of Black popular music up so that our young people want to reach that quality, not by sampling, but by actually performing and playing instruments and singing again. See, Prince is connected to a whole wonderful tradition of great singers. I mean, what's that ballad he does, the new one where he has the Jazz guitar in the background?

CK: "Damn U."

WB: "Damn U." What a lovely ballad! That's a great ballad, man! That ballad Ella Fitzgerald could be doing, or Sarah Vaughan could be doing or Billie Holiday, or certainly Luther Vandross. But he really understands the quality of our Black arts tradition and maintains that quality. To answer your question, that is how I would respond to him. I wouldn't go that way to the moral thing, you know. I know we would disagree there. I would say, "Hey, let's suspend our judgment on that stuff and let's just deal with the quality of the music. He's a great poet.

CK: Yes he is.

WB: Let's come up with some lyrics that just deal with love and relationships and saving the world and bringing the power of music . . . like the way [George] Clinton used to do it. He used to talk about the funk. Even though it had political overtones there was still this notion of the funk, on the music being the paradigm for life. There were some drug problems up in the George Clinton thing, you know, "Make my funk the p-funk, I want to get funked up." "Uncut funk," that had to do with cocaine use and what have you. In a sense with Prince, though, I would just like to move toward dealing with bringing the quality of the music up and putting that out there as a model for people to emulate.

CK: So you don't think that any of his lyrics carry that message? The positive message that you are talking about?

WB: Well, you tell me. You know every song he ever wrote.

CK: Almost.

WB: Almost. Well, he's got hundreds, so which tunes do that?

CK: Well, I'm thinking of the song "America," which is stuck in my head. It talks about the problems of life today and, I can't recall right now if it talks about the value of the music, but through the music it makes a comment that tries to take us to another place. Then I think back to the songs about going to another place like, "I Wish U Heaven."

WB: Well, see now, Crystal, we're going to go on with this conversation even longer because now you are going to have to unpack "other world," you have to unpack "heaven," you have to unpack "God," you have to unpack "messiah," you have to unpack "salvation," and "he's coming." Who is coming? All these biblical references like "Seven," "God," you have to unpack each one of those to find out what he's talking about. I don't think that what he's talking about is the same thing that the Word, in traditional language, implies.

CK: I'm thinking about his song "Positivity" now. The song is called "Positivity" and asks, "Have you had your plus sign today?" It is a whole commentary on affirming life, basically, in this world which, we know, people say all the time is hell. And it is. We talked about that the other day. There is so little in life that is really good. Life is hard, it's difficult, and it's ugly. But he's always talking about looking for the good things in life.

WB: Okay.

CK: So what do you do with that?

WB: I think it is so minimal in comparison to his other message that I don't even consider it a spark of light in the darkest room in the world.

CK: Oh really?

WB: Really. You and I just disagree there at this point. I just am not able to find enough here in his songs and his message to redeem the problematic issues that I find present in much of his work.

CK: Now I'm thinking about songs like, "Money Don't Matter 2 Night," where he talks about how you've got to get your soul together. It's not the money that is going to save you, it is how you relate and how you deal with other people, that whole notion of the value of other people.

WB: Value, value. For every one value you can find I can find 50 problematic values in Prince. We've talked about it! You are aware of these! Why do you run from the issue?! Why?!

CK: Which issue do you want to put on the table?

WB: Why do you run from my particular questioning of Prince's moral value message in his art? Why do you try to say that there are, equally on the other side, good positive messages, when you know almost every lyric that he ever wrote? You are familiar with them. Why do you dismiss the problematic ones in order to put forward the positive ones?

CK: I don't dismiss the negative aspects, they are there. He says they are there when he says he has two sides. He puts it right out there in front of you.

WB: Satan. [Laughs]

CK: OH STOP!

WB: Satan knows right from wrong.

CK: Uh huh, Satan? [Laughs]

WB: SATAN! What does the Church Lady say? "Must be, sounds like, uhm, perhaps, uhm, SATAN?!"

CK: Okay, we've talked about this before! You want to put it on the table, here it is! You said yourself that Satan is attractive to everybody. I've already said that Prince is not attractive to everybody.

WB: I didn't say Satan was attractive to everybody.

CK: Yes.

WB: I said if there was . . . I don't know who Satan is or what he is. I don't even know if there is a Satan. But, mythically speaking, Satan represents the attractive model of something that leads the people astray, away from the light, supposedly. This is the biblical way it is presented. So here comes Prince attracting people towards this new generation, this new mode of ethics, away from those things that are positive, even though he couches . . . as he explains what those positive things are he says, "Oh, they are boring." Like for instance when he talks about, in "Sexuality," or is it "Automatic," which is it where he talks about all the tourists who don't even take a picture with flash? They are boring.

CK: Right. "Tourists, what no flash again? Eighty-nine flowers on their back, inventors of the accujack."*

WB: Yeah. Well, he characterizes all of the boring, moral, straight and narrow people as tourists. He talks a little bit about "Let me take you to another world."*

CK: Right. "Let me take you tonight."*

WB: Sexuality is all that you need. "Sexuality, let your body be free. Stand up, this is your life. I'm talking about a revolution, we've gotta organize."* Who is this "we" who has to organize? He fits the mold, basically. Let's just break it down and put him in a category biblically.

CK: Okay.

WB: He fits into this group that is spoken about in Revelations that is supposed to be a wave of powerful people who lead the people away from good things, righteousness, or the way the power of God would have people go. So when he talks about this new generation he very easily fits into the whole prophetic notion of the evil days when you will have a wave of evil prophets who lead people astray. So his way of leading you astray, as he pronounces in "1999," is that we are on the edge of doom anyway, so why don't we just party like there is no tomorrow. And the banner of this code of ethics is sex, music and . . .

CK: Dance and romance.

WB: Right, dance and romance, this is the way of life. So, in other words, you can dismiss all other concerns because the gettin' off is the real thing. [Sings] "Gett off, 21 positions in a one-night stand. Gett Off."

CK: Twenty-three.

WB: Twenty-three positions, sorry. This is his message. It is clear in every tune.

CK: I want to ask you something, though. Let's go back to "Sexuality." Who was in office then? Who was president?

WB: Probably Reagan.

CK. Probably Reagan, okay. Prince makes a lot of political commentary in his work. I think that what he was doing was reacting to the Reagan regime that continued through Bush. That's where the song "America" fits into this. Prince, I believe, was trying to warn people about following that '80s mentality that said this is what life is all about; it's not how you treat each other, it's how much money you can amass. It's how much power you can get. He's addressing the talking heads who showed up in the media and were telling Americans this is what life is all about, the greed that was running rampant at the time. And I'm thinking that is what he reacts against. Now, if you want to talk about devils, demons, etc., you need to start looking at our politicians. There were a lot of nasty things going on. America was all over the world wreaking havoc. I think that Prince is very astute. For one thing, he travels all over the world and he may have had access to some of the things that we, sitting here, complacent, didn't see. He has the gift, the power, the talent, to bring that to us. And that's what he did.

WB: That's one thing that he did. I still don't think it dismisses the other stuff. But you're right, I mean, if we are talking fairly we have to look at all sides of the meaning of the artist. I see those political, powerful, positive things that he says. But for me, if you had to lay all the cards on the table, the others just don't stack up.

CK: We can argue from here to eternity . . .

*Lyrics from *Controversy* (Warner Brothers Records, 1981)

Crystal Keels now serves as assistant editor of Black Issues in Higher Education.

·36·

The Day I Met Flavor Flav
(Public Enemy and the Boyyy!!!!) (1994)

As usual, when I was leaving Detroit to teach, friends teased me and said something like, "Well, what's going on down South between a cornfield and a cow in the middle of nowhere?" For them, southern Indiana is a long way from the cultural mecca of Detroit, and they are right. But this day was one I would remember because it was the day I met Flavor Flav.

I was invited to a little gathering, a surprise birthday party for Mellonee Burnim, who was then the chairperson of the Indiana University African American Studies Department. The dinner took place at a local restaurant. Well-dressed, a bit reserved, and definitely Black, we were dining out in southern Indiana surrounded by white diners. Beneath my own sedate exterior, however, thoughts of Public Enemy flew through my mind.

The very next week I was to give a paper entitled "Rap Music: The Expression of Rebellion and Diversity" for the College Music Society in San Diego. My thoughts landed on a striking image of Public Enemy, Chuck D and his "clown companion" Flavor Flav, that appeared on the cover of *Spin* magazine. I was in the restaurant thinking about the paper and how great it would be to get a chance to talk with Flavor Flav.

My impression of him was that he was the most cartoonlike character since Pee-Wee Herman. In fact, Flavor Flav is Pee-Wee Herman urban style. I could see Flav on the front of a lunch box, or on a cereal box—Chocolate Marshmallow Publix Corn Flakes. I knew they could make a million off of this cat. I could just see it. There was homie on a box of cereal, head tilted to the side, the clock, the hat, the voice, "What's for breakfast boyyyyyyyyy!" These thoughts ran through my head. Then I wondered how Flavor Flav would respond to my critique of his image. I wondered if this "clown" ever said anything on his own instead of simply responding to Chuck D's rhetoric. I sat there at the table with these thoughts while I enjoyed the company of my dinner companions.

My eyes slowly circled the table and then the room. Nice folks, white diners, wait . . . What the . . . ? No way! It was Flavor Flav sitting directly across from us in a Bloomington restaurant on a Sunday afternoon! There he was, big hat, sunglasses, big clock, gold teeth, frowning smile, leaned to the side engaged in a conversation at a table full of White students who seemed to be his, yes, his friends. I yelled over, "Yo Flava, what up Mo?!" I excitedly told my friends, "Hey, that's Flavor Flav!" "What flavor, who?" was their puzzled reply. I quietly went into culture shock.

As Flavor Flav left the restaurant, I jumped up to follow him into the parking lot. What could I possibly say to him? I certainly didn't want to come off as an out-of-touch-wanna-be-Negro. I was well aware of the animosity between professors of the urban beat and professors

231

of the ivory towered university. I said, "Flavor Flav, how you doing man?" and I introduced myself with reservation. He responded, "Hey man just call me William. We have a lot in common already."

He was a gentle spirit and he was genuinely interested in my role as a young Black professor. I started in on him about the *Spin* article. Flavor Flav said he thought that was the best article that had been done on Chuck D and Public Enemy. Flav was interested in keeping in touch and gave me his card. We shook hands, he jumped into his car, and drove off with his friends.

I was floored, hard hit, standing on the concrete. In a daze, I looked up to God, the ultimate comedian, thinking, "Wouldn't you know it, not only is Flavor Flav intelligent and warm, his name is William." Who was really the clown? I knew I was as I stood there staring straight ahead for at least five minutes in the middle of the lot. I will never forget the day I met Flavor Flav. Life has great lessons.

· *37* ·

Rap Music on Trial (1994)

FROM THE *INDIANAPOLIS RECORDER*, MARCH 12, 1994

*W*ith the most recent arrests of Black Rap artists Snoop Doggy Dog, Dr. Dre, Tupac Shakur, and Flavor Flav, the question about the role of these artists and the pervasiveness of the glorification of the criminal hero through radio and video media becomes a major social issue facing all Americans. People are concerned.

Other issues that have arisen from the artistic standpoint is the lack of "real" musicianship, and the age-old question of the validity of art. And if the volume of worldwide sales is any indication of the validity of the previously mentioned artists' worth, then one could come easily to the conclusion that hard-core Rap artists are some of the most important voices in contemporary American culture. Has contemporary popular music, particularly Black popular music, fallen into the hands of a blind, insensitive commercialism which projects harmful images at the cost of exploiting young, innocent "wanna-be" poets and musicians?

And what of the cultural issues? Black artists have left a long, lasting, and deep mark of artistic excellence on American culture, which all Americans can be proud of. But, today some people are asking what one should make of this new wave of hard-core Rap and the much too sexually explicit R&B musical groups that have emerged. Have we come to a point where the tracing of the seeds of the cultural decline leads us to creative surges?

Music has always played a significant role in the shaping and construction of productive and life-affirming communities in American society, especially in lives of African Americans. Unfortunately, we have gotten to the point where too much popular cultural musical expression is not simply a reflection of an artistic vision of cold realism, but artists with the help of an insensitive and money hungry recording industry are involved in the game of cultural destruction through projection.

This projection leads to the internalization of some extremely harmful value and belief systems which target the impressionable young and fuels a rage that simmers just below the surface of society. As far as artists go, there must be a prophetic block of young commercially wise musicians who refuse to lower their standards of excellence for commercial success, and this of course must be done in partnership with ethically minded movers and shakers in radio, TV, and the recording industry, along with communities of parents, churches, and educators who are concerned enough to say: "Stop the madness! Our people are being destroyed!" We all must find more constructive ways to critique the social system that causes inequalities, change the awful reality and eliminate the shallow reactionary tendencies of the misguided

---

Article appears courtesy of the *Indianapolis Recorder*.

Rap rage, and the short-lived message of overcoming the blues with the easy fix of sexual saturation and satisfaction.

Cornel West from his writing *Prophetic Fragments* states:

> The impact of mass culture, especially through radio and television has diminished the influences of the family and the church. Among large numbers of youth it is Black (urban popular) music that serves as the central influence regarding values and sensibilities. Since little of this music is spiritually inspiring, Black people have fewer and fewer resources to serve them during periods of crisis. With the invasion of drugs in the Black community, a new subculture among Black youth has emerged which thrives on criminal behavior and survives on hopelessness. This spiritual crisis cannot go unheeded, for there can be no economic or political gain without spiritual resources.[1]

Despite what has been projected by the media as the cultural and artistic norm of African American urban communities (rapping hooded clowns thrusting fingers of hate), Black people are tired of images and themes which suggest that these images represent the entire community. Rap music is not the CNN of the Black community as some have suggested.

American consumers must realize that the recording business has taken advantage of this crisis in our culture, and that it exploits rappers and then throws them away only to quickly find another. The end result is that young consumers buy into an array of disrespectful, hateful, immoral behaviors and belief systems.

Again, one possible solution to all of this is to find more constructive ways of criticizing the social system which causes such inequalities to occur. A strong message must be sent to the radio and recording industries that Americans will not support these kinds of expressions within our communities if such destructive tendencies continue to impact our youth. The Rap medium is a valid artistic creation which fits easily into African American artistic genres, but the content of the messages heard primarily in the lyrics must be critiqued and challenged, and this is not censorship, but good common sense.

· 38 ·

A Brush with Teddy: Riley's Last Words (1994)

I walked the streets of downtown Indianapolis late in the summer of 1994. People were everywhere. Many of them had come to attend the Black Expo, you know, the one where Mike Tyson (the Bomber) went down for the count (or a number of them). Tyson wasn't the only celebrity in town; there were a lot of stars hanging around that day. I saw a group of young kids flood the lobby of the Omni Hotel. I decided to go with the flow, followed them, and found Teddy Riley and Guy. They sat on the cement edge of the fountain in the lobby, where they were admired by every PYT who could get within sniffing range.

I stood back, watched and waited patiently. I had BIG PROBLEMS with "Rump Shaker," Riley's most recent release. I couldn't come off on him about that but I was still searching for opportunities to speak with Black artists about their experiences. I would probably get only one shot with Riley and that exchange needed to be positive. After all, Teddy Riley was Miles Davis's new pivot point into yet another branch of Jazz expression. Boy got to be given his propas'. It came to me. I had a question for him and it was something I really wanted to know. As Riley signed the last autograph and moved toward the door with his driver I squeezed in between some young women and followed the entourage to the limo. He hugged the last "honey," I stepped in his path and said, "Hey, Teddy man, what's up? Man, I really enjoyed your work on the *Dangerous* album. How was it to work with Mike [Michael Jackson]?" "Thanks man," he replied, "it went really smooth. Mike was down."

Riley slid down into the limousine and it sped off. This situation was starting to seem very familiar. There I was again, stargazing. I stand there, a car whisks off with some famous person. There is a theme there somewhere. Bernstein, Flavor Flav, and now Riley. The fleeting remarks of famous folks figure into some sort of pattern. My short brush with Teddy revealed two more things about "moving" stars. The meaning of the experience lies in the realization that simple artistic presence itself sometimes states what an artist thinks. Sometimes Miles played only one note. Sometimes a brush of experience can be as illuminating as a short stroke of blue against a white canvas; you get color.

96 Hemmingway: The Boston Daze (1994)

$\mathcal{B}$oston, from 1978 to 1985, was one of the most potent developmental places for young Jazz artists since Harlem in the Bebop days of Parker, Davis, Monk, and Gillespie. None of us would have ever believed it or even thought about it at the time, but Boston produced an incredible amount of young world-class Jazz artists who are leaders in the field today. Almost as famous as those who occupied it is the address 96 Hemmingway, which was the apartment building many of these artists shared while in Boston.

I had come from Detroit, along with Mark Ledford, Terry Connely, Mark Mitchell, Derry Allen Kelly, Jeff Stanton, Regina Carter, and Carla Cook. We were all drawn to Boston and we were all so ready to ignite the world. The list of musicians is long and many of those same people are now famous as top Jazz and progressive Black popular musicians.

It was an extremely rich community filled with talented young musicians. Our exchanges coupled with the cultural climate nurtured so many sprouting musicians. Music poured from the walls and the windows. Trumpets blasted down streets, people sang, and, everywhere, guitars and drums blared. To us it was musical heaven. We were all about 18 and 19 years old. Only history looking back at herself will be able to reveal the reason why Boston was so fertile in those days. Boston clubs like Pooh's Pub, Michael's, Wally's, Springfield's, 1369, Riley's, and the Willow cooked continuously! The cats were gigging!

None of us, ironically, had any real young role models except perhaps Wynton Marsalis. Marsalis ushered in a whole wave of young, high-profile Jazz artists. He made the image of the young serious musician fashionable. His success, whether through exposure or exploitation, helped give credence to many careers. Never before in history had so many Jazz artists cornered the market as headliners. Prior to this period, Jazz had been an "old man's" and "seasoned lady's" market. Fame was not necessarily the goal, but young artists certainly flooded the market. Today an "old man" or an "old cat" would have to struggle for a record deal. What a switch! Wynton Marsalis is responsible for the renewed interest in the young Jazz musician. The other attraction in Boston was the number of Jazz masters who taught there. Allan Dawson, Jacki Byard, Mic Goodrick, Miroslav Vitous, George Russell, Tom McKinley, and a host of others too numerous to list imparted their wisdom and craft to eager students.

Volumes could be written about 96 Hemmingway and the musical renaissance in Boston. A chronicle of the incredible number of young Jazz players who erupted on the scene during this time has great historical implications. Many musicians from New York, Philly, Jersey, Boston, and Detroit got their start hanging out in Boston. Branford Marsalis is probably the most famous musician to emerge from this period. I saw Branford Marsalis for the first time during a gig I headlined at Pooh's Pub. Najee was my saxophonist that night and he was probably the reason Marsalis was there. I looked out into the audience and saw Marsalis seated directly in front of me. The next time I saw Marsalis I was playing in the streets with singer Lynne Fiddmont (now Lynne Fiddmont Linsey). Fiddmont and I were one of the most popular street duets. Marsalis came by, dropped a dollar in my case, and kept walking. Fiddmont said, "That was Branford. You don't know Branford? That's Wynton Marsalis's little brother!" Of course Wynton is the little brother, not Branford.

In the last decade, Boston harbored great Jazz musicians. Another port for musicians was 96 Hemmingway, which has both literal and symbolic significance. This house functioned as a microcosm of Boston. Out of this small space stepped many of today's Jazz giants: Donald (Duck) Harrison, Victor Bailey, Gene Jackson, Mark Ledford, Jean Touissant, Walter Beasley, and Jeff "Twain" Watts, all whom have gone on to become major Jazz greats, shared that one little apartment.

The list of Boston musicians goes on and on. Figures like Branford Marsalis, Najee, Smitty Smith, Kevin Eubanks, Wallace Roney, Monty Croft, Greg Osby, Cyrus Chestnut, Frank Lacy, Cindy Blackman, Don Byron, Terri Lyne Carrington, Nelson Rangell, Rachel Nicolazzo, Rachelle Ferrell, and Bobby Broom honed their talents by the bay. James Williams, David Dyson, Lenora Zenzalai Helm, Cecilia Smith, DelFeayo Marsalis, Armstead Christian, Lynne Fiddmont Linsey, Keith Robinson, Tommy Campbell, Jerry Etkins, Byron Brown, Mike Stem, Jeff Berlin, Billy Kilson, Jeff Stanton, and more musicians too numerous to mention made their mark. Intellectual Jazz circles were not the only productive places. There were also some local musicians well versed in the more popular "folk traditions," like Tracy Chapman, in the streets, the neighborhood bars, and the local talent shows. Tracy Chapman, Maurice Starr, the New Edition crew—including Bell Biv Devoe, Ralph Tresvant, Bobby Brown, and New Kids on the Block—struggled in Roxbury and Dorchester pre-1981.

Boston soil generated a great number of the industry's bright young musical stars in both the elitist Jazz market as well as in the young Doo-wop generation. This generation of kiddy Doo-wop was kicked off by the New Edition. Groups like Jodeci, Color Me Badd, and New Kids on the Block, as well as girl groups like TLC, Jade, and SWV, soon followed the tradition established by the New Edition and expanded the current musical trend.

I don't know what it was but from 1978 through 1986, Boston was the incredible pot where this century's greatest young musicians brewed and stewed a mess of talent. And 96 Hemmingway is the house where so many sleeping giants laid their young heads. The Boston daze and 96 Hemmingway represent, for me, a monumental moment of music making that has yet to be matched. That time in Boston was a fabulous flurry of fecundity that continues to influence contemporary musical trends.

· 40 ·

Gordon Parks: An Artist Celebrating the Human Spirit (2000)

I chose my camera as a weapon against all the things I dislike about America—poverty, racism, discrimination.

—Gordon Parks[1]

It was 6 P.M. or so, September 21, 2000, and I had just left the premiere of my brass work which was commissioned by the University of St. Thomas for the naming of their Roach Center for the Liberal Arts. The work went well and fitted within the tune of the event: the dedication to learning and celebration of the human spirit. This theme would continue ringing on throughout my evening.

As soon as the event was over, I rushed out to my car to head across the bridge to another gathering at the Anderson Library on the University of Minnesota campus. I was invited by dear friends who had been promising me an introduction to one of this past century's most important Americans, Gordon Parks. I had spent the last two years dreaming of what I would say or could say to this living prophetic voice of our times. He's a man who captured on film and paper several generations of people stories. As a photojournalist, composer, author, social critic and activist, movie director, poet, and humanitarian, Gordon Parks was the one human being whose feet I longed to sit at and who I longed to learn from. Parks had covered on film, word, and music World War II, poverty in America, Paris in the 1950s, segregation in the South, the Civil Rights era, police brutality in New York, Duke Ellington, Malcolm X, Ingrid Bergman, Barbra Streisand, and Leonard Bernstein. He had written about American society and directed the film *Shaft* (the original!).

I knew he would provide me with answers to question I sought as a researcher of culture: What must we as contemporary artists be doing? How can we continue the traditions set before us and still write new chapters? As Americans, people of color, what responsibilities do we have? Who are we accountable to as we document and share culture? My heart began beating faster as I approached the library where Gordon Parks was speaking.

The occasion was a dinner and reception sponsored by the Givens Foundation and Literary Collection, at which Parks was speaking as an advocate of their efforts to document the culture and preserve the traditions of Black literature.

His presentation in a crowded room of people was profound and moving, as Parks told of his humble beginnings . . . a poor boy from Kansas, the last and youngest of 15 children. He spoke of his mother's wisdom and concern for him; she believed he had something special that should be protected, so she sent him away to St. Paul to live with an older sister.

He spoke of his determination, and not genius in his words, but exceptional luck to be the recipient of the benevolence of a few people who gave him a chance. This occurred at every crucial point in his long and productive career. He recounted his first job as a photojournalist at *Life* magazine, the honor of being the first Black American to have a piano concerto performed by a major symphony, and his experiences as Hollywood's first African American film director, producer, and screenwriter. In every instance he said someone simply gave him an opportunity. This is why, he said, he could not turn down the Givens Institute's invitation to come and address Minneapolis.

His humor and wit, humaneness, and simple message were so moving. When asked by someone what was the most important lesson his life and experiences had taught him, he responded: "In all my years, near 90, the thing I have learned, what most matters, is love. Loving all the people and giving of yourself, extending yourself and helping someone, and liking giving more than getting."

He went on to say that so many people had extended themselves, reached out and helped him with no explanation. And so he admonished us to always be ready to help somebody else. Here is a man who can write the history of the twentieth century in several languages, art forms, and medium, a man who has more than 40 honorary doctorates and a presidential medal. This man has dined with and been an associate of many major figures of the last century. From this great human being, his best lesson was that in this life the most rewarding thing you can do is reach out to somebody else. This was for me the greatest lesson learned.

Parks's camera, words, music, books, and social commentary were the lens of the entire second half of the twentieth century. As a composer, he asked me what kind of music I was working on, and I described my opera, which is based on "Soul Gone Home" by Langston Hughes. Parks knew Hughes, the most important chronicler, in my view, of Black culture. I stood amazed, honored, in awe, and exhilarated.

I left the room knowing that I would probably never again have the great privilege to be in the presence of such a prophetic instrument. I knew that his illuminating message would forevermore be stamped on my mind and soul. Parks had given us all a map for our lives. From Parks we are given a recipe for doing our work—not profound in rhetoric, rhyme, philosophy, or jargon, but potent enough to move the world for many generations to come.

Ralph Ellison, *A Raisin in the Sun*, We Bamboozled: Some Thoughts (2004)

I may be Black, Poor, and I may even be ugly, but I'm here.

—Alice Walker[1]

In his teaching/lecture film, *Representation and the Media*, sociologist and cultural theorist Stuart Hall opens with the questions: Do media images help us understand how the world works? What kinds of images of Black people are we presented with? Then the film continues with the scenes from Robert Townsend's *Hollywood Shuffle*, in particular his spoof on Hollywood, the Black Acting School. In Townsend's short clip, in the school you can study epic slave roles, Jive Talk 101, Black walk taught by White professors. Hall explores a comic classic, but it as well underlines the importance of our critique and interpretation of cultural products, especially in image mediums.

Like music, film and literature have been places where a lot of questions about art, image, meaning, and the presentation and preservation of cultural integrity within the American culture arise.

My experience in exploring cultural expressions such as *The Invisible Man*, *A Raisin in the Sun*, *The Color Purple*, or Spike Lee's *Bamboozled* is that many times we just miss the richness, complexity, diversity of Black American cultural intellectual, spiritual, social, artistic experience and expression as well as the biting critiques. White folks don't get it, and many of us haven't been exposed nor educated beyond Harriet Tubman, the Blues, and a Black History Month program.

And so the range, the depth, the complexity, sensitivity, the beauty, and the diversity of Black people's experiences and culture are misinterpreted, misrepresented, dismissed (dissed), and seen as a miserable "Blues life," or with no family identity or legacy beyond our slave culture. There is in Black arts an attempt to be seen and depicted like other people's experiences as noble, relevant, or the narratives being further expressions of the universal continuum of human experience, although complex and varied.

From Black people there continues to as well be a suspicion and the rejection of yet another Hollywood version of the same theme of a White man saving the last samurai, Private Ryan, Native Americans, Mississippi's burning, New York's gangs, General Bush's universal police, or Captain Kirk's noble galactical explorations.

So, *Invisible Man*, a Blues-song like Louis Armstrong's "Black and Blue," Billie Holiday's performances of "Strange Fruit," Hansberry's *A Raisin in the Sun*, or Spike Lee's *Bamboozled* are all literary, poetic, visual movements in sound and variety of Black life and culture seen in multiple forms and forums lived in by multidimensional people.

Ms. Hansberry said of our work, "The most ordinary human being has with him elements of profundity, of profound anguish. You don't have to go to the kings and queens of the earth. . . . Every human being is in enormous conflict about something, even if it's about how you get to work in the morning."[2]

In literature, *Invisible Man* is at once specific to a Black male narrative and as universal as any of our common quests for identity and clarity in pursuit of self-definition. Remember the invisible man's last lines, "On the lower frequencies I speak for you."

In American culture since the ridicule and envy of Black people by Whites, our images, narratives, experiences have been so consciously degraded that the humane, the intelligent, the sensitive, the artful, the deep in value is so invisible to most in this culture, seen as marginal or exceptional coincidence, certainly not common.

So Ralph Ellison, a generation before him and following, these conscious Black intellectuals, artists, poets, painters, dancers, writers, have over the last 160 years been called upon to address, using their expressive powers to continuously explore the depth, range, rage, and beauty of the Black narrative. *Invisible Man* shines through as one of the most complex and creative; *A Raisin in the Sun*, a complete triumph; and still to become visible to mainstream culture is Spike Lee's contemporary satire on Black identity and image degradation, *Bamboozled*.

Black American experience, the narrative is completely unique as stories go. From the richness and variety of West African culture, languages, customs, to the slaves' experiences in the West Indies to Georgia and New Orleans, the transfer and transformation of Black Southern migrations from the South to northern cities, the synchronization of French, German, English, and American White culture has created an expressive, strange, deep, compelling, and beautiful story that artists have attempted to narrate, orchestrate, direct, dissect, rap, dance, formulate, finance, sing, and play through. That's what *Invisible Man* and most other comprehensive Black texts are attempting to do.

They are as well a necessary critique and correction upon what many times goes on unchecked as well in mainstream White American culture, and why we can only suspect our education and culture is so frightened of the Black perspective. Black gaze upon the hypocrisy in this culture stings and bites, and that inside lighted view, having in Ellison's words, "a slightly different sense of time, a certain ability to see within," this American dark cave, the 1,369 lights, the ability to suggest ways again in Ellison's words, to "solve the problem" that bothers a lot of people. Slavery, lynching, segregation, discrimination, un-civil rights, would have likely gone on longer in America had it not been for the eloquent voicing of these narratives. So, these narratives become more huge, more beautiful, more inclusive of the experiences of many more common people than we think, yet they speak with new colors, brilliance, shapes, and sound of the variety of our collected human experience.

A FURTHER LOOK DIRECTLY INTO SOME OF THE HEART OF THE TEXT OF *INVISIBLE MAN*

It has been said that Black narratives, creative work, creates a space that holds at bay the damages and attack of the ugliness of a falsely constructed, White supremacy practiced in America. And so in the 1940s, Ellison creates a character that is betrayed, humiliated by all, so he hides, becomes "invisible" in order to discover who he is without the imposed definition of others. His invisibility becomes a metaphor for anyone who sits on the margins of society, "on the lower frequencies," and the book becomes one of the great models in American literature.

My Top Ten Reasons Why Invisible Man *Is One of the Great Black Art Texts*

1. This is Black Peoples' great book about themselves, their map to surviving a cruel White world attempting to ignore their humanity and erase them. "Son, [the grandfather] after I'm gone, I want you to keep up the good fight. . . . Our life is war. . . . Live with your head in the Lions mouth. Overcome 'em with Yes, undermine 'em with grins, agree 'em to death and destruction, let 'em swoller you till they vomit or bust open wide. Learn it to the youngins." "Brother and Sistas, my text this morning, is the Blackness of Blackness. That blackness is most Black, most black."
2. Ellison as quintessential race man of the early twentieth century. He believes in the public example of Black exceptionalism. "Instead of uplifting the race, you've torn it down. . . . But in return, you dragged the entire race into the slime."
3. It is Black peoples' self-renaming ritual—"Since you never recognize me even when in closest contact with me. You no doubt hardly believe that I exist, I've illuminated the blackness of my invisibility." In other words Ellison empowered each reader to examine their nameless, selfless self, reflect, then have your own naming ceremony.
4. Poses the important questions of identity and self-knowledge. "You often doubt if you exist. You wonder whether you aren't simply a phantom in other people's minds. You ache with the need to convince yourself that you do exist in the real world. . . . You curse and you swear to make them recognize you." "Without light, one is not only invisible, but formless . . . to be unaware of one's form is to live a death. I did not become alive until I discovered my invisibility." "It took me a long time and much painful boomeranging of my expectations to achieve a realization everyone else appears to have been born with."
5. "Black Wisdoms," Ellison cautions about the world, "To Whom it May Concern, Keep This Nigger-Boy Running." "Why the dumbest black bastard in the cotton fields knows that the only way to please a white man is to tell him a lie!" "You let white folk worry about pride and dignity—you learn where you are to get yourself power, influence, contacts with powerful and influential people—then stay in the dark and use it." "Two things our people must do is accept responsibility for their actions and avoid becoming bitter. Son, if you don't become bitter, nothing can stop you from success. Remember that."
6. Ellison's critique on the insensitivity of White American racism.

   "I can hear you say, What a horrible irresponsible bastard. Who was responsible for that near murder—I? He bumped me. He insulted me. Shouldn't he for his own personal safety have recognized my hysteria? I should have used my knife to protect the higher interests of society. Some day that kind of foolishness will cause us tragic trouble.

   "These white folks have newspapers, magazines, radios, spokesmen to get their ideas across. If they want to tell the world a lie, they can tell it so well that it becomes the truth."

7. Quoting and romancing freely the Black vernacular—"What did I do to be so Black and Blue?" This Armstrong rendition and actual "spin" on Fats Waller's classic is about the social, psychological being in the world for every Black American.

8. A warning of the dangers of "massa's poison" the pitfalls of Black integration at the cost of losing self:

> Behold, a walking Zombie. Already he's learned to repress not only his emotions but his humanity. He's invisible, a walking personification of the Negative. You cannot see or hear or smell the truth of what you see. He believes in that great false wisdom taught slaves and pragmatists alike, that White is right.

9. Ellison's belief in the ultimate fix of a broken American society, a fraternity between the groups of Black and White Americans. From the 1981 preface he states:

> So my task was one of revealing the human universals hidden within the plight of one who was both black and American . . . conveying my personal vision of possibility, a way of dealing with the sheer rhetorical challenge involved in communicating across our barriers of race, and religion, class color and region-barriers which consist of the many strategies of division that were designed, and still function to prevent . . . the natural recognition of the reality of black and white fraternity.

10. My best quote from the book: "Come out of the fog young man. . . . And remember you don't have to be a complete fool in order to succeed. Play the game, but don't believe in it. Play the game, but play it your way. Learn how it operates, learn how you operate." Be your own father young man. And remember, the world is possibility if only you'll discover it . . . last of all, leave the Mr. Nortons alone."[3]

BAMBOOZLED

In Spike Lee's *Bamboozled*, Pierre Delacroix opens with a definition of this work as satire. He describes it as a literary work in which human vice, folly is ridiculed or attacked scornfully, the brand of literature focusing in on such activity. Where irony, derision, and caustic wit is used to expose such folly, vice, or stupidity. He evokes author Mark Twain and says satire is the way, a certain way to promote racial healing. So from the start we are served up an explanation of the movie *The Man Tan New Millennium Minstrel Show*. With White audience members, for instance, Italians, bragging of being a "bigger Nigger than anybody" and the "I'm a Nigger, You're a Nigger, we are all Niggers on this farm" rhetoric of the show, I wonder how many Americans got this? Other questions *Bamboozled* addresses in American cultural complexities are:

- Race relations
- Media exploitation
- Identity
- The undressing of the American soiled history
- Power and influence of popular culture to manipulate and distort truth
- Costs of assimilation
- Social inequality

- Rights of artistic voice, freedom of speech
- Definition of art
- Power of popular culture to influence culture
- The creation and maintenance of negative stereotypes
- The relentless cyclical struggle of Black identity in a radicalized society

And whose narrative is this, though told in the voice of Delacroix? Is it the Mau Maus's story of their rise and death, is it the betrayal of loyal Sloan, a commentary on the diversity within contemporary Black American family values, that is, Sloan, educated, assimilated, vs. her brother (Big Black Africa) as a Hip Hop radical, Man Tan and Sleep and Eats' exploration of their relationship, search for identity, their brush with the realities of the vacuousness of fame and glory, a sad commentary on the soiled psychology of big media or a way of depicting a forgotten history of the practices of minstrel, blackface, or Black collectible dolls and figures? *Bamboozled* has to be one of the most important films of my generation and fits the Black American model of a celebration of culture and the simultaneous critiquing of Black culture and expression, inner-cultural pathologies and myths as well as the larger societal framework.

All of these can be defined as the continual quest for authentic expression of Black identity up against the continual degradation of Black humanity in America. Again, our art does its best as a dual function always, cultural creation and cultural critiques from the Spirituals to Hip Hop and Black film and literature have been the great partner in this ongoing narrative.

CONCLUSION

What I think we can appreciate most from Ellison in particular is the profundity of his social analysis. It is American, it is Black wisdom and Black creativity, it is relevant and poignant American social critique and it is timely and timeless. It is timeless in that it teaches through decades, across boundaries of race, class, ethnicity, and it is timely in that we live in a most critical time of unprecedented media, macrocultural slicing, dicing, and distortion of public truth in human history. We are seduced by the power of Mr. Norton, Mr. Bledsoe, and bumped into and stepped on consciously by that "rude, insensitive man" Ellison almost killed. And yet for our sakes, he did identify him, and a plan for illuminating his atrocities. We should heed Ellison's mostly hopeful reading to live life to be illuminating the truth, coming out from under the stifling veil of our invisibility, and to keep in tune and in time with the "lower frequencies."

TAKING IT TO THE BRIDGE: THE FUTURE OF BLACK POPULAR MUSIC VISITED

"The Violence against Us" by James Zeke Tucker

The Future of Black Popular Music:
A Theory of Contemporary Interpretation

$\mathscr{T}$he following essays actually stem from reflections first published in the Black Minneapolis weekly, *Insight News* (2001–2004). In these essays I dealt with the future of Black music and values carried in music culture. In these essays, many of the themes this book wrestles with have been tussled out in plain view of a local reading and listening audience—listening because my radio show is called *Essays of Note*. On the radio show I play examples of the music and culture I write about.

Recently, as a researcher and teacher I have been consumed with the idea of the future of Black American music. Actually, while finishing my work as a W. E. B. DuBois Fellow at Harvard during the spring of 2001, Henry Louis Gates Jr. challenged me, "You should be dealing with the future of Black music. That's what we need to know about."

In the *New York Times*, dated April 22, 2001, a piece yelled out at me: The Blues is Dying in the Place it was Born. The article traced a narrative of three of the "last" living Delta Bluesmen. One Bluesman shared with the interviewer, "The Blues is about peoples, and as long as it's peoples, there will be the Blues. . . . Hip Hop don't tell the story . . . the Blues is about things."[1] These "things" really interest me. The people who tell about the "peoples' things" really interest me. I was chosen by the Mobile Museum of Art, Mobile Opera, Mobile Symphony and National Museum Loan Network for a partnership and series of commissioned works to celebrate the museum's expansion and to commemorate Mobile's 300th anniversary in 2002. In addition to composing the new work, time was spent traveling with the museum staff to select artworks from some of the nation's leading museums to celebrate the opening. This is part of an effort to increase interdisciplinary discussions among the nation's educators, artists, and institutions. What does this have to do with Black music? Well, the holding place for culture, the preserving spaces, make me revisit how our cultures are carried. A future for this art form means we have to make people aware and responsible for carrying on traditions. History, future, reporting on, "peoples' stories."

The idea crystallized for me: to pull and pool these resources and inquiries together in a way that would benefit my research through a series of documents for sharing this information.

As I state later on, the future of Black music relies upon the delicate balance of the convergence of authentic narrative, historic practice, contemporary expression, and innovations in artistic expression. This is precisely what I witnessed among the young Jazz–Hip Hop artists jamming in Philadelphia, a movement well known in the industry.

For addressing the larger questions coming out of the Delta, the birthplace of Black popu-

Article courtesy Insight News, Inc., Minneapolis, MN.

lar music, if it is dying, where do we go from here? What implications does this have for the future of Black American music and the stories and storytellers of the next generation's stories? Does the folk/vernacular narrative in art have a place or a space amongst the visual and market-driven music and culture of this century? Have we done service or some damage to ourselves and our traditions, the age-old question of the costs of progress? My premise is that while this inquiry is not new territory, it is rarely initiated by musicians themselves. I wanted to talk the talk with these older Black people and learn the inside story, to face some hard realities about the future of Black American music, a national treasure and culture.

I simply share these as the evolving reflection of Black music and contemporary music culture. In my mind it's all a part of the ongoing process of dealing as a musician in the world who is concerned about the quality of life and the way in which the music "sounds off" in the world, and how that art is being celebrated, received, and dealt with.

HOW TO READ THE FUTURE

In April of 2001, I traveled to Philadelphia to participate in a conference on American and popular culture. I had been thinking about the connections between young Black musicians and our culture. Schisms, styles, and generational divides. I have been asking, "Where are the young Black musicians?" I have been listening and moved by Musiq SoulChild and Jill Scott and the Philly movements. A buddy of mine, Guy Ramsey, professor of music at Penn University, took me out to hear some local Philly players in a club. Bam! There was Musiq SoulChild sitting in with the young Jazz players. All the strategies for Black music making were there: the jamming, the innovative spirit, playing a mix of styles. Here was traditional, straight-ahead Blues and wrapped tight around a Hip Hop backbeat. Bam! All Black, incredibly gifted, upholding the traditions in full style, representing. It was just like the stuff Aretha sang about thirty years ago: "To be young gifted and Black, and that's a fact, with our Souls intact." I was Done! These questions, though, still ran deep in my mind and in the conversational exchange of so many artists, educators, and just the folks. What is happening to the music? Does Black popular music have a future worth hoping in? Is this just older people's concerns?

Considering the future paths of, in particular, Black popular music rests squarely in the problem of how to define and talk about the who, the what is of contemporary artists. Paul Gilroy has spoken well when calling this particular problem the puzzle of how and what analytical aesthetic social inroads to choose when talking about Black music. Because of its breadth, height and depth, and the length of its canons, it's difficult to find the floor in a time when the floors are constantly shifting beneath us. This is a daunting task. Gilroy asks, "How are we to think critically about artistic products and aesthetic codes which though traceable to a distinct location, have been changed either by the passage of time or by displacement, relocation or dissemination through networks of communication and cultural exchange?"[2] For me, it's tough dealing with the problems in finding similarities and differences in these styles and types across the record bin divides, diasporic waters, breaking through class and generational divides. Exploring the "is we" and the "who is" in art within the Black music family feud takes some listening, but it must be done. Black music culture is not an "on the side study," but an extremely complicated and rich matrix of cultures, technologies, advances, and voices and deserves full study.

Black popular music in my mind is in danger. It is being eaten by the sharks of market saturation, which is driven by profit and leaves the music to being diluted into a popular culture wasteland where thugs, hoods, and bad musicians, through tricky and hefty marketing ploys, stole the soul of contemporary audiences. Black music audiences are settling for trendy noise and a lot of tired profiling and posturing. Before these words are lumped historically with the rhetoric of critics, like Alan Bloom, Calvin Butts or Delores Tucker, let me say that Hip Hop culture is the most important musical tradition of our day. It is ours, it's Black, it's American, and it is music.

Its artists are innovative, tied to the Black music tradition and capable of carrying the arts tradition into the twenty-first century.

It's clear to me that Black artistry will continue to carry and project Black experiences, and that this form of expression (music, video, marketing) within the culture is the most humanely textured of the arts. But its future simply as a music product depends upon maintaining current linkages between practicing artists bound to all aspects and development of the culture; and education and jamming in tradition across generations where social linkages can be made and maintained. The future of Black creativity in music per se is not in jeopardy, but there are more basic questions like: where are the musicians, the bands (Earth Wind and Fire, Kool and the Gang)? I wonder if the criteria of what we want to continue to hear no longer exists?

Secondly, apart from the search for musical or social/cultural or artistic value comes quite another challenge from the outside perimeter. Artists of all stripes have now to compete with a generation of computer programmers who have their fingers on the pulse of innovation, creativity, technology, and popular culture. So we now live in an age where music culture is being generated by nonmusicians. And it sounds so good, but it ain't real! Notions of musical value and the lack of musical innovation, creative ingenuity and musicianship are coming up in a consistent conversation that will not go away.

HOW TO HEAR THE FUTURE

Each new generation of artists that emerges has to face the management question. Where is the music going? What is the future of our musical activity? If Black music tradition is going to step up, what are younger musicians doing these days with the traditions? Is the art heart pumping in a healthy manner? As I have stated before, the music that lives with the majority of Black people all over the world is youth music. As Quincy Jones has stated, "It's [Black music] the music that the entire world has adopted as the voice of its Soul."[3] So important is this "sounding," that the future of Black music does not lie in the hands of any of us who, above the age of 30, stand mockingly on the sidelines and point fingers. The future of Black music, that which stands, crawls, raps, grooves, and sings, belongs to young, creative people. As I am listening to contemporary music, in particular Black popular music, it seems to me there are several windows of value that get at what it is, and where it is going. The consideration, appreciation, and the evaluation of the future of contemporary Black popular music has to be viewed from a wider parameter of experiences. We have to look at the total package because technology, visual and mass marketing means music, the artist performing the music is not the sole driving value anymore. Music is:

A. Music and the beat
B. Words and message (through which new value systems are being worked out)
C. Visual enterprise and technological support

    D. A product created by market demand

    E. A voice of expression through artistic, visual stylin' or representin'

In my "old" mind, when I listen to Marvin Gaye's *What's Going On?* Earth Wind and Fire or Chaka Kahn's recordings, I get it all in the song itself: words, great music, a message, the beat. I don't need all that market hype stuff. With the growth of the Hip Hop market into clothes, sports culture overlaps, video, poetry, and now at least five subcultures within Hip Hop (Old School, Gangsta, Christian, New School, and Hip Hop Soul), taking in any popular music seriously requires a broader pallet of filters for the ears and for music comprehension and enjoyment. It is important for the future of Black popular music to do as it has always done; it has allowed people to live in the balance, keeping it real, and keeping it beautiful and human. So much of our dialogue has been a search for a way to critique problematic values and to determine a present path for contemporary Black popular music. It's important to know how the path is presently being trod, where Black music is walking, and what it is saying in its talking.

HOW TO PROJECT THE FUTURE

I do think there are enough examples of new artists connected with a thick sampling of older traditions of the best of Black popular music to ensure a future in Black music. For my money, the most innovative, fresh sounds released between 1999 and 2002 were Lauryn Hill and Erykah Badu. They are both market smart but not artist dumb. They both drew, in their first projects, on multiple levels of Black artistry. They were global, they had something to say that is compelling, and their voices are original. Their productions were not industry conveyer belt products. They sang in conventional forms but were nonconventional record formats.

The March 2001 issue of *Jet* magazine states:

> There is a revolution underway in the world of music. A new squad of artists raised on old-school tunes are on a crusade to put feeling, the meaning, the soul back into music . . . their sounds are distinctive, innovative, has roots in soul but branches that spread far and wide into all genres of music. Their sounds sung with a shot of blues, a dash of gospel, a jazzy riff, a disco beat, a funk laced chord, some spoken word and a bit of rock or metal; musical gumbo for the soul" [Lauryn Hill, Jill Scott, Musiq SoulChild, Common, Macy Gray, and D'Angelo].[4]

Writer Kelefa Sanneh in an April *New York Times* piece, entitled "R&B Is Reborn," called it, "new found audacity, re-invigorated spirit, re-invented sense of identity . . . new trail for American pop."[5]

I like Common (produced by members of the Roots); his musical mix (Jazz, Hip Hop, Soul), the poetry as griotness, his paying proppers to the culture. Jill Scott is beautiful, the music is all that. *Who is Jill Scott?* (2001) made me believe in the artistic spirit in popular music again. This product made me feel like a musician.

D'Angelo is like Prince, a musical "monster." Another young brother who can sing. Actually, while there are no new things going on with most of these new "revolutionaries," Jill Scott and Musiq SoulChild kind of present a joy-filled, clean love lyric (i.e., "Just Friends," "A Long Walk"), which are really refreshing with things like "maybe we can just go and see a movie, or walk in the park, or listen to the Roots." This makes us believe in that lost innocence author

Alexs Pate talks about needing to reclaim. This is the most revolutionary act among these singer/poets, that they put great Black music back on the radio!! Common, Jill Scott, Musiq SoulChild, and Lauryn Hill all open their albums with an "ID" song: a song about who "I be" representin', I guess? But I have to ask, what's with all the need to say who you are? Just sing, do music, and we'll figure out that your name is spelled "C-O-double M-O-N. I just listened to a two-year review of lots of Hip Hop hits. Too much darkness, still! Every cut I listened to, from L. L. Cool J to DMX to Lil' Kim, was saturated with dirt and keepin' it real. For what?

Paying my bills is about as real as I need to get. When will music transport us again, and allow us to dream, wonder, and achieve as a "peoplehood"? That's the "hood" I want to be about! I am wondering if the criteria, styles, values, musical sensibilities have all changed too drastically. Seems like you either have to deal with it, or listen to the oldies stations.

There does seem to be in all this a growing number of contemporary popular artists who define their music within broader multiple categories; Hip Hop, Jazz, Euro, and global beats. I call this time in popular music, "Free Styling." A patchwork musical identity where the fall-out, the style or movement will result into a form. What that will be is up to the artists. Every other movement that preceded Hip Hop saw a similar twenty-year development which was preceded by "Free Stylin'." Ragtime, New Orleans march music, and Blues mixtures created classic Jazz in the 1920s, which blossomed into Big Band Jazz. Smaller big bands with Gospel quartet singers flirted within the sounds of Louie Jordon, which blossomed into R&B.

During these "free stylin'" periods artists are more fluid in their choices, more open and progressive in their aesthetic and artistic identity. Today's young musicians/poets are now marked by digital cultural shifts and marketing phrase lines such as: "Be different," "Obey your thirsts," "Dare to be different," "Aggravation by innovation," and "Don't fear change."

Macy Gray is this Black generation's Cyndi Lauper, who herself in look, voice growl, and attitude was on the edge, but people went for it. As Macy Gray states, from her album *How Life Is*, "There is a conversation I need to have with me . . . it's just a moment to myself." The concern for ownership now of independent choices and control of the shaping of ones (I)den-tity is what comes from so much of the popular music narratives. This is where society is and where the music resonates. As writer Robin Kelley pointed out in a *New York Times* piece "Listening across the Generational Divide," "Art and music and our cultural institutions must address (society) in terms of the expression(s) needing to be relevant in terms of serving peo-ple's experiences."[6]

Our concern, our task, is to solve the puzzles of how to listen, critique, and hope for a future of Black popular music is more daunting than ever. Because now Black music is not one thing, does not come from one place, has no one aesthetic fiber, one shade, one style or espe-cially now, one marketplace. Its future largely depends upon our broadening and our constant watch and keep. I think the future relies on a musical practice based on the command of the craft of the art, and the alliances with the needs of Black people as well as a diasporic connec-tion. That is, seeing art, styles, and need from the larger Black family as music is made in West Africa, Jamaica, Brazil, and so on. Therefore the narratives, the literature of common Black people's play, prides, passions, and pronouncements, no matter how removed we are from them, somewhere inside this yell, our own narrative is there. We are, as Dr. King put it, "in an inescapable network of mutuality."[7] Somehow, buried deeply, "You through my I" is always in the song. Our experiences are carried in the narrative or at least we recognize the pain and emptiness that is so compelling, so absolutely human that we are drawn there. Many are stick-ing there.

The work of Hip Hop culture in popular music is powerful and compelling and I think it illustrates and underlines many of the earlier points about the contemporary functionality of Black popular narrative. Where the dominant themes of authenticity, image, and identity underpin and wrap around the video and artists is what makes it good, effective in the navigation of identity and image projection. It is music, word and message, and commercial market product. It is a great example of giving voice to human expression and experience through a particular kind of urban popular stylin' that now is incorporated as the best of what our art can offer many.

I am cautious though, because my concern is how many messages and messengers can we take in, before the saturation of product becomes a blur? I doubt that if we are not watchful, the ball that is pitched right to us will be one we can't catch.

CONCLUSION

The future of Black music relies upon, in my mind, the delicate balance of the convergence of authentic narrative, contemporary expression, historic practice, and innovation in expression. This is precisely what we are witnessing in the young Jazz/Hip Hop/R&B convergence. I'm feeling better about music because of these few voices. The dark rain of negative imagery in too much Rap music from mainstream popular Black culture has had recently a few moments of sun.

Again, as I have written before, when musicians and artists become focused and take their art to the next level of inspired, passionate, individual innovation and not "copy-ation," then we can hope, together, in a future of Black popular music. We must jam together. As the hip hoppers have continued to do, Black artistry must be tied to the needs of Black people. But this generation needs to be better grounded by more musical skills. It needs to keep in touch with the practices of the past which linked musical values and practices. It was those links, rooted in excellence, that secured our culture against crisis. It is at this point that the quality of the music, our aesthetics, philosophies, performances, that the hope and future of Black music will be recognizably distanced from a bleak emptiness. As Cornel West has written, the future of Black music may hang on the quality of the response to our contemporary social challenges depending on not just the talents, but moral visions, social analyses, and political strategies which highlight personal dignity. Toni Morrison's beautiful discussion of our great Black music literature sums it up best: "a sustaining force, which healed, nurtures and translates Black experience into above all else, art. My parallel as a writer is Black music because all the strategies are there. . . . It makes you hungry, it slaps, it embraces, music is the mirror that gives necessary clarity . . . and literature ought to do the same thing."[8]

· 43 ·

Tracing the Seeds of Our Cultural Decay

$\mathcal{O}$n the record "Superstar," from the 1998 release *The Mis-Education of Lauryn Hill*, Ms. Hill states, "Come on baby light my fire. Everything you drop is so tired. Music is supposed to inspire, how come we ain't getting no higher? Now tell me your philosophy on exactly what the artist should be? Should they become someone with prosperity and no concept of reality?" In my last writing I asked several questions. What must contemporary artists of color be doing? What responsibilities as people of color do we have? Are we accountable in our work to the community?

Through their musing, artists provide a space for people to be moved, touched, and inspired through song and performance. As John Lovell has written in his *Black Song: The Forge and the Flame*, "Song always expands the person who creates it and through song people are inspired. Without song through the ages we would be dwarfs, working at our best only to fulfill tasks at hand."[1] Many claim too much of our music today, our "projections," are in part the cause of a culture in decay and wonder what this signals as we move further into a new century. Cultural critic and author Cornel West hinted at this in his early writing *Prophetic Fragments*. It is so powerful I have to use it here again:

> The impact of Mass culture, especially through radio and television has diminished the influence of the family and church. Among large numbers of Black youth, it is Black music that serves as the central influence regarding values and sensibilities. Since little of this music is spiritually inspiring, people have fewer and fewer resources to serve them in periods of crisis.[2]

I can't help but to agree with Steve Harvey's hilarious appeal in *The Kings of Comedy* film: "Old school man, old school. We used to talk about loving somebody." Marvin Gaye's "What's Going On" asks, "Brother, brother, there's too many of you dying. You know we've got to find a way, to bring some love in here today. What's going on?" Among today's generation, there seems to be a feeling of ambivalence toward these people, community concerns. From the bridge of so many R&B and Hip Hop artists the message seems to be, "Its all good, as long as my crew is living large." There's little at risk here because so much is possible and accessible, and anyway the world's not worth changing. The best way to deal is to just adapt to it, by any quick, easy way. This societal ambivalence is acceptable. Without sounding too to the "right" or soft, the notion of "values," working for excellence, self-determination, pride, and a care for a community to which one "belonged to" has been lost. Whatever we thought was gained socially as a culture after the Civil Rights movement, and the 1970s and 1980s, we have lost at the close of the century. Where does one find our "truth platform" today? We must face the

---

Article courtesy of Insight News, Inc., Minneapolis, MN.

reality that these new values and cultural constructs in music and contemporary sensibilities engage a growing many of us, more faithfully than our once tried and true foundations. One advertiser calls the Internet "the dominant force of our future."

Those ugly 20 or so days of the Bush/Gore presidential race of 2000, which was more of a farce than an election, was clearly an indication that from every way we look at it, be it cultural, economic, and megacultural (politics and society), we continue to push close to the edge of total uncharted territories in our societal grappling. This is good, some argue, because we are growing. But in all this where do Black people stand? Productively, in the eye of the storm, as we've done in decades and centuries past, or are we unimaginatively detached on the margins, voiceless, unempowered, desensitized, uninformed, and unconcerned? The real answer to this question, for Black culture, for any culture, is to chart the lives of young people. This is where the answer and future lies. If the truth be told it has to come from charting the experiences and outcomes of this very important group. As an artist, I spend all my time looking at culture through the eyeglasses of music.

In a *Newsweek* special report (October 9, 2000) entitled "Rap on Rap," the writers featured in the report revealed some interesting and troubling perspectives from contemporary artists and the Black communities where they are from and whom they claim to represent. The *Newsweek* report led with this line: "Is rap increasingly driven by sex (getting some or bling bling), violence and money? Is it going too far?" To that question I say, "Gone too far, and we are headed fast down the road every great culture traveled with similar problems to our ultimate cultural/spiritual death."

In a similar piece from *Time* (February 8, 1999), rapper Chuck D, in a piece called "The Sound of Our Young World," commented that "it's difficult to stop a Cultural Revolution that bridges people together. By discussing differences through artistic communication and sharing interests in a common bond—rap music has achieved that in twenty years." I agree, but I am more concerned with the more pervasive problematic values that we seem to be less critical of and should be on the watch for. The senseless dumbing down, or as it is called, "being real" or "being ghetto," is really allowing far too many young Black people a "space" to conform to and to be comforted in. This "cultural zero-hero-zone" is frightening to many of us. We must be on watch! Cultural critic and Hip Hop writer Kevin Powell, in a piece from the same *Time* issue entitled "My Culture at the Crossroads," states,

> None of this would matter as much to me if videos didn't pump visual crack into the minds of young people across the planet. Or if urban radio actually played something other than the same 10–12 songs every day. Or if some of our fabulous hip hop magazines didn't make constant references to marijuana, liquor and 'niggas' under the guise of keeping it real.

Don't get the message wrong here: Rap and Hip Hop music and culture are the most valuable and important popular mainstream music(s) today. But as a musician, I have to say that there is too much nonmusic going on, headed up by industry slaves who pimp *only* our pathologies and problems as music and "our culture." This is madness, and time yet again, for Black people to say something, to not allow our young people to be living with and in these problematic message and image identities. I like to think of Black music culture as a clock, a map, and the bloodline, because the music and art making in its various forms are illustrative of a culture's health, reflecting ills and genius. The music is rich, elastic, and strong enough to deliver as well. It always has.

So as a point of conversation, where do we go from here? Again:

1. Combat by challenging the media saturation of negative and shallow rhetoric, images and ideology of contemporary Black popular culture which does not examine and/or celebrate the fuller expression and experience of Black people, culture, and image(s).
2. Appreciate and celebrate the significance of popular voices and culture, seeing the value of their workings but as well to challenge and expect the artists to be more accountable for the images and messages inherent in their popular expression.
3. Be on watch in order to deal with the social/spiritual complexities of our time. We need to be able to decode the "monsters" that left unchecked will ultimately lead to a cultural, intellectual, and spiritual demise of our most vulnerable.

Tracing the seeds of cultural decay for this musician begins at present with a more critical look toward one of our most important cultural bloodlines: the music. Sister Lauryn Hill is correct: "Music is supposed to inspire . . . so how come we ain't getting no higher?"

We're Representin': The Hope for the Future of Black Popular Music

The music business has finally figured out how to do music without musicians. . . . Today more pop is created not by conventional musicianship, but by digital editing to stitch together prerecorded sounds. The industry belongs to people who don't play instruments. It used to be that musicians owned a few trusty guitars, they made sounds; today they buy them.[1]

This was a segment from a recent *New York Times* article called, "Strike the Band." Kind of sad when we think about it. Apart from the myriad of young rappers and R&B singers, as a musician I have to say we don't have the numbers we used to of practicing, playing young Black musicians. Remember all those bands, Earth Wind and Fire, Ohio Players, the Time, even our local (Minneapolis) Mint Condition? For a people who have cultivated and provided this past century's most important music(s) to the world, our musicians of the future have not been surfacing in the popular music marketplace. The most innovative musicians like Gospel's Sister Rosetta Tharpe, Jazz's Dizzy Gillespie and Mary Lou Williams, Rock and R&B's Jimi Hendrix and Patrice Rushen, or Meshell Ndegeocello, and D'Angelo are not commonplace. Who's playing the guitars and saxophones, flutes, and pianos? What happens when the griot's beats and strums are taken away? Cultural critic/historical Paul Gilroy has written that "Black musicians and musical arts have been an important part of our cultural refinement and development in the west. By producing numerous expressive and artistic forms, enhanced modes of communication beyond words spoken or written, their work is continuously presented as living symbols of the value of self-activity."[2]

There is no doubt about it, Black American music is one of our treasures. The numerous forms of Black music and the amalgamates of forms from the Spirituals, Blues, Jazz, orchestral to Hip Hop, have impacted the world not only in terms of artistic achievement, but also by spurring social and artistic movements of marked significance. Writer Portia Maultsby pointed out, "The Soul era in particular, was a productive period for Black Americans. The music created by Blacks and for Blacks during this era communicated a general philosophy of refusal to accept the undesirable and a determination to create a better future."[3] When considering all that has been done in Black music culture, the breadth, vitality, and fluidity of styles, the artists and forms, it's clear that music has been properly representin'. The future of Black creativity in music per se is not in jeopardy, but there are more basic questions like, where are the musicians, the bands, and, I wonder if the criteria of what we want to continue to hear and be nourished from is nonexistent?

Article courtesy of Insight News, Inc., Minneapolis, MN.

If Black music tradition is going to step up and along again, what are younger musicians doing these days with the traditions? Is the art heart pumping in a healthy manner? This is the arts/culture issue I want to share in the community.

As the Puffy Combs (now P. Diddy) trial added another glimpse into the trifling downward spiral our contemporary artists are falling, I still feel very comfortable in this dialogue asserting that we are losing our creative soul. Could our music be literally, killing us? The music that lives with the majority of Black people all over the world is youth music.

So important is this "sounding," as I have said before, that the future of Black music does not lie in the hands of any of us who, above the age of 30, stand mockingly on the sidelines and point fingers. The future of Black music, that which stands, crawls, raps, grooves, and sings, belongs to young creative people. Ahmir Thompson, drummer of the old school Hip Hop group Roots, in a recent article stated: "mainstream pop music is losing its Soul."[4] And in a related call to the culture bearers and the community, in his recent book *How to Make Black America Better*, Tavis Smiley, host of a provocative BET show, challenges us all with saying, "Each of us must bear the burden of trying to save the Soul of Black America." As a musician and arts educator, I take brother Tavis's challenges seriously and rather personally. There is no way to talk about making anything better, hoping for a future without a real, sometimes tough but necessary, tight relationship with today's young people and their cultural practices. Education, music, and cultural arts are the most important carriers of public values. Black music is our people's most cherished cultural expression. Many educators, musicians, and artists are very committed to getting together and sharing ideas. We must take a very serious look at our music(s) with the young arts community and ensure that we eradicate the current downward spiral. This can be done through education, the development of a shared aesthetic theory and/or platform (a hope and criteria of what we like and expect our art to do), and by jamming with younger musicians.

EDUCATION

In many instances, if young people are not in school programs, community arts, or studying privately, younger musicians are not being educated about music or Black music culture outside of BET and MTV, which are fast ways to cultural death in terms of the future of music making. There is much blame to be put at the foot of the industry who simply doesn't look for or support the nurturing of creative young voices outside of new Rap or R&B or Gospel artists. In most cases these are simply singer projects. Younger musicians really need to see how deep and rich being in music is, and be exposed to our great legacy of musicians. Somehow we have got to hook up with the church, after-school and artists residency initiatives where practicing musicians of all stripes, but of professional competency, will help to ensure that new generations of musicians are inspired and directed to cultivate their talent. Rev. Carl Walker's Walker West Academy in St. Paul, Minnesota, is an excellent example of local Black music teachers committed to ensuring community excellence in music. In the last year at least four students went to prominent Jazz music programs in New York and Boston including Manhattan School of Music, the New School, and Berklee College of Music.

AESTHETIC PLATFORM

Much was shared in a very rich conference recently held jointly by Macalester College and the University of Minnesota, by the Departments of African and African American Studies. The conference keynote speaker Manning Marable's call was consistently echoed, "Every generation needs a moral assignment." Every generation of Black creative musicians created a manifesto: Langston Hughes did in the 1930s; Duke Ellington did with "It don't mean a thing if it ain't got that swing"; Amiri Baraka did it with the Black arts movement in the 1960s; and George Clinton did it with "One Nation under the Groove."

From GURU's 1995 *Jazzmatazz* release, he says, "Hip Hop is a way of life . . . with a history, culture . . . origin and a set of principles, acting as a safety valve in society . . . to let out the frustration of how young people feel today."

In all these cases it seems there is an attempt to link the social and aesthetic philosophy as a cultural and even in many cases moral assignment, at least in terms of an assumed collected belief and performance idea. This is what's missing, a consistent dialogue. Do we have some sense of what's good or meaningful anymore? The commercial mind-set is basically folks know if the beat is good, or the babes are "phat" enough, and the video is showing enough of the crew living large. Gold chains, cars, getting paid, and running with the crew is just stupid. This is all we see as a visual, cultural image of musicians. Everybody is singing and rapping Ghetto Fabulous! Anybody, and most young people can see that, it's just that there is so much commercial reward for that kind of stupidity. And so much of mainstream culture is steeped in the same mud while masked in conscious insidious ways. Again, if younger Black creative people knew how to define and find artistic value in what their traditions were (West African griots, slave musicians and preachers, the beboppers, Gospel artists who maintained active spiritual and socially sectarian visions and lives, and the sixties and seventies musical social goals), Hip Hop culture could do so much more and sustain its worldwide popularity. At the present rate of escalating stupidity and waste of our young peoples' energies and talents, Hip Hop could exhaust itself and burn out. An acute and consistent understanding of what is good and hip and progressive and meaningful about Black music culture for younger musicians is what is needed.

There are exceptions; artists like Mos Def, Talib Kweli, and Common. In a recent *Essence* magazine article on the Hip Hop agenda, Hip Hop big brother Chuck D stated, "Hip hop's social energies have been redirected by commercial success and corporate marketing . . . seduced by the ethic of getting paid . . . these celebrities lose focus and think it's all about them instead of collective thought."[5] In short, too much of the messages about "keepin' it real" or living the ghetto fabulous life suffocates the possibilities of long-standing music making traditions that unite art with activism, community responsibility, and accountability.

I'm a musician. My job, task as it were, is to look at Black music making and culture. My observations have been that too much of our popular arts are wobbling away from the high pedestal of cultural accomplishment Gilroy is talking about to a kind of low road, a titillating thud and low noise wrapped in whines, moans, and wimpy, sappy vocal lines, vacuous lyrics, and robotronic drum loops. The real sad part is that consumers accept these spit out, plastic, today a hit, tomorrow throwaway remake star wanna-bes. We, along with younger musicians, have not insisted on an evolving criteria for music value apart from the beat and its commercial sensuality.

JAMMING

I think both education and aesthetic theory can be combined in an active cultural sharing of older poets/writers and musicians and dancers, by all jamming with each other. Create local spots where the older artists can share with and perform together with younger artists. So, in this way our traditions and our culture can be enhanced, and things that should be valued and passed along can be. Plus, the older artists need to learn from the younger. Each week I work with sections of a 200-member boy's choir on improvisation, composing, and musical styles. I also produce a monthly Jazz jam series called Patrick's Jazz Jam with local professionals. Lots of younger musicians are coming down to sit in. We're jamming!

When the contemporary Black community and its artists demand and support the further development of our talented musicians, and when we share collective passion(s), I think we can refashion our aesthetic/cultural voices to make Black America better, and to ensure the power and meaningful purpose that our music has had. Secondly, when musicians and artists become focused and take their art to the next level of inspired, passionate, individual innovation and not copy-ation, then we can hope, together, in a future of Black popular music. It is at this point that the quality of the music (our aesthetics, philosophies, performances) that the hope and future of Black music will be recognizably distanced from the bleak emptiness it is headed fast toward in its present downward spiral. As Cornel West has written, the future of Black music may hang on "the quality of the response to our contemporary social challenges depending on not just the talents, but moral visions, social analyses, and political strategies which highlight personal dignity."[6] By doing this, as Gilroy suggested, we can continue to present our lives, our arts, our communities, and our nation as living symbols of the value of self-activity.

Who Stole the Souls of Black Folk?

*N*ever let 'em attempt to step on or crush your dignity mon . . . this is what we Jamaicans have learned and valued, that which keeps us. We are a deeply proud people." This is what an old Jamaican friend shared with me recently. My entire mind and soul have been wrapped around this idea of what our people value today. As I hung out in the upper region of Brownstown, Jamaica, in the mountains at the local people's village markets (as opposed to the tourist traps), I was reminded of how we are an alive, vibrant people, full of life, expression, spirit, beauty, power, and value. Our life breathes with vitality and peoplehood. I wonder if we here in the States have lost this? I see too many of our young brothers and sisters maddened, angry with forbidding looks and a seemingly permanent growl and "tudes" deeply buried in their faces. How can, as author Alexs Pate has asked, we find our innocence again? To walk around with an assumed guilt means too much of our time is wasted on breaking out of or through an America that despises us. Yet America still fancies our expressions of "play." So, I hear very clearly DuBois's notion in several directions, *The Souls of Black Folk*, and I hear and feel it rubbing against Public Enemy's question, "Who Stole the Soul?" What about the minds, the inner souls of Black folk, what do we value most? What is our home space? What is it that is keeping us?

Black people, our culture and cultural products, our souls, have impacted the world. We changed, shaped, and challenged problematic notions previously held about human value since the beginning of our integration within the Western story, dating from European memoirs as early as the fifteenth century and certainly earlier. The world as we know it would simply be a different place without Black presence and contribution in numerous ways. The expression and contribution certainly of our arts, which carries our experiences and expressions, innovation and values, have been a hinge upon which modernity has swung upon (pun intended).

An interesting search for a center, a direction, the resonating of our souls in contemporary culture is arising in conversations about what our expressions are saying about who we are and what we value. Our communities are multivalued, generational, and multivoiced. A difficult terrain to survey for sure.

In our ongoing discussion of contemporary Black life, our images, history, our value, music, our "soul," while emanating from us, is projected and controlled by the "cultural apparatus" (Harold Cruse term), the media. So who stole the soul as Larry King proclaims N'Sync to be the "band of the new millennium"? Our soul, I think is both a sound thing and a value thing.

Article courtesy of Insight News, Inc., Minneapolis, MN.

SOUL AS SOUND

Sound is an essential qualifier for Black culture. How things rub, resonate, growl, how blue they are, define the essence of Soul. In Black music, we want sound, style, and feel. This is where much of our social and spiritual centers have been. How many times have you been in a Black church and seen an older person tear up, sway, and say, "Thank you Jesus" at just the hearing of one chord? Kenny G is today sold as Jazz, or Soul, yet I believe many of our young musicians and listeners would do well to know about Grover Washington Jr. Being from Detroit and a Jazz musician, I prefer, our Kenny G: Kenny Garrett.

Today, I find fewer examples of a qualifiable Black arts initiative, objective collected Black Arts Value, a Soul. Not even a movement (Post–old school, Hip-Hop), or spokesperson(s). I yearn for an occasional Bob Marley, or Sister Souljah, a sustained Lauryn Hill or a Paul Robeson. These are artists whose art "represents" a cause, a value of innovation and dignity, some collected value, a soul. I wish the artists, especially musicians, songwriters, and singers of this generation would rise collectively and say something of value to American society besides "Who let the dogs out?" or "Say my name, say my name." There was a time not so long ago when music as the voice and consciousness, the soul of young Black artists, were many times turned towards advocacy and care for one another, our community, where our people were headed, what they were facing, what they valued, and how they needed to overcome. This is one of the things, next to loving your "baby," that was number one in the song content. What happened? What will it take for us to grasp and again insist upon that kind of value in our expressions? For me the public value mirror is in our arts, our projections. What do we see when we look in the mirror of our expressions?

SOUL AS VALUE

Soul is a multipronged and textured terrain. As a recent *Newsweek* reported, "What color is Black? The markers of racial (and cultural) identity, ideology, attitude and pigmentation are of every conceivable hue."[1] Some would argue these questions are unimportant and too difficult because we want many things and our accomplishments, diversification, and our many points of light are marks of our arrival. I think I liked it better when I knew what Black people were all about, because we were "sounding off" in some clear collected value places. As an artist, I saw these times as memorable, impressionable moments, a clear picture and stream of multiple expressions of concrete Black, and human experience, deep. They were serious, and I placed my identity, my strength, and my values in those expressions and images. In every creative period in our history, the Harlem Renaissance, Bebop, the Civil Rights and Soul era movements (Free Jazz, Black arts movements, Motown, AACM in Chicago), all were spearheaded and carried by young artists.

The styles (Soul), steps, attitudes, performance practices, and aesthetic ideas were expressed in songs and lyrics that carried collective ideas, which gave people meaning, identity, value, and self-worth. Black cultural expressions (music, comedy, literature, dance and arts) are so inextricably connected to what we value and who we are in every era. So today where are our Soul Centers? The Black church? BET? Rap and Hip Hop? The NAACP? Is it what Oprah thinks? Is it the NBA? Where is the place where our collected values, if any, are displayed as our best efforts? As the political terrain thickens with figures like J. C. Watts, Colin Powell, and Condoleezza Rice, well, "I'm about to lose my mind up in here!"

Chuck D's question, "Who stole the soul?" and Dr. Martin Luther King Jr.'s "Where do we go from here?" seem aptly appropriate. At our present pace there will simply be more division, less concrete definable spaces, fewer places where a collected community can resonate together. What happens when everybody wants to sound like us, look like us, walk like us, and style like us, but then ultimately move on beyond us? What happens to a people, a community, whose soul is diluted and sold? Sound, soul is a value center where we associate meaning(s), not a commodified style. For Black people those soul places have always been revered and understood. We are selling so much of our soul in the marketplace that I'm afraid we've saturated the market and the value of our products have been diminished. We don't know the worth anymore, we're all cashed out. Identity, innovation, soul, value, center, and sound as our most vibrant resonating places are all but faint. They are not completely absent. There are young artists who are in the mix keeping the flames alive, but still, they are only flickering beacon lights in a real dense storm of "otherness." I do see N'Sync (Justin Timberlake), Britney Spears, the Backstreet Boys and other media appropriations as being clear examples of our cultural soul, or urban American style. Who stole the soul?

NEGROPHILIA

Equally interesting is the ongoing question of how others view us and perceive our values. How do others see Black people and our dislocated souls? Again the media and education from where I work continue to dominate the discussion and cultural cooking. Actually the world has always been fascinated with Black people and has exploited them, and then there is an attempt to disregard and discard. The same cycle is bound to crop up again. Spike Lee's *Bamboozled* was a brilliant exercise in calling it out modern media style. He hit it, again! Likewise, in her recent book, *Negrophilia*, author Petrine Archer-Straw puts it this way as she is concerned with "how Black forms were appropriated, adopted, vulgarized by whites and raises the question about motives and reasons for interests about the personalities whose lives, loves, images and ideas pioneered the passion for Black culture."[2] Negrophilia, as she suggests, means a love for Black culture. When viewing this period, the beginning of the last century, in the twenties in Europe and Harlem where Whites visited clubs to seek the Black exotic, it was clear that Black expression helped to define modernity. Black expressive culture typified humanity. This was a precious value. What does Black culture in music, film, literature, and media images represent today?

Has Josephine Baker's exoticism been replaced by images of Black athletes in a Nike commercial? Or a hooded, chain-wearing, thug-representin' youth, blasting the sound waves in search of getting paid? Will the real Mr. Mathers please stand up? As Macalester College professor El-Kati recently stated, "Black popular culture is America's biggest export." Funny that the power of the intangible is unattainable to most, but it is just this power that our culture is tapped directly into. That's soul.

CONCLUSIONS

Values are no longer an A, B, C or 1, 2, 3 proposition. A recent *St. Paul Pioneer Press* feature (January 7, 2001), entitled "American Values Are No Longer So Clear," emphasized the differences between two groups: cultural conservatives and cultural innovators who sometimes move very closely to a center. (The previous election bears this out.) Political scientists in the report find that we are less likely to trust one another, less likely to trust traditional institutions, and more concerned with self-expression, experiences, and the meaning of life. Mainstream American social/political value may be seen, determined, and even directed by politics, policies, and programs. Black peoples' interests are definitely a part of this. But while we are reflected in this, this is not the arena where our values are most projected. The most profound arena historically has been our indigenous cultural leadership. So where is the cultural leadership? As Harold Cruse wrote years ago, "In advanced societies it is not the politicians who create new ideas and images of man/woman, that role belongs to the artists and intellectuals of each new generation."[3] Or as Paul Gilroy says, musicians and artists are "living symbols of the value of self activity."[4]

Equally interesting is the fact that many of the artistic expressions in popular music and the arts, aided by technology and the media, are mainly (I)dentity and narrative driven. Many relate to "your experience as seen through my story." Rap narrative in terms of sales and interest figure in high here. Any way that art addresses "you through I" sells as a contemporary, "music/culture value." Writer Robin Kelley pointed out in a (January 6, 2001) *New York Times* piece, "Listening across the Generational Divide," "Art and music and our cultural institutions must address this in terms of the expression(s) needing to be relevant in terms of serving people's experiences." If this is so, and we want to be honest about where we are, then we cannot ignore the emerging value systems that pervade so much of our contemporary Black culture.

I am frighteningly aware of my own distance from this 1990s generation in terms of value construct. Consequently as I struggle with these questions and I am appreciative of what I am learning about my own strengths and weaknesses as I fuss with, and enjoy, contemporary cultural expression. I am aware of the fact that history teaches us that evolution, change is good, and inevitable. History also teaches us that yesterday's most cherished idea is today's old school norm. In the past, some of the most contested and feared conventions and values are today's most important foundations. Also, if value construction and expression is a goal, the reality is that today our values are constantly shifting. I'm learning that you can't teach "moving forward" by only "looking backward." One has to make contemporary failures accountable to the possibilities of a bleak future, and not a rich past. So, some very important lessons are bound to arise from today's contemporary sensibilities, styles, sayings, and songs that carry values. These are vital to the future. But the questions that we should not forget having to do with the Souls of Black Folk, is where are we going from here and is this journey, this value place important for our future, our next breaths?

I think we must reach across the tracks of our ideological divides and talk with each other and younger people, constantly and consistently, despite class, age, political preference, and education. All of our experiences considered together equate value. We do not have to agree with what every value is or should be, but we should agree that the discussion of and the search for construction of values is what connects us and what will make us a cultural force to be reckoned with. Only in this way will we be a people whose cultural values, projections, and leadership are admired.

Treading Turbulent Waters: Being an Invisible Black Artist in Contemporary American Culture—Foundations for Cultural Theory (2004)

> I am an invisible man. No, I am not a spook like those who haunted Edgar Allan Poe; nor am I one of your Hollywood-movie ectoplasms. I am a man of substance, of flesh and bone, fiber and liquids—and I might even be said to possess a mind. I am invisible, understand, simply because people refuse to see me.
>
> —Ralph Ellison[1]

PART I: THE PROBLEM; ARTISTIC INVISIBILITY

I wonder, as a consumer in American culture what do you really see and want anyway? Images that are generated in our society through the popular culture apparatus make huge impressions on how we have come to see the world and value our understanding of life. More than 50 years after that famous Ellison opening articulating a common experience of Black invisibility, many expressions of Blackness are still invisible in America today. Many are concerned with the role of the media/industry and its curious reluctance to provide more visibility and market spaces for all kinds of Black imagery and expressions. As a Black creative person, one is virtually invisible unless of course you are an athlete, a rapper, a Hip Hop or younger R&B singer, or anyone who utters the "most important" cultural catchphrase of this generation, "Yo, I'm just trying to keep it real, know what I'm saying." No, I'm not bitter or playa hating, but I must admit this is a real source of frustration because I guess many of us thought we were building upon and representing the best aspirations of so many Black people who had gone on before. But today in a market-driven culture where identities are constructed and commodified for dollar gain only, any varied and realistic range of Black images of substance is counterprofitable and therefore worth zero in this marketplace.

It feels as though we are witnessing certain functional parts, voices of our culture beginning to disappear. For example, I have collected and surveyed the Sunday *New York Times* Arts and Leisure sections for the past three years. The majority of Black arts articles to appear in this section cover Hip Hop artists, R&B adolescents, a Jazz dead person, or an occasional mention of the stirring of an Aretha Franklin. (The *Times* did do pieces on Steve Coleman, avant-garde saxophonist; and Jazz pianist Jason Moran.) I've never seen a piece or review feature on a Black contemporary composer, conductor, scholar/author, sculptor; these are places and spaces reserved for "White artists only." The first *New York Times* Sunday Arts and Lei-

---

Article courtesy of Insight News, Inc., Minneapolis, MN.

sure section of 2004, featured Black artists or spotlighted? Zero. The lead story (a great one) was on Punk music's new mission. Ironically, the classical lead story was on nineteenth-century Bohemian composer Dvorak's influence in America, yet Black artistry, which he advocated, is not a part of this feature, at all. Today the tremendous range and impact of Black culture in all fields of the arts is evident yet the lens of that reporting is very narrow. Black artists of various stripes are overwhelmingly absent from mainstream coverage at the national level.

It breaks my heart to have read recently in a mainstream magazine (*Newsweek*) about a star rapper's porn and reality TV interests. In this piece the Rap artist brags that he is "making it happen just living out the American Dream." Man, what dream is he living out of? Sounds to me worst off than Malcolm's notion of the American nightmare gone bizarre and berserk. But this is what the majority of the American media still want to see us as, it seems. *Newsweek*, for example has focused on: "The Negro in America: What Must Be Done" (1967), "Can the Children Be Saved? Battle against Drugs and Despair" (picture on front is of a young Black child; September, 1989), "America's Prison Generation" (picture on front is of Readell Johnson, a young Black male, with a subheading, "one of 14 million mostly black, Latino Americans"; November 2000), "Affirmative Action, Do We Still Need It?" (January 2003). This is the reason for so many "invisible" Black men and women.

As long as the perpetuation in this culture of negative and the same ole' information exists concerning Black culture and a flow of images of us as "America's problem," stupid, unsuccessful, monkeying around with foolish jive talking, the American public seems happy as if this is normative. Unfortunately many young people fall into these "culture traps." And while our communities, parents are as much to fault, the cultural entertainment we support, push these points over the edge to our sure fall. Of note, one Hollywood formula for a successful film, still in practice, is that in the movie the monster always kills the indispensable Black man first (*Jurassic Park I* and *III*, *Resident Evil* [in which the first person killed is a Black female and the second a Black male], *Hulk* 2003). Today a popular contemporary Black narrative is almost always centered around, as my niece puts it, "them bustas and their my baby's mama drama." And not all but too many Hip Hop narratives are hopeless, almost always crude, hard and "ghetto" as style and content, and again using in the defense of too much trash today, "Oh we just keepin' it real."

The Black narrative is justifiably inclusive of the fights that people continue to wage against hopelessness, poverty, and the ills in this system. This is absolutely crucial and has been one of the creative fires and backbone of much Black art with social/spiritual consciousness. This is what cultural critic Cornel West has often called the Black Spiritual-Blues impulse. But this (we just keepin' it real) is probably one of the most overused, overrated, and damaging cultural slang banners we've seen in popular culture, because it attempts to justify complacency, especially when "real" is shorthand for as many have mentioned, "real stupid." What about those Black entrepreneurial empires with names like "Death or Murder"? This is America, brothers got the right to exercise privilege, but please more images, icons, and identities, please. I am like many Black artists working hard to "be" and "represent." The artists/performers of the 1930s, 1940s, Paul Robeson, Lena Horne, Duke Ellington, and Harry Belafonte, as Alan Pomerance points out, "changed the public image of Blacks" and served as a pivotal cultural transformation, a true pre–Civil Rights movement. One has to ask if the images of gangsters, and hoods, half-dressed rump shakers, and half-witted Steppin' Fetchit–like Black males with gold teeth chasing tire rims and gold chains really has done anything more than set back Black public imagery at least 50 years? Today, how could we expect to reach a younger generation (outside of academic circles) when a diversity of options is virtually invisible to them in this culture? This frustration about invisibility is shared by many artists these days outside of the hegemonic (invading forced commercial dominance) mainframe of commercial popular music. Record companies, radio and retail, concert venues have dreadfully tied themselves to advertising mechanisms that drive everything.

And while my focus is on artistic expression and product, disregard of the positive and constant view of workers in education, business and finance, politics, medical work, and science equally are feeling the veil of this larger cultural invisibility.

In the arts, I see this identity of invisibility more clearly each year as the music industry has made another "slave for sale on the auction blocks" of public commodities: mean-looking young Black males with shirts off. Our current generation of artists are being sold, bought out with stupid money, and this price will probably never allow us to buy back again a sense of worth lost to fame, fortune, and this big media moment. When a market places value on vacuousness and the artists have nothing to say except "It's your birthday," messages like "Fight the power" will go on unheard and unheeded. Invisibility, as Ellison points out, means people may look at you but not see your worth and dignity as a human being, your fight, your substance, and meaning(s).

Your value in this way of invisibility is reduced to a dollar figure and bottom line gain data. What do you say then, that's keeping it real?

I can't read Ellison's *Invisible Man* today without shaking my head. At 40 when I read this, I'm so acutely aware of the biting relevance of this landmark work. I do experience Whites in passing who consciously it seems look away from me. As if I weren't there. It's as if they looked upon me they would be immediately reminded of the tear and rip in the fabric of our social formulas. When or if they were to look into my eyes they would be as well acutely and painfully aware of their poisoned social plight, their socially constructed, inherited, and continually imposed "social raise" and the imposed and acted out downward spiral many others slid upon. While I do recognize we are in a time as well of unprecedented Black images, likenesses of me (Black males) which are pervasive, the meaning(s) implied in the invisibility I speak of are so visible for sure.

PART II: THE DELIGHT AND DILEMMA OF BEING YOU

Now more than ever these divided generations [baby boomers, b. late 1940s, 1950s; post Civil Rights kids, b. 1960s; Hip Hop, b. 1980s] must begin to understand the ways that the new Black youth culture both empowers and undermines Black America. . . . The older generation must realize they cannot claim any real victory if the hip-hop generation cannot build significantly on those gains.

—Bakari Kitwana[2]

I have said to my students many times, "I don't understand what it is you think you are doing that is so new, different, or really meaningful as a cultural movement in Hip Hop and contemporary Black popular culture. Everything is borrowed, not even the political messages have nearly the relevance of the Civil Rights or Black arts movement. Spoken word is sometimes empty rhetoric and lacks depth, and the music lacks real creativity and innovation." I say this in hopes to tease a class and evoke a real in-depth search and discovery for the hippest stuff going on out there. Don't get me wrong here, there is creative Hip Hop and R&B artistry in the contemporary marketplace to speak of.

Speaking as a musician (even an invisible one can hear), Hip Hop music culture is the important music movement of the last part of the twentieth century. The groove, absolutely slamming, and the harmonic pulses, "phraseology" brought to it by musicians like Teddy Riley, D'Angelo, Erykah Badu, Meshell Ndegeocello, or the intricate flow of a KRS-1 or Busta' Rhymes has revolutionized musical phrasing, clearly. There is even some singing talent when you really look hard for it or when they let one surface every 100 records and videos or so. But, are these gains enough to make good on the musical and cultural innovations of the past?

Russell Simmons's work is impressive. A recent business section feature of *Newsweek* reads, "Russell Simmons made Hip Hop into an unstoppable cultural force. Now he's turning up the volume in politics and business."[3] He is truly making headway into using the visibility of his assets to say something. Simmons and several Hip Hop moguls who are following his lead to their credit are redefining the entrepreneurial model in the marketplace, and in Simmons's case is now committed to social consciousness.

But American media mechanisms, the industry, have no intention of or interest in highlighting Black creative agency outside of what sells (newspapers, TV ads) and gains a profit first.

These formulations largely prescribed by corporate gatekeepers are driving creativity into the ground. There seems to be no or little market space for so many really talented musicians. If you can believe this, Wynton Marsalis took me out for dinner a few weeks ago in New York. On the way walking to a restaurant we passed a flyer advertising Wynton Marsalis and the Lincoln Jazz Orchestra. It was on the ground, ripped, dirty and wet and in a funny way to us was a euphemistic moment symbolizing this new invisibility. Wynton looked down at it and said, "See that's the way it is for us now. We are marginalized in what we do." As successful as he and other musicians of my generation have become, all are feeling the pinch of a force which is not valuing a fuller range of artistic creation in the market place anymore. But American media outlets won't have an intelligent Black artist speak will they? As the recent *Ebony*, *Black Enterprise*, and *Newsweek* magazines show and point to, Master P, P. Diddy, Russell Simmons, Missy Elliot, and Jay-Z, their one-half billion dollar Hip Hop empires, rapper Eve's and Snoop Dogg's multimedia spray as TV show hosts now barking with "Big Bow Wow's," this is where the creative juice is today.[4]

One has to ask today, what is the real victory for Black imagery? Is the increased global pervasiveness of Black popular artistry a positive enough pulse that it should silence this critique? Is the most pervasive idol an Eminem ("American Idol; Eminem for Everybody," *New York* magazine feature, November 2002) or a 50 Cent, a talented rapper, a survivor who overcame nine bullet shots? This is the high mark today of Black artistic excellence?

If Bakari Kitwana's claim is correct, what kind of future can this generation build upon if the foundation, the house rests upon questionable and shaky pillars?

PART III: THE CONTENT OF OUR CULTURE

Our conversations about nature and about ourselves are conducted in whatever "languages" we find it possible and convenient to employ. We do not see nature or intelligence or human motivation or ideology as "it" is but only as our languages are. And our languages are our media. Our media are our metaphors. Our metaphors create the content of our culture.

—Neil Postman[5]

I don't go to *Ebony*, *Jet*, *Essence*, or *Vibe* for this kind of musical diversity on a regular basis. These magazines while providing a much needed constant gush of pictures, stories, and insights on Black popular faces and themes, could do much more to give readers interesting stories and highlights on a wider variety of productive, influential Black artists.

Unfortunately, the current growth, interest and popularity of the services and liturgies in the Black church are driven not by traditional hymns, Spirituals and the grassroots communal theology of the Gospel songs. The message is carried and driven now by the amplification it takes to truly bury good vocal sound and to "produce" the pump of contemporary Hip Hop Gospel. So the Bobby Jones Gospel-like shows smother and saturate the screen with 200-plus choirs all yelling in three-part, catchy one lines about Jesus and the three ways he wants to help us out of our troubles and miseries. Not all, but too many of the contemporary Gospel works have a theological vision that has the depth of a comic book one-liner. The good book tells us to, "Study to show thyself approved unto . . ." As pervasive and important as our Gospel music tradition is, it too in these waters must be weary of massa's poisons! The power of this great cultural theater will soon be diminished to just another commodified reality show for network hire.

During the late summer of 2003, the Tavis Smiley Foundation hosted a positive gathering of Black youth leaders of the future in D.C. The number one question these gifted young people asked: "What can be done to regain again control and unplug the media's manipulation and distortion of Black people's images?" No CNN, NBC, or WB there.

Well, these encounters are reflective of some of the content of our culture and as well some of the waves we paddle against as invisible Black artists. Despite these turbulent waves, there are a thousand islands out there of people who are sick and tired of dis mess on all fronts.

Its time the industry stop pimping folks and rather support, develop, distribute to and promote larger more reflective niches of the American buying public. It's almost too late as this generation has found many gratifying and less expensive ways to create, self-promote, and distribute their own creations and find works that interest them. And while we can benefit from the technological information highway, this still does not absolve the major companies who distribute in the traditional markets of their responsibility. We cannot allow us to be amused and confused to death.

PART IV: PUSHED TO THE EDGE, FALLEN INTO THE JUNGLE

Hip Hop is a way of life with a history, culture, origin and a set of principles, acting as a safety valve in society . . . to let out the frustration of how young people feel today.

—Guru[6]

The genius of Black people is that you ain't seen rap coming. We keep reinventing ourselves through our expressions. Just as when the White industry begin to appropriate Jazz music and commodify it so that it was taken away, so much so that Blacks had less access to their own music because of the technologies . . . musicians came up with Bebop to challenge the narrow minded museum-like character of Jazz. To appropriate it again through the lens of Black street discourse. So Bebop, Charlie Parker, was an attempt to resist the mainstreaming of Jazz music. The reality is that the different styles that young people invent is an attempt to mark their own particular environments with the style they are accustomed to. And style is an attempt to put your stamp on your existence. Whites can't just simply appropriate that, because Black people keep inventing and re-inventing, asserting and re-asserting so that we can mark our own existence through the prism of style and give some sense weightiness of our existence. But we should not resist the edifying character of Hip Hop Culture as a tool of aesthetic, economic and social expression for young people.

—Michael Eric Dyson[7]

You know I think something happened in the transfer, change over of culture and power between 1980 and 2000. Somewhere in the policy and presidential switches between Reagan, Ford, Carter, Bush (1), Clinton, and Bush (2), we got hit below the knees and our footing got slippery.

We took our attention away from the weaker more vulnerable communities because our hopes were high, our examples high (Cosby), the perceived victories and voices of the 1960s and 1970s were on our minds and in our grasps and we didn't continue to address our poorer community's hopelessness.

That hopelessness was heard clearly in a new form in Grand Master Flash's, "The Message" (1982), but that message got truncated and transformed into commodified aesthetic rhetoric that flowered a profitable new market concept. Instead of the message being a critical concern it has become a mind-set and a concretized glamorized state of living called "hood life," or "ghetto," or "thug life," or "keeping it real for the peeps."

So what happened that we didn't listen when Grand Master Flash said, "Don't push me cause I'm close to the edge, I'm trying not to lose my head"? Many fell all the way over the edge and got trapped in the "jungle." Those of us that benefited from the 1970s gains in the larger cultural formula rode into colleges or position of influence, but there were not enough it seems left in the mix of the common folk to raise and rattle the message. That message was co-opted into Rap where words began to lack vision and no victory in sight. Somebody marketed that narrative, rage, into a multibillion-dollar commodity called Hip Hop. I think this is what happened to our Black contemporary popular artistry.

These metaphors, image, and messages heard now in hundreds of Hip Hop, R&B productions are forming too much of the content of our culture today. Reader, we are pushed over the edge and have lost our heads.

PART V: WHAT IS CULTURAL THEORY?

What are these songs, and what do they mean? . . . I know these songs are the articulate message of the slave to the world.

—W. E. B. DuBois[8]

The main thing for a musician is to give a listener a picture of the wonderful things he senses in the world.

—John Coltrane[9]

What does a cultural theory mean today, in musical terms and why do we need them? I look at the world through the lens of artistic interpretation and expression. I'm interested in the themes, the messages artists "sing" about and the maps of meaning, the processes of construction. I spend all of my time creating music, studying music of Black culture, the artists, times, the styles and movements, and larger cultural responses. I'm interested in the meaning, the values, and cultural associations people invest in artistically. I believe these expressions are about the mind, beliefs, and activity of people, in culture and in time. I am firmly committed to the culture of the everyday and its central task to, as Cornel West has written, "dislodge, critique . . . consolidate communal resistance."[10] This is my spiritual, intellectual, and moral agenda. My recent articles in this way asked: How do we trace the seeds of cultural decay? And most importantly, who stole the souls of Black folks? We need a constant flow of cultural theory (talk) about what we want, artists do, and what society values in this exchange.

Engaging cultural theory (talk) is so important. From the other side it has been used against people of color and helped to undermine Black life and devalue our humanness heard through racist arguments which have devastated Black opportunities in education, business, housing, and political and social life. Frederick Hoffman published in 1896 his cultural theory on race traits and tendencies of the American Negro. In this theory Hoffman argued that Blacks have "downward tendencies" which would lead to their natural extinction in American society. Upon this kind of recommendation the United States Supreme Court found documented support for the disregard for Black life and was able to legalize segregation, thereby instituting a real American banner; the for "White Only" signs which marked the American landscape until the 1960s. It didn't end there as Hitler's evil regime found hope in American race theory and literally exterminated six million of its "minority and ethnic problems." By the way, Hoffman was actually working for and providing this information for an American life insurance company at the time (the industry). Black people, their value, worth have clearly been at the center of American debates and dilemmas about itself, its industries, its markets, itself as a modern civilized nation. On that historical fact alone, makes Black destiny inextricably bound with what America is and will become.

In contemporary cultural theory four general schools of thought have erupted in the past decades: (1) The British school and their focus on power and the relevance of the peoples' own subjective voices who found cultural spaces to just "be" in relation to oppressive social structures. (2) American cultural historians focus on the American historical narrative and its most salient theme of manifest destiny, the American dream, city set out on a hill, the spirit of conquest and exploration, the land of freedom, home of the brave, its peoples and republic in this huge cultural assimilating, percolating, melting pot. (3) The ethnic and postmodern cultural studies models (i.e., African American, Asian American, woman's studies) which developed largely out of the Civil Rights movement. It looks at human experience, expression, and the fight and creation of newer identities within a history of American hegemony (the righteous fight against "the man"). (4) And lastly, popular cultural theory looks at folk and mainstream popular artifacts such as magazines, comic books, TV ads, and music which surround, inform, and shape our contemporary cultural identity and beliefs. These are called sites of examination, places and times where the formation of our culture is talked about.

Michael Eric Dyson, bell hooks, Tricia Rose, Gerald Early, Stanley Crouch are all writers who speak about the folks wrestling with cultural, social-political, and artistic meaning in society. In his recent book, *Race Music*, musicologist Guthrie Ramsey argues for an interpretation of our music making reality as "cultural theaters," that is the roller-skating rink, the church, the club, the house party. These are all sacred places he argues where one can best understand our music as a participating, engaging community in which meaning and music are inextricably bound. This should ensure that we keep in documentation, mind, the relevance, meaning and reverence we have to hold in place of our exchanges, our expressions, and rituals as valued and sacred.

One has to ask in light of the DuBois notion, "What is the articulate message of Blacks to the world today? What would at least one of the top messages on our list be? What form and forum would it be delivered in?"

PART VI: THE ARCH OF HUMAN EXPERIENCE

I'm goin' represent the African American interests while being critical of them. I'm going to speak to the larger, universal themes of Black American culture while being critical of the ways we fail to live up to our obligation to defend our own people—and I'm going to hit the themes that the larger American culture can resonate with, because Black folk are not orangutans living outside the arch of human experience.

—Michael Eric Dyson[11]

I recently sat down to watch the 14 episodes of the PBS *Eyes on the Prize* series. It's thick. The one thing that comes across out of this entire period in our history, 1954 to the 1980s, is that Black people and this nation were involved in the most serious and important cultural debates, policies, and definitions of modern society the world has ever known. Black preachers, beauticians, college students, lawyers, politicians, schoolteachers, janitors, and maids, common folk sincerely took their living in their hands and remolded the times with total commitment and engagement. What a great lesson for our current times. And for me, the music was an equal participant in the struggle for power, meaning, and the search for Black and national souls. Music historian, singer/composer, activist Dr. Bernice Johnson Reagon stated that during this period the music allowed people to become empowered and unparalyzed by the hatred and stiff resistance to justice the nation showed Black people. As pointed to earlier, this important music period of Soul between 1965 and 1975 represented for Black people and artists many things: cultural and political empowerment, a musical category, spiritual/expression depth and meaning, race pride, and social and civic responsibility and accountability. This was articulated in the concepts of Soul music, soul brother, having soul, soul food, soul hair, singing with soul and getting down to the soul of the matter.

I don't think this is an old folk's search for the romanticized mythical moral note. I clearly remember, not long ago, what Black music culture felt and breathed like. Music was a part of the oxygen of the times, because, as I indicated in the opening of this book, music mattered because it meant something, it was about something.

Every era of culture has cultural memory which helps to recover and bring back essential meanings about what the people and times were about. Each era then, generation needs cultural theory (ways of talking), banners, new ways of seeing why, when, how, and where we are headed. I believe the most important question that one of our cultural critics posed was in 1967. In his late work, *Where Do We Go from Here: Community or Chaos?* Martin Luther King Jr. writes, "We are faced with the fact that tomorrow is today . . . there is such a thing as being too late . . . this well may be mankind's last chance to choose between chaos and community."[12]

My honest feeling is that his death which happened less than a year after *Community or Chaos* signaled that we were in our last chance mode. We now sit in chaos. Things, technology, and terror it seems have replaced and far escalated beyond the visible examples we have of human decency and care being given in our culture. I believe it's time that our cultural agencies produce and make room for more artistic vision imbued with meaning(s) that restore community, value, excellence at every level and time for our culture to abhor stupidity, excess, and indecency. We do not live on the outside of the arch of human experience (Dyson), naked, barren, and unable to grasp the lifelines that draw us closer to one another.

PART VII: TIME TO GET TO WORK

This is what we are saying: If the Black man must create, create a new music brother. . . . If you are a free man, then speak to the free idiom. Make your poetry that speaks to the new. Then you are creating a new thing that the world must come to. Then you're the original man again.

—Louis Farrakhan[13]

All of what I do is to burn bad karma and help people live better. I just go to work every day and enjoy it.

—Russell Simmons[14]

I think it is time again for a new Black declaration of independence (Locke, *The New Negro*; Hughes, *The Negro Artist and the Racial Mountain*; Baraka, *Blues People*; selected writings from the Black arts movement; Harold Cruse, *The Crisis of the Negro Intellectual*). Time to get to work again. Bravely, somehow a number of Black artists and scholars need to create ensembles, "race records" outlets and labels, book and film venues, arts and dance sites for the singular purpose to maintain cultural "talk and song" teaching, us. This is what we should go to work and do every day. Alain Locke, writing in 1925, stated that Black life in Harlem was, "The first concentration of so many diverse elements of Negro Life."[15] The greatest experience of this group was "finding each other." One of my mentors is author Harold Cruse, who in 1967 wrote that the true cultural leaders of every generation are the artists. Most of our leading Black writers, from Toni Morrison to Cornel West, from Bernice Johnson Reagon to Michael Eric Dyson, all refer to and work within the models of artistic excellence, exhibited by the examples of musical artistry in particular. But what would happen if the young artists could no longer be allowed to shine, shimmer, no longer have anything worthy to say or be allowed to be heard, when they lose their "voices"? This is what concerns me most, and the question is real. The industry has virtually silenced, muted, made invisible significant Black voices except for rambling religious zealots, inarticulate and loud sports figures, commentators, and of course their modern Black cultural cash cow, the rapper.

Music culture has real meaning. It represents certain ideas, ideals, values; it engages certain sensibilities. When will Hip Hop creation/producers face up to its lack of meaning related to excellence, communal activism? Will it be able to shed its sonic symbolism of "badness', bad dude, playa, homey keeping it real" shackles? When will Hip Hop artistry as a movement in art turn back or center towards its value of old, Grand Master Flash message music, teaching music and get up, wake up, and be somebody music?

We are tired of entertaining for public gaze and White extended fantasy, setting in place Black nightmares. That is what is happening as a result of too much contemporary productions. Instead music making should be about the investment in inspiring dreams, moving people, crushing stereotypes, challenging society, figuring out how to give people something more than just a sideshow. Not all music needs to be so lofty and honorable, but there needs to be in place a balance. There is such a palpable emptiness in today's music making. The dominant themes in 2004, in addition to the teen angst of alienation, fear, abandonment, are also some whacked love stories, adolescent sensory search for materiality or sex and thug brute stupidity. Just too much ignorance and being concerned with "dumb stuff." Are we proud of this? Today there is clearly an absence of spiritual reflection, common respect for living with and caring for others. The overwhelming anger and disregard for one another is disturbing at all levels. Our world can only be changed by a generation of young people who get and stay turned onto something of value and sustaining substance like the love of neighbor, the pursuit of justice, the inspiration to be somebody, not parading in loud-mouthing and stupidity and claiming that this is cool, or being Black, or in, or real.

At the close of 2003 and into 2004, we had music artistry in madness. Phil Spector kills, R. Kelly and Michael Jackson arrested for problematic sexual charges, James Brown, George Clinton, Diana Ross all arrested for various ills, Janet plays silly with a younger Justin (a real wasteful move), rappers doing almost-porn videos for sale on TV, Madonna and Britney's televised kiss (meaning?), a huge album is titled *Get Rich or Die Trying*, lawsuits about accusations of murder attempts by music moguls, rappers arrested on more murder charges, Kobe loses it, Rosa Parks is suing OutKast?! We still must have hope in this generation to change it all.

To me, that's this generation's greatest challenge to discover the meaningful center of its cultural meaning beyond the superficial emptiness which much of the music is wrapped in. Russell Simmons, now 45, wants to return for himself (as well as Hip Hop) to values, led by spiritual convictions and maturity that he is now guided by. But he's "old" now and it's too late for Hip Hop to follow suit, perhaps. Hip Hop as an art movement has invested almost all of its remaining capital into shallow holdings of commercialism. What now? We are far beyond King's equation and insistence on community. We are in the zones of chaos. If you look at the great family of Black music, yes, Blues, Jazz (from Swing to Bebop to Modern, Free) R&B, Reggae, Soul, Funk, and Urban Contemporary, all dipped and dabbed into the stream of commercial folly. But all these musics kept a stronger footing in a championing place for Black people to survive, to believe in us, to be proud and to keep our culture up baby up. In this way Hip Hop music has failed its family heritages of "Say It Loud, I'm Black and I'm Proud." Hip Hop, perhaps in some ways, is becoming a step backwards for "Black culture," unfortunately. As a cultural form and forum it is now gnawing away at the crucial centers of values that give the Black community its musical meaning. Hip Hop has got to change. One of art's and culture's primary functions in society is to allow people to dream and create visible, viable, and real cultural agency. Yes, cultural expression gives place for societal critique and rage, but that rage is to embolden us to make a better way.

As a Black musical force in American culture, Hip Hop music and artistry, R&B included, has certainly landed on a certain kind of cultural mission as an emerging voice now 25 years old. But it must in line with Franz Fanon's challenge, fulfill its inherited epochical mission. This generation is evolving, just as Jazz evolved to contain over a 60-year period so many different styles within. Honestly, as an artist I do see Hip Hop artistry being fully big, bad, and beautiful enough to provide the place and space for that kind of depth and relevance on the many levels discussed here.

But our cultural theory, talk, representation, artifacts, rituals, and manifestos must move out of the current commercial state of these zones of chaos and must be the source and fuel of our forthcoming cultural projections toward these goals. Then and only then can a recognizable stability of communities, values, identities, and ideologies of substance be visible. It's time to get to work, all of us, and transform the cultures of chaos into moments, monuments, and movements of meaning. This will be the transforming times when the invisibility of the necessary expressions of substance within our culture illuminate and dismantle the barriers that keep a generation blinded by the "evils" of this current chaotic era.

· *47* ·

Still Black Notes: Reporting from the 2004 BET (Black Entertainment TV) Awards Show

(Portions broadcast on MPR, July 3, 2004)

Today's music makes me want to go out and buy old school music even more. Today's music makes me appreciative of what I did in the '80s, George Clinton, James Brown, the Gap Band did . . . because right now all these youngsters are doing is taking our stuff, sampling it, and putting a bunch of rap on it.

—Rick James[1]

In a modern cultural environment of terrorism, occupations, feisty and combative elections, beheadings, and the popular cultural resonances of *Fahrenheit 9/11*; *White Chicks*; *I, Robot*; *King Arthur*; *Spider-Man 2*; *Catwoman*; rappers/movie stars posing as FBI agents and jacking cars, again, the question comes up: What kind of world are we finding ourselves in? And as an artist I ask, What's the right note to link into this recent chain of events which challenge us?

Sitting watching the BET (Black Entertainment Television) awards show rehearsals, then live at the Kodak Center in Los Angeles, summer 2004, I noticed a few niches and notches in our current examples of contemporary Black music expressions. I was again reporting for MPR on invitation from my dear friend music director Patrice Rushen, and I think what I saw in general is reflective of where we are today in mainstream Black popular music.

We got "major game" now, got stage, largely due to the unprecedented power and market punch of Hip Hop youth music culture. The market investments are huge and several of the young Black men and women heading a number of recording/production companies are multi-millionaires; *the first time in music history any single group of Black entertainers generated and controlled so much, money in the mainstream popular marketplace.*

But the questions I pose are: What is the cost to "be in" the game? What is specifically being said, what are the messages in the music, and do they suggest we hope and believe in anything significant? I wonder, because for all the gas and glitter, it does not provide the "gold" (the music) with much weight beyond shine and shimmer.

The Twin Cities gave the world of popular music in the eighties a new unique sound and Prince who has emerged again, more kingly than ever (this year inducted in the Rock and Roll Hall of Fame), set the stage for some new and relevant questions. There is that line from his new *Musicology* (2004) CD, "Wish I had a dollar for every time they say, 'Don't you miss that feeling music gave you back in the day?'"

At the 2004 BET Black Music Awards show I was seeking out some answers. I was as well interested in had the political climate aroused any relevant thinking among the new generation of songster/performers? As well how is the industry with so many restrictions and market

275

formulas for making "chartable hits" is reacting to the consciousness of artists who want to say something, politically, musically, creatively? Would the show reflect and respond to some of these resonances? I was hoping to have a conversation with some performer/insider about some of this.

Well, I got eyeball, and earful. Anyway you look at it, whether it's Elvis's hips in the late-1950s, Bob Dylan's political consciousness call, or James Brown's "Say It Loud, I'm Black and I'm Proud," the relevance of popular artists' song, sentiment, and singles ring true to what significant impulses there are all around our society.

At accepting their award for best group, OutKast spoke to a crowd of several thousand reminding them to go out and vote and made a plug for *Fahrenheit 9/11*, the Michael Moore documentary film. This was a good sign.

So, I'm sitting there watching the rehearsals with Alicia Keys. India.Arie, Usher, the Isley Brothers, Janet Jackson, Jay-Z, OutKast, Kayne West, Doug E. Fresh, Melle Mell, the Sugar Hill Gang, Ludacris, 50 Cent, Teena Marie and Rick James, Smokie Norful, Yolanda Adams, and I'm thinking, "My God this room has within it the most performed young Black musical entertainers on the planet!" There is an incredible pounding on the ground that is still being made by these contemporary voices.

I must admit, as I have said before, many of the strategies are there. India.Arie sings a tribute to Ray Charles, there's a tribute to Barry White, a musical tribute to the Isley Brothers and they perform a medley spanning 50 years of their hits! There is a very powerful tribute to 25 years of Hip Hop culture on wax, ending with a stunning performance of Public Enemy's "Fight the Power." After hearing that, I could only think of the social critique usually heard in music, back in the day, perhaps still has a place.

One guest host noted, "Hip Hop is a worldwide phenomenon and there are emerging new stories that need to be told. The Hip Hop artists are the new storytellers."[2] I think that is an impactful point that is being made, undeniably.

Watching Usher, you cannot miss the torch being passed in front of our eyes, from Bo Jangles, Sammy Davis, Gregory Hines, or Michael even.

Music in many of today's contemporary forms are driven largely by visual performance mediums than simply music sounding, in notes. We just have to take on different filters for viewing where this music is coming from and heading. There is plenty to hope for in the future of Black musical artistry. That being said, we can certainly expect more technology, more spectacle, cross-fertilization of styles and audiences and yet more Black youth exploitation, uncensored sex narratives, more anger, disregard of traditional systems, values, well it's just "Rock and Roll" anyway, right?

One powerful example in the opening of the show was a performance by rapper Kayne West from the Hip Hop side. He utilized the social-political rhetoric of the Black Gospel church. He had 120 people on stage, a choir, dancers, walk-on extras, high school marching band drum corps, and Gospel diva Yolanda Adams doing his number, "Jesus Walks."

This was a pretty fantastic show opener and a great example of the crisscrossing and merging of styles that contemporary artists are again pushing the envelopes on.

I am a fan of Country music; it is real and rich. I love as well Classical and Rock and Roll, this is great, great music. But throughout time, even casual observers have noted the extraordinary gifting of Black artistry. From reports on the West African musician parades and festivals, to Southern slave singing at camp meets, old Bluesmen, the swinging of the Count Basie band, the grace and fluidity of Ella Fitzgerald to the phrase dexterity of rapper Ice Cube, there is nothing quite like Black performance artistry. The fervency and fluidity of the expressions, the performance energy, the meeting and melding of earthliness, spiritual exuberance in a Gospel riff, again all the strategies are still in place. Black people doing their music is an extraordinary human experience of expressions. To be in the presence of Black artistry is simply indescribable, and I'm a Black musician.

I guess most of my questions posed were answered. Music back in the day is still providing these young artists with great examples to emulate that benefit us all. And, there are plenty of opportunities for young artists to speak up and out socially and politically.

Now, this being the last reporting of Black music culture before I close this book down, I do want to leave on a positive affirmation for the future of Black music culture. But, there still remains the work we have to do to address what we should be doing and hoping in, beyond the glitter of charts, TV millisecond, and sells.

And again, while this may very well be an appropriate question for politicians, parents, teachers, and church/culture leadership, there has and should always be a dipping into the pool of artistic thought and practice imbued with the dynamics of a vision.

BLACK MUSIC DOING; DO THEY GET IT?

In its current spin, will the creation and marketing of this art be continued to be nurtured to grow its more creative side, its innovative side? The values we have instilled in music making as Black music has seemingly been dissipated, been watered down to mostly commodity entertainment packages. Traditional questions of "values" sometimes dragged up as old school (or "the school" as I call it) are usually a tributary museum moment. But so much of music making as I see it is rehashed, looped, and made to sell on the shelf.

The now very familiar complaint that too many of these young artists are not musicians at all but entertainers for the camera moment is at this point very real. You cannot believe how much time and money is spent to rehearse and produce a three-minute spectacle for a TV show, just to "come out correctly." These are some very expensive notes being made or generated these days! Perhaps the musicians all come around record making time, but by the time the show producers create $100,000 stage production sets there's no money left for musicians in the budget. One can imagine after Janet Jackson's wind machine tunnel, Ludacris's 25-foot mermaid video screens, and Usher's bungee jumping routines and fire sets, I guess it's just cheaper to throw on a prerecorded track. Alicia Keys and Jay-Z had live musicians (Questlove, Kid Rock, Sheila E), and Patrice Rushen's house band played live for Smokey Norful, but all else was prerecorded walk-ons and tracks. Backstage, the dressing rooms are all for the dancers, and everyone else is a singer or a rapper, extra, and their crew. Still, in this kind of environment, I could ask, where are the young Black musicians, bands, a horn player or guitarist? This was a Black popular music show principally! This is not good.

THE SOIL AND WELL OF BLACK MUSIC

Many of my colleagues—musicians, producers, music educators—are concerned and have concluded that despite the indifference or nonknowledge of the deeper implications of this "Black youth entertainment super moment," people are moved into action, pseudopolitical consciousness, identity surges, and some moral agency, anyway. Why? Because the foundation of this music is based on symbols and meanings which have been "deeply planted." Again, the strategies are there (Morrison), the values although disrupted are still there and the symbols and icons erected stand in our minds. These pop into our stream of consciousness for many even though these young performers' performance practices, their delivery, styling yes, is oversexualized and sinister looking at times. This work is still Black artistic activity and that has certain cache in the world and meaning(s). These young entertainers are handling and stumbling onto and into traditions of power and public prestige attributed to the best. (We will miss Ray Charles, Elvin Jones, Barry White, Ray Brown, and Nina Simone, all master musicians who died in 2003 or 2004.) This is frustrating to my generation of musicians and music educators because too many young artists today in the moment react to this old school ideology of music making, with rhetoric like "We're just trying to keep it real." "I'm not trying to playa' hate by dissing my homies." "My dogs expect me to keep it true to the game." Granted this enactment is couched in a Hip Hop jargon and a generalization, but it is really hard for those of us trying to train and instruct younger musicians that they must remember and study the role of the master artists of past generations.

MTV, BET, Vibe, and the Internet have made even in the music docu-pieces, this music, anything older than 1990, a past faded reality. The only value that is valued in this present moment is youth identity, largely in Black music through Hip Hop and Hip Hop R&B. And we have heard Mr. Johnson's well-quoted line, "The E in BET stands for entertainment."[3] From a larger cultural view, the reach and influence that a media outlet has still means that this is a moment where ensuring the relevance and future rides on the waves not just of profit but what will ensure traditions to hold onto and pass on. Money is not the bottom line in this discussion of culture. The future is based on ensuring those strategies for living that have been the first bottom line of Black creative culture and survival; representation of identity, spiritual/moral agency, social/cultural critique and celebration, party, ritual and dance, musical and artistic integrity respected throughout the world. That's what from a cultural view should be the bottom line for our cultural production and projections.

Strictly from a musician's view, we have to keep "edumusicating" hoping to imbue the coming generations with the richness and meaning and practices of true musicianship and artistry.

No matter what, as I have said before (see chapter 46), the future of Black music is not in the hands of any of us 30 years or older; the future of Black music is in the working hands of younger musicians. But every generation of musicians comes out of a community. So in terms of mainstream popular music by the end of 2004, we have to commend young artists who proudly represented Black music traditions, like India Arie, Usher, Brandy, Norah Jones, Alicia Keys, Floetry, Beyonce, Pharrel Williams, Anthony Hamilton, Smokey Norful, and Robert Randolph and the Family Band, because these kinds of examples keep the flame burning brightly. This two-step dance between artistry and its commitment to, representation of, and connection to the expression and the well-being of Black people is another bottom line that is essential in our art. I'm reminded of how one of our modern griots, Dr. Bernice Johnson Reagon, speaks about our experience giving and receiving in Black culture. She spoke of how ritual in the Black church service functions. When we go to church we assume we are there to get something from that experience, but we go as well to participate in creating it. There is in this cultural continuum no such thing as just coming, sitting down in your seat, and having something come to you from the stage. In Black traditions you come in with a need and understanding that what you got out of the experience would be determined by how open you were to receiving, and giving. I believe audiences are expecting to get something but give back, report back as well. In our current chaos, there are needs today that performers must read and see beyond the commodity of the price of a concert ticket, about helping to inspire and imbue these communities with meaning again. That connection to audience, community, artistry is one of the strategies that must be kept in play and in place to ensure that the bottom line is there.

I've lived and listened now through the race riots in the 1960s, Watergate and Nixon, Reaganomics, Iran-Contra, an honest peanut farming presidency, Bush Gulfing, Ken Starr, Whitewater and Clinton clashes, in our current political climate one can hear loudly the discontent being expressed. It is being reported by some that *we are in the most deceitful, disgraceful social environment mechanized and manipulated by legislation and political ideology and farce, ever.*

Many of the empty values in popular culture are amplified I believe to sound out as loud, blaring and uncaring, rude and disrespectful, and musically dishonest artistry. Popular culture is a "very expensive staged show" and young artists seem to be puppets in the commodification wheel produced and pinned up for daily purchase and consumption. Dishonest artistry happens due to these popular performers just "rehearsing an act" and when they have no real grounded attachment to values and/or what it takes to study, develop the craft of musicianship.

One hundred years from now, actually much sooner than that, we will be able to point to a dysfunctional and corrupt political ideology and consumer-driven mentality that fueled it, and funded it.

STILL BLACK

American cultural developments have been influenced by the Negro presence. Since a cultural philosophy has been cultivated to deny this truth, it remains for the Negro intellectual to create his own philosophy and to bring the facts of cultural history in focus with the cultural practices of the West. That role belongs to the artists and intellectuals of each generation.

—Harold Cruse[4]

The task in cultural studies discussions like this is to decode, unveil the cultural apparatus so we can find hidden meaning that otherwise undetected distorts, debases free will, moral grounding, and intellectual and creative pursuits. This kind of thinking, line of questioning is to enliven to wake up, to give a voice back again to individuals in culture to speak, sing, play, and live. Black music has always done this.

Today, one cannot dismiss the power of Black music culture, particularly Hip Hop music culture. As a cultural force in the world its vibrancy is felt. And while too many Black notes are twisted, contorted, and the performers delivering are blinded by materialism and the high of "flashes and fame for the minute" in many ways, it is still (Black music) an unstoppable, impenetrable force in societies across the globe in the United States, Europe, Brazil, and Japan, which are just a few examples. What this means in my hearing is that this music is alive and still being stirred (some by creative young artists, some by market forces and industry) and still brewing, and so some great young artists, singing, playing, conceptualizations will continue to bubble up to the top. This is because despite market forces and demands, the brew, the root is good. That root is Black artistry, and the notes are still Black. I'm not alone in my love of this great music artistry certainly, and there are many deserving and talented artists who will emerge.

As a cultural reporter though I have to play the game, to be in it. I buy the tickets, sit in the bleachers with the fans, I go down and fuss at the owners, I jump on the field with the players, I run, pitch, catch and bat the ball, and I always ask, "Did we have a great time?" and "Why?"

Our task now is to just keep encouraging excellence, making great music, and keep the fire on so people are provided with examples and opportunities to hear Black music doing.

If people are exposed to Black music performances, younger musicians, singers, songwriters will be encouraged to move toward that music making "center," not just being entertaining, and here is where the future has to be refocused, reshaped now.

7

CONCLUSIONS: THE TURNAROUND

"Seashore" by James Zeke Turner

· 48 ·

Staying Tune-Full: From Where I Have Walked, Final Reflections, and the Hope(s) in the Future of Black Music Culture

𝒮t seems right to speak at the close of this book specifically about my own life, walking in it as a musician. A hope in the future of a culture's music can be seen from the bridge of one's own constant engagement. I am persuaded by and committed to the shaping of our music because of my own involvement and work in it as an artist. This whole thing for me began with an interest in emulating a hero, Jimi Hendrix, who I saw on TV playing his electric guitar. I saw this incredibly gifted musician who looked like me, doing something that sounded extraordinary. He commanded his instrument, he was playing his music his way, and he was in control of his image. Without knowing all the trappings and what factored into the Jimi Hendrix "experience," I just knew as an eight-year-old I had to have a guitar so that I could be like Jimi Hendrix. This had to be in the late 1960s.

But I was always in church singing, playing the piano, doing those Sunday school plays and reading the Scriptures in front of the church. Probably most of the Black musicians from my generation and earlier began in a similar way, nurtured by Black communities rich in cultural activities, many times exclusively in the church. But as well, my parents went to the symphony and the plays and took us to the *Nutcracker* ballet every year. My earliest recollection of wanting to mix music up was upon hearing the symphony series the "Young People's Concerts" with the Detroit Symphony in the early seventies. The conductor was Paul Freeman, a Black man. So, I simply thought I could write Jimi Hendrix music for the symphony. This all seemed logical to me then, and still does. My mother told me then, "One day that orchestra is going to be playing your music." That day arrived in 1995 when the Detroit Symphony premiered my *Essay for Orchestra* in Detroit's Orchestra Hall. And that conductor, Paul Freeman, some thirty-plus years later, conducted and recorded my *Essay for Orchestra* in Chicago during his 2002 symphony season. So this nurturing and this flirtation with multiple strands of Black music culture, from Gospel to R&B, to Rock and Roll, to Jazz and contemporary avant-garde music, and to writing operas, has been an integral part of my music mapping. I just had always seen Black music and "cultural doing" painted in broad strokes of color. I always understood that Black is "best" because it encompassed all. It's the deepest and richest color.

Junior high school was a breeze because of the music programs. Music helped us to do well and was seen as part of the nurturing, our growing. I have no delusion about it now; the public schools in Detroit made my friends and me who we are because of music programs. Playing in the bands, singing in the choirs, later in high school going to state festivals and slammin' all those suburban schools gave us the images of productivity, discipline, and artistic integrity. Most of our high school and junior high school teachers were great Black musicians; trained, tough and loving. I know it was in the music program at Cass Tech High School in Detroit that most of my clearest memories about my identity as a serious musician began. Out of Cass Tech and similar public school music programs came: Ron Carter, Curtis Fuller, Diana Ross, Earl Klugh, Geri Allen, Janet Williams, Kenny Garrett, and later James Carter, Regina Carter, and Carla Cook, to name a few.

As stated earlier, the future of Black artistry has to come from younger musicians. Where you find healthy, innovative, Black music culture within a supportive and nurturing community, there you will find the best evidence for where the music is heading. It will come not out of the radio and marketing ploys, but neighborhood music, church-community programs, and jams.

My good buddy Mark (Trent) Mitchell and I started the Cass Tech Jazz Festival Jam, which had to be around 1975 or so. We went to the Detroit Public Library's Azalia Hackley Collection and studied about so many heroes documented there. We plowed through old news clips, record reviews, and obituaries of hundreds of famous and local Jazz artists. The difference I see between then and now is that we listened to and were interested in all kinds of music. Our radio programs had everything from Elton John and George Clinton to Boston, Kiss, and Earth Wind and Fire, Luther Vandross, Steely Dan, and the Carpenters. It was all popular music and it was all good. For our festival we packed the music rooms with musicians, pre-med students, computer science majors, football players, and chemistry majors, and opened our concerts with lectures about Mary Lou Williams and Duke Ellington. Billy Strayhorn's niece Robin Strayhorn was in our class so we had some connection to the history. Detroit was a big Jazz town way back in the day, when Lionel Hampton, Miles Davis, Duke Ellington, and all the cats stopped in and hung out. One of my compositions, a big band piece called "And What Would You Like to Hear Little Lady?" was actually what Duke Ellington said to my mother in 1944 when, as a young woman, she heard him play in Detroit. But Cass Tech had many great musicians who went with us and before us, providing fertile soil for our nurturing. I often tell university and high school students that I don't see the drive and passion for music doing that I remember being such a driving force in our lives. We lived to do music all the time and we jammed together.

In 1978, I received a fellowship grant at 17 to study music abroad. I chose the guitar capital of course, Mexico. I think it was here that this Detroit boy began to see the world from larger spaces and places. I studied guitar at the Federation of Musicians in Acapulco, performed concerts and lived the culture. For the first time, I saw and hung out with Black people who looked just like me but were very different, spoke different languages, and were mixed with more than just my African American and Native American bloods. These folks were Spanish, West African, Chinese, French, the whole mix! But true to its universality, music was a common chord, practice, and community builder.

In the tenth grade I started a group called the Concept Jazz Orchestra. This was a 17-piece Jazz band that I was already booking and doing performances with in some major clubs at 16. We had a great group of young musicians who participated. Our pianist was Vernon Fails, who later went on to play for and write a good number of Anita Baker's late-1980s hits. Regina Carter, our little sister, was already making a name for herself playing in a group called Brainstorm that opened up for Michael Jackson. Kim Jordan went on to be the music director for Gil Scott Heron. From this young Detroit experience, a whole group of us went to Boston to attend the New England Conservatory and the Berklee School of Music. Even back then my hometown newspaper dubbed me "Little Quincy."

Thinking back on it now, that we were a recognizable flock of young musicians poised for doing something of note is very significant. That flock included Regina Carter, Jeff Stanton, Carla Cook, Derry Alan Kelley, Mark Mitchell, Mark Ledford, and many, many others. The year was 1979.

We settled into our college music studies in Boston, and there is no doubt in my mind that this was the most important music college town, ever. So many extraordinary musicians and movements were developing there. I would be willing to bet that there have not been too many other places and times more potent for the development of so many young musicians— other than, of course, Harlem in the 1920s, the Bopper's New York during the late-1940s, and Chicago's creative nurturing of the AACM. It is history now, but clubs like Pooh's Pub, Michael's, Wally's, 1369, Riley's, and the Willow Club cooked nightly. The other attraction was all the great Jazz masters still living and teaching there during this period, 1979 to 1988 or so. Allan Dawson, Jackie Byard, Mic Goodrick, Miroslav Vitous, William Thomas McKinley, Ran Blake, and George Russell were a few. Boston was the training ground and then they were off to New York. Some began to get picked up by GRP Records; Wynton (while not studying in Boston at this time, he was a constant presence) and Branford were picked up by Columbia; and of course at that time Art Blakey was still a drop-off point for a number of cats we knew then.

My earliest memory of a major artist who came to perform in Boston was Patrice Rushen. Patrice was the Janet Jackson of our day. She was one of the most famous musicians of the time and one of the most influential on our development; probably to this day she is one of the most respected musicians, particularly on the popular music scene in Los Angeles, where much of the heartbeat of the industry lies. We knew her not only as a hit song maker ("Forget Me Nots"), but also as a great Jazz pianist. I still have the ticket from that concert, Berklee Performance Center, Boston, April 11, 1980. I remember being so blown away. She opened up for Gil Scott Heron and after her performance I went up to the balcony to look down on the stage during intermission, and standing right there was Patrice Rushen! I couldn't believe it. I very shyly introduced myself and she asked me what I wanted to do with my music. I was so stunned and I probably said something stupid like, "I want to be just like you Ms. Rushen." She encouraged me to stay on. Some 15 years later as a professor of music and African American studies at Indiana University, I received a call from Patrice Rushen; she was interested in getting some help from me with circulating her name and works among concert music circles I was involved in. I couldn't believe it. Consequently I invited Patrice as an artist to Indiana to perform and talk about her work in the industry. We have collaborated on several projects together since. But this is an example in my mind of the importance of musicians sharing, passing torches on, and of how crucial it is to foster music participation so that the cultivation of traditions can be maintained. Imagine the great irony and the joy for us old-siders to see Will Smith remake the song we danced to at our senior proms, now renamed "Men in Black," for which Ms. Rushen received great new honors and some cash I'm sure.

Just a cursory flashback reveals so many young musicians training at the same time in Boston. My first gig in Boston was with Smitty Smith, now the drummer for the *Tonight Show* band with Jay Leno. I vividly remember my attempts to pay rent working as a street musician, playing my guitar in Copley Square, Boston Commons, Downtown Crossing, the train stations, and Harvard Square, singing with Lynne Fiddmont Linsey, who went on to sing with Stevie Wonder. My first band in Boston (1980–1983) had Najee playing E-flat sax, flute, and soprano sax; and he subsequently went on to be one of the most important sax voices in smooth Jazz, before Kenny G.

My pianist was Rachel Niccolazzo, known now as Rachel Z. Her roommate Regina Carter is today the preeminent Jazz violinist of this generation. Our camps were divided among the two schools, Berklee College of Music and New England Conservatory, but we all gigged together. From my class (1979–1983) two other Jazz greats emerged, my roommate and dear friend Nelson Rangell and clarinetist/composer Don Byron. My first composition at the NEC (New England Conservatory) was called Don Lee, composed for Don Byron.

There was an apartment building on the corner of Westover and Hemmingway Street. I promised when I got a chance in later years I would be the first to tell the story of 96 Hemmingway. This apartment will be remembered as the place that housed some of the greatest young Jazz musicians from this period. They all lived in that house! Going to visit was like going to the musician's club of Boston: Donald (Duck) Harrison, Walter Beasley, Mark Ledford, Victor Bailey, Jean Touissant, Clyde Hunt, Dwayne Cook Broadnaux, Gene Jackson, and Jeff "Twain" Watts. The list still goes on of those studying, gigging, and hanging out together in Boston: the Marsalis brothers (Wynton, Branford, DelFeayo), Kevin Eubanks, Terri Lyne Carrington, Gregg Osby, Curtis Williams, Cindy Blackmon, Bobby Broom, Carla Cook, Lenora Zenzalai Helm, Monty Croft, Cyrus Chesnut, Damon Duewhite, Cecilia Smith, Lynne Fiddmont, Rachelle (Barnes) Ferrell, James Williams, Jerry Atkins, Tommy Campbell, Billy Kilson, Mike Stern, Jeff Berlin, and I know I'm missing a few dozen more. This was just the Jazz lions set. At the same time, in the Folk and early developing teen pop market was Tracy Chapman and Maurice Starr's crew, who set off a megamovement that Back Street Boys, N'Sync, and all the other copy boy bands can't touch. These young men, who came to be known as the New Edition, were actually high school students; one of them was in my music class. By this point in 1981 I was a 19-year-old, full-time high school music teacher in the Boston public school system (hired illegally I bet) teaching at Madison Park High, Roland Hayes Division of Music, in Roxbury, the "hood." The New Edition, including Bell Biv Devoe, Ralph Tresvant, Bobby Brown, as well as another White version, the multimega-dollar group New Kids on the Block, were all in Boston developing their market acts and concepts. Both groups developed in the hoods of Roxbury and Dorchester, Massachusetts, and were trained by pre–Puff Daddy mogul Maurice Starr, who, by the way, was a great musician. Boston was rich.

The New England Conservatory was a place where Jazz and Classical music were taught side by side in partnership due to the extraordinary vision of composer/historian Gunther Schuller. Third Stream (the combination of classical and Jazz conventions) ideology ran thick. All my teachers spoke multiple languages—my composition teachers, George Russell (Lydian Chromatic Concept), William Thomas McKinley, and Mic Goodrick, my guitar teacher. During this time I met, through an exchange program at Tufts University, the man who introduced me to the idea of being a composer, T. J. Anderson. It was T. J. who hipped me to the academic avant-garde of twelve tone, aleatoric, and modern ideas of mixed media, multiple performance platforms, non-notated scoring, and so on. Also he was the first serious Black composer I had ever met. He changed my life and planted the seed for the next directions which were to shape my thinking, music, and activities from the age of 22 to 40 and beyond.

I continued on making music, gigging, and establishing ties. Because I was already booking recording dates and producing my mixed-bag works (Jazz, funk with string quartets and vocals), I decided to form my own recording company, BMagic Records. But it was this kind of contact with musicians that inspired me to think about music from a broader scope: music making (performing, composing and arranging, publishing, recording and producing), education, and the music industry. I have always been clear on the potential of these connections. At 22 I had received a bachelor's degree in music from the New England Conservatory, I was a full-time music teacher and the president of my own record company. NDN distributors out of New York distributed us. My company, with a gift of $4,000 in liquidated stock from my parents, had a small staff, a roster of artists, and a running contract with the Port Authority Train/Bus Station in New York. We were hired by a friend who worked there to bring down groups from Boston to play in the station. Myself and a couple of my in-house producers (Lester Goodwine) generated money by doing demos for high school kids who wanted to be "recording stars." Rap was just hitting and everybody wanted to do a New Edition–like demo or a Rap demo. We honestly thought Rap was the stupidest thing ever! Where was that mess going to take anybody? We were clueless! The company was going well, and so after graduation I decided to quit my post as a public school music teacher and run the company full-time.

In Boston during this time there was more money and public funding available for educational partnerships. So I began to write grants for funding the record company, which subsequently grew into YADI (Young Artists Development Inc.). A good buddy of mine from Detroit grade school came east to study Jazz composition at the University of Massachusetts at Amherst. Stephen Newby and I would form a series of artistic partnerships that would help us develop as musicians and best friends. With Stephen's help as an undergraduate music education major, we decided to start a school. We raised some $30,000 between 1985 and 1987 for the school, moved into the Boston Community Music School, and when money ran out we operated YADI in the basement of my church, Union United Methodist on Columbus Avenue.

We created an after-school community arts education/performing school and ensemble. We had classes in music history, popular music production, voice, and ensemble coaching. It was a great effort of which I was extremely proud. My thinking at the time was that the school would be able to generate more interest in the philanthropic community and subsequently channel those funds into my recording company.

Somewhere in here I decided that I needed to train in theology and philosophy to better understand where all this was taking me. The years in public school teaching made it evident that the crossroads of music and reaching younger people was part of my own calling. I applied in 1985 knowing nothing about aesthetics or philosophy to Boston University's School of Theology, minoring in composition studies. I immediately fell into another world, intellectualizing about meaning(s)—concept papers on the history of religion, epistemology, ontology, aesthetics, Paul Tillich, Karl Barth, and systematic theology! While working on the master's, I was also a room-service waiter at the Hyatt in Cambridge (I turned this into a vehicle to do a music showcase in the hotel's restaurant) and substitute teaching. Stephen came down from Amherst and we would run YADI on the weekends. During this time I met a whole group of very brilliant aspiring preachers and future philosophers at Harvard Divinity School. I was allowed to study there because all the schools of divinity in Boston, through the Boston Theological Institute, provided cross-school registration. This group included Drs. Anthony Pinn and Allan Callahan. My theology and preaching courses were done at Harvard and my church history and advanced composition courses were done at Boston University. My final master's thesis was the study of Richard Wagner's operas, arguing the case of a "theological music" based on the idea of a European superartist heroism model and the stage as a moral institution.

During this time I took a group of musicians through a Boston University–sponsored program to Dakar, Senegal, in 1988. Stephen Newby and Jazz vocalist Carla Cook were on this trip as well. Being there confirmed for all of us the functionality of music in traditional West African culture as we attempted to understand the cultural, historical, and practical teaching/performing applications. Performances and teachings from West African master musicians confirmed our understanding of the root of Black American African retentions apparent in our musical traditions: call and response, polyrhythmic pulse, community, and most importantly the crucial role of the master drummer and singer/philosopher, griot. I knew from this incredible experience it would not be difficult for me to return to my master's thesis board and argue my theory on theological music. I was wrong. Boston University's theology faculty rejected my first thesis. They found my thesis, which argued for theology based on West African functionality, untenable and based on premises that were impossible to argue or prove, which in their minds was the didactic role of music in culture. They further asserted that my findings were not based on traditional theories of music aesthetics. Can you believe that? We fought over it hard at my thesis defense but they finally after three years let me graduate and make the claim.

Their approval came only after I switched the focus of my cultural paradigm to European models based on the writings of Nietzsche, Schopenhauer, and the music of a western European composer. I am now proving all that I argued was correct, and I got the model from traditional West African and Black American music practice. The basis of this entire writing is the active role of artists in shaping contemporary society. We Are the World, the biggest artist/humanitarian concept to date, raising millions for hungry people, didn't come from Nietzsche's idea of a superman. This is an example where as a Black American musician I have had to join the fight within the traditional academy to point to and get up off exclusionary thinking and understanding—that is, to see that the rest of the world participates in, creates, and celebrates art in very different ways than Bach, Brahms, and Bruckner. The return to the States was eye-opening. At any rate, by day I was pursuing a master's in theology, but my work continued in Boston as a by-night record producer, and I was as well writing a few song cycles and string quartets.

One teacher, Donal Fox, has become a very close colleague. Donal is a contemporary new music composer who, among other things, experimented with mixing Bach fugal themes and approaches with Bebop and Free Jazz chords, structures, and improvisations based on this mixture. He's winning critical acclaim for his effective fusing and performances. Donal introduced me to more worlds of compositional insights and new music. Even before I entered the master's program studying composition with Greek avant-garde composer Theodore Antiniou, I was working out structure, analysis, and process problems with Donal.

Another opportunity that arose out of my connections with music and the public schools was being hired to be the music director of the Days in the Arts Program with the Boston Symphony and schools, which was housed in Lenox, Massachusetts, at the famous Tanglewood summer festival. Here I heard all kinds of music, taught art and music, wrote new kids' musicals every week, and watched Seji Ozawa conduct that great Boston Symphony Orchestra. I ran the program from 1982 to 1988, along with buddy Stephen Newby, who also taught in it later. I learned arts administration as well as interdisciplinary and cross-cultural tactics, which fueled my hunger for ways to do music in the world. Our kids taught us great lessons. We saw, directed, and coached hundreds of young minds and souls during those summers. This was a great time. I was also flirting with record companies in New York, trying to get a record deal primarily from Dr. George Butler, then the head of Jazz A&R at Columbia Records.

And while Wynton and Branford had things all tied up there, George seemed really interested in having me join the camp. Didn't happen. I got the big runaround and immediately begin to reroute my entries into the industry. My company was still doing business, YADI was in session, two records got notable mentions in *Billboard* magazine, and even some of the musicians were coming up to my office bringing charts and wanting to write for our artists. One client was Harvard's Divinity School. I negotiated with the help of my Harvard partners the deal to actually carry on the BMagic label, our first and only Gospel album. The artist was a Divinity School student whom I had actually worked with as an undergraduate at NEC, Garth Fletcher. Garth was an early BeBe Winans, I guess, with a kind of all-encompassing Pop/Jazz/Gospel bent. But this allowed my small company to see a full album project through the stages of artwork, packaging, and putting product in some local stores.

My exit from Boston in 1988 happened due to sheer exhaustion and frustration with trying to get a record deal, trying to keep YADI and BMagic afloat, and trying to be an academic. Crazy! Dr. George Butler had moved as far as to tell industry friends I was going to be signed. We set up a showcase, and DelFeayo Marsalis was actually assigned to be my producer. On the day of the showcase at the Hyatt in Cambridge, George Butler didn't show! I was devastated, along with my band, which included Rachel Z on keyboards, Billy Kilson on drums, and Greg Jones on bass. There was even an almost fight between my drummer and the young Marsalis. I got the "sign" from the Lord that I was being prepared for something else. My teacher at the time, T. J. Anderson, told me, "We don't need any more 'Wyntons' doing this. What we need is more Black composers. Go get your doctorate and study."

I had already by this time been accepted into the doctoral program in composition at the University of Michigan in Ann Arbor, but the lure of a recording contract blurred a small and steady compositional voice that would later emerge and be the entry point into a more national artistic identity. Actually, Stephen Newby, after finishing his graduate degree at University of Massachusetts, also headed out to the University of Michigan. This is another point that underscores the importance of the camp and crew idea. Most of the people I began with in the middle 1970s in high school and the many I named here are still making music strong, and we keep in touch. This point really hits home for me when I think of the graduate school friends, because from this group you tend to hear about jobs and research projects; you travel together to conferences and advise one another through the difficult terrain of the academy and the music business.

I entered the University of Michigan doctoral program in 1988 (I had to stay in Boston an extra year to complete and rewrite my Boston University thesis), and being back on Michigan soil made me feel like a kid who had left home, then returned to old familiar playgrounds. Immediately the connections were made with family, friends, and Detroit institutions, as well as a completely new environment in the college town of Ann Arbor. The group that Stephen and I both bonded with as we crossed the sands included Chicago pianist and musicologist Guthrie Ramsey, vocalist and musicologist Kyra Guant, singer/pianist Louise Toppin, and so many others. The five of us remain very much connected in academia and in music. Guthrie is a professor of music history at the University of Pennsylvania, Dr. Kyra Guant at New York University, and Dr. Louise Toppin is a voice professor at East Carolina University at Greensville. Louise actually took over the Boston-based Videmus/Visionary recording and concert/education company in 1997 and asked if I would serve as the executive director of the record company, along with composer/conductor Julius Williams.

In 2001 we released our first symphonic record with the Prague Radio Symphony and Washington Symphony. One of the works that was released on that CD project was Stephen Newby's Gospel symphony. The important thing about this group at the University of Michigan in the graduate programs in music, between 1988 and 1995 or so, is that it was probably the largest and most supported group of Black doctoral students in music, ever. Most of those people graduated and are professors and artists teaching and performing all over the United States. The other thing was that the institution funded us. We were all on incredible fellowships, and we could hold teaching posts as well. If you change the funding structure, place the priority on embracing people's work and nurturing their creativity, you will produce successful results in numbers. Two were responsible for bringing us there: musicologist Dr. Raelinda Brown and Dr. Willis Patterson. Brother Newby and I met Raelinda as we cotaught with her sister Carlene Brown, a systematic musicologist at Tanglewood. Raelinda acted as big sister, keeping us all in line and setting the example for young Black scholars in music. The real foundation layer for Black graduate recruitment and retention at the University of Michigan was Dr. Willis Patterson. A monument should be erected to honor his incredible work and dedication to supporting so many great Black musicians in Ann Arbor. He also is responsible for probably one of the most dynamic classes of Black music scholars and artists across at least two or three generations, as he provided leadership as a voice professor, and then dean in the school for 30-plus years.

Black music cannot be done without Black scholars and teachers in the field. Music is a special enough field, but can you imagine the world without Black music leadership? Oftentimes I think we would have the industry mislead us into the fantasy that Black music is well on all levels. We are losing great Black training. There aren't enough Black technicians, and the development of young performers (musicians) in major cities has declined so rapidly over the last three decades that there is bound to be a serious shortage of "serious" Black musicians. This is clearly due to the lack of school programs, the draw of more competitive industries, and the lure of spotlight-popular music traditions, which are mostly producing Rap and kiddy R&B singers. Forget the Classical music scene, it has not grown up out of its racist, exclusionary, elitist governing to become a safe, warm, encouraging environment to support large numbers of young Black artists. But we have to encourage, push, and inspire more young musicians of all interests and stripes to stay on, stay on. This is what we all did and are doing. I hope we continue to pass on the torches.

At the University of Michigan as a graduate teaching fellow I taught 180 undergraduates in American Religion and the African American Church Experience. This is where I got my chops as a college instructor, and it was here that I brought together history, aesthetics, and the socially charged evolution of Black people in the church and in music. Now keep in mind I was a young brother and still am! Perhaps I was in my late 20s. The other class I taught occasionally after taking it was Harold Cruse's American Culture and Gender course. In Harold Cruse's class I learned a more critical approach to cultural studies and about the powerful African American narrative. Harold Cruse taught like a master teacher and was preparing me to actually carry the torch. He subsequently invited me to assistant teach his course, which I did each year, handling the sections dealing with Black music. His book *The Crisis of the Negro Intellectual* will long be hailed as one of the most important writings of Black American cultural critique.

At the doctoral level I studied composition with Leslie Basset, then William Albright, Bill Bolcolm, and a little sharing with American composer Michael Daughtery. This was the coming together of all the worlds I had known as a musician and later as an aspiring scholar and student in the culture of Western art music. I had a lot of catching up to do, as my master's was not in composition proper. But, I was already writing as much if not more concert music than my colleagues. I had finished my first guitar concerto at 19 and it was premiered, with me as soloist, when I was 23 with the Detroit Metropolitan Orchestra in the venerable Symphony Hall. My second guitar concerto was completed not long after I arrived in Ann Arbor and was again premiered in Detroit.

At this time, 1989 or so, I was also hired at Hartford Memorial Baptist Church in Detroit on the ministerial staff, conducting the chamber orchestra and teaching in their Biblical Studies Institute. I guess coming back to Detroit in the church, doing music in probably one of the nation's premier Black churches, plus working on doctoral studies, allowed me to see yet another view of what I should be doing with music and culture. Seeing it all played out around and within the culture of Black life in Detroit was an epiphany, revelatory and prophetic for me all at once. I worked under Dr. Charles Adams, the "Harvard Hooper," as he is called, and James Abbington, one of the finest church organists and Black choir pedagogists in the country. Our pianist from high school, Vernon Fails, was and still is there at Hartford, and the church organist was the music director for Aretha Franklin. I tell this story all the time. Vernon was then writing, arranging, and playing for Anita Baker, and Darrel Houston was the music director for Aretha Franklin! Music at Hartford Memorial was a most incredible experience. Jimmy, by the way, was doing doctoral work at the University of Michigan in organ studies. The music at the church went from Black traditional Baptist anthems, to traditional hymns, to Spirituals, to a Bach cantata with orchestra, to Richard Smallwood and the Winans, all in one service, performed and sung by incredible musicians and one of the best trained Black church choirs anywhere. There probably will never exist a Black music program like that again. It was truly incredible. When the church installed its new pipe organ, it flew in a Russian organist to inaugurate it. Yes, pretentious, yes bourgeoisie, and yes big Black church tradition—truly rich and powerful! Jimmy did all the music for the national progressive Baptist conferences and accompanied Pastor Adams all over the world doing Black church music traditions. I required all of my 90 or so students to go on a field trip once a year to Detroit. Hartford's spiritual and musical service changed lives. Since then, as a professor of music, I have always taken my classes to the Black church, the absolute most important carrier of Black music tradition.

During this time I was also playing in Detroit clubs and was actually seen in 1991 or so by a talent scout at a record company. I had no intentions of pursuing the matter, but received a call from Ramon Hervey, then manager of both Vanessa Williams and Andre Crouch. The industry seduces me back again! Ramon encouraged me to come out to Los Angeles. I did and I signed a management contract under which we recorded an album. It was produced by ex-Rufus drummer Andre Fisher, son of the famous orchestrator Claire Fisher. The demo record was followed up with a showcase in a rehearsal studio somewhere in Burbank. Most of the young green-light guys in the emerging smooth Jazz market were invited. I had honestly not made the jump to smooth Jazz and was caught in an awful no-man's zone of stylistic eclecticism, which these new young record executives didn't get. And dig this, on bass I had Alphoso Johnson; on drums, Ndugu Leon Chancelor and the then music director of Frankie Beverly's Maze, Wayne Lynsey. He was, by the way, married to my old bandmate and street performer partner, the singer Lynne Fiddmont Linsey. We actually performed a piece together for the first time in ten years. Whenever you see any big-name Black singers on the Jay Leno *Tonight Show*, Lynne nine times out of ten will be singing lead backup. At any rate, all were L.A. big-time music industry veterans. Still, no deal.

The time in L.A. with Ramon was great because at that time Vanessa Williams was huge and Ramon managed the club R&B Live, where so many big Black names hung out. My old saxophone player and buddy Najee was sitting in on R&B Live during the time I was in town, so yet another connection. I met the Wayans brothers, who were huge, as *In Living Color* was blowing up. There hanging when I was there were Wesley Snipes, Babyface, John Salley, Robert Townsend, you name them—all the Black big names came to R&B Live. This was my first taste of Hollywood. I loved it, and it poisoned or flavored my pallet for the industry. Somewhere in here I met my number one idol, Quincy Jones. During this first meeting, he even said David Baker had mentioned me, but that he couldn't speak with me for at least three years. I met up with Quincy and reminded him of that broken promise at a concert that David invited me to with his Smithsonian Jazz Orchestra. David did an all Quincy Jones concert in July of 2001 at the Lincoln Theater in D.C. But what that initial L.A. trip did was give me a very wide view of music making from all angles: the professional world of being a musician, running a record company, publishing, recording. By this time I could appreciate L.A.'s industry, Classical concert music circles, the academy, and the Black church.

While I have many heroes and she-roes, models, mentors, and people I just idolize, Leonard Bernstein is probably one of the examples that shone brightest for me. When I met him I couldn't believe it. I had seen him several times working at Tanglewood, but at the University of Michigan he was there to meet five conductors and five composers, and I was chosen, as well as Stephen Newby. I still have the letter. This was the winter of 1988. After Lenny conducted an incredible concert at Hill Auditorium in Ann Arbor, we were invited to a small gathering at the university president's home. There he (Lenny) was in all his regalia, with his wit and charm. But this evening he didn't seem to be interested in hanging with that crowd at all. As a matter of fact, he cornered Stephen and me and, unbeknownst to our professors and the university president and other guests, encouraged us to get him out of there.

So, if you can believe this, we called his driver to the side door, Stephen, myself, and another New York composer, Todd Levin, and Lenny, after politely excusing himself as tired, hopped into his limousine with us, and we rushed to a local tavern for drinking. We secretly spread the word to the music students that we were taking Lenny Bernstein downtown to hang! We sat there with him all night listening to his stories, each one of us getting personal advice and instruction. And then, Lenny turned to me and really shared. I know it's the "Black and Jewish thing"; that is, there has been and will always be a synergy and connection, a shared history between Black American and Jewish people because of our horrific histories and marginalization. And there is our deep, spiritual music center. Leonard Bernstein gravitated toward me that night in sincere and honest brotherhood to share. He sensed I believe in my own questions, particularly the search for the center of artisthood and culture—in Blackness, the vernacular, the academy, and reaching a marketplace. He encouraged me to express what he called, "your Blackness. . . . It is what makes you beautiful and different, and somehow as an artist you simply must bring this Blackness out in your music as a composer." Not long after, I remember on a drive to Detroit hearing on the radio that the great composer, the American maestro Leonard Bernstein had died. This was 1990, and I cried all day. He meant that much to me for all the many reasons I have already stated. As artists, we must have living examples of individuals who exemplify these principles of artistry, creativity, passion, dedication, drive, and the making of music that brings people to wholeness. That's what Leonard Bernstein represented to me; I really admired his artistic spirit.

Leonard Bernstein was the second non-Black concert music composer (the other was German composer Hans Henze, whom I met and shared my early work with as a much younger composer at Tanglewood) I met who truly understood the crossroads and the dilemmas of being a Black American and being a composer and wanted to talk about it freely. The problem with too much of academic Classical music training is that it is anti-Black and even antimusic. It is as if Black people didn't matter, shouldn't matter; there are, in the traditional music academy, very few links, sidebars, or references to the rich, deep, and varied traditions of Black music doing and its implications for concert music doing. As a composer I figuratively came to blows with and brushed up against these thorns too many times. That conversation with Lenny Bernstein changed my perspective, and once again I was, as my teacher T. J. had charged, pointed toward a mission in the academic and concert music fields, holding up the torch of Black music artistry as a creator, not just as a performer.

Studying composition at the University of Michigan, I finished string quartets, song cycles, chamber music, and a lot of Jazz charts. I researched the history and writings of Black music pioneers and became committed to charting the lives of Black music thinkers, especially after getting a hold of David Baker's *The Black Composer Speaks*. Finding that book, published by Scarecrow Press in 1978, I couldn't believe it. A book on Black composers? David Baker immediately became the focus of my attention toward securing links to the long legacy of Black composers, who they were, where they lived in America, and what music they were writing.

All we ever heard of was William Grant Still, who was a path breaker, but it was David Baker who became my "Quincy Jones of the academy." I wanted to emulate his academic, Jazz, and concert music writing and scholarship. As it turned out, Scarecrow Press later asked me to write the follow-up to David's book, which became the vehicle for introducing me to many composers, led to the radio interview formats I developed, later resulted in the formation of the Undine Smith Moore Collection of scores and manuscripts by Black composers, and gently pushed me into Black music scholarship in general. I sought David Baker out when I was invited to Indiana University to have one of my pieces performed there in the fall of 1989. After meeting with him, I was determined that I wanted to be a Black music professor. Up until that point, even through my first year or so of doctoral studies at the University of Michigan, I had wanted to return to the East Coast and seek a life running around New York chasing the broken and short-lived dreams that all too many burned-out musicians are forced to accept. Discussions with David Baker and Portia Maultsby convinced me to pursue the life of the academy.

I completed my dissertation, which was my Symphony No. 2, ("Dream Realized/Nightmare Resolved"). Symphony No. 2 is a 40-minute work with chorus, speakers, and tenor saxophone that aesthetically, in musical form, looks at the differences and similarities between the philosophies of Malcolm X and Dr. Martin Luther King Jr. Infused among the sections of the symphony are various excerpts from the speeches, highlighting what I have identified as the central themes of their legacies: spirit, revolution, brotherhood, integration/nationalism, dream and nightmare. This symphony was chosen the year of my graduation, 1992, by the Utah and University of Utah Symphonies in a national contest and was subsequently premiered there. This was a huge piece that brought together my concert, Jazz, and contemporary dissonant languages that were refined from all the doctoral studies of Arnold Schoenberg, serialism, and Coltrane. And simultaneously, this symphony put together social and spiritual principles and music, which have provided me with the foundations of my work as a composer. In 1992, I was the first Black man ever to graduate with a doctorate in composition from the University of Michigan—a damn shame! Only two or three more since have completed the program, and Stephen Newby was also one of them.

After graduating from the University of Michigan, I was actually recruited, due to David and Portia, to Indiana University in 1992. I was hired as an assistant professor in the Department of African American Studies, was composer in residence with the African American Arts Institute, and later taught in the Department of Music at the Indianapolis campus. The move to Bloomington, Indiana, was extremely difficult. Going from a graduate student to a professor was like going from diapers, in some ways, to wearing a wrinkled suit. Nobody really teaches you what to expect. I knew nothing about salary negotiation, arranging to pay for my moves, housing, computer needs—nothing! My father and I packed up an old pickup truck and drove down. I moved into a one-room apartment on the top of a flower shop next to a Burger King. My windows during the summer constantly received the fumes of flamed broiled burgers, fries, and onion rings. I had no clue that this was really just student living and I should have purchased a house or condo. I wasn't just another graduate student; I was now a 31-year-old professor at one of the most respected universities in the country and teaching students who attended the world's biggest music school. Clueless!

I taught my signature course, the Art Music of Black American Composers, a general Western music history course, and directed the Black Popular Arts Ensemble, then named the Indiana University Soul Revue. Portia Maultsby founded the group and course in the 1970s making it the first academic/performing course in Black popular music. When I arrived I changed the name to "Black Popular Arts Ensemble." I was cursed at for doing this, but Soul music was no longer existent, and I wanted to give the ensemble and our music a proper designation within the academic setting. This was radical at the time because the White scholars in the Department of Music looked at the group with scorn, and Black folks thought of it as a holy historical dinosaur not to be messed with. The ensemble, some 35 members, toured around Indiana, Chicago, and Detroit, doing some 20 performances a year. Unheard of! Again, I was clueless. Most university ensembles do two or three concerts a year and rarely leave the campus. We were on the road! Here I was a young Black classical music composer forced to do Black vernacular music (and loving it). My kids only wanted to do current stuff: Tony Toni Tone, Boyz II Men, Whitney Houston, Mariah Carey, Jodeci, SWV (Sisters with Voices), TLC, Ralph Tresvant, Heavy D and the Boys, and the onslaught of Hip Hop culture in the 1990s. I revised the performance curriculum and for the six years I directed the ensemble. I had it doing music from Jazz to Motown, 1970s revolutionary work to Hip Hop and Kirk Franklin. As well, I made my students do research papers on the music they were performing and attend "other music" concerts. I was caught in another cultural revolution or market swoosh, first with smooth Jazz, then Hip Hop culture. Hip Hop is Black music family. But, due to its posture in the industry, the focus around young Black urban poets who use (sample, loop) records that I grew up on, as well as its completely different audience base, in many ways it's a very different artistic orientation. This old school R&B and Jazz guitarist from the 1970s, aspiring to be a classical concert composer, now teaching 18-year-olds how to do Janet Jackson choreography and 1990s Doo-wop R&B ballads? Wow! By immersing myself in our vernacular, first languages I grew back into myself as a Black musician, but I must admit it was the emergence of Hip Hop Black music culture that really brought me back to myself. You have to give as an artist.

To study traditional academic Classical music culture too often is to study non–music giving. As lofty and as rich as that tradition is, it is, because of the academy and Classical music industry practice, snobbery, and pretension, actually an antimusic practice and just sad attempts at European museum music replication. Its not Europe's fault, nor the musicians'; there are just too many pretentious academics and hangers-on who feel that to be involved with European-based music of old is a status and knowledge marker. That's not what the music is for. Being in Black music at that point got me back into why we even do music: to delight, to inspire, to speak to, and to move people! I taught at Indiana University from 1992 to 1997.

I taught hundreds of students, engaged with both music and African American Studies colleagues, began the Undine Smith Moore Collection and the extensions of the Tradition Concert Music Series (both still staples of Black music research at Indiana University), and wrote a lot of music. I completed my symphonies nos. 3–6 during this time, as well as a percussion and tuba concerto, had my sixth symphony commissioned and recorded by the Akron Symphony on TelArc, my fifth symphony commissioned by my alma mater the University of Michigan, composed large chamber works and first my three operas, and co-orchestrated, along with David Baker, my first musical, *Eyes*, by stellar poet Mari Evans. All this was during the time at Indiana University. I grew because I was inspired by my students, music teachers, and an active academic/musical environment in the Afro-American Arts Institute that fostered excellence and music community among young people. I owe a lot to my colleagues in the AAAI and the Department of Afro-American Studies at Indiana University (Dr. Charles Sykes, James Mumford, Iris Rosa). They taught me so much about teaching music culture and how to survive in the academy. One of the major music partners I met during this time was the incredible classical percussionist Tim Adams, with whom I composed a percussion concerto for the Indianapolis Symphony. Not only have we become great partners, creating a band called Black, touring and recording an album together (released in 2004), but we were both born in 1961 and share similar navigation struggles with doing Black music, participating in Classical culture, and being concerned about the values in artistry. These kinds of concerns among our generation of artists will surface more and more frequently as we become the power players in American music culture. We must hope, anyway! In this great mix I also met my wife Krystal, who is from Detroit and a former music student at Cass Tech. See, full circles.

Now by 1996 I had become, while teaching at Indiana University, really active as a concert music composer. So I was traveling back and forth across the country having premieres, doing residencies, conducting Jazz big bands, speaking and giving papers, and establishing connections with orchestras, foundations, and universities, making friends in multiple circles, never recognizing that any boundary existed between the industries of recording, doing colleges, composing concert music, and gigging. My first professional commission (it was for $5,000) was from a recommendation from David Baker in 1992. It was my third symphony, called *Job's Song*, commissioned by Phillip Brunelle and the Plymouth Music Series of Minnesota. This was not only my first of many trips to the Twin Cities, it was my first connection to Mr. Brunelle, who would subsequently commission a series of works, including my seventh symphony, and connect me, ultimately, to that community in some permanent ways.

In 1996 I was nominated for a Guggenheim and Cal Arts Award, but received a Mc-Knight Fellowship from the American Composers Forum (ACF), actually founded in Saint Paul. The project I created allowed me to work in residence at the Ramsey School for the Performing Arts in Minneapolis. For the entire school year, every month I drove 800 miles (one way) back and forth between Bloomington, Indiana, and Minneapolis. I proposed to the ACF that I write a large cantata based on the words of the English classes, using their band, choirs, and orchestra. The final concert as well included members of the Minnesota Orchestra, the Saint Paul Chamber Orchestra, and the Plymouth Music Series. We had, for *Life Suite*, over one hundred kids on stage performing and singing this 20-minute work. That year culminated with many school visits and lectures in my then future institution, The University of Saint Thomas. At the same time, Bobby McFerrin and the Saint Paul Chamber Orchestra were there as a part of their Connect Residence Series, working in Minneapolis public schools. I actually had first met Bobby as a graduate student at the University of Michigan. He had come to Ann Arbor to study conducting with Gustav Meyer. Now, some ten years later, I met him as the artistic chair/conductor of the Saint Paul Chamber Orchestra. So I had the opportunity to get to know and work with one of the most important artists of the twentieth century, Bobby McFerrin. Bobby and I developed a very close friendship, and he has helped to confirm every aspect of what I have been saying about artistry in our world.

We spent many hours over meals and hanging out talking about music, artists' citizenry, and our culture. He is a great model for me. This model was too overwhelming. The Twin Cities was for me at that time a "model" arts community. It was reported then that Minneapolis/Saint Paul was second in arts activity only to New York. Consequently I left Indiana University officially in 1997 and headed north and west out of Southern Indiana to polar territory! In 1998 I was appointed as the endowed chair in arts and humanities, associate professor of music at the University of Saint Paul in Saint Paul, Minnesota. My teaching continued and I developed courses (the Theology of American Popular Music, Rhetoric and Music in Popular Culture, Popular Arts Choir, Introduction to American Cultural Studies, Black American Music: A Historical Survey, Creative Construction: Composition Seminar) which were dead center of my research interests and artistry.

Not long after I arrived, with the help of a very energized faculty in humanities studies, I organized an American cultural studies program with some 30 courses examining American cultural experience, and was awarded a National Endowment for the Humanities Focus Grant, and later encouraged to apply for a near million-dollar support grant. The appointment and living in the very artistic Twin Cities provided me with incredible opportunities to bring all of my work and interests full circle. Minnesota by culture and practice is one of the most important cities for the arts by virtue of its aggressive and sincere advocacy for the arts. No wonder Bobby McFerrin settled there, Libby Larsen, Stephen Paulus, Dominique Argento, author Alexs Pate, and too many others to name. I settled in and began to get to know the culture. In addition to commissions, including works from the Minnesota Opera, the Minnesota Orchestra, the University of Minnesota commemorating the building of the Wabash Bridge in Saint Paul, my undergraduate alma mater commissioned my eighth symphony. I published articles, and I continued to give lectures on the role of artists in contemporary popular culture.

I thought it was important, if I was going to be dealing with culture from these larger vantage points, that I should as well address my own Black community here in the Twin Cities. I had always thought that the Black community had too few hometown critics. I love that scene in *Hollywood Shuffle* where the two principle characters, one played by Robert Townsend, decide to be "real brothers" as movie critics. The Twin Cities paper is *Insight News*. I approached them with the idea of writing a cultural commentary on contemporary music. Many of those pieces are published in this book as they appeared in print.

I organized my BMagic orchestra and began playing at local clubs, the Dakota, the Mall of America, and finally running our own concert series at a local arts theater called Patrick's Cabaret. This was a remarkable thing for us because we were the orchestra in residence and invited younger players and musicians to sit in a real music community Jazz orchestra, with radio and foundation support. During this time I was approached by the music producer (Ben Roe) of National Public Radio's *Performance Today* to host a special series of programs which I called *Landscapes in Color: Conversations with Black American Composers*. This was my first national radio broadcast program.

Soon after I was approached by another public radio station, WCAL at Saint Olaf College, Northfield, Minnesota, to write and produce an original show where I could explore any aspects of my artistry and teaching. I called that program *Essays of Note*. The show's philosophy was based on my interpretation of music as boundary-less and having as a criteria for excellence only a continued stream of human expression from multiple places. One of the openings went,

> I understand as a concert music composer the world of Classical music and its historical place. But as a contemporary artist and educator I'm faced with the daunting task of making music live now and of making it useable and accessible—while still pushing the boundaries of art and expression. Furthermore, I'm interested in breaking down the categorical barriers that separate too much great music. So, in *Essays of Note*, I want to tie Beethoven's rhythms to Prince's rhythms, and Bob Dylan's songwriting to Schubert's, as well as Ellington's orchestrations to Ravel's. I want to look at the relevance of Hip Hop verse as poetic structure and see Carole King's writing as monumental to the shaping of American musical culture.

Another huge meeting of musical minds for me was hooking up with Morris Hayes. Morris is one of the most gifted and beautiful brothers I know. Morris had served as Prince's music director and was introduced to me through some mutual friends and, specifically, Craig Rice, Prince's former manager. Craig, a huge player in the Twin Cities, served as the head of the Minnesota Film Commission. Craig produced the award-winning documentary on Gordan Parks. Morris and I made a musical pact to help each other. His studio is the one our dreams are made of. Probably Prince and anyone else in that whole musical camp has been and worked in Morris's studio and has been impacted by his technical and musical wizardry. Morris produced my first commercial release as a Jazz recording artist (2004, *Striking Balance*, Innova Records). So, Morris helped produce Prince's road sound, then he produced little me. Clearly my connection with him brought my 20-plus-year bumpy road in the popular music industry to some meaningful resolutions. I am indebted to him for bringing a certain part of my dream to reality and keeping me real.

More on writing music: this idea that there is a drama always to be told in multiple languages came to be tested in what has been my largest work to date, the opera *Luyala*. The work, which was budgeted at $400,000, was commissioned and financed by Duke University, Triangle Opera, and the Lila Wallace Foundation. It was conceived by librettist and fundraiser Penelope Bridgers and was danced by Chuck Davis and the African American Dance Company. The cast included Jazz legend Nnenna Freelon, opera tenor Bill Brown, and my dear friend Louise Toppin singing the lead role. Clearly the loving ghosts of my past came to conjure up this work, those being Wagner, Africa, and T. J.'s baptisms in modern music. I had to make all this work, and this opera exposed me to the power and potential of large-scale works. Again, this was an opportunity that you don't usually get before 40. I was commissioned at 34. It took six years to complete. The opera was premiered at Duke University in April of 2000.

This same year my first commissioned piano concerto was performed and recorded by the Grand Rapids Symphony; the solo pianist was Patrice Rushen. Classical pianist Leon Bates, in New York, as well performed it in February of 2000. This was my first New York performance, and a *New York Times* critic said great things! "Rigorous organization with harmonization that could be read as typically jazz or typically Bartokian with a combination of gracefulness."[1] As a matter of fact, cultural critic Stanley Crouch met Leon Bates, composer/pianist Donal Fox, and myself at the Village Vanguard that night and congratulated me on the premiere. We ended up hanging out 'til four the next morning talking about the role of Black people in the next moves to shape the culture! I learned a lot from Stanley Crouch that night and we have maintained our dialogue since then. The brother is always in pursuit. Even Wynton Marsalis the next day apologized to me for missing the concerto performance. He invited me to attend a rehearsal of his Lincoln Jazz Orchestra, which was preparing for their China tour. Wynton also born in 1961 too, and as you can imagine has been the focus of much of my admiration and envy. I was very appreciative of that soft moment.

As an active academic during the first years in Saint Paul (1997–2000), I received awards and sat on panels, did conferences (Opera America, American Symphony Orchestra League) and residencies teaching my perspectives on Black music and cultural studies at Morehouse, Atlanta University, Spelman College, North Carolina Central, the University of North Carolina, Duke University, the University of Texas, Bowling Green State University, the University of Pennsylvania, Carnegie Melon University, and Hamilton and Hunter Colleges in New York.

During the summer of 1999 I was invited by Marian Wright Elderman to have a work of mine performed (my *Spiritual Songs for Tenor and Cello*, sung by Bill Brown and played by cellist Ron Crutcher) to inaugurate the John Hope Franklin Library and Maya Angelou Reading Room on the Alex Haley Farm, owned and operated by the Children's Defense Fund, in Clinton, Tennessee. Both Maya and Dr. Franklin attended, and Hilary Clinton officiated the overall celebration that week. It was another full circle. I ended up the next year being invited to be the first scholar in residence on the farm. I wrote the major portions of this book while in residence for one week—no one else was on the entire farm! It was scary, but I was at complete peace by myself in the hills of Tennessee. I was able to determine that at that point I wanted to pull together some of the seemingly disjunct, yet harmonious, portions of my musical struggle to find the right note.

Henry Louis Gates Jr. invited me to be a W. E. B. DuBois scholar at Harvard during the 2000–2001 school year. He actually challenged me to write a much-needed book that would address the future of Black music! During this year I wrote two more operas, one based on Gertrude Stein and the other, *Soul Gone Home*, based on a 1936 text by Langston Hughes. For my final required lecture as a fellow, gathered in the crowd were people who had known me in Boston as a freshman from some 20-plus years earlier. So many times back then I dreamed while walking around the campus, but never dreamed that I would be able to study there, and certainly never dreamed that I would be invited to share my music and research as a scholar. So this event was cathartic for me in many ways; I had become recognized for doing what had been so difficult to make sense of for nearly 20 years, and I was doing it within the halls of what is thought to be the citadel of American intelligentsia. The final page of this music/academic/art chapter was a call from Nobel Prize–winning author Toni Morrison, who had heard my work (she was present at the Clinton farm performance) and received further recommendations from poet Yusef Komunyaka. I was invited to be the 2002 Atelier artist in residence at Princeton University. Our work was a dramatic music piece with text by Yusef on nineteenth-century Black sculptor Edmonia Lewis. In 2003 and 2004 came commissions from the National Loan Museum Network, National Endowment for the Arts (NEA), and the American Composers Forum (ACF) Continental Harmony for new symphonies in Mobile and Pineville/Alexandra, Louisiana. The Mobile Symphony premiered my *Structures in Sound and Soul* to inaugurate the opening of the Mobile Art Museum. I was in residence in the South for the 2002–2003 academic year. The NEA commission was to commemorate the 100th birthday of Harlem Renaissance writer, archivist, and librarian Arna Bontempts. I used his poem "Hope," which won him the *Crisis* Magazine Award in 1924 and brought him to New York as a young man, along with all the other young Black artists who seized this cultural time and created one of the most important arts and culture movements in history. That I have written my ninth symphony using Bontemps' words, as Beethoven used in his ninth symphony the words of Goethe, really rang home for me. Ellis Marsalis agreed to be the piano soloist. This symphony with Jazz, voices, Black text, and musical styles marks, I think, a real pulling together of the major thrusts of my work up until the publication of this book in 2004.

My final academic test was to deliver parts of my thesis, "The Post Album Age," at the citadel, the birthplace of American popular culture theory, Bowling Green State University in Ohio. I was invited by Dr. Angela Nelson, chair of the program, and Dr. Ray Browne, the founding father of American popular culture studies. I went there in late February 2004 to present my findings and discuss them with students in graduate seminars and faculty; they gave me my last, "You go boy." I began this writing in 1999 alone in a secluded cabin on Marian Wright Elderman's farm in Tennessee, and ended it actually writing in a secluded and quiet university home provided to me by Bowling Green State University, with, if you can believe this, two dear ladies (Vi and Mary) who would come cook and clean each day! This was living large!

With all this I wanted to say that being in the arts is all wide and all fulfilling and that all of us are examples of people who are dedicated, focused, and absolutely rewarded first by the ways in which our music reaches, inspires, and completes people, and that this activity of music making is what makes us whole too.

We continue to struggle and explore. I end here only at the beginning of a long journey to stay in the fight to keep the music right, and moving, and with meaning and purpose sounding in a sometimes hard-of-hearing and hard-of-loving world. I felt it was important to illustrate portions of the walk and my current walking as I wrestle with finding peace in my own sounding spaces as an artist. Probably the biggest stretch for any aspiring and growing artist is how to reach the mark of the high calling of artistry, measuring your own inabilities, failures, and insecurities against that call, and keeping your head in place as you encounter your few leaps and successes. And in 2004 and beyond, despite what seems like a world crumbling before our eyes, in this post 9/11, post-album age, we are challenged to maintain hope with a vision toward fighting and working for a better world. Or at least we can try to save the one we are in with our small battles for love and taking care of one another. I am one who still believes the art will keep a crazed world saner.

This is only chapter 1 for me attempting to engage with the ongoing maps of this music culture, charting and paving new roads. Baraka's words so dearly and clearly come back to instruct the end of this sharing, as they did the beginning:

> Writing the book confirmed ideas that had been rolling around in my head for years and that now, given the opportunity, flashed out upon the page with a stunning self exhilaration and certainty. That is, how to measure this world in which we find ourselves, where we are not at all happy, but clearly able to understand and hopefully, one day transform. How to measure my own learning and experience and to set out a system of evaluation, weights and meaning. . . . This is the history. . . . This is your history, my history and the history of the Negro people. The Music. The Music, this is our history.[2]

We must stay tune-full.

· 49 ·

Coda and Cadence

$\mathscr{W}$hen we from our various spaces are done singing and playing and composing about the loving, the lost dream, the exhilarating experiences, and when we are done listening to these "lived stories," it is time to live, something we all do. It is this understanding of our common lived experience that artists speak and produce about that is our common ground. So I decided to move away from just my own read and look at the larger Black artistry, history, speak to some artists and industry heads. This has been one attempt to stay close to cultural shifts and to come to some understanding, interpretation of musical culture in this post-album age.

A society that loses its connection with the beat and songs and scream of the common folk is one that cannot stand, no matter how vulgar or loud or disturbing the screams are. Musical art is an expression that has the ability to raise the Spirit and speak to the common humanity of a society. Musicians and artists don't make music to change a society, but their vehicle of expression, the music, is an example of a transformative activity. Given the extraordinary history of American music, particularly the relationships between Black music and American social and cultural evolution, how do we interpret our current popular expressions in music? Where is this all going as we see generations of new artists emerging in so many different arenas of musical expression with so many different influences, impulses, and needs to generate music? I asked these questions and shared this narrative clearly with a predisposition toward the idea that one cannot separate artistic expression in popular music and American societal evolution. These two go hand in hand. I needed to revisit the most dramatic rise of a social-cultural group within the larger society, noting that group's social progress from the bottom of American society. Clearly we can see this by tracing the development of Black American music, pointing to the work of several exemplary creative artists inextricably bound to cultural and societal construction. One cannot take one's eye and ears off of popular culture if one wants to keep one's foot on solid ground. When the beat shifts, and you miss it, you will fall down, because the floor, the foundation has moved. Contemporary popular creation simply reflects the pulse, the heartbeat of a society despite mainstream society's appropriation, exploitation, and commodifications of it. Popular music is always a commercialized vernacular expression. It's folk music, always has been always will be. And "folk" properly understood is where the people are.

Musical performance, the art of the stance, imaging, the posturing in performance delivery of Black music traditions makes real what you're saying and the ideas that are put forth. In this mix of refining and defining style, performance practices, and traditions mass-marketed for popular consumption you have the simultaneous creation of conscious cultural constructs that contain authentic images that project, protect, and hold onto identity. When people within "lived in" contexts provide for themselves living examples, structures of expression of who they are, what they hope for, dream of, and protest, there you have culture of marked significance.

My underlying agenda is to ensure that Black creative expression, particularly in music, is documented and preserved as culture.

I have seen too many frightening attempts to minimize these important and meaningful expressions and this language as diversions of the simpleminded, emotional-driven, entertaining Negroes. Western culture from the academic and literate traditions has clearly done by non- or misdocumentation everything possible to devalue Black thought while immortalizing even minute gestures of expression, sayings, and images in White cultural creation. White cultural creations are elevated and museumized, placed under glass in the sacred halls, or continuously projected as cultural icons to be emulated and imitated for infinitude. In many cases these may be in fact examples of greatness in human achievement. But Black greatness in aesthetic form is usually marginalized, reduced to entertainment at best. John Wayne, Marilyn Monroe, and Mozart are not the defining cultural image, and "To be or not to be" is not the only question. My passion for pulling back the lids of these cultural discussions as an artist is to make sure that "somebody says Amen."

For every literary epoch, generation, and decade there needs to be the continuous study, analysis, recording, and confirmation of significant accomplishments or creative bodies of musical expression. Artists through authentic imaging connected with a sincere understanding of their role in contemporary culture have the possibility of projecting and cementing cultural identity that is reflective of the best that our times have to offer. The arts are always about our attempts to understand and appreciate human activity. These expressions are exemplary of our ability as a society to move for the better causes of our fellow citizens; this movement comes by hearing the "voices" and by moving to address, evolve, change, and make real a living condition beneficial to all participants in the society. Music is a great model, as Christopher Small has noted; he prophetically points out that "every voice, every sound, is of equal importance with every other, yet gains its full significance only in the relationship with other sounds, like members of a truly just society."[1] The biggest lesson we learn from the popular artist is about human living in the world. The logical answer to the question "What's the right note in a post-album age?" is that the right note is the one that sounds for human social illumination, celebration, commentary, critique, and empowerment.

Be well,
Bill Banfield

Trying to keep in step with the time. Author with his cousin Charles Wilson, keyboardist with Justin Timberlake. Backstage, Timberlake/Aguilera Tour, Oct. 2003, St. Paul, MN

Younger author with guitar at 10 years old in 1971

With Q and David Baker

With Dr. Ray Browne

Sweet Honey in the Rock with Bernice Johnson Reagon, Ysaye Barnwell

Author with Gordon Parks

Quincy Jones

Bobby McFerrin

With composers John Costa, Stephen Newhy, Leonard Bernstein, Denise Ince

A Gathering of Contemporary Black American Composers (Alvin Singleton, Wendal Logan, Olly Wilson, Author, George Walker, T. J. Anderson, Dwight Andrews)

Branford Marsalis

Wynton Marsalis

Regina Carter

Patrice Rushen

Nnenna Freelon

Recording with producer Michael Powell

Harold Cruse

Dr. Billy Taylor

Author with Henry Louis Gates Jr.

Author with Alexs Pate, John Wright, Cornel West, Allan Callahan

Amiri Baraka

Dancer Aleta Hayes, Yusef Komunyaka, and Toni Morrison with author

Notes

CHAPTER 2

1. Nelson George, *Hip Hop America* (New York: Viking, 1998), 51, 52.
2. Imamu Amiri Baraka (LeRoi Jones), *Blues People: Negro Music in White America* (New York: Morrow, 1999).
3. Album notes, the Ojays, *Message in the Music*, 1976.
4. Albert Murray, *The Hero and the Blues* (New York: Vintage, 1995), 14.

CHAPTER 3

1. Cornel West, *Prophetic Fragments* (Grand Rapids, MI: Eerdmans, 1988), 36.
2. "Don't Hate Me Because I'm Ghetto Fabulous," *GQ* (August 1999): 144.
3. John Lovell Jr., *Black Song: The Forge and the Flame; The Story of How the Afro-American Spiritual Was Hammered Out* (New York: Paragon House, 1986), 6.

CHAPTER 4

1. Eileen Southern, *The Music of Black Americans: A History* (New York: Norton, 1997), 93.
2. Vincent Harding, *There Is a River: The Black Struggle for Freedom in America* (New York: Vintage, 1983), xii.
3. Henry Louis Gates Jr., *The Signifying Monkey: A Theory of Afro-American Literary Criticism* (New York: Oxford University Press, 1988), ixx, xxiv.
4. From the CNN special *Impact, Marsalis: Blood on the Fields*, which aired April 6, 1997.
5. John Miller Chernoff, *African Rhythm and African Sensibility: Aesthetics and Social Action in African Musical Idioms* (Chicago: University of Chicago Press, 1979), 154.
6. Olaudah Equiano, *The Interesting Narrative of the Life of Olaudah Equiano* (New York: Norton, 2001), 21.
7. Ray Pratt, *Rhythm and Resistance: The Political Uses of American Popular Music* (Washington, DC: Smithsonian Press, 1994), 59.
8. Roger D. Abrahams, *Singing the Master: The Emergence of African American Culture in the Slave South* (New York: Penguin Books, 1992), xxii, xxiii.
9. Anton Dvorak, taken from David Ewen, *The World of Great Composers* (New York: Prentice Hall, 1962), 370–71.
10. Paul Oliver, *Blues, the New Groove* (New York: Norton, 1986), 61, 62.
11. Alain Locke, *The New Negro* (New York: Macmillan, 1925), 221, 222.
12. Anton Dvorak, *New York Herald*, May 24, 1893.
13. Locke, *New Negro*, 6, 7.

14. Leslie Gourse, *Dizzy Gillespie and the Birth of Bebop* (NewYork: Maxwell Macmillan International, 1994), 66.

15. Ben Sidran, *Black Talk* (New York: Dacapo, 1971), 18.

16. Portia Maultsby, "Soul Music: Its Sociological and Political Significance in American Popular Culture," *Journal of Popular Culture* 17 (Fall 1983): 54.

17. *New York Times*, August 22, 1999.

18. Henry Louis Gates Jr., *The Signifying Monkey* (New York: Oxford, 1988), 4, 5.

CHAPTER 5

1. Thomas Rochon, *Culture Moves* (Princeton, NJ: Princeton University Press, 1998), 22.

2. Jack Nachbar, *Popular Culture: An Introductory Text* (Bowling Green, OH: Bowling Green State University Press, 1992), 5, 6, 7.

3. John Berger, *Ways of Seeing* (London: British Broadcasting Corporation; Harmondsworth, UK: Penguin, 1972), 142.

4. Michael Eric Dyson, *Open Mike* (New York: Basic Civitas Books, 2003), 227.

5. Neil Postman, *Amusing Ourselves to Death* (New York: Penguin Books, 1986), 15.

6. Farai Chideya, *The Color of Our Future* (New York: William Morrow, 1999), 15.

7. Ronald Takaki, *A Different Mirror* (Boston: Back Bay Books, 1993), 2, 17.

8. Albert Murray, *The Hero and the Blues* (New York: Vintage Books, 1973), 13–15.

CHAPTER 6

1. Vincent Harding, *There Is a River: The Black Struggle for Freedom in America* (New York: Harcourt, Brace, Jovanovich, 1981), 11.

2. Gayraud S. Wilmore, *Black Religion and Black Radicalism* (Garden City, NY: Doubleday, 1972), vii.

3. Eugene D. Genovese, *The Political Economy of Slavery* (New York: Vintage Books, 1967), 7–8.

4. James Mellon, *Bullwhip Days: The Slaves Remember; An Oral History* (New York: Weidenfield and Nicholson, 1988), xv.

5. Mellon, xvii.

6. James H. Cone, *The Spirituals and the Blues* (New York: Seabury Press, 1972), 3–6, 42.

7. John Hope Franklin and Alfred P. Moss, *From Slavery to Freedom: A History of Negro Americans* (New York: Knopf, 1956), 31.

8. Cone, *Spirituals*, 6.

9. *The Portable Thomas Jefferson*, ed. Merrill D. Peterson (New York: Viking Press, 1975), 190.

10. Wilmore, *Black Religion*, ix–x.

11. Mary Francis Berry and John W. Blassingame, *Long Memory: The Black Experience in America* (New York: Oxford University Press), 5.

12. Charles K. Meeks, in Berry and Blassingame, 6.

13. Berry and Blassingame, 10.

14. Robert L. Harris Jr., *Teaching African American History* (Washington, DC: American Historical Association, 1985), 14.

15. Harris, 11.

16. Harris, 14.

17. Wilmore, *Black Religion*, 53.

18. J. H. Kwabena Kenatia, *The Music of Africa* (New York: Norton, 1974).

CHAPTER 7

1. Francis Anne Kemble, *Journal of a Residence on a Georgian Plantation in 1838–1839* (New York: Harper, 1864).

2. Henry Louis Gates Jr., *The Signifying Monkey* (New York: Oxford University Press, 1988), xix–xx.

3. A. M. Jones, *African Rhythm* (London: International African Institute, 1965), 290–97.

4. John Miller Chernoff, *African Rhythm and African Sensibility* (Chicago: University of Chicago Press, 1979), 155.

5. Traditional Negro Spiritual.

6. Interview with T. J. Anderson by William C. Banfield, 1992.

7. From "The Undeniable Groove," an unpublished poem by William C. Banfield.

CHAPTER 8

1. Hugues Panassié, *The Real Jazz*, trans. Anne Sorelle Williams (New York: Smith and Durrell, 1942).

2. Suzanne K. Langer, *Philosophy in a New Key* (Cambridge, MA: Harvard University Press, 1942), 235.

3. Christopher Small, *Music, Society, Education* (Hanover, NH: University Press of New England, 1996), 5.

4. From Ken Burns's documentary *Jazz*, Episode 9, "The Adventure," which aired January 29, 2001.

5. Burns's *Jazz*, Episode 9.

6. Quincy Jones, *The Autobiography of Quincy Jones* (New York: Doubleday, 2001), 41, 42.

CHAPTER 9

1. As quoted in Eric Maisel, *Artists Speak* (San Francisco: Harper, 1993).

2. As quoted in Maisel, *Artists Speak*.

3. As quoted in Maisel, *Artists Speak*.

4. From Media One and AT&T, 1999.

5. Cal Thomas, Associated Press, March 1998.

6. Henry Louis Gates Jr., *Loose Canons: Notes on the Culture Wars* (New York: Oxford University Press, 1992), xv.

7. Lyrics from Marvin Gaye's "What's Goin' On."

8. Institute for Civil Society Survey, 1998.

9. Michael Eric Dyson, *The Theology of American Popular Music: A Post-Modern Afro-American Secular Spirituality; Michael Jackson* (Durham, NC: Duke University Press, 1999), 101.

10. Howard Gardner, *Art Education and Human Development* (Los Angeles: Getty Center for Education in the Arts, 1990).

11. Christopher Small, *Music, Society, Education: A Radical Examination of the Prophetic Function of Music in Western, Easter, and African Cultures with Its Impact on Society and Its Use in Education* (London: Calder, 1980).

12. Small, *Music, Society, Education*, 5.

CHAPTER 10

1. Michael Eric Dyson, sermon (Mt. Olive Baptist Church, Ft. Lauderdale, FL), June 25, 2000.

2. Paul Tillich, *Theology of Culture* (New York: Oxford University Press, 1959), 50.

3. Paul Gilroy, *The Black Atlantic* (Cambridge, MA: Harvard University Press, 1993), 79.

4. John Miller Chernoff, *African Rhythm and African Sensibility* (Chicago: University of Chicago Press, 1979), 154.

5. Kenneth Gamble and Leon Huff, liner notes from *The O'Jays: Message in the Music* (LP), Philly International Records, 1976.

6. Lyrics from Guru's "Hip-Hop as a Way of Life," *Jazzmatazz* (CD), Chrysalis Records, 1995.

7. Anthony Pinn, *Why Lord? Suffering and Evil in Black Theology* (New York: Continuum, 1995), 116.

8. Pinn, *Why Lord?*, 116.

9. Tillich, *Theology of Culture.*

10. Tricia Rose, *Black Noise: Rap Music and Black Culture in Contemporary America* (Hanover, NH: University Press of New England, 1994), 17–20.

11. Rose, *Black Noise*, 2.

12. Albert Murray, *The Hero and the Blues* (New York: Vintage Books, 1973) 13–15.

13. See chapter 28.

14. Neil Postman, *Amusing Ourselves to Death* (New York: Penguin Books, 1985), 15.

15. Susan Langer, *Philosophy in a New Key* (Cambridge, MA: Harvard University Press, 1957), 235.

16. Chernoff, *African Rhythm.*

17. Francis Bebey, *African Music: A People's Art* (New York: Lawrence Hill Books, 1969), 17.

18. Bebey, *African Music*, 22.

19. Bebey, *African Music*, 26.

20. Bebey, *African Music*, 33.

21. Lyrics from Duke Ellington's "It Don't Mean a Thing If It Ain't Got That Swing," 1932.

22. Neil Strauss, "The Hip-Hop Nation: Whose Is It?: A Land with Rhythm and Beats for All," *New York Times* (August 22, 1999).

23. Russell Simmons, *Life and Def: Sex, Drugs, Money, + God* (New York: Crown, 2001), 4.

24. Simmons, *Life and Def*, 83.

25. As quoted in *Say It Loud: A Celebration of Black Music in America*, produced by Patrick Milligan, Shawn Amos, and Quincy Newell, 2001.

26. Carlos Santana, liner notes from *Supernatural* (CD), Arista Records, 1999.

27. Lyrics from Lauryn Hill's "Superstar," *The Mis-Education of Lauryn Hill* (CD), Rough House Records, 1998.

28. Lyrics from Notorious B.I.G.'s "Juicy," *Ready to Die* (CD), Bad Boy Records, 1994.

29. Lyrics from Mary J. Blige's "No More Drama," *No More Drama* (CD), MCA Records, 2001.

30. Chuck D., *Rap, Race, and Reality* (New York: Delta Books, 1977), 5.

31. Tupac Shakur, *The Rose That Grew from Concrete* (New York: Pocket Books, 1999), 150.

32. Cornel West, *Prophetic Fragments* (Grand Rapids, MI: Eerdmans, 1988), 187.

33. As quoted in Gilroy, *The Black Atlantic*, 78.

CHAPTER 11

1. Na'im Akbar, "Making Black America Better through Self Knowledge," in *How to Make Black America Better*, ed. Tavis Smiley (New York: Doubleday, 2001), 133.

2. Ralph Ellison, *Invisible Man* (New York: Vintage Books, 1980), 3.

3. Amiri Baraka, *Blues People* (New York: William Morrow, 1999), vii–viii.

4. Tricia Rose, *Black Noise: Rap Music and Black Culture in Contemporary America* (Hanover, NH: University Press of New England, 1994).

5. As quoted in Branford Marsalis, liner notes from *Bloomington* (CD), Sony, 1993.

6. As quoted in Bakari Kitwana, *The Hip-Hop Generation: Young Blacks and the Crisis in African American Culture* (New York: Basic Civitas Books, 2002), 23.

7. As quoted in Kitwana, *The Hip-Hop Generation*, xi.

8. Lyrics from Grand Master Flash's *The Message* (LP), Sugarhill, 1982.

CHAPTER 12

1. As quoted in Bakari Kitwana, *The Hip-Hop Generation: Young Blacks and the Crisis in African American Culture* (New York: Basic Civitas Books, 2002), 23.

2. Christopher John Farley, "Hip Hop Nation," *Time* (February 8, 1999): 54–64.
3. Lyrics from Grand Master Flash's *The Message* (LP), Sugarhill, 1982.
4. Allan Bloom, *The Closing of the American Mind* (New York: Simon and Schuster, 1987), 74–75.
5. See chapter 29.
6. Interview by William C. Banfield.
7. Interview by William C. Banfield.
8. Interview by William C. Banfield.
9. Michael Eric Dyson, sermon (Mt. Olive Baptist Church, Ft. Lauderdale, FL), June 25, 2000.
10. Interview by William C. Banfield.
11. Albert Murray, *The Hero and the Blues* (New York: Vintage Books, 1973), 13–15.

CHAPTER 13

1. Lyrics from Guru's "Hip Hop as a Way of Life," *Jazzmatazz* (CD), Chrysalis Records, 1995.
2. Michael Eric Dyson, sermon (Mt. Olive Baptist Church, Ft. Lauderdale, FL), June 25, 2000.
3. Francis Bebey, *African Music: A People's Art* (Chicago: Lawrence Hill, 1969), 17.
4. Bebey, *African Music*, 26.
5. *New York Times*, August 22, 1999.
6. Russell Simmons, *Life and Def: Sex, Drugs, Money, and God* (New York, Crown, 2001), 4.
7. Simmons, *Life and Def*, 83.

CHAPTER 14

1. Miles Davis, *Miles: The Autobiography* (New York: Simon and Schuster, 1989).
2. Davis, *Miles*.
3. Davis, *Miles*.

CHAPTER 19

1. Quincy Jones, *Q: The Autobiography of Quincy Jones* (New York: Doubleday, 2001).
2. Jones, *Q*.
3. Jones, *Q*.
4. Jones, *Q*.

CHAPTER 21

1. F. Scott Fitzgerald, *The Jazz Age* (New York: New Directions Bibelot, 1996), 4–5.

CHAPTER 23

1. As quoted in Regina Carter, liner notes from *Regina Carter* (CD), Atlantic Records, 1995.

CHAPTER 25

1. From the magazine *LA Jazz Scene*.

CHAPTER 27

1. David Ewen, *The World of Great Composers* (New York: Prentice Hall, 1962), 121.

CHAPTER 37

1. Cornel West, *Prophetic Fragments* (Grand Rapids, MI: Eerdmans, 1988).

CHAPTER 40

1. Gordon Parks, *A Choice of Weapons* (New York: Harper and Row, 1966).

CHAPTER 41

1. Spoken by Celie (Whoopi Goldberg) in the film *The Color Purple*, a Guber-Peters production, written by Alice Walker and directed by Steven Spielberg, 1985.
2. From the PBS film *I'll Make Me a World*, a Blackside, Inc., production in association with Thirteen/WNET, written and directed by Tracy Heather Strain, 1999.
3. All quotes in this list from Ralph Ellison, *Invisible Man* (New York: Vintage Books, 1947).

CHAPTER 42

1. Rick Bragg, "The Blues Is Dying in the Place It Was Born," *New York Times* (April 22, 2001).
2. Paul Gilroy, *The Black Atlantic* (Cambridge, MA: Harvard University Press, 1993), 80.
3. Quincy Jones, *Q: The Autobiography of Quincy Jones* (New York: Doubleday, 2001).
4. "The Rebirth of Soul," *Jet* (March 26, 2001).
5. Kelefa Sanneh, "Responding to Rap, R&B Is Reborn," *New York Times* (April 8, 2001).
6. Robin D. G. Kelley, "Listening across the Generational Divide: A Doubting Dad Yields in the Radio Wars," *New York Times* (December 24, 2000).
7. As quoted in James Washington, ed., *Testament of Hope* (San Francisco: Harper and Row, 1986), 269.
8. Gilroy, *The Black Atlantic*, 78.

CHAPTER 43

1. John Lovell Jr., *Black Song: The Forge and the Flame: The Story of How the Afro-American Spiritual Was Hammered Out* (New York: Paragon House, 1986), 6.
2. Cornel West, *Prophetic Fragments* (Grand Rapids, MI: Eerdmans, 1988), 36.

CHAPTER 44

1. Tony Scherman, "Strike the Band: Pop Music without Musicians," *New York Times* (February 11, 2001).
2. Paul Gilroy, *The Black Atlantic* (Cambridge, MA: Harvard University Press, 1993), 79.
3. Portia Maultsby, "Soul Music: Its Sociological and Political Significance in American Popular Culture," *Journal of Popular Culture* 17 (Fall 1993).
4. As quoted in Scherman, "Strike the Band."
5. Chuck D., *Rap, Race, and Reality* (New York: Delta Books, 1977).
6. Cornel West, *Prophetic Fragments* (Grand Rapids, MI: Eerdmans, 1988), 187.

CHAPTER 45

1. Tom Morganthau, "What Color Is Black?," *Newsweek* (February 13, 1995): 63–65.
2. Petrine Archer-Straw, *Negrophilia* (New York: Thames and Hudson, 2000), 9, 10.
3. Harold Cruse, *The Crisis of the Negro Intellectual* (New York: Quill, 1984), 96.
4. Paul Gilroy, *The Black Atlantic* (Cambridge, MA: Harvard University Press, 1993).

CHAPTER 46

1. Ralph Ellison, *Invisible Man* (New York: Vintage Books, 1980).
2. Bakari Kitwana, *The Hip-Hop Generation: Young Blacks and the Crisis in African American Culture* (New York: Basic Civitas Books, 2002).
3. Johnnie L. Roberts, "Beyond Definition: Russell Simmons Branches Out," *Newsweek* (July 28, 2003): 40–43.
4. Letter from William C. Banfield to Gerald Early.
5. Neil Postman, *Amusing Ourselves to Death* (New York: Penguin Books, 1986), 15.
6. Guru, liner notes from *Jazzmatazz* (CD), Chrysalis Records, 1995.
7. Michael Eric Dyson, sermon (Mt. Olive Baptist Church, Ft. Lauderdale, FL), June 25, 2000.
8. W. E. B. DuBois, *The Souls of Black Folk* (New York: Vintage Books, 1990), 182.
9. From Ken Burns's documentary *Jazz*, Episode 9, "The Adventure," which aired January 29, 2001.
10. Cornel West, *Prophetic Fragments* (Grand Rapids, MI: Eerdmans, 1988).
11. Michael Eric Dyson, *Open Mike* (New York: Basic Civitas Books, 2003), xviii.
12. Martin Luther King Jr., *Where Do We Go from Here?: Chaos or Community* (Boston: Beacon, 1967), 191.
13. As quoted in S. H. Fernando Jr., *The New Beats: Exploring the Music, Culture, and Attitudes of Hip-Hop* (New York: Anchor Books, 1994), 120.
14. As quoted in Johnnie L. Roberts, "Beyond Definition: Russell Simmons Branches Out," *Newsweek* (July 28, 2003): 40–43.
15. Alain Locke, ed., *The New Negro: Studies in American Negro Life* (New York: Atheneum, 1968), 7.

CHAPTER 47

1. As quoted in Hank Stuever, "James' Legacy: A Song Whose Ubiquity Is . . . Well, Freaky," *Washington Post* (August 7, 2004).
2. Mekhi Phifer, BET Awards, 2004.
3. As quoted in Brett Pulley, *The Billion Dollar BET: Robert Johnson and the Inside Story of Black Entertainment Television* (Hoboken, NJ: John Wiley, 2004).
4. Harold Cruse, *The Crisis of the Negro Intellectual* (New York: Quill, 1967), 96.

CHAPTER 48

1. Allan Kozinn, music review, *New York Times*, February 15, 2000.
2. Amiri Baraka, *Blues People* (New York: Quill, 1999), introduction.

CHAPTER 49

1. Christopher Small, *Music, Society, Education* (Hanover, NH: Wesleyan University Press, 1996), 118, 119.

Index

About the Author

William C. Banfield holds the Endowed Chair in Humanities and Fine Arts at the University of St. Thomas, Minnesota. He is also director of the American Cultural Studies program and associate professor of music. He is the author of *Musical Landscapes in Color: Conversations with Black American Composers* (Scarecrow Press, 2003). His wide view of Black music culture is shaped by his work as a contemporary composer, educator, radio host, columnist, and recording Jazz musician.

FOR LIBRARY
USE ONLY